# Editorial PEER REVIEW

# *Editorial* PEER REVIEW

## ITS STRENGTHS AND WEAKNESSES

### *Ann C. Weller*

## asis&t
**American Society for
Information Science
and Technology**

**ASIST Monograph Series**

**Information Today, Inc.**
**Medford, New Jersey**

*Editorial Peer Review: Its Strengths and Weaknesses*

*Second Printing, 2002*

**Library of Congress Cataloging-in-Publication Data**

Weller, Ann C.
    Editorial peer review : its strengths and weaknesses / Ann C. Weller.
        p.cm. – (ASIST monograph series)
    Includes bibliographical references and index.
    ISBN 1-57387-100-1
Scholarly periodicals—United States—Editing. 2. Scholarly publishing—United States.
Peer review—United States. I. Weller, Ann C. II. Title. III. Series.

Z286.S37 W45 2001
    808'.027—dc21

                                        00-047204

Publisher: Thomas H. Hogan, Sr.
Editor-in-Chief: John B. Bryans
Managing Editor: Janet M. Spavlik
Production Manager: M. Heide Dengler
Copy Editor: Robert Saigh
Designers: Lisa M. Boccadutre, Jacqueline Walter
Indexer: Sharon Hughes

Dedicated, with love to
Glenn, Stephanie, Valerie, and Andy


*The power is in the balance:*
*we are our injuries*
*as much as our successes.*

*~ Kingsolver, The Poisonwood Bible ~*

# Acknowledgments

My acknowledgment starts with one who encouraged most. My husband receives special thanks: for ideas generated over dinner conversations, his faith in me and, especially, his constant and sincere support. Eileen Fitzsimons, editor *par excellence*, carefully read the manuscript and brought fresh insights, clarifications, and suggestions.

Special thanks to the past editor of the *Journal of the American Medical Association*, Dr. George Lundberg, whose pursuit of truth and quality in journal publishing whetted my appetite for the subject and has inspired me to pursue editorial peer review as a topic in need of investigation.

My colleagues at the University Library at the University of Illinois at Chicago have a collegiality that, I believe, must be unique. Their assistance with ideas, critiques (given in good humor), coupled with a willingness to give of their time in reading drafts, discussing ideas, sharing knowledge, pursuing an understanding of scientific communication, and the thoughtful discussions of the organization, methodology, and analysis of this work leave me with a deep appreciation of their scholarship and generosity.

Particularly, I will mention those who regularly attended the library research discussion groups and gave invaluable input: John Cullars, Jo Dorsch, Joan Fiscella, Karen Graves, Julie Hurd, Bill Jones, Carol Scherrer, Rama Vishwanatham, and Stephen Wiberley. A special word of appreciation is made to the interlibrary loan staff at the Library of the Health Sciences who cheerfully tracked down obscure items. Thanks to all of you.

# Table of Contents

**PREFACE** . . . . . . . . . . . . . . . . . . . . . . . . . . . . . . . . . . . . . . . . . . . . . . xii

**CHAPTER 1**
## Introduction to the Editorial Peer Review Process . . . . . . . . . . 1
Evolution of the modern editorial peer review process . . . . . . . . . . . . . 3
The literature of editorial peer review . . . . . . . . . . . . . . . . . . . . . . . . . 8
Study of editorial peer review . . . . . . . . . . . . . . . . . . . . . . . . . . . . . 10
International Committee of Medical Journal Editors . . . . . . . . . . . . . . 13
Definition of a peer-reviewed journal . . . . . . . . . . . . . . . . . . . . . . . 15
Editors' views of peer review . . . . . . . . . . . . . . . . . . . . . . . . . . . . 16
Discussion . . . . . . . . . . . . . . . . . . . . . . . . . . . . . . . . . . . . . . . . . . 17
References . . . . . . . . . . . . . . . . . . . . . . . . . . . . . . . . . . . . . . . . . . 27

**CHAPTER 2**
## The Rejected Manuscript . . . . . . . . . . . . . . . . . . . . . . . . . . . . . 43
Medical journals and the news media . . . . . . . . . . . . . . . . . . . . . . . 44
The rejection process . . . . . . . . . . . . . . . . . . . . . . . . . . . . . . . . . . 46
Reasons for manuscript rejection . . . . . . . . . . . . . . . . . . . . . . . . . . 49
Rejection rates by disciplines . . . . . . . . . . . . . . . . . . . . . . . . . . . . 54
Rejection rates over time . . . . . . . . . . . . . . . . . . . . . . . . . . . . . . . 60
Authors' responses to rejected manuscripts . . . . . . . . . . . . . . . . . . . 62
Quality of journals that accepted rejected manuscripts . . . . . . . . . . . 67
Conclusions about rejected manuscripts . . . . . . . . . . . . . . . . . . . . . 70
References . . . . . . . . . . . . . . . . . . . . . . . . . . . . . . . . . . . . . . . . . . 71

**CHAPTER 3**
## Editors and Editorial Boards:
## Who They Are and What They Do . . . . . . . . . . . . . . . . . . . . . . . 79
Role of editors . . . . . . . . . . . . . . . . . . . . . . . . . . . . . . . . . . . . . . . 80
Role of appointed editorial boards . . . . . . . . . . . . . . . . . . . . . . . . . 81
Editorial appointments . . . . . . . . . . . . . . . . . . . . . . . . . . . . . . . . . 83
Social Sciences and Psychology . . . . . . . . . . . . . . . . . . . . . . . . . . 85
Nursing . . . . . . . . . . . . . . . . . . . . . . . . . . . . . . . . . . . . . . . . . . . . 89
Medicine and the Sciences . . . . . . . . . . . . . . . . . . . . . . . . . . . . . . 90
Editors' publication criteria . . . . . . . . . . . . . . . . . . . . . . . . . . . . . . 92
Bias of editors . . . . . . . . . . . . . . . . . . . . . . . . . . . . . . . . . . . . . . . 96
Editorial peer review process . . . . . . . . . . . . . . . . . . . . . . . . . . . . 100
Editorial guidelines . . . . . . . . . . . . . . . . . . . . . . . . . . . . . . . . . . . 105
Conclusions from studies of editors and editorial board members . . . . . 110
References . . . . . . . . . . . . . . . . . . . . . . . . . . . . . . . . . . . . . . . . . 111

**CHAPTER 4**
**The Authorship Problem** ............................... 119
  Coauthorship ........................................ 120
  Selecting journals for manuscript submission .................. 129
  Value of the editorial peer review process to authors ........... 133
  Authorship guidelines and definition ...................... 136
  Conclusions about authors ............................. 141
  References .......................................... 143

**CHAPTER 5**
**The Role of Reviewers** ............................... 151
  Reviewer selection .................................. 152
  Reviewer characteristics .............................. 154
  Reviewers' reports .................................. 158
  Guidelines for reviewers .............................. 160
  Value of reviewers' reports ........................... 166
  Conclusions about role of reviewers ..................... 172
  References .......................................... 173

**CHAPTER 6**
**Reviewer Agreement** ................................ 181
  Statistics used to analyze studies of reviewer agreement .......... 185
  What can be learned from reviewer agreement studies ........... 193
  Guidelines for reviewer agreement ...................... 197
  Conclusions about reviewer agreement studies ............... 199
  References .......................................... 201

**CHAPTER 7**
**Reviewers and Their Biases** .......................... 207
  Editorial policies on anonymous and blind review .............. 209
  Name recognition ................................... 214
  Reviewer bias and name recognition ..................... 218
  Bias of ideological framework ......................... 223
  Gender and ethnicity biases ........................... 225
  Signed reviewers' reports ............................. 232
  Guidelines for addressing reviewer bias .................. 234
  Conclusions from studies of bias of reviewers .............. 238
  References .......................................... 240

**CHAPTER 8**
**Peer Review and Statistical Review** .................... 247
  Editorial use of a statistical reviewer ................... 249
  Statistical review of manuscripts ...................... 251

Statistical review of published studies .......................... 254
Complexity of statistical tests in published studies ................ 263
Publication bias and replication studies ........................ 267
Studies with statistically significant outcomes ................... 268
Publication of approved studies ............................. 270
Fabricated manuscripts ..................................... 272
Replication studies ........................................ 273
Guidelines and checklists ................................... 273
Efforts of individual journals ............................... 277
Additional published statistical review guidelines ................ 281
Conclusions about statistical review .......................... 283
References ................................................ 285

## CHAPTER 9
# Peer Review in an Electronic Environment .............. 295

Models of editorial peer review in an electronic environment ....... 296
A model in medicine ...................................... 296
A model in high-energy physics-theory ....................... 298
A model in psychology ..................................... 300
Emerging models ......................................... 300
Studies of peer review in an electronic environment ............. 301
Conclusions about peer review in an electronic environment ....... 303
References ................................................ 304

## CHAPTER 10
# Conclusions about Studies of Editorial Peer Review ...... 307

Design of studies of editorial peer review ..................... 309
Weaknesses of studies of editorial peer review ................. 310
Strengths of studies of editorial peer review .................. 312
Areas for future research .................................. 315
Recommendations for improving studies of editorial peer review ..... 315
Current model and alternate models of editorial peer review ........ 316
Peer review is essential .................................... 321
References ................................................ 322

## ABOUT THE AUTHOR ...................................... 325

## INDEX ................................................... 327

# Figures and Tables

## FIGURES

Figure 1-1: Path of a manuscript through the editorial peer review process . . . 2

Figure 1-2: Number of references to editorial peer review by decade . . . . . 10

Figure 4-1: Average number of authors per article in medicine . . . . . . . . 122

Figure 4-2: Principles and definitions of authorship . . . . . . . . . . . . . . . . 138

Figure 8-1: Types of statistical errors . . . . . . . . . . . . . . . . . . . . . . . . . . . 257

Figure 8-2: Scatter diagram of statistical problems in articles over time . . . 263

Figure 8-3: Percentage of medical articles with no statistics . . . . . . . . . . . 266

Figure 8-4: Statistics section. Uniform requirements for
manuscripts submitted to biomedical journals . . . . . . . . . . . . 282


## TABLES

Table 1-1:  Summary of results of database searches . . . . . . . . . . . . . . . . . 9

Table 1-2:  Editors' description of their editorial peer review process . . . . . 18

Table 2-1:  Editors' ranked reasons for rejecting manuscripts . . . . . . . . . . . 50

Table 2-2:  Actual reasons for rejecting manuscripts . . . . . . . . . . . . . . . . . . 52

Table 2-3:  Journal rejection rates by discipline . . . . . . . . . . . . . . . . . . . . . 56

Table 2-4:  Final publication outcome of rejected manuscripts . . . . . . . . . . 66

Table 3-1:  Professional status of editors and editorial boards . . . . . . . . . . . 86

Table 3-2:  Ranking of publication criteria . . . . . . . . . . . . . . . . . . . . . . . . . 94

Table 3-3:  Editorial peer review process:
Surveys of editors by discipline . . . . . . . . . . . . . . . . . . . . . . 102

Table 3-4:   Suggested editorial guidelines ........................ 106

Table 4-1:   Changes in the average number of
             authors in medical articles over time ................... 121

Table 4-2:   Ranking of journal selection criteria by authors .......... 131

Table 4-3:   Value of the editorial peer review process to authors ........ 135

Table 5-1:   Reviewers' workload ............................. 156

Table 5-2:   Relation of status of reviewers to quality of reviews ........ 159

Table 5-3:   Reviewer guidelines ............................... 163

Table 5-4:   Value of reviewers' reports .......................... 168

Table 6-1:   Multiple reviewer ratings of one manuscript .............. 182

Table 6-2:   Studies of reviewer agreement ........................ 186

Table 7-1:   Blind review and anonymity:
             Surveys of editors by discipline ....................... 212

Table 7-2:   Blind reviewing: Identification of authors ................ 216

Table 7-3:   The quality of blind versus nonblind reviews ............. 219

Table 7-4:   Gender differences in evaluation of fabricated manuscripts ... 228

Table 7-5:   Gender differences in blind
             and nonblind manuscript reviews ..................... 231

Table 8-1:   Surveys of statistical review in medical journals .......... 250

Table 8-2:   Statistical evaluation of manuscripts ................... 252

Table 8-3:   Statistical shortcomings of published articles ............ 256

Table 8-4:   Complexity of statistical tests
             in published articles in medicine ...................... 264

Table 8-5:   Evidence of publication bias and
             replication studies in published articles ................ 269

Table 8-6:   Evidence of publication bias in research project outcomes ... 270

Table 9-1:   Descriptions of peer review practices of ejournals ........ 297

# Preface

Almost all scholarly and research articles published in the journal literature undergo the editorial peer review process prior to publication. This process is straightforward. The authors' peers evaluate the contents of each manuscript and recommend to the editor that the manuscript be published, revised then published, or rejected. The goal of this process is to ensure that the valid article is accepted, the messy article cleaned up, and the invalid article rejected. The editor can either accept or reject the reviewers' recommendations. For editors, editorial peer review adds considerable work to the journal publication process. It also requires countless hours on the part of reviewers who could be spending those hours on their own research and scholarship. Authors are burdened with revisions. Does editorial peer review really work as it should, and does it justify the tremendous time and effort that goes into it?

The purpose of *Editorial Peer Review: Its Strengths and Weaknesses* is to conduct a systematic review of published studies on the editorial peer review process. Although there have been many individual studies, no one work has comprehensively analyzed the editorial peer review literature.

*Editorial Peer Review: Its Strengths and Weaknesses* is intended for anyone interested in the scholarly communication process. It should be particularly interesting to those who directly influence the publication process: editors, reviewers, publishers, professionals from learned societies, writers and scholars, and librarians and vendors who distribute, purchase, and make available scholarly material. Those who have questions about the editorial peer review process might find that the monograph generates ideas for further investigation in this field. A study of the editorial peer review process at this time might prove to be valuable as scholarly communication itself continues to evolve in an electronic environment and the scholarly publication process is undoubtedly about to transform dramatically. This work examines the editorial peer review process comprehensively to identify what elements of it add a value to scholarly communication and what elements might be modified or eliminated in an electronic environment. The results of this analysis of the cumulated data on editorial peer review should provide direction for shaping emerging models.

*Editorial Peer Review: Its Strengths and Weaknesses* covers English language studies published between 1945 and 1997. The simple reason for the beginning date is that I located no studies about the editorial peer review process published prior to 1945. Although some retrospective studies have examined data from journals earlier than 1945, most 1997 publications should have been indexed during 1998 and 1999, giving me the time needed to locate relevant material. Each chapter or chapter section is arranged in a similar manner. First, after an introduction to each topic, a question or two related to editorial peer review is asked;

for example, what is known about the quality of manuscripts that are rejected? Which studies to include was determined by a set of criteria. Did this group of relevant studies on peer review investigate similar questions, try to solve the same problem, or have the same study characteristics, design, or analysis? For the above example, a requirement for inclusion was that any study had to compare the quality of published articles vs. the quality of rejected manuscripts. Second, a systematic review of the studies within this defined set of investigations was undertaken. Within any one section similar studies are grouped in chronological order. Findings and limitations of the studies are discussed, conclusions are drawn, and suggestions for further research are proposed. Each chapter concludes with a discussion of any proposed guidelines for improving editorial peer review based on the data.

When data are sufficient, a group of studies can be statistically analyzed with the goal of drawing conclusions about the accumulated data; this third step is usually called a "meta-analysis." In the field of editorial peer review, groups of studies on the same topic did not fit neatly together, often did not ask the same question or had a slightly dissimilar design, and could not be analyzed using this strict methodology. When appropriate, similar data from a group of studies have been averaged, but not statistically analyzed using meta-analysis.

The studies are organized in the following broad categories: general studies of rejection rates, studies of editors, studies of authors, and finally studies of reviewers. The analysis begins with a study of rejection rates since the rejection rate of a journal is considered a measure of its rigor, value, or importance. Some studies of rejection rates compare different disciplines, while others evaluate the quality of the published articles vs. the quality of the rejected manuscript. Three types of studies of editors exist: studies of the professional status or credentials of editors compared to other scholars in the same field, reports of the operations of individual journals by their editors, and surveys of editors, usually within one discipline, to analyze or codify any number of operational or decision-making issues. Author studies center on their decisions to select a certain journal and their perception and experience with the editorial peer review process. The impact of this process on a single- vs. multiple-authored work is examined. Studies of reviewers focus on the role of the reviewers, their professional status, reviewer agreement, bias of reviewers, and statistical review of manuscripts. One chapter is devoted to the issues related to editorial peer review in an electronic environment. This work concludes with an examination of new models of editorial peer review. These models could help enhance the scientific communication process as it moves from a print to an electronic environment.

This work is concerned solely with the editorial peer review process. It does not include any studies of the peer review process that funding institutions use. Grants and contracts have specific criteria in addition to the scholarly and scientific value of a proposed study. Nor are there studies of the review process used for monographs. These must meet institutional or financial criteria. Ethical, legal, and economic aspects of journal publishing are mentioned when the editorial peer review process has a direct impact on them. Fraud, plagiarism, and duplicate publication, which are extremely important issues, are discussed in terms of the role editorial peer review might play in preventing publication. Commentaries on the technical aspects of writing, editing, or the structure of a scientific article also have been excluded, unless directly related to editorial peer review.

An annotated bibliography published in 1993 that covered all aspects of editorial peer review, including book reviews and grant reviews (Speck, 1993) helped to identify relevant literature. Speck did not list his criteria for the 643 references included in the journal articles section other than their focus on the topic of editorial peer review. However, he did note that "many of those sources articulate opinions and advice about peer review that are not grounded in empirical research" (p. vii). I agree with this sentiment. Within *Editorial Peer Review: Its Strengths and Weaknesses*, I have concentrated on the empirical research in this area.

I became interested in the topic of editorial peer review in the early 1980s while I was working with the editorial staff of the *Journal of the American Medical Association*. This experience left me fascinated with the journal publication process and the role of editorial peer review within it. Given that editorial peer review is not discipline-specific, but covers virtually any scientific and scholarly field, there was no limit to the number of places to search for material on the subject. A strategy somewhat akin to Sherlock Holmes' methodology was needed to identify and locate all studies in this field. With an eagerness similar to Holmes' enthusiastic, "The game is afoot," I relentlessly tracked down all leads. When I serendipitously located (in a journal titled *PS*) an article that I had been searching for in a journal cited as *Political Science*, I felt the satisfaction of winning the game. When (as happened all too often) I came upon a relevant article or editorial other than the one I was searching for in a particular issue or volume of a journal, I understood the true futility of identifying all relevant references.

In the game of tracking down all relevant material that eventually grew to almost 1,500 citations, the first step was a search of the literature. I searched standard scientific online databases using relatively similar search strategies, altering the strategy only as dictated by the capabilities of particular databases. Some of the leads did not end satisfactorily while others ended in discovering a gem of a study. As any searcher of the literature can appreciate, citations listed in the references of published articles often contained very limited or incorrect information. Once citations were deciphered, it was not unusual for journal issues to be missing from library shelves. Nor was it unusual for the contents of the article, once in hand, to be either irrelevant to this work or one that I had already hunted down and deemed to be of no value. Locating an irrelevant article for the second or third time happened frequently enough to lead me to create my own database of "not relevant" literature that eventually contained almost 300 citations. There were a few very relevant sounding citations that never could be located, even with the assistance of the diligent interlibrary loan staff at the Library of the Health Sciences at the University of Illinois at Chicago. However, except for these few instances (which are noted) the primary document was always used.

Many of the studies were located not through traditional database searching, but from citations in relevant articles. One of the most reliable confirmations that (almost) all studies for a particular topic had been located occurred when bibliographies uncovered no new studies. The availability of SCI's online version, *Web of Science*, greatly helped with citation searches of frequently cited or classic works.

In descriptions and conclusions, one is limited to the depth and breadth of the study being analyzed. I have taken great care not to reach conclusions beyond the intent of the author(s), the data supplied by the author(s), or the limitations of the studies. And I end with the usual, but difficult to write, statement of responsibility: any interpretations (or misinterpretation) of studies, conclusions drawn, and outright mistakes or errors are entirely my own.

Ann C. Weller

Speck, B.W. (1993). *Publication peer review; an annotated bibliography* (Vol. 7). Westport, Connecticut: Greenwood Press.

# Chapter One

# Introduction to the
# Editorial Peer Review Process

*The referee is the lynchpin about which the whole business of*
*Science is pivoted.*

(Ziman, 1968, p. 111)

Some form of prepublication review has been part of the journal production process since the first scientific journals appeared over 300 years ago. Primary responsibility for the earliest English language journal, the *Philosophical Transactions of the Royal Society*, was given to the secretary of the Society Council who was instructed by the Council to print the *Transactions* on " ... the first Monday of every month, if he [had] sufficient matter for it: and [after it was] ... first reviewed by some member of the ... [Council]" (Zuckerman & Merton, 1971) (pp. 68-69). The Council wanted some control over the contents of the *Transactions*, and this decision represents the earliest recorded use of the refereeing system. Several well-researched, informative articles provide an excellent overview of the evolution and early use of the editorial peer review process and summarize the development of the scientific journal, scholarly communication, and the journal publication process. Burnham summarized information on the transition to editorial peer review by a number of journals (Burnham, 1990). Kronick reviewed the role of professional societies in the move to peer review in the eighteenth century (Kronick, 1990). Both Lock and Arndt provided a history of the peer review process in medical journals (Lock, 1991) (Arndt, 1992).

Today editorial peer review is fairly well defined (Figure 1-1). An aspiring author sends a manuscript to a journal's editorial office. The journal editor, or for large journals one of the associate editors, logs in the manuscript, selects two or three reviewers to evaluate the manuscript, and sends each a copy. Reviewers are asked to assess the manuscript and make a recommendation to accept, accept with revisions, or reject the manuscript. The editor or associate editors then decide if they will accept the recommendation of the reviewers. If the reviewers

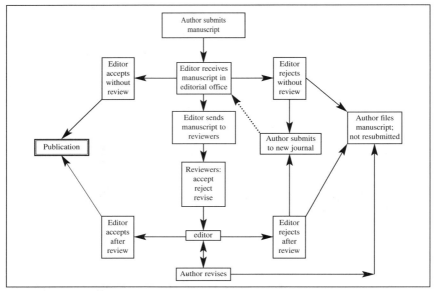

**Figure 1-1: Path of a manuscript through the editorial peer review process**

disagree, the editor may subject the manuscript to another round of reviews, or the editor may adjudicate, deciding without further review if the manuscript should be accepted or rejected.

Within these standard parameters, many variations exist. Sometimes editors accept or reject a particular manuscript with no input from reviewers. Reviewers may come from the editorial board of a journal or be selected from names of potential reviewers known to the editor, who often keeps a file of reviewers' names in the editorial office. During the review process, the editors usually, but not always, use anonymous review (the author is not provided the names of the reviewers). They are less likely to use blind review (the authors' names have been removed from the manuscript). Editors may provide a form for reviewers to complete, they may supply several pages of guidelines for the reviewers, or they may simply ask for comments. The reviewers' reports are handled in a number of ways: they may be returned to the author exactly as written, the comments may be summarized by the editor, or the editor may simply give the author the final recommendation without the reviewers' comments. Reviewers are advisors only; editors can and do reach decisions contrary to all reviewers' recommendations. They may decide to publish a manuscript because the topic is timely, interesting, thought provoking, or controversial. Often editorials, proceedings, symposia, invited manuscripts, and special-topic journal issues with a guest editor are not refereed. Once accepted, the manuscript is placed in the queue for publication. If the manuscript is rejected, several options exist for the author: appeal to the editor, submit it to another journal exactly as written, revise and resubmit it to the same or another journal, or permanently set the manuscript aside. Editors may change their minds and accept an earlier rejected manuscript for publication, if the author presents solid arguments for the manuscript's acceptance or has made acceptable alterations to it.

As publication moves from print to electronics and the editorial peer review process may undergo change as a result, now is an excellent time to examine the cumulated information on editorial peer review and critically evaluate the entire process. This chapter briefly reviews the modern evolution of editorial peer review, the adoption of the practice by scientific and scholarly journals during the past century, and the growth of the literature on editorial peer review. During the latter half of this century as peer review became a more or less standard practice, the process itself began to be investigated. Researchers and editors wanted to have data to verify or refute the validity of certain practices. As attention to editorial peer review increased its exact definition has been the subject of some discussion. A number of professional organizations have pressed for a precise definition and several have emerged.

Editors frequently write about editorial peer review in their own journals. What they say about their own process provides an introduction to the many issues related to this topic and the areas that editors consider important, problematic, or in need of explanation. The major issues discussed in these editorials each comprise a chapter of this monograph: rejection rates, studies of editors and editorial boards, authors, and finally reviewers and the many facets of the review itself, including reviewer agreement, reviewer bias, and statistical review.

## Evolution of the modern editorial peer review process

As scientific and scholarly journals have steadily increased in numbers during the latter half of this century, editorial peer review has evolved into a well-defined, codified practice quite different from the process that was first mentioned 300 years ago. The following list provides a glimpse into when a few scientific and scholarly journals began to use some form of editorial peer review and how the process has been adopted.

- In the nineteenth century, both *Nature* and the *British Medical Journal* (*BMJ*) adopted some form of peer review similar to the *Philosophical Transactions of the Royal Society* (Lock, 1992).

- In 1905, the editors of *Surgery, Gynecology, and Obstetrics* announced that "practical surgeons, gynecologists, and obstetricians will direct editorially the trend of policy" (p. 1324) for the journal. As pointed out by Burnham, "direct editorially" meant that any reviewing would be carried out by the in-house staff (Burnham, 1990).

- In 1910, the *American Journal of Diseases of Children* had an editorial board of "four to six pediatrists, who shall have editorial control of the journal in a manner similar to that of the Editorial Board of the *Archives of Internal Medicine*" (p. 1326) (Burnham, 1990).

* In 1915, the *New England Journal of Medicine* (then the *Boston Medical and Surgical Journal*) had two groups of board members: the consulting editors and the advisory committee (Burnham, 1990).

* Through the 1930s and 1940s, the *Journal of the American Medical Association* (*JAMA*) relied on a small internal staff for editorial decisions (Burnham, 1990).

* In 1942, editorial review of manuscripts for *Anesthesiology* took place in the editorial office between the editor and two associate editors (Cullen, 1964).

* Also in 1942, the *Journal of Clinical Investigation* began using editorial peer review when the editor, Gamble, "instituted the policy of sending papers to experts outside the Editorial Board for evaluation" (p. xvi) (Wilson, 1974).

* In 1944, the entire first volume of a new journal, the *Journal of Neurosurgery*, was written by a "most select group of authors" (p. 162). By 1964, "every manuscript submitted for publication in the *Journal* is reviewed by every member of the Editorial Board" (p. 163) (Bucy, 1994).

* Ingelfinger maintained that the first editor of the *American Journal of Medicine*, which began publication in 1946, used limited peer review and decided on 95 percent of all submissions within a week or two of receiving a manuscript (Ingelfinger, 1974).

* For the first time in 1948, the *Journal of Pediatrics* published a list of editorial board members who were to "maintain high standards for acceptance of articles to be published" (p. 4) (Nelson, 1982).

* In the 1950s, because of the rapidity with which new "V particles" in high-energy physics were found, coupled with the need to make this information available quickly, physicists felt that publication could not wait for the usual delay associated with the publication process. They began sending pre-prints to colleagues. By the time these new discoveries were published in *Physical Review*, almost everyone in the field already knew about each new particle. The solution for physicists at that time was the addition of a new journal—*Physical Review Letters*—which had a policy of rapid publication. The editor, Pasternack, admitted that it was "difficult (but essential) to determine whether the work submitted to us has importance and urgency as basic physics …We expect that some of the Letters we publish will turn out to have flaws and occasionally major errors because they are hastily prepared" (Pasternack, 1960). By 1961, *Physical Review Letters* was receiving too many submissions in the eyes of the editor who cautioned authors that the editors would be "stricter and thus more arbitrary in our rejection policy"

(p. 588) (Goudsmit, 1961). Years later, the editor of *Physical Review Letters* conceded that "during the frenzied days of the 1960s, we never published without at least the motions of peer review" (p. 262) (Roberts, 1991).

- From 1954 to 1972, the editor of the *Southern Medical Journal* "used an extensive editorial board for modern peer reviewing," (p. 1327) seeking reviewers from members of the Southern Medical Association (Burnham, 1990).

- In 1958, with the announcement of a new journal, *The American Journal of Cardiology*, the editor said he looked to the editorial board to "guide the Editors in their selection of material and help to keep the scientific standards of the journal at a high level. Many of the presentations will be in the form of symposia and seminars to be arranged and edited by members of the Editorial Board and other authorities in their particular field" (p. 1). He also assured readers that the editors would be unbiased when they decided to accept or reject a manuscript (Dack, 1958).

- In 1958, the new editor of *Circulation Research* informed the readership that manuscripts would be "reviewed by a distinguished board of editors" (p. 1) (Schmidt, 1958).

- In 1962, the editors of the *Archives of Dermatology* found they needed to "search widely for authorities with sufficient detailed knowledge to serve as critical and constructive editorial referees. During the past year the Editorial Board of the Archives of Dermatology has embarked on a program seeking such review of every manuscript submitted" (p. 413) (Blank, 1963).

- In 1962, the International Council of Scientific Unions Abstracting Board conducted a study of well-known primary journals from 10 countries. Sixteen percent of editors said their journal was not peer reviewed and another 8 percent gave equivocal answers. Other details of the study (criteria for inclusion, journal titles, response rate, subject of journals, etc.) were not supplied by Porter (Porter, 1963). The original report was presented at a conference and no publication from this study was located.

- From 1965 to 1978, Braceland was editor of *American Journal of Psychiatry*. In a discussion of these 13 years, he implied that editorial peer review had not been used prior to his tenure as editor: "early on we opted for the referee system, i.e., sending our manuscripts out for peer review" (p. 1150) (Braceland, 1978).

- In 1966, a study of 166 journals in the humanities revealed that 9.6 percent of the editors made an acceptance or rejection decision themselves. The remaining editors agreed that as a general rule each manuscript was reviewed by two or three readers (Lavelle, 1966).

- In 1974, *Lancet* used its editorial staff to decide on 90 percent of all manuscripts (1974a). Douglas-Wilson, a longtime editor of *Lancet*, openly questioned the assumption that peer review is essential: "I am a convinced opponent of routine peer review of articles" (p. 877) (Douglas-Wilson, 1977). He tempered this remark by outlining categories of manuscripts that should be reviewed, singling out those manuscripts that made therapeutic claims of pharmaceuticals with potentially adverse effects and those that reported on new drugs.

- In 1977, the new editor of *Parapsychology* "quietly moved the *Journal* to a more formal use of outside referees" (p. 31). The previous editor had been opposed to outside peer review (Broughton, 1987).

- By 1985, about 30 percent of manuscripts submitted to the *Lancet* were sent for outside review (1985). In 1989, an editorial in *Lancet* claimed "in the United States far too much is being demanded of peer review. Careers and the viability of whole departments now depend on publication in peer-reviewed journals." The editorial concluded: "peer review works best when you do not ask too much of it" (p. 1116) (1989a).

Two studies with contradictory findings examined the adoption of the editorial peer review process of journals in the nursing profession (Clayton & Boyle, 1981), (Fondiller, 1994). In a 1994 survey of U.S. nursing journals Fondiller asked editors to provide the date their journals began to use editorial peer review. Editors responded that few nursing journals used peer review in the 1960s. Only 3.8 percent of the editors surveyed knew that the review process began prior to 1970. Over 30 percent of the editors did not know when peer review had been instituted in their journals. About 20 percent began peer reviewing material between 1970 and 1979, and almost half of the 53 responding editors knew that peer review had begun after 1980. In an earlier survey by Clayton (1981, thirteen years before the Fondiller study), 23 of 25 (92 percent) of responding editors stated that their journal was peer reviewed. One of the two journals whose editor said it was not using peer review in the Clayton survey, the *Journal of Nurse Midwifery*, was actually using peer review in 1981 (Shah, 1981). Because raw data were not provided in the Fondiller study, a comparison of actual titles that did or did not use peer review was not possible.

Fondiller received responses from the editors of 53 nursing journals while Clayton's study included 30 titles. Thirteen titles overlapped. The seemingly contradictory findings of these two surveys may well rest on an imprecise definition of editorial peer review, the difference in the nursing journal titles used in the two surveys, or the difficulty of receiving reliable answers to questions about editorial practices of former editors. The two surveys of nursing journals attempted to determine when peer review was begun, and the studies showed that the history was not well documented.

All these examples suggest that the practice of editorial peer review evolved over time. As articulated by Manske: "It was not until the post-World War II period, some 200 years after its inception, that the process became universally accepted. Just as there is no specific time when the concept of peer review was adopted, so also the process of peer review has never taken a standardized form and continues to vary from journal to journal" (p. 768) (Manske, 1997).

Even when peer-reviewed, most, if not all, journals contain some material that bypasses the editorial peer review process. "No journal is fully peer reviewed: all have sections containing material that has been scrutinised only in the editorial office" (p. 360) (Lock, 1993). Some of the non-peer-reviewed material is rather easy to identify—news items and regular columns—while with others it is less clear. Editorials, symposia, conference proceedings, solicited manuscripts, commentaries, even letters to the editor may or may not be peer reviewed. Letters to the editors serve to balance peer review by providing a forum to discuss studies after their publication (Spodick, 1981). Published "symposiums sponsored by drug companies often have promotional attributes and are not peer-reviewed" (p. 1135) (Bero, Galbraith, & Rennie, 1992).

In 1979, a survey of 400 editors of history journals listed in *Ulrich's International Periodical Directory* disclosed that about 12 percent of them used outside reviewers (Stieg, 1983). A survey of a sample of journal editors from journals indexed in *Index Medicus* revealed that between 56 percent to 65 percent of published articles in journals from four subject areas (dermatology, neurology, orthopedics, and otolaryngology) were actually subjected to the peer review process (Colaianni, 1994). Also in medicine, Eldredge examined two directories, *Ulrich's International Periodical Directory* and *The Serials Directory*, for discrepancies of information about peer reviewed clinical medicine titles (Eldredge, 1997). Almost half (46 percent) of the titles were unique to one of the two directories. He found varied practices of journals that described themselves as peer reviewed. Eldredge concluded that there was "widespread confusion about the actual identities of peer-reviewed clinical medical journals" (p. 418).

Some journals published by learned societies give preference to material presented at the society's annual conference. Early in this century, *JAMA* published all papers presented at the annual AMA meeting (Hollender, 1983). When the *American Journal of Public Health* began publication in 1911, "virtually all its content was derived from APHA [American Public Health Association] meetings or meetings of the Massachusetts Association of Boards of Health" (p. 810). Until 1963, speakers at the annual APHA meeting were given a "first chance" (p. 810) to have their presentations published in the *American Journal of Public Health* (Yankauer, 1986). In 1965, the psychology journal, the *American Psychologist*, also considered its "first responsibility...to chronicle the affairs of the Association" (p. 121) (Brayfield, 1965). This same editorial by Brayfield, which discussed manuscript submissions, revisions, and editorial decisions to accept or reject, made no mention of an editorial peer review process. If associations did not regularly engage in the practice of publishing conference material in their journal, meeting presenters were not necessarily successful in getting their material published in other journals. A study by Lin and colleagues revealed that only about 47 percent of presenters at an American Sociological Society meeting in 1966 had published the same material four years later (Lin, Garvey, & Nelson, 1970). Relman, citing a study by Goldman and Loscalzo, supported the view that one should not automatically publish abstracts from meetings, when research showed 35 percent of them were never published (p. 278) (Relman, 1980).

## The literature of editorial peer review

One goal of this monograph was to identify all the studies on the subject of editorial peer review published through 1997. Since editorial peer review is not a discipline-specific field, literature on the subject could and does exist in almost every scholarly field with a journal publication outlet. The task of tracking down all relevant articles was a little daunting and, in the end, probably outright impossible.

Table 1-1 summarizes the results of 19 database searches. The table lists each database searched along with the subject headings or keywords and the number of postings retrieved for each search. It also lists the number of possibly relevant postings. As any searcher of the literature knows, some retrieved citations will be obviously irrelevant and easy to eliminate. For many of the postings, the actual article or document itself needed to be perused to determine if it was relevant to the study of editorial peer review. The table might give the impression that the literature searches were an orderly process. In reality, many of the search results listed in the table were performed relatively late in this project, supplementing results of earlier searches. These later searches often served to fill in gaps or to confirm that no new, relevant material had been indexed on a particular topic.

Literature searches on the topic of editorial peer review produce many false drops or irrelevant postings. The phrase "peer review" itself is used in a number of disciplines with a meaning unrelated to the editorial peer review process: physicians' clinical practice procedures undergo peer review, hospitals have quality assurance programs, educational and governmental organizations are subjected to evaluations, faculty are assessed by their peers, etc. Other, more specific terms related to the editorial peer review process also have meanings in other disciplines. For example, "rejection rate" is a term from the organ transplantation literature, "referee" is common in the sports literature, and "statistical review or evaluation" can apply to mathematics. To further encumber an already imprecise nomenclature, many of the titles of articles did not use the term "peer review" or other relevant terms. Titles like "Does it work effectively?" (a commentary on one of the AMA's conferences on editorial peer review) (Anderson, 1989); "Lifting the pernicious veil of secrecy" (a news item recommending the elimination of the practice of anonymity) (Berezin, Gordon, & Hunter, 1995); and even "Our thanks to our consultants" (an editorial acknowledging the work of reviewers) (Huth, 1982) needed to be examined firsthand before deciding if they were relevant.

| DATABASES | YEARS SEARCHED | SUBJECT OR KEYWORDS | POSTINGS | REFINED SEARCH | POSTINGS | RELEVANT POSTINGS |
|---|---|---|---|---|---|---|
| Wilson, Business | 1983-5/98 | peer review | 407 | referee, editorial, statistics, bias, reviewer | 18 | 2 |
| | 1983-9/98 | rejection rate(s) | 94 | | | 0 |
| Wilson, Library | 1984-6/98 | peer review | 38 | | | 27 |
| | 1984-9/98 | rejection rate(s) | 1 | | | 0 |
| Wilson, Readers Guide | 1983-5/98 | peer review | 301 | | | 31 |
| | 1983-9/98 | rejection rate(s) | 45 | | | 1 |
| Wilson, Art | 1983-6/98 | peer review | 8 | | | 1 |
| | 1983-9/98 | rejection rate(s) | 0 | | | 0 |
| Wilson, Biol & Ag | 1983-6/98 | peer review | 57 | | | 12 |
| | 1983-9/98 | rejection rate(s) | 2 | | | 0 |
| Wilson, Gen Sci | 1984-6/98 | peer review | 397 | referee, editorial, statistics, bias, reviewer | 45 | 23 |
| | 1984-9/98 | rejection rate(s) | 22 | | | 0 |
| Wilson, Humanities | 1984-6/98 | peer review | 9 | | | 2 |
| | 1984-9/98 | rejection rate(s) | 1 | | | 0 |
| Wilson, Social Science | 1984-6/98 | peer review | 81 | | | 15 |
| | 1984-9/98 | rejection rate(s) | 28 | | | 3 |
| Wilson, Applied Sci & Tech | 1983-6/98 | peer review | 261 | | | 35 |
| | 1983-9/98 | rejection rate(s) | 63 | | | 0 |
| Current Contents | 1994-2/98 | electronic peer review | 2 | | | 2 |
| | 1994-2/98 | rejection rate | 120 | | | 1 |
| | to 8/97 | peer review | | | | 18 |
| MathSci | to 8/98 | peer review | 123 | | | 2 |
| Math Rev | to 8/97 | peer review statistical review | 0 | | | 0 |
| CINAHL | to 2/98 | editorial peer review | 6 | | | 6 |
| | to 2/98 | peer review refereeing | 56 | | | 30 |
| | to 9/98 | rejection rate(s) | 33 | | | 1 |
| Article First/OCLC | to 8/97 | statistical review | 112 | | | 1 |
| ERIC | 1984-5/98 | peer review | 540 | referee, editorial, statistics, bias, reviewer | 53 | 8 |
| | 1984-9/98 | rejection rate(s) | 35 | | | 6 |
| IPA | to 2/98 | editorial peer review | 4 | | | 4 |
| | to 2/98 | peer review journals | 11 | | | 11 |
| | to 9/98 | rejection rate(s) | 12 | | | 0 |
| PAIS | 1972-5/98 | peer review | 72 | | | 2 |
| | 1972-9/98 | rejection rate (s) | 3 | | | 0 |
| PsycINFO | 1967-3/98 | peer review | 352 | | | 23 |
| | 1967-3/98 | reviewer bias | 4 | | | 4 |
| | 1967-9/98 | rejection rate(s) | 234 | | | 8 |
| | 1887-66 | rejection rate(s) | 36 | | | 0 |
| | 1967-3/98 | statistical review | 13 | | | 1 |
| | 1967-7/97 | statistical review | 32 | | | 4 |
| | 1967-10/98 | normative & criteria | 212 | publish/journal | 3 | 0 |
| MEDLINE (PubMed) | 1966-3/98 | author/duplicate | 67 | | | |
| | | editorial peer review | 41 | | | 41 |
| | 1966-9/98 | rejection rate | 10,000 | | | |

**Table 1-1: Summary of results of database searches**

Often very general subject headings were the index terms of choice; such terms as publishing, journals, editors, or authors were frequently the only term under which a relevant article was indexed. The index term was at other times limited to the discipline of the particular study or discussion. Undoubtedly, partially due to the continuous improvement in the online searching software, and since some of the late literature searches did identify previously unknown references, there are still unidentified studies on this topic.

The database compiled for this work contains 1,439 references that incorporate 1,485 individual authors who contributed to 405 different journals. Figure 1-2 graphs the number of references in this database against the year of publication. Not all of the references in the database are cited in this monograph. Approximately 300 references initially identified as relevant, but ultimately not cited in this work, tend to be letters to the editors, commentaries peripherally related to editorial peer review, or items that simply add nothing new. Those topics peripherally related to editorial peer review covered such areas as how to write, journal rankings, industry support of research, publication delays, fraud, economics, ethics, scientific misconduct, review of grant applications, author's potential conflict of interest, etc. These references were all carefully scrutinized to determine the degree of relevance or importance to this work.

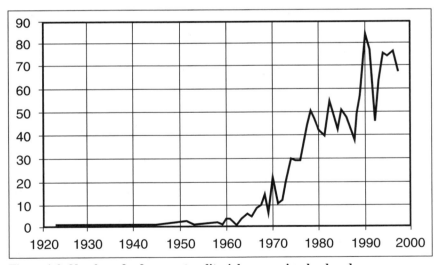

**Figure 1-2: Number of references to editorial peer review by decade**

## Study of editorial peer review

In 1974, Franz Ingelfinger, renowned editor of the *New England Journal of Medicine*, made the first appeal for research into the field of editorial peer review.

Ingelfinger maintained that, if the editors of the prestigious *Lancet* could reach a decision within a few days, data were needed to justify the American process that "faithfully and meticulously depended on a system of peer review" (p. 687) (Ingelfinger, 1974). He added:

> *That data on the performance of the reviewing system are lacking is all the more astounding in view of the momentous influence the system exerts on the lives of those who write biomedical articles* (p. 687).

The first studies in the field of editorial peer review were conducted in the middle of this century. Interest in the process has steadily increased during the latter half of this century. Patterson and Bailar identified 79 studies indexed by *Index Medicus* from 1966 through October 1981 that investigated the peer review process, covering such topics as inter-referee agreement, biases of referees, authors' characteristics, and editors' influence on fairness (Patterson & Bailar, 1985). They also identified 40 studies indexed in *Social Sciences Citation Index*, 20 in *Psychological Abstracts*, nine in *Science Citation Index*, six in the National Clearing House for Mental Health and none in both *Biological Abstracts* and *Chemical Abstracts*. Bailar and Patterson called for the adoption of a research agenda in the field of editorial peer review in 1985 (Bailar & Patterson, 1985). They suggested that studies of editorial peer review "have languished largely ... because there has been little high-level interest, no identifiable source of funds for such work, and no comprehensive public analysis of needs. As a result, the work we found was often poorly conceived, methodologically weak, based on small samples, undertaken by persons without a major long-term commitment to studies of journal peer review or related matters, and irrelevant to policy." While admitting that they had a "high regard for the journal peer review system," they wanted data to prove it worked as it should.

The First International Conference of Scientific Editors was held in Jerusalem in 1977 (Balaban, 1977). This conference covered a broad range of editorial topics including the growth of the scientific literature, publication styles and standards, economics and organization of scientific publication, international publication issues, unconventional scientific literature, and the relationship between primary and secondary publication outlets. The conference also included a number of reports on peer review of the scientific literature (Gordon, 1977), (Keller, 1977), and (Kochen & Perkel, 1977). These are discussed in the Chapter Four on the role of the reviewer.

The first monograph on the subject of editorial peer review in biomedical publications was published in 1985 by Lock, then editor of the *British Medical Journal* (*BMJ*), and included 281 references (Lock, 1985). This monograph detailed the procedures he employed at the *BMJ* and presented considerable data regarding *BMJ*'s process. The studies identified by Patterson and Bailer as well as the *BMJ* study are discussed in detail in the following chapters.

By the late 1980s, increased interest in the editorial peer review process was evident. The Council of Biology Editors frequently discussed relevant editorial peer review topics at its annual meeting. In October of 1988, the Council organized a conference on this topic (Relman, 1990). In 1990, the American Medical Association (AMA) sponsored the First International Conference on Peer Review in Biomedical Publications (Rennie, 1990). This conference brought nearly 300 editors, scientists, journalists, librarians, academicians, and publishers together to report on the outcome of research into the editorial peer review process. Approximately 70 percent of the 35 presentations and poster sessions were the results of investigations into various aspects of journal publication. Of the selected proceedings published in *JAMA*, nine studies were directly related to editorial peer review ((Evans, Nadjari, & Burchell, 1990), (Gardner & Bond, 1990), (Garfunkel, Lawson, Hamrick, & Ulshen, 1990a), (Garfunkel, Ulshen, Hamrick, & Lawson, 1990b), (Hargens, 1990), (Lock, 1990) (McNutt, Evans, Fletcher, & Fletcher, 1990), (Weller, 1990a), and (Yankauer, 1990)). Other publications from the selected proceedings included reports on unpublished clinical trials, fraudulent research, and citation studies. Overall, although isolated research endeavors were certainly taking place, the congress failed to uncover a large, coordinated research effort in the field of editorial peer review in biomedical publications. The AMA has continued to sponsor the International Conference on Peer Review in Biomedical Publications with a second congress in 1993 and a third one in 1997. A meeting in 1994 at Vanderbuilt University (Weeks & Kinser, 1994) brought scientists, editors, and others together to share information on the value of refereeing. This conference focused on the process of editing and reviewing as well as some of the ethical issues relevant to editorial peer review.

An annotated bibliography on peer review published in 1993 included 780 references of which 643 covered the journal peer review literature and the remaining were citations to the literature on book reviews and grant reviewing practices (Speck, 1993). References cited in Speck's monograph include studies of the editorial peer review process as well as a range of others types of publications, including editorials, commentaries, news items, and letters to the editor. Speck did not index studies of editorial peer review as such, but they can be identified from details in the annotations.

All these endeavors have served to encourage research into the field of editorial peer review. One of the interesting features of the study of this process is that it encompasses all disciplines with a scientific or scholarly journal publication outlet. However, studies of the editorial peer review process itself tend to exhibit discipline dependency. Most studies on editorial peer review have been conducted in medicine, the social sciences, and psychology, with specific areas for studies associated with particular disciplines. For example, studies that examined review of statistical methodology of manuscripts were usually generated from medicine; studies on the bias of reviewers usually came from psychology and sociology; and studies of rejection rates often originated in the social sciences. Researchers investigating this topic tend to be an eclectic group who for a number of reasons have become intrigued enough or puzzled in one way or another by the process that they began to investigate it.

After reviewing some of the more recent studies on editorial peer review and repeating what Bailar and Patterson had called for 15 years earlier, Fletcher and Fletcher argued that more studies are needed to establish the actual benefits of peer review (Fletcher & Fletcher, 1997):

> *Few studies have put to the test, through scientific research, be-*
> *liefs (hypotheses) that what peer reviewers and editors do to*
> *and for manuscripts improve the outcome. This kind of research*
> *is needed to establish a strong basis for editorial policies ... It*
> *is possible to do hypothesis-testing research on peer review and*
> *editing practices. There are a growing number of examples,*
> *though not a well-developed body of information* (p. 38).

Suggested topics for research included: define exactly what constitutes a good review in a scientifically rigorous and useful way; evaluate strategies to improve peer review (blinding reviewers, paying them, or publicly thanking them); study how peer review improves the quality of an accepted or published article; or, examine the relationship between authors and journals (Fletcher, 1991).

Studies that have been conducted on editorial peer review have run the gamut from an editor's examination of certain aspects of his or her own journal to comparisons of journals within a single discipline and to large, interdisciplinary comparisons of many facets of the editorial peer review process. Studies are usually limited to one perspective: the perspective of the editor, the author, or the reviewer. Given the confidential nature of the editorial peer review process, certain types of data could only come directly from editors who have either examined their own files or have made data from their journal available to researchers.

## International Committee of Medical Journal Editors

A group of editors meeting for a slightly different purpose have probably been responsible for encouraging some of the recent research into the editorial peer review process. Biomedical journal editors met in 1978 in Vancouver, Canada, to begin a process of establishing standard guidelines for authors submitting manuscripts to their journals. This group was initially referred to as the "Vancouver Group" to reflect the original meeting site although its formal name is now the International Committee of Medical Journal Editors (ICMJE). From the 1978 meeting, the ICMJE developed a set of guidelines called the *Uniform Requirements for Manuscripts Submitted to Biomedical Journals.*" The *Uniform Requirements* is a document written for authors on how to prepare manuscripts; it does not include guidelines for editors on publication style, on how manuscripts should be reviewed, or on which criteria to use for accepting manuscripts for publication. The first *Uniform Requirements* was published in 1978 shortly after the Vancouver meeting and was endorsed by a "tentative list" of 19 participating journal editors who agreed to receive manuscripts prepared and submitted according to the requirements (International Committee of Medical Journal Editors, 1978).

ICMJE encourages distribution of the *Uniform Requirements* and the document has never carried a statement of copyright. It was updated five times between 1978 and 1997. By 1997, over 500 editors of biomedical journals agreed to cite the *Uniform Requirements* in their instructions to authors. The *Uniform Requirements* have focused, as the title suggests, on manuscript preparation including stylistic components such as information on the title, pagination, abstract, text, arrangement of sections of the manuscript, acknowledgments, and references. The most recent revision has broadened its scope "to increase clarity and address concerns about rights, privacy, descriptions of methods and other matters" (p. 270) (International Committee of Medical Journal Editors, 1997). Some of these supplementary statements are relevant to the publication of journal articles and the editorial peer review process. These include statements on retraction of research findings, confidentiality, competing manuscripts based on the same study, order of authorship, the popular media, conflict of interest, advertising, supplements to journals, the correspondence column, citing the uniform requirements, and the definition of editorial peer review.

A new organization, the World Association of Medical Editors, was planned by a group within the ICMJE with the purpose of organizing a global network of medical journal editors who would work within the existing structure of four associations: the Council of Biology Editors, the European Association of Science Editors, the International Federation of Science Editors, and the ICMJE. The primary purpose of the organization is to "promote the science and art of medicine and the betterment of health" (p. 1757). One of the specific goals is "to promote peer review as a vehicle for scientific discourse and quality assurance in medicine and to support efforts to improve peer review" (p. 1757) (Squires, 1995). The Association met for the first time in September 1997, elected officers, and established a committee structure.

Three years before the ICMJE first met, Hess reported that the American National Standards Institute (ANSI) Committee Z 39 was about to appoint a subcommittee to propose standard reviewing practices (Hess, 1975, September). Both Juhasz and colleagues and Miller and Serzan recommended the establishment of ANSI standards for peer review (Juhasz, Calvert, Jackson, Kronick, & Shipman, 1975) (Miller & Serzan, 1984). According to the only reference to Hess' publication, Hess believed that peer review tends to suppress the publication of new ideas (Schauder, 1994). A year after Hess' announcement, McCartney proposed a Council of Editors to address editorial concerns within sociology journals (McCartney, 1976). McCartney wanted this council to focus on the economic and structural problems of sociology journals, suggesting there should be more coordination and cooperation among these journals. The National Science Foundation provided funding for an initial workshop for 35 editors to investigate forming such a council. The outcome was a proposal for a council with three major purposes: information sharing, cooperation, and policy considerations. The only apparent reference to this workshop was a remark by Schwartz on one of the suggestions: McCartney's proposal to have editors resubmit rejected manuscripts to editors of similar journals was rejected (Schwartz, 1994). The implication in this discussion was that the council has never been formed.

These examples of efforts and proposals illustrate a variety of attempts by editors and scholars to pursue an understanding of and investigation into the value of editorial peer review. Some groups have apparently met with more success than others following proposals to form organizations or committees for the specific purpose of investigating or establishing policies on editorial peer review. Other organizations and learned societies have stated policies on particular procedures for the review process. For example, the American Psychological Association (APA) has a policy on anonymous blind review that is discussed in the chapter on reviewer bias (American Psychological Association, 1972).

## Definition of a peer-reviewed journal

Since editorial peer review is a process, its definition can and does vary according to how the process is envisioned. Much of the literature on editorial peer review assumes a very general definition—a review of a manuscript by someone other than the editor. Literally, of course, there is an obvious definition of peer review: "evaluation by one's peers." Beyond that, a number of definitions include the requirement that manuscripts are sent outside the editorial office before a journal can be considered peer reviewed.

After a study of nursing journals, Swanson and McCloskey proposed that a peer-reviewed journal be defined as:

> *one that uses individuals with the professional expertise to evaluate a manuscript. These experts are selected by the journal staff in accordance with the expertise needed or are composed of a preestablished group of reviewers. The decision on the manuscript is based on a minimum of three reviews, and the ultimate responsibility for the decision on the manuscript is with the editor. The editor also routinely shares with the author the reasons for rejection and reviewers' comments* (p. 75) (Swanson & McCloskey, 1982).

Lewis, editor of *Nursing Outlook*, also used the concept of reviewers outside the editorial office as the cornerstone of a peer-reviewed journal (Lewis, 1980). Bailar and Patterson defined "'journal peer review' as the assessment by experts (peers) of material submitted for publication in scientific and technical periodicals" (p. 654) (Bailar & Patterson, 1985). In a survey of editors, Weller defined a peer reviewer as someone "other than the editor, co-editor, or associate editors" (p. 266) (Weller, 1990b). DeBakey concentrated on the term "peer" when

he considered the definition of editorial peer review (DeBakey, 1990). "'Peer reviewing' has become a stock term, but is the reviewer of a manuscript … always
a peer: a person who has equal standing with another, as in rank, class, or age?"
(p. 347). Lock considered that "the expert assessment of articles for publication" (p. 359) was a good working definition of peer review (Lock, 1993).

The ICMJE defined a peer-reviewed journal as one:

> *that has submitted most of its published articles for review by*
> *experts who are not part of the editorial staff. The numbers and*
> *kinds of manuscripts sent for review, the number of reviewers,*
> *the reviewing procedures, and the use made of the reviewers'*
> *opinions may vary, and therefore each journal should publicly*
> *disclose its policies in its Instructions to Authors for the ben-*
> *efit of readers and potential authors* (p. 1030) (International
> Committee of Medical Journal Editors, 1992).

Pettigrew and Nicholls' definition articulates the ambiguity of the term:

> *"Refereed journal" is not a precise term, but rather covers a*
> *continuum of peer-controlled quality assessment that reaches*
> *its most strict definition with double-blind peer review by sev-*
> *eral scholars working in the research area, and minimal abil-*
> *ity of the editor to override clear decisions by the peer re-*
> *viewers on which articles are appropriate for a given journal*
> (p. 144) (Pettigrew & Nicholls, 1994).

These definitions contain a common element in that they each require some
type of review of a manuscript other than the editor. Some definitions are more
prescriptive than others, incorporating a number of processes and requirements.
These definitions do not address such issues as the percentage of material in a
journal that should be peer reviewed, any recommended level of peer review, or
many other details of the process. The working definition of peer review for this
monograph is intended to be as inclusive as possible:

> *A peer-reviewed journal is one that has a portion of submit-*
> *ted manuscripts evaluated by someone other than the editor*
> *of the journal.*

## Editors' views of peer review

Many editors have taken the opportunity to use editorials in their journals as a
vehicle to describe their own editorial peer review processes. The first step in the
analysis of the literature and studies of editorial peer review is an examination of
journal editors' descriptions of their own procedures, policies, guidelines, and
opinions. Some editors regularly use editorial pages to discuss editorial peer

review policy or outcome, providing detailed procedures and guidelines for either reviewers or authors. A review of these editorials serves as an introduction and overview to most of the many issues related to the editorial peer review process.

*Question*

How do editors describe their own editorial peer review process in their journals?

*Criteria for inclusion*

~ any editorial or commentary in which an editor discusses some aspect of editorial peer review procedures.

To be included in this section, editorials and commentaries have to be written by the editor, give some details regarding their process for the particular journal, and contain some explicit statement that the journal was peer reviewed. Editorials that include a more detailed study of the journal's process with some data analysis are discussed in later chapters.

## Discussion

Table 1-2 is a list of journals whose editors have written about their editorial peer review process. Journals are categorized by discipline and alphabetically within each discipline. Medical titles are listed first, since they comprise about one-half of all journals in this list. These descriptive editorials were frequently written at either the beginning or the ending of the editors' tenure or as part of an annual report to subscribers. They range in length from a few sentences to several pages. While some of these editorials were located through database searches, most were located through references in related articles or serendipitously.

The information provided in Table 1-2 represent some of the more common issues discussed by the editors, and these topics are discussed in detail in the following chapters. Most journals publish "instructions to authors" that provide those preparing manuscripts with information on submission requirements or refer authors to the *Uniform Requirements*, if a medical journal. Many of the editorials in Table 1-2 also address subjects unrelated to editorial peer review, including details about the journal's circulation, subject coverage, international scope, citation patterns, financial information, policies on advertisements, publication procedures, flow of manuscripts through the editorial offices, publication time tables, explanations of interest to association members, or biographical sketches of editors.

These editorials cover a wide variety of editorial peer review issues. Some editors wrote about the importance of the review process and how they viewed their roles in that process. Some editorials are directed to reviewers: asking readers to volunteer as reviewers, thanking reviewers, or describing the difficult task of reviewing. Some are directed toward authors: stressing the need for quality submissions, reiterating that reviewers only recommend, explaining why manuscripts need revisions, describing procedures when reviewers disagree, reporting on the probability of rejection, or informing authors of an appeals process. Some *anonymous review: the author is not provided the names of the reviewers; blind review: the authors' names have been removed from the manuscript*

| Journal Titles | Rejection Rates | Reject Without Review; Reasons | Policy on Anonymous and Blind Review* | Additional Discussion and Policy Topics | References |
|---|---|---|---|---|---|
| **Medicine and Health** | | | | | |
| *Academic Radiology* | ~50% | | | | (Franken, 1997) |
| *Acta Obstet & Gynecol Scandinavica* | | | double-blind | reviewer checklist | (Fischer-Rasmussen, 1996) |
| *American Journal of Cardiology* | | | | | (Roberts, 1987) |
| *American Journal of Diseases of Children* | | | | reviewers' form | (Fulginiti, 1984) |
| *American Journal of Gastroenterology* | 50-56% | | | | (Zetterman, 1996) |
| *American Journal of Health-System Pharmacy* | | | | | (Talley, 1996) |
| *American Journal of Infection Control* | ~50% | if out of scope | double-blind | thanks to reviewers; statistical review | (White, 1993) |
| *American Journal of Medical Technology* | | | | | (Roe, 1978) |
| *American Journal of Ophthalmology* | | some are | anonymous | reviewer guidelines | (Newell, 1990) |
| *American Journal of Public Health* | ~80% ~80% 80% 80% 80% 80% | ~20% ~33% if acceptance unlikely | double-blind, if feasible double-blind double-blind guidelines for authors; statistical review | reviewer agreement thanks to reviewers statistical review | (Yankauer, 1977) (Yankauer, 1978) (Yankauer, 1979) (Yankauer, 1982) (Yankauer, 1983) (Yankauer, 1984) (Yankauer, 1987) (Yankauer, 1989) (Yankauer, 1990) (Northridge & Susser, 1994) |
| *American Journal of Roentgenology* | 58% 56-60% | | double-blind double-blind | thanks to reviewers | (Beck, 1991) (Beck, 1992) (Chew, 1993) (Friedman, 1995) |
| *American Review of Respiratory Disease* | | | | thanks to board and reviewers editorial policies | (Murray, 1974) (Murrary, 1975) |
| *Anesthesiology* | 54-69% | | | | (Saidman, 1995) |
| *Annals of Allergy* | | if incomplete | anonymous | thanks to reviewers reviewer guidelines | (Sly, 1989) (Sly, 1990) (Sly, 1991) |
| *Annals of Emergency Medicine* | 72% 71% | | double-blind | thanks to reviewers | (Waeckerle, 1996) (Waeckerle & Callaham, 1996) |
| *Annals of Internal Medicine* | 85% | ~50% | | thanks to reviewers editorial policies; statistical review reviewer agreement | (Huth, 1982) (Fletcher & Fletcher, 1991) (Fletcher & Fletcher, 1993) |

**Table 1-2: Editor's description of their editorial peer review process**

| Journal Titles | Rejection Rates | Reject without review; reasons | Policy on anonymous and blind review* | Additional discussion and policy topics | References |
|---|---|---|---|---|---|
| Archives of Dermatology | | | | thanks to reviewers<br>thanks to reviewers<br>thanks to reviewers | (Blank, 1963)<br>(Arndt, 1984)<br>(Arndt, 1989) |
| Archives of Surgery | 60%<br>65% | rarely are<br>54% of all rejected | anonymous<br><br>anonymous | reviewer guidelines and editors; appeal process guidelines for editorial board | (Warren, 1973)<br>(Baue, 1985)<br><br>(Baue, 1993) |
| Australian and New Zealand Journal of Psychiatry | 50% | 4% | | reviewer agreement | (Parker, Barnett, Holmes, & Manicavasagar, 1984) |
| Beta Release | | | double-blind | | (Nichol, 1993) |
| Biological Psychiatry | | | anonymous | | (Brady, 1985) |
| British Journal of Occupational Therapy | | | double-blind | reviewer agreement | (Drummond, 1993) |
| British Journal of Surgery | 65% | rarely are<br>18% | | share reviewers' reports | (Dudley, 1989)<br><br>(Farndon, Murie, Johnson, Earnshaw, & Guillou, 1997) |
| British Medical Journal/ BMJ | 79%<br>81.6% | if two editors agree if not original or seriously flawed; ~50% | anonymous<br><br>anonymous<br><br>anonymous | editorial committee | (1974b)<br><br>(Lock, 1976)<br>(Smith, 1982)<br>(Lock, 1985)<br>(Smith, 1993) |
| Canadian Journal of Occupational Therapy | | if unsuitable subject | double-blind | | (Weiss-Lambrou, 1991) |
| Canadian Journal of Surgery | | | | reviewer guidelines | (Meakins, 1996) |
| Canadian Medical Association Journal | ~50%<br><br>~50%<br><br><br>83% | <br><br><br><br>~50%<br>~50% | anonymous<br><br>anonymous<br><br><br><br>double-blind, reviewer can sign | editorial policies<br><br>appeals process<br><br>statistical review<br><br>reviewer guidelines<br><br>reviewer guidelines for review articles<br>reviewer guidelines | (Morgan, 1981)<br>(Morgan, 1984)<br>(Bolster & Morgan, 1986)<br>(Squires, 1987)<br>(Squires, 1989a)<br>(Squires, 1989b)<br>(Squires, 1989c)<br><br>(Squires, 1989d)<br><br>(Squires, 1989e) |
| Chest | | | <br><br>anonymous, reviewer can sign | biostatistical review<br>appeal process | (Soffer, 1968)<br>(Soffer, 1978)<br>(Soffer, 1979) |
| Circulation Research | ~71% | | | | (Vatner et al., 1996) |
| Communicable Disease Report | 11.5% | rarely are | anonymous | | (Handysides, 1996) |
| Comprehensive Virology | | | no, reviewers sign | | (Fraenkel-Conrat, 1974) |

**Table 1-2: Editor's description of their editorial peer review process (continued)**

| Journal Titles | Rejection Rates | Reject Without Review; Reasons | Policy on Anonymous and Blind Review* | Additional Discussion and Policy Topics | References |
|---|---|---|---|---|---|
| Developmental Medicine & Child Neurol. | | | Anonymous | | (Pountney, 1996) |
| Diabetes Care | | | anonymous | appeal process | (Service, 1983) |
| Health Care for Women International | | If hopeless | double-blind | editorial process | (Stern, 1996) |
| Infection Control & Hospital Eplidemiology | | | anonymous | statistical review; solicited manuscripts | (Hepker, 1991) |
| International Journal of Cancer | ~50% | | | | (Saxen, 1976) |
| International Journal of Epidemiology | | | anonymous | | (1974d) |
| JAMA | | | | | (Talbott, 1969) (Barclay, 1976) |
| | 81% | | anonymous | thanks to reviewers thanks to reviewers; reviewer guidelines | (Lundberg, 1984) |
| | 82% | 54% | | thanks to reviewers thanks to reviewers; statistical review | (Lundberg, 1985) (Lundberg & Carney, 1986) |
| | | | | thanks to reviewers | (Carney & Lundberg, 1987) |
| | 83.8% | 54% | | thanks to reviewers | (Lundberg & Williams, 1991) |
| | 84.2% | 45% | | thanks to reviewers | (Williams & Lundberg, 1996) |
| Journal of Adolescent Health Care | | | double-blind | | (Litt, 1990) |
| Journal of the American Academy of Physician Assistants | | | | call for reviewers | (Kole, 1989) |
| Journal of the American College of Cardiology | | | | announcement of new journal conflict of interest; thanks to reviewers | (Dack, 1983) (Parmley, 1995) |
| Journal of Chronic Diseases | | | anonymous | editorial policy ethical issues | (Feinstein & Spitzer, 1983) (Feinstein, 1986) |
| Journal of Clinical Epidemiology | | | | thanks to reviewers; share reviewers' reports thanks to reviewers | (Feinstein & Spitzer, 1989) (Feinstein & Spitzer, 1991) |
| Journal of Clinical Investigation | | | | | (Wilson, 1974) |
| Journal of Clincal Psychiatry | | | | editorial policy | (Easson, 1979) |
| Journal of Endocrinology | 43-51% | | anonymous | | (1978) |
| Journal of General Internal Medicine | | 27% | anonymous, reviewers asked to sign | reviewer guidelines | (1988) |
| Journal of Hand Surgery | | | anonymous | guidelines for authors | (Manske, 1997) |
| Journal of Laboratory & Clinical Medicine | | | anonymous, 2/3 of reviewers sign anonymous, reviewers can sign | | (McDuffie, 1978) (Knox, 1981) |

**Table 1-2: Editor's description of their editorial peer review process (continued)**

| Journal Titles | Rejection Rates | Reject Without Review; Reasons | Policy on Anonymous and Blind Review* | Additional Discussion and Policy Topics | References |
|---|---|---|---|---|---|
| Journal of Neuropathology & Neurology | | | double-blind, if possible | identification of authors by reviewers | (Moossy & Moossy, 1985) |
| Journal of Nutrition Education | | if obvious flaws | | | (Glanz, Axelson, & Brinberg, 1994) |
| Journal of School Health | ~70% | | double-blind | survey of reviewers | (Pigg, 1987) |
| Kidney International | 57-72% | | | | (Andreoli, 1997) |
| Lancet | ~85% | 70% | | | (1985) |
| Medical and Pediatric Oncology | | | | statistical review | (Mauer, 1985) |
| Medial Care | | yes | | | (Neuhauser, 1997) |
| New England Journal of Medicine | 85% | | | thanks to reviewers | (Ingelfinger, 1970) (Ingelfinger, 1972) (Ingelfinger, 1975) (Ingelfinger, 1977) (Relman, Rennie, & Angell, 1980) (Relman, 1981) (Angell & Relman, 1989) (Relman, 1989) (Angell & Relman, 1989) |
| | 90% | ~20% | | | |
| | 88-90% | 5-10% | anonymous, can sign | editorial policy anonymous, can sign | |
| | 88-90% | 5-10% | anonymous, can sign | | |
| Obstetrics and Gynecology | ~75% | 5% | 2-3% of reviewers sign 1-2% of reviewers sign | role of reviewers | (Pitkin, 1993) (Pitkin, 1993) (Pitkin, 1995) |
| Ophthalmology | | | | | (Lichter, 1990) |
| Pediatric Neurosurgery | | none are | anonymous | reviewer guidelines | (Humphreys, Reigel, & Epstein, 1995) |
| Physical Therapy | | | | thanks to reviewers | (Rothstein, 1991) |
| Physiotherapy | | | anonymous | role of reviewers; reviewer selection | (Arnell, 1986) |
| Physiotherapy Canada | | | | checklist for reviewers | (Cleather, 1981) |
| Plastic and Reconstructive Surgery | | | anonymous, reviewers can sign | reviewer bias | (Goldwyn, 1989) |
| Postgraduate Medicine | 75-80% | | anonymous | | (Hoffband, 1990) |
| Psychopharmacologia | 40% | | | guidelines for authors | (Kornetsky, 1975) |
| Psychopharmacology | 5% | if not in scope | | thanks to reviewers | (Jacobsen, 1980) |
| Qualitative Health Research | | if no merit or out of scope | | authors responses to reviewers' comments | (Morse, 1996) |
| Radiology | | | | reviewer guidelines | (Siegelman, 1988) |
| Respiratory Care | | if incomplete | double-blind | | (Fluck & Hess, 1988) |
| **Business/Manufacturing** | | | | | |
| Administrative Science Quarterly | | 43% | | | (Weick, 1983) |
| Ceramic Bulletin | | | double-blind, if requested | reviewer guidelines | (Stull, 1989) |
| Journal of the Operational Research Society | | | anonymous | functions of referees | (Amiry, 1983) |

**Table 1-2: Editor's description of their editorial peer review process (continued)**

| Journal Titles | Rejection Rates | Reject without Review; Reasons | Policy on Anonymous and Blind Review* | Additional Discussion and Policy Topics | References |
|---|---|---|---|---|---|
| **Communication** | | | | | |
| Communication Quarterly | | | double-blind | bias of review process | (Chesebro, 1987) |
| **Dentistry** | | | | | |
| General Dentistry | | | double-blind | | (Winland, 1997) |
| Quintessence International | | | | | (Simonsen, 1996) |
| **Economics** | | | | | |
| American Economic Review | ~85% | | double-blind, if possible double-blind | thanks to reviewers | (Borts, 1974) (Ashenfelter, Campbell, Gordon, & Milgrom, 1991) |
| Journal of Economic Literature | | | | thanks to reviewers | (Perlman, 1974) |
| **History** | | | | | |
| American Historical Review | 62% | | anonymous in 1969 | | (Stieg, 1983) |
| **Library Science** | | | | | |
| Art Documentation | | some are | | guidelines for authors | (Smith, 1993) |
| Bulletin of the Medical Library Association | | | anonymous | reviewer guidelines | (Crawford, 1988) |
| College & Research Libraries | 51.8% | if out of scope (3.5%) | | reasons for rejection | (Hernon, Smith, & Croxen, 1993) |
| Information Processing & Management | | if not in scope | anonymous anonymous, reviewers can sign | editorial policies reviewer guidelines, thanks to reviewers | (Saracevic, 1985) (Saracevic, 1986) |
| Journal of the American Association of Information Science | | if not in scope | anonymous anonymous | reviewer guidelines reviewer guidelines | (Meadow, 1980) (Kraft, 1987) |
| Library Quarterly | ~70% | | double-blind | reviewer guidelines | (Harter, 1993) |
| **Nursing** | | | | | |
| American Journal of Nursing | | | | | (Schorr, 1979) |
| Applied Nursing Research | | if not appropriate | | thanks to reviewers | (Fitzpatrick, 1995) |
| Contemporary Nurse | | | double-blind | | (Tregoning, 1993) |
| Critical Care Nurse | | | double-blind | reviewer guidelines | (Alspach, 1994) |
| Gastroenterology Nursing | | | | | (Puetz, 1995) |
| Journal of Continuing Education in Nursing | | | | thanks to reviewers | (Wise, 1995) |
| Journal of Nephrology Nursing | | | | | (Binkley, 1984) |
| Journal of Nurse Midwifery | | | double-blind double-blind | | (Shah, 1981) (Shah, 1988) |
| Nurse Education Today | | | double-blind | | (Johnson, 1996) |
| Nursing Outlook | | | | reviewer guidelines | (Dickerson, 1984) |

**Table 1-2: Editor's description of their editorial peer review process (continued)**

| Journal Titles | Rejection Rates | Reject Without Review; Reasons | Policy on Anonymous and Blind Review* | Additional Discussion and Policy Topics | References |
|---|---|---|---|---|---|
| *Nursing Research* | ~80% | if hopelessly flawed | blind review anonymous | reviewer guidelines statistical review | (Carnegie, 1975) (Downs, 1979) (Downs, 1988) |
| *Nursing Times* | | | | | (Dunn, 1978) |
| **Political Science** | | | | | |
| *American Political Science Review* | 94.6% 93.5% | | anonymous | editorial policies; thanks to reviewers reviewer agreement | (Jones, 1977) (Finifter, 1997) |
| *Journal of Politics* | | | double-blind | | (Livingston, 1971) |
| **Psychology** | | | | | |
| *American Psychological Association, journals* | | | anonymous not blind | ask authors not to appeal | (American Psychological Association, 1972) (American Psychological Association, 1975) |
| *American Psychologist* | | | | thanks to reviewers | (Hunt, 1971) |
| *Journal of Clinical Neuropsychology* | | | | brief reports for "failure to replicate" studies | (Rourke & Costa, 1979) |
| *Journal of Experimental Psychology: Human Learning and Memory* | | | blind review, if requested | editorial policy | (Shiffrin, 1980) |
| *Journal of Experimental Social Psychology* | | | | editorial policy | (Zanna, 1992) |
| *Journal of Personality and Social Psychology* | 80-90% | | blind review, if requested | editorial policy; thanks to reviewers | (Greenwald, 1976) |
| *Personality & Individual Differences* | high | | | guidelines for authors | (Eysenck, 1980) |
| *Personality and Social Psychology Bulletin* | 80% | | | reviewer agreement, thanks to reviewers reviewer agreement, thanks to reviewers | (Hendrick, 1976) (Hendrick, 1977) (Jackson & Latane, 1978) |
| *Psychological Medicine* | | | anonymous | | (Wessely, 1996) |
| *The Psychologist* | | if obviously unacceptable | | | (Eysenck, 1989) |
| *Psychopharmacologia* | 40% | | | | (Kornetsky, 1975) |
| **Science** | | | | | |
| *Analytical Chemistry* | 25.4% | 2.2% | | | (Petruzzi, 1976) |
| *Angewandte Chemie* | 26% | | anonymous | | (Daniel, 1993) |
| *Ground Water* | 55% | | double-blind | reviewer guidelines and editors reviewer guidelines and authors | (Lehr, 1991a) (Lehr, 1991b) |
| *Journal of Geophysical Research* | | | anonymous named in article | | (Reid, 1974) |
| *Journal of Organometallic Chemistry* | | | | | (King, 1994) |

**Table 1-2: Editor's description of their editorial peer review process (continued)**

| Journal Titles | Rejection Rates | Reject Without Review; Reasons | Policy on Anonymous and Blind Review* | Additional Discussion and Policy Topics | References |
|---|---|---|---|---|---|
| IEEE Spectrum | | yes, some are | | editorial policy | (Christiansen, 1974)<br>(Christiansen, 1975)<br>(Christiansen, 1978) |
| International Journal of Insect Morphology and Embryology | | | anonymous | thanks to reviewers; ethical issues; appeal process | (Gupta, 1996) |
| Magnesium Research | | | | author guidelines | (Durlach, 1995) |
| Nature | | none should be | anonymous | editorial code of practice | (1974c)<br>(1975) |
| Physical Review | ~20% | if crackpot papers | | | (Pasternack, 1966)<br>(Goudsmit, 1969) |
| Physical Review Letter | | | anonymous and blind review, if asked | appeal process | (Trigg, 1979)<br>(Lazarus, 1980) |
| Physiologia Plantarum | | | double-blind, reviewers can sign | | (Murphy & Utts, 1994) |
| Protein Science | | | | ethical guidelines | (1994) |
| Science | 80%<br>87% | 60%<br>60% | | editorial policy<br>editorial policies | (Koshland, 1985)<br>(Abelson, 1994) |
| Science, Technology, & Human Values | | | double blind | | (LaFollette, 1983) |
| **Sociology** | | | | | |
| American Journal of Sociology | 38%<br><br>29% | if poor or marginal | | processing of manuscripts | (Goodrich, 1945)<br><br>(Schwartz & Dubin, 1978) |
| American Sociological Review | 63%+21% | | | | (Bakanic, McPhail, & Simon, 1990) |
| Contemporary Sociology | | | | editorial policies<br>thanks to reviewers | (Glenn, 1978)<br>(Glenn, 1979) |
| Human Organization | 73% | 12% | double-blind | | (Bernard, 1980) |
| Journal of Health & Social Behavior | 64% | | | | (Kaplan, 1982) |
| Rural Sociology | | | double-blind | reviewer guidelines | (Bealer, 1974) |
| Social Psychology Quarterly | 74% | | | | (Bohrnstedt, 1982) |
| Social Science and Medicine | | | | reviewer agreement | (1989b) |
| Social Work | | | blind review<br>double-blind | ethical issues | (Meyer, 1983)<br>(Hopps, 1989) |
| Social Work Research and Abstracts | | | double-blind | | (Kirk, 1993) |
| Sociological Quarterly | | 4% | double-blind | reviewer guidelines<br><br>reviewer selection | (McCartney, 1973a)<br>(McCartney, 1973b)<br>(McCartney, 1973c) |
| Sociological Theory | 83% | | | | (Collins, 1982) |
| Sociology of Education | 70%<br>84% | | | | (Sussmann, 1966)<br>(Kerckhoff, 1982) |
| Sociometry | 85% | | | reviewer guidelines | (Seeman, 1966) |

**Table 1-2: Editor's description of their editorial peer review process (continued)**

offer detailed descriptions of their processes with specific information on rejection rates, number of reviewers per manuscript, the use of solicited material, or policies on anonymous or blind review. Some address the journal readership in general announcing a new procedure, for example, double-blind reviewing, explaining why letters are an important addition to the review process, describing reviewer selection, or discussing policy changes.

Topics frequently discussed and most germane to the current investigation include information on rejection rates, rejection without review, and the use of anonymous or blind review (Table 1-2). The second to last column of Table 1-2 lists additional topics discussed by the editors related to editorial peer review, such as reviewers' or authors' guidelines, reviewer agreement, acknowledgment of reviewers, statistical review, and an appeals process. Most of the data provided are from one year only. *The American Political Science Review* published an annual report in *PS*; only the first and most recent are included in Table 1-2. Information in Table 1-2 could be viewed as the results of a large focus group comprised of editors from a variety of disciplines. As in a focus group, interest, trends, and problem areas can be ascertained. Of the 139 journal titles in this table:

- About one-half (51.8 percent) of the editors used the editorial as an opportunity to present their views on anonymity of either reviewers or authors; 28.0 percent mentioned anonymity for reviewers only, 2.8 percent mention only blind reviewing, and 23.0 percent said they use double-blind review.

- 34.5 percent told their readers the journal's rejection rate (usually for unsolicited manuscripts only).

- 28.7 percent discussed their editorial policy on rejecting manuscripts before outside editorial peer review; 12.9 percent gave percentages of manuscripts rejected without review (the practice of rejecting a manuscript without review with the percentages ranging from 2.2 percent of manuscripts to 70.0 percent).

- 16.5 percent thanked their reviewers, often listing the names of those who had reviewed for the journal in a given time period (this group was probably the easiest to miss since these editorials seemed the least likely to be indexed. Many more editors periodically publish a list of reviewers without any commentary; these are almost impossible to identify and have not been included unless there was also some commentary from the editor).

- 17.3 percent gave detailed guidelines or checklists for reviewers (often a copy of the material reviewers received when asked to evaluate a manuscript).

- 6.5 percent stated that at least some manuscripts underwent statistical review.

- 4.3 percent provided supplemental instructions or advice to authors in addition to the formal instructions to authors. Since almost all editors provide some type of instructions to authors, it is not surprising that only 4.3 percent address this in their editorials.

Just over half (50.4 percent) of the journals came from medicine. However, this is only an indication of the number of journals with editorials about peer review. One cannot conclude that the frequency with which medical journal editors write editorials on peer review is an indicator that medicine is more concerned about the process or does a better job with it than economics, for example, a field in which editorials were located in only two journals. Nor is it necessarily indicative of greater interest in editorial peer review among medical journal editors. Although there has been increased attention to peer review in medicine due to the ICMJE and a number of conferences focused on editorial peer review. The fact is *Index Medicus* seems to index editorials more regularly than the indexes to the literature of other disciplines, making editorials in the field of medicine easier to locate. The increased attention editorial peer review has received in the medical community has no bearing on the degree or level of seriousness with which other professions or disciplines view or use the editorial peer review process; it has simply received more visibility.

Through these editorials, editors were supporting their viewpoint and letting their readership know their opinions, procedures, the decision-making process, or outcomes. While this is not a complete picture of editorial practices, Table 1-2 gives insight into which issues editors consider important. Editors are usually limited to a certain number of pages for each issue, and probably do not take lightly the fact that these editorials are published at the expense of pages dedicated to the journal's subject or discipline.

Information from Table 1-2 should be welcomed by the readership and potential authors who might want to know policies or guidelines for particular journals. New editors should find some of these editorials helpful when wrestling with the difficult issues of policies and guidelines.

Limitations of information in Table 1-2:

- Table 1-2 includes journals whose editors have intentionally made a public statement about their journals. These editors of course had control of the communication and decided what they would or would not address. Therefore, the information in this table is not a comprehensive picture of editors' views on the subject. It is simply what a given editor decided to address in a given editorial and is sometimes rather limited or singled minded.

- The editors might, in fact, have been addressing not their own readers, but the "competition" (editors of journals in similar fields) pointing out how selective, highly cited, important, or prestigious their journals were. Or, they might want to inform their readership of the excellent job they were doing. Editors might also have written with the purpose of encouraging potential authors to submit manuscripts by explaining the benefits (high circulation, important topics covered, etc.) of publishing in the journal.

- Editors revealed only what they wanted their readership to know. As can be gleaned from Table 1-2, while some provided detailed information and guidelines, others did not use these editorials as an opportunity to provide the reader with a comprehensive description of their procedures, detailed statistics about manuscript submissions or rejections, their decision-making processes, or their strict editorial guidelines. Of course, this in no way implies that no statements on policies and procedures exist for a particular journal. Such information is often found elsewhere, such as incorporated in the instructions to authors or included in the packet of material sent to reviewers with a manuscript. Editors tended to discuss controversial topics in these editorials, letting their readership know where they stood on such issues as anonymity, level of rejection rates, or the tendency to reject manuscripts without review.

- Relatively few journals are represented in this table given the thousands of English-language scholarly and research journals published. As a group they tend not to be indexed, but one hopes they are representative of similar editorials not uncovered through literature searches and cited references.

At the end of his tenure as editor of *Communication Quarterly*, Chesebro made an appeal to editors to provide the readership with an explicit definition of how they use peer review, to assess the outcome of the process, to use reviewers who favor innovation, and to find editorial board members who insist that articles make a contribution to the field (Chesebro, 1987). There appears to be a trend in this direction, with an obvious benefit to both journal readers and scholarly communication as a whole.

Some editorial control was used with the first scientific publications a few hundred years ago, but by any one of a number of definitions of peer review the current process has been codified only in the latter half of this century. The exact dates journals began using a formal editorial peer review process appear to be difficult to determine. There are many variations in the process and room for individual styles and approaches. During the last 50 years, the process of editorial peer review has been the subject of a growing number of investigations.

Every day, approximately 6,000 to 7,000 scientific articles are written (Arndt, 1992). The enormity of the editorial peer review process is astounding, coupling this vast number of articles with the review of each one of them. In 1990, Relman estimated that for the *New England Journal of Medicine* alone the review process cost about $1 million a year. In addition to this, he added an estimated $1.5 to $2 million of reviewers' time (Relman, 1990). Is all that time and money worth it, he wondered. One purpose of this monograph is to answer that question.

## References

(1974a). Are referees a good thing? *Canadian Medical Association Journal, 111*(9), 897-898.

(1974b). Both sides of the fence. *British Medical Journal, 2*(5912), 185-186.

(1974c). In defense of the anonymous referee. *Nature, 249*, 601.

(1974d). Editorial. *International Journal of Epidemiology, 3*(3), 203-204.

(1975, November 6). Do scientific journals need code of practice? *Nature, 258*(5530), 1.

(1978, January). The refereeing system in the Journal of Endocrinology. *Journal of Endocrinology, 76*(1), 9-19.

(1985, December 14). Editors' decisions. *Lancet, 2*(8468), 1340.

(1988, July-August). Writing and editing. *Journal of General Internal Medicine, 3*(4), 412-414.

(1989a). Peers reviewed. *Lancet, 1*(8647), 1115-1116.

(1989b). Editorial. *Social Science and Medicine, 29*(7), i-ii.

(1994, January). The Protein Science code of ethics. *Protein Science, 3*(1), xi.

Abelson, P. H. (1994). Enhanced challenges for editors. In R. A. Weeks & D. L. Kinser (Eds.), *Editing the refereed scientific journal* (pp. 204-211). New York: IEEE Press.

Alspach, G. (1994, December). What journal editors would like from reviewers. *Critical Care Nurse, 14*(6), 13-16.

American Psychological Association. (1972, June). Eight APA journals initiate controversial blind reviewing. *APA Monitor, 3*(5), 1,5.

American Psychological Association. (1975, September). Publication in APA journals: advice from the editors. Council of editors. *American Psychologist, 20*(9), 711-712.

Amiry, P. (1983). Refereeing for JORS. *Journal of the Operational Research Society, 34*(11), 1025-1026.

Anderson, A. (1989, May 18). Does it work efficiently? *Nature, 339*(6221), 164.

Andreoli, T. E. (1997, June). Report of the editor, July, 1984 - June, 1997. *Kidney International, 51*(6), 1663-1668.

Angell, M., & Relman, A. S. (1989, May 4). Redundant publication. *New England Journal of Medicine, 320*(18), 1212-1213.

Angell, M., & Relman, A. S. (1989, September 21). The Journal's peer-review process. *New England Journal of Medicine, 312*(12), 837-839.

Arndt, K. A. (1984, August). Reviewers for 1983. *Archives of Dermatology, 120*, 1015-6.

Arndt, K. A. (1989, February). Peer review, the Archives, and Harvey Blank. *Archives of Dermatology, 125*(2), 285-286.

Arndt, K. A. (1992, September). Information excess in medicine. *Archives of Dermatology, 128*, 1249-1256.

Arnell, P. (1986, November). Communication through publication: the role of reviewers. *Physiotherapy, 72*(11), 530-533.

Ashenfelter, O., Campbell, J. Y., Gordon, R. H., & Milgrom, P. R. (1991, December). Editorial statement. *American Economic Review, 81*(5).

Bailar, J. C. & Patterson, K. (1985, March 7). Journal peer review. The need for a research agenda. *New England Journal of Medicine, 312*(10), 654-657.

Bakanic, V., McPhail, C., & Simon, R. J. (1990, Winter). If at first you don't succeed: review procedures for revised and resubmitted manuscripts. *American Sociologist, 21*(4), 373-391.

Balaban, M. (1977). *Scientific Information Transfer: the editor's role*. Paper presented at the First International Conference of Scientific Editors, Jerusalem.

Barclay, W. R. (1976, December 20). An expression of thanks to our loyal reviewers. *JAMA, 236*(25), 2887.

Baue, A. E. (1985, August). Peer and/or peerless review. Some vagaries of the editorial process. *Archives of Surgery, 120*(8), 885-888.

Baue, A. E. (1993, December). Reflections of a former editor. *Archives of Surgery, 128*(12), 1305-1314.

Bealer, R. C. (1974, Spring). On journal reviewing procedures: a statement. *Rural Sociology, 39*(1), 6-11.

Beck, R. N. (1991, December). Recognition of manuscript and book reviewers for 1991. *American Journal of Roentgenology, 157*, 1349-1351.

Beck, R. N. (1992, August). Report of the editor, 1991. *American Journal of Roentgenology, 159*, 415-418.

Berezin, A. A., Gordon, R., & Hunter, G. (1995, February 11). Lifting the pernicious veil of secrecy. *New Scientist, 145*(1964), 46-47.

Bernard, H. R. (1980, Winter). Report from the editor. *Human Organization, 39*(4), 366-369.

Bero, L. A., Galbraith, A., & Rennie, D. (1992, October 15). The publication of sponsored symposium in medical journals. *New England Journal of Medicine, 327*(16), 1135-1140.

Binkley, L. S. (1984, September/October). From manuscript to published paper. *Journal of Nephrology Nursing, 1*(2), 117-119.

Blank, H. (1963, April). The summary moves forward. *Archives of Dermatology, 87*(4), 41.

Bohrnstedt, G. W. (1982, March). *Social Psychology Quarterly. ASA Footnotes, 10*, 12.

Bolster, A. & Morgan, P. P. (1986, February 15). How CMAJ controls the quality of its scientific articles. *Canadian Medical Association Journal, 134*(4), 301-303.

Borts, G. H. (1974, May). Report of the managing editor *American Economic Review*. *American Economic Review, 64*(2), 476-481.

Braceland, F. J. (1978, October). On editing the Journal: Ave atque vale. *American Journal of Psychiatry, 135*(10), 1148-1155.

Brady, J. P. (1985, August). Journal referees: gatekeepers of science. *Biological Psychiatry, 20*(8), 823-824.

Brayfield, A. H. (1965, February). Editorial note. *American Psychologist, 20*(2), 121-122.

Broughton, R. S. (1987, March). Publication policy and the *Journal of Parapsychology.* *Journal of Parapsychology, 51(*1), 21-32.

Bucy, P. C. (1994, January). Commemorative article, The Journal of Neurosurgery; its origin and development. *Journal of Neurosurgery, 80*(1), 160-165.

Burnham, J. C. (1990, March 9). The evolution of editorial peer review. *JAMA, 263*(10), 1323-1329.

Carnegie, M. E. (1975, July-August). The referee system. *Nursing Research, 24*(4), 243.

Carney, M. J. & Lundberg, G. D. (1987, July 3). We've come a long way—thanks to peer review. *JAMA, 258*(1), 87.

Chesebro, J. W. (1987, Fall). The peer review system. *Communication Quarterly, 35(*4), i, iv-v.

Chew, F. S. (1993, February). Manuscript peer review: general concepts and the *AJR* process. *American Journal of Roentgenology, 160*(2), 409-411.

Christiansen, D. (1974, July). Who gets published? *IEEE Spectrum, 11*(7), 33.

Christiansen, D. (1975, November). Judging the judges. *IEEE Spectrum, 12(*11), 29.

Christiansen, D. (1978, May). The perils of publishing. *IEEE Spectrum, 15*(5), 27.

Clayton, B. C., & Boyle, K. (1981, September). The refereed journal: prestige in professional publication. *Nursing Outlook, 29(*9), 531-534.

Cleather, J. (1981, September/October). Manuscript review and the editing process. *Physiotherapy Canada, 33*(5), 283-286.

Colaianni, L. A. (1994, July 13). Peer review in journals indexed in Index Medicus. *JAMA, 272*(2), 156-158.

Collins, R. (1982, March). Sociological Theory. *ASA Footnotes, 10,* 12.

Crawford, S. (1988, January). Peer review and the evaluation of manuscripts. *Bulletin of the Medical Library Association, 76*(1), 75-77.

Cullen, S. C. (1964, July-August). An account of the history of the journal Anesthesiology. Anesthesiology, 25(4), 416-427.

Dack, S. (1958, January). Looking ahead. *American Journal of Cardiology, 1*(1), 1-2.

Dack, S. (1983). *The Journal of the American College of Cardiology*: editor's perspective. *Journal of the American College of Cardiology, 1*(1), 3-4.

Daniel, H-D. (1993). An evaluation of the peer review process at *Angewandte Chemie.* *Angewandte Chemie, 32*(2), 234-238.

DeBakey, L. (1990, March). Journal peer reviewing. Anonymity or disclosure? *Archives of Ophthalmology, 108*(3), 345-349.

Dickerson, J. K. (1984, July/August). Guidelines for peer reviewers. *Nursing Outlook, 32*(4), 232.

Douglas-Wilson, I. (1977, April 14). Editorial Review: peerless pronouncements. *New England Journal of Medicine, 296*(15), 877.

Downs, F. S. (1979, July-August). My manuscript—myself. *Nursing Research, 28*(4), 197.

Downs, F. S. (1988, September-October). You and I. *Nursing Research, 37*(5), 260.

Drummond, A. (1993, September). Review: another obstacle to publication? *British Journal of Occupational Therapy, 56*(9), 319.

Dudley, H. A. F. (1989, March). Editorial process at the *British Journal of Surgery*. *British Journal of Surgery, 76*(3), 211-212.

Dunn, A. (1978, October 5). How to make the editor's life easier. *Nursing Times, 74*(40), 1635-1636.

Durlach, J. (1995). Editorial policy of *Magnesium Research*: general considerations on the quality criteria for biomedical papers and some complementary guidelines for the contributors of *Magnesium Research*. *Magnesium Research, 8*(3), 191-206.

Easson, W. M. (1979, August). Prompt review—early publication. *Journal of Clinical Psychiatry, 40*(8), 331.

Eldredge, J. D. (1997, October). Identifying peer-reviewed journals in clinical medicine. *Bulletin of the Medical Library Association, 85*(4), 418-422.

Evans, J. T., Nadjari, H. I., & Burchell, S. A. (1990, March 9). Quotational and reference accuracy in surgical journals. A continuing peer review problem. *JAMA, 263*(10), 1353-1354.

Eysenck, H. J. (1980). Editorial. *Personality and Individual Differences, 1*(1), 1-2.

Eysenck, H. J. (1989, March). Refereeing in psychology journals: a reply from Hans Eysenck. *Psychologist, 2*(3), 98-99.

Farndon, J. R., Murie, J. A., Johnson, C. D., Earnshaw, J. J., & Guillou, P. J. (1997, July). The referee process of *The British Journal of Surgery*. *British Journal of Surgery, 84*(7), 901-903.

Feinstein, A. R. (1986). Some ethical issues among editors, reviewers and readers. *Journal of Chronic Diseases*, 39(7), 491-493.

Feinstein, A. R. & Spitzer, W. O. (1983). Variance and dissent. *Journal of Chronic Diseases*, 36(4), 299.

Feinstein, A. R. & Spitzer, W. O. (1989). The peer-review process—and an acknowledgment of our peerless reviewers. *Journal of Clinical Epidemiology, 42*(1), 1-4.

Feinstein, A. R., & Spitzer, W. O. (1991). An expression of gratitude to the *Journal*'s reviewers. *Journal of Clinical Epidemiology, 44*(1), 1-4.

Finifter, A. W. (1997, December). Report of the editor of the *American Political Science Review*, 1996-97. *PS, 30*(4), 783-791.

Fischer-Rasmussen, W. (1996). The scientific reviewers. *Acta Obstetricia et Gynecologica Scandinavica, 75*, 693-694.

Fitzpatrick, J. L. (1995, February). The making of a manuscript. *Applied Nursing Research, 8*(1), 1-2.

Fletcher, R. H. & Fletcher, S. W. (1993, April 15). Who's responsible? *Annals of Internal Medicine, 118*(8), 645-646.

Fletcher, R. H. & Fletcher, S. W. (1997). Evidence for the effectiveness of peer review. *Science and Engineering Ethics, 3*(1), 35-50.

Fletcher, S. W. (1991). Research agenda for medical journals. In S. Lock (Ed.), *The future of medical journals: in commemoration of 150 years of the British Medical Journal* (pp. 93-97). London: British Medical Journal.

Fletcher, S. W., & Fletcher, R. H. (1991, April 15). Early release of research results. *Annals of Internal Medicine, 114*(8), 698-700.

Fluck, R. R., Jr., & Hess, D. (1988, May). What happens to your manuscript after you send it to *Respiratory Care*? Peer review and all that. *Respiratory Care, 33*(5), 329.

Fondiller, S. H. (1994, March). Is nursing at risk? *Nursing & Health Care, 15*(3), 142-148.

Fraenkel-Conrat, H. (1974, March 1). Is anonymity necessary? *Nature, 248*, 8.

Franken, E. A., Jr. (1997, October). Peer review and *Academic Radiology. Academic Radiology, 4*(10), 663-664.

Friedman, D. P. (1995, April). Manuscript peer review at the *AJR*: facts, figures, and quality assessment. *American Journal of Roentgenology, 164*(4), 1007-1009.

Fulginiti, V. A. (1984, April). On the editorial process in the medical literature. *American Journal of Diseases of Children, 138*(4), 337-339.

Gardner, M. J. & Bond, J. (1990, March 9). An exploratory study of statistical assessment of papers published in the *British Medical Journal. JAMA, 26*(10), 1355-1357.

Garfunkel, J. M., Lawson, E. E., Hamrick, H. J., & Ulshen, M. H. (1990, March 9a). Effect of acceptance or rejection on the author's evaluation of peer review of manuscripts. *JAMA, 263*(10), 1376-1378.

Garfunkel, J. M., Ulshen, M. H., Hamrick, H. J., & Lawson, E. E. (1990, March 9b). Problems identified by secondary review of accepted manuscripts. *JAMA, 263*(10), 1369-1371.

Glanz, K., Axelson, M. L., & Brinberg, D. (1994, December). Peer review: indispensable or a crap shoot. *Journal of Nutrition Education, 26*(6), 258.

Glenn, N. D. (1978, January). Statement of the new editor. *Contemporary Sociology, 7*(1), 5-6.

Glenn, N. D. (1979, November). Accountability and the journal article review process. *Contemporary Sociology, 8*(6), 785-787.

Goldwyn, R. M. (1989, February). Peer review for publication. *Plastic and Reconstructive Surgery, 83*(2), 398-399.

Goodrich, D. W. (1945, December). An analysis of manuscripts received by the editors of the *American Sociological Review* from May 1, 1944 to September 1, 1945. *American Sociological Review, 10*(6), 716-725.

Gordon, M. D. (1977). *Refereeing reconsidered: an examination of unwitting bias in scientific evaluation*. Paper presented at the First International Conference of Scientific Editors, Jerusalem.

Goudsmit, S. A. (1961, June 1). Editorial. *Physical Review Letters, 6*(11), 587-588.

Goudsmit, S. A. (1969, May). What happened to my paper? *Physics Today, 22*(5), 23-25.

Greenwald, A. G. (1976, January). An editorial. *Journal of Personality and Social Psychology, 33*(1), 1-7.

Gupta, A. P. (1996, January/April). The peer review process, multiple publications, and the overcrowded by-line: roles of editor, reviewer, and author. *International Journal of Insect Morphology and Embryology, 25*(1/2), 19-24.

Handysides, S. (1996, November). CDR Review's editorial process: a survey of papers published in 1995. *Communicable Disease Report, 6*(12), R176-8.

Hargens, L. L. (1990, March 9). Variations in journal peer review systems. Possible causes and consequences. *JAMA, 263*(10), 1348-1352.

Harter, S. P. (1993, July). The peer review process. *Library Quarterly, 63*(3), v-vi.

Hendrick, C. (1976). Editorial comment. *Personality and Social Psychology Bulletin, 2*, 207-208.

Hendrick, C. (1977, Winter). Editorial comment. *Personality and Social Psychology Bulletin, 3*(1), 1-2.

Hepker, R. R. (1991, January). *Infection Control and Hospital Epidemiology*: the formal review process. *Infection Control and Hospital Epidemiology, 12*(1), 11-13.

Hernon, P., Smith, A., & Croxen, M. B. (1993, July). Publications in *College & Research Libraries*: accepted rejected, and published papers, 1980-1991. *College and Research Libraries, 54*(4), 303-321.

Hess, E. L. (1975, September). Effects of the review process. *IEEE Transactions on Professional Communication, PC-18*(3), 196-199.

Hoffband, B. I. (1990, February). Conversation piece: the medical journal editor. *Postgraduate Medical Journal, 66*(772), 153-154.

Hollender, M. H. (1983, July 8). The 51st landmark article. JAMA, 250(2), 228-229.

Hopps, J. G. (1989, January). Peer review: A trust, not a vault. *Social Work, 34*(1), 3-4.

Humphreys, R. P., Reigel, D. H., & Epstein, F. J. (1995, May). The editor's labours: separating the wheat from the chaff. *Pediatric Neurosurgery, 22*(5), 23-27.

Hunt, E. (1971, March). Psychological publications. *American Psychologist, 26*(3), 311.

Huth, E. J. (1982). Our thanks to our consultants. *Annals of Internal Medicine, 96*(1), 119.

Ingelfinger, F. J. (1970, August 28). Medical literature: The campus without tumult. *Science, 169*(3948), 831-837.

Ingelfinger, F. J. (1972, December 21). Season's greetings. *New England Journal of Medicine, 287*(25), 1301.

Ingelfinger, F. J. (1974, May). Peer review in biomedical publication. *American Journal of Medicine, 56*(5), 686-692.

Ingelfinger, F. J. (1975, December 25). Charity and peer review in publication. *New England Journal of Medicine, 293*(26), 1371-1372.

Ingelfinger, F. J. (1977, June 30). The *New England Journal of Medicine*: Editor's report, 1967-77. *New England Journal of Medicine, 296*(26), 1530-1535.

International Committee of Medical Journal Editors. (1978, May 20). Uniform requirements for manuscripts submitted to biomedical journals. *British Medical Journal, 1*(6123), 1334-1336.

International Committee of Medical Journal Editors. (1992, June 15). Statements on electronic publication and on peer-reviewed journals. *Annals of Internal Medicine, 116*(12 pt 1), 1030.

International Committee of Medical Journal Editors. (1997, January 15). Uniform requirements for manuscripts submitted to biomedical journals. *Canadian Medical Association Journal, 156*(2), 270-277.

Jackson, J. M., & Latane, B. (1978, July). On the displacement of authors by editors. *Personality and Social Psychology Bulletin, 4*(3), 381-382.

Jacobsen, E. (1980). Authors, reviewers, and editors. *Psychopharmacology, 71*, 111-115.

Johnson, M. (1996). On refereeing journal articles. *Nurse Education Today, 16*, 161-162.

Jones, C. (1977, Fall). Report of the managing editor of the *American Political Science Review*, 1976-77. *PS, 10*(4), 448-453.

Juhasz, S., Calvert, E., Jackson, T., Kronick, D. A., & Shipman, J. (1975, September). Acceptance and rejection of manuscripts. *IEEE Transactions on Professional Communication, 18*(3), 177-185.

Kaplan, H. B. (1982, March). *Journal of Health & Social Behavior. ASA Footnotes, 10*, 11-12.

Keller, M. (1977). *Editorial judgment in scientific periodicals.* Paper presented at the First International Conference of Scientific Editors, Jerusalem.

Kerckhoff, A. C. (1982, March). Sociology of Education. *ASA Footnotes, 10*, 11-12.

King, R. B. (1994). Editorial aspects of the *Journal of Organometallic Chemistry*. In R. A. Weeks & D. L. Kinser (Eds.), *Editing the refereed scientific journal* (pp. 54-66). New York: IEEE Press.

Kirk, S. A. (1993, June). The puzzles of peer perusal. *Social Work Research and Abstracts, 29*(2), 3-4.

Knox, F. G. (1981, January). No unanimity about anonymity. *Journal of Laboratory and Clinical Medicine, 97*(1), 1-3.

Kochen, M. & Perkel, B. (1977). *Improving referee-selection and manuscript evaluation.* Paper presented at the First International Congress on Scientific Editors, Dordrect, Holland.

Kole, L. A. (1989, May/June). Between hammer and anvil. *Journal of the American Academy of Physician Assistants, 2*(3), 162-163.

Kornetsky, C. (1975). Thoughts of an ex-editor. *Psychopharmacologia, 42,* 1-4.

Koshland, D. E. (1985, January 18). An editor's quest (II). *Science, 227*(4684), 249.

Kraft, D. H. (1987, March). The peer review process for the *Journal of the American Society for Information Science (JASIS). Journal of the American Society for Information Science, 38*(2), 81-82.

Kronick, D. A. (1990, March 9). Peer review in the 18th-century scientific journal. *JAMA, 263*(10), 1321-1322.

LaFollette, M. C. (1983, Fall). On fairness and peer review. *Science, Technology, & Human Values, 8*(4), 3-5.

Lavelle, J. (1966, November). Facts of journal publishing, IV. *Publications of the Modern Language Association of America, 81*(6), 3-12.

Lazarus, D. (1980, November 10). Authors, editors and referees. *Physical Review Letters, 45*(19), 1527-1528.

Lehr, J. H. (1991a, March/April). The peer review system according to *Ground Water. Ground Water, 29*(2), 167-168.

Lehr, J. H. (1991b, May/June). More on the peer review process according to *Ground Water. Ground Water, 29,* 327-330.

Lewis, E. P. (1980, April). A peerless publication. *Nursing Outlook, 28,* 225-226.

Lichter, P. R. (1990, December). Journal accountability. *Ophthalmology, 97*(12), 1581-1582.

Lin, N., Garvey, W. D., & Nelson, C. E. (1970, February). Publication fate of material presented at an annual ASA meeting: Two years after the meeting. *American Sociologist, 5*(1), 22-25.

Litt, I. F. (1990, July). Blind review: why not? *Journal of Adolescent Health Care, 11*(4), 287.

Livingston, W. S. (1971, February). Editorial note. *Journal of Politics, 33*(1), v-viii.

Lock, S. (1976, November 6). How editors survive. *British Medical Journal, 2*(6044), 1118-1119.

Lock, S. (1985). *A difficult balance. Editorial peer reviewed in medicine.* Philadelphia: ISI Press.

Lock, S. (1990, March 9). What do peer reviewers do? *JAMA, 263*(10), 1341-1343.

Lock, S. (1991). As things really were? In S. Lock (Ed.), *The future of medical journals: in commemoration of 150 years of the British Medical Journal* (pp. 21-35). London: British Medical Journal.

Lock, S. (1992). Journalology: evolution of medical journal and some current problems. *Journal of Internal Medicine, 232,* 199-205.

Lock, S. (1993). *Quality assurance in medical publication.* Paper presented at The Royal Society of Edinburgh, Edinburgh.

Lundberg, G. D. (1984, February 10). Appreciation to our peer reviewers. *JAMA, 251*(6), 758.

Lundberg, G. D. (1985, March 8). Thanks to our 1984 peer reviewers/referees. *JAMA, 253*(10), 1446-1451.

Lundberg, G. D. & Carney, M. J. (1986, June 20). Peer review at *JAMA*. *JAMA, 255*(23), 3286.

Lundberg, G. D. & Williams, E. S. (1991, March 6). The quality of a medical article. Thank you to our 1990 peer reviewers. *JAMA, 265*(9), 1161-1162.

Manske, P. R. (1997, September). A review of peer review. *Journal of Hand Surgery, 22A*(5), 767-771.

Mauer, A. M. (1985). Editorial review policies for manuscripts. *Medical and Pediatric Oncology, 13*, 113.

McCartney, J. L. (1973a, Spring). Selecting reviewers. *Sociological Quarterly, 14*(2), 287-288.

McCartney, J. L. (1973b). Manuscript reviewing. *Sociological Quarterly, 14*(3), 290, 440-446.

McCartney, J. L. (1973c, Winter). Preparing manuscripts. *Sociological Quarterly, 14*, 2, 144.

McCartney, J. L. (1976, August). Confronting the journal publication crisis: a proposal for a council of social science editors. *American Sociologist, 11*(3), 144-152.

McDuffie, F. C. (1978, January). A progress report. *Journal of Laboratory and Clinical Medicine, 91*(1), 1-2.

McNutt, R. A., Evans, A. T., Fletcher, R. H., & Fletcher, S. W. (1990, March 9). The effects of blinding on the quality of review. *JAMA, 263*(10), 1371-1376.

Meadow, C. T. (1980, September). On refereeing of *JASIS* papers. *Journal of the American Society for Information Science, 31*(5), 307-308.

Meakins, J. L. (1996, June). The review process. *Canadian Journal of Surgery, 39*(3), 180.

Meyer, C. H. (1983, January-February). Responsibility in publishing. *Social Work, 28*(1), 3.

Miller, A. C. & Serzan, S. L. (1984, November/December). Criteria for identifying a refereed journal. *Journal of Higher Education, 55*(6), 673-699.

Moossy, J., & Moossy, Y. R. (1985, May). Anonymous authors, anonymous referees: an editorial exploration. *Journal of Neuropathology and Experimental Neurology, 44*(3), 225-228.

Morgan, P. P. (1981, March 15). Author, editor and reviewer: how manuscripts become journal articles. *Canadian Medical Association Journal, 124*(6), 664-666.

Morgan, P. P. (1984, November 1). Anonymity in medical journals. *Canadian Medical Association Journal, 131*(9), 1007-1008.

Morse, J. M. (1996, May). Revise and resubmit: responding to reviewers' reports. *Qualitative Health Research, 6*(2), 149-151.

Murphy, T. M., & Utts, J. M. (1994, November). A retrospective analysis of peer review at *Physiologia Plantarum*. *Physiologia Plantarum, 92*(3), 535-542.

Murray, J. F. (1974, January). On assuming the editorship of the American Review of Respiratory Disease. *American Review of Respiratory Disease, 109*(1), 1-3.

Murray, J. F. (1975). Progress report. *American Review of Respiratory Disease, 111*(11), 1-3.

Nelson, W. E. (1982, July). The first 50 years of the *Journal of Pediatrics*. *Journal of Pediatrics, 101*(1), 1-4.

Neuhauser, D. (1997, April). Peer review and the research commons. *Medical Care, 35*(4), 301-302.

Newell, F. W. (1990, February 15). Peer review. *American Journal of Ophthalmology, 109*(2), 221-223.

Nichol, H. (1993, June). Manuscripts: from peer review to your review. *Beta Release, 17*(2), 8.

Northridge, M. E. & Susser, M. (1994, May). The paper route for submissions to the journal. *American Journal of Public Health, 84*(5), 717-718.

Parker, G., Barnett, B., Holmes, S., & Manicavasagar, V. (1984, March). Publishing in the parish. *Australian and New Zealand Journal of Psychiatry, 18*(1), 78-85.

Parmley, W. W. (1995, May). Peer review or poor review? *Journal of the American College of Cardiology, 25*(6), 1470-1471.

Pasternack, S. (1960, February 1). Editorial. *Physical Review Letters, 4*(3), 109-10.

Pasternack, S. (1966, May). Is journal publication obsolescent? *Physics Today, 19*(5), 38-43.

Patterson, K. & Bailar, J. C. (1985). A review of journal peer review. In K. S. Warren (Ed.), *Selectivity of information systems: Survival of the fitest* (pp. 64-82). New York: Praeger.

Perlman, M. (1974, May). Report of the managing editor *Journal of Economic Literature*. *American Economic Review, 64*(2), 483-487.

Petruzzi, J. M. (1976, September). Peer review in *Analytical Chemistry*. *Analytical Chemistry, 48*(11), 875A.

Pettigrew, K. E. & Nicholls, P. T. (1994). Publication patterns of LIS faculty from 1982-92: effects of doctoral programs. *Library and Information Science Research, 16*, 139-156.

Pigg, R. M. (1987, January). Comments on the Journal peer review system. *Journal of School Health, 57*(1), 5-7.

Pitkin, R. M. (1993). Referees: their roles, rights, and responsibilities. *Obstetrics and Gynecology, 82*, 464.

Pitkin, R. M. (1993, August). The peer-review system. *Obstetrics and Gynecology, 82*(2), 304-305.

Pitkin, R. M. (1995, May). Blinded manuscript review: an idea whose time has come? *Obstetrics and Gynecology, 85*(5, Part 1).

Porter, J. R. (1963, September 13). Challenges to editors of scientific journals. *Science, 141*(3584), 1014-1017.

Pountney, M. (1996, December). Blinded reviewing. *Developmental Medicine and Child Neurology, 38*, 1059-1060.

Puetz, B. E. (1995, May/June). The *GNJ* review process. *Gastroenterology Nursing, 18*(3), 85-86.

Reid, G. C. (1974, May 17). Referees in print. *Nature, 249*(5454), 206.

Relman, A. S. (1980, July 31). News reports of medical meetings: how reliable are abstracts? *New England Journal of Medicine, 303*(5), 277-278.

Relman, A. S. (1981, October 1). The Ingelfinger rule. *New England Journal of Medicine, 305*(14), 824-826.

Relman, A. S. (1989, September 21). The Journal's peer-review process. *New England Journal of Medicine, 321*(12), 837-839.

Relman, A. S. (1990, November). Peer review in scientific journals—what good is it? *West Journal of Medicine, 153*, 520-522.

Relman, A. S., Rennie, D., & Angell, M. (1980, December 25). Greetings - with regrets. *New England Journal of Medicine, 303*(26), 1527-1528.

Rennie, D. (1990, March 9). Editorial peer review in biomedical publication. *JAMA, 263*(10), 1317.

Roberts, L. (1991, January 18). The rush to publish. *Science, 251*, 260-263.

Roberts, W. C. (1987, April). Reviews of classic books and ineptness of reviewers: lessons for judges of medical manuscripts. *American Journal of Cardiology, 59*(8), 922-923.

Roe, I. L. (1978, May). Peer review. *American Journal of Medical Technology, 44*(5), 365.

Rothstein, J. M. (1991, February). Peer review. *Physical Therapy, 71*(2), 88-89.

Rourke, B. P., & Costa, L. (1979). Editorial policy II. *Journal of Clinical Neurosychology, 1*(2), 93-95.

Saidman, L. J. (1995, July). What I have learned from 9 years and 9,000 papers. *Anesthesiology, 83*(1), 191-197.

Saracevic, T. (1985). Changing of the guard—editorial policies of information processing and managment. *Information Processing & Management, 21*(1), 1-3.

Saracevic, T. (1986). The refereeing process at *Information Processing & Management*. *Information Processing & Management, 22*(1), 1-3.

Saxen, E. A. (1976, March 15). International Journal of Cancer—a ten-year report of the editor-in-chief. *International Journal of Cancer, 17*(3), 289-291.

Schauder, D. (1994). Electronic publishing of professional articles: attitudes of academics and implications for the scholarly communication industry. *Journal of the American Society for Information Science, 45*(2), 73-100.

Schmidt, C. F. (1958). On changing editors. *Circulation Research, 6*(1), 1-3.

Schorr, T. M. (1979, October). Peer review and the AJN. *American Journal of Nursing, 79*(10), 1731.

Schwartz, B. & Dubin, S. C. (1978, April). Manuscript queues and editorial organization. *Scholarly Publishing, 9*(3), 253-259.

Schwartz, C. A. (1994, March). Scholarly communication as a loosely coupled system: reassessing prospects for structural reform. *College and Research Libraries, 55*(2), 101-114.

Seeman, M. (1966, November). Report of the editor of *Sociometry. American Sociologist, 1*(5), 284-285.

Service, F. J. (1983, March-April). Manuscript review. *Diabetes Care, 6*(2), 208-209.

Shah, M. A. (1981, January/February). Yes! *JNM* is a refereed journal. *Journal of Nurse Midwifery, 26*(1), 3.

Shah, M. A. (1988, March/April). Who referees the referees? A dilemma for peer reviewed journals. *Journal of Nurse Midwifery, 33*(2), 55-56.

Shiffrin, R. M. (1980, July). Editorial. *Journal of Experimental Psychology: Human Learning and Memory, 6*(4), 439-440.

Siegelman, S. S. (1988, February). Guidelines for reviewers of *Radiology. Radiology, 166*(2), 360.

Simonsen, R. J. (1996). Peer review—it should mean something. *Quintessence International, 27*(8), 509.

Sly, R. M. (1989, August). Contribution of peer review to scientific progress. *Annals of Allergy, 63*(2), 85.

Sly, R. M. (1990, October). Blinding reviewers improves peer review. *Annals of Allergy, 65*(4), 243.

Sly, R. M. (1991, January). How to review a scientific manuscript. *Annals of Allergy, 66*(1), 3.

Smith, B. K. (1993, Winter). The journal article—conception to publication. *Art Documentation, 12*(4), 159-162.

Smith, R. (1982, October 30). Steaming up windows and refereeing medical papers. *British Medical Journal, 285*, 1259-1261.

Smith, R. (1993, January 2). Auditing *BMJ* decision making. *British Medical Journal, 306*(6869), 3-4.

Soffer, A. (1968, November). Alienated readers and frustrated editors. *Diseases of Chest, 54*(5), 3.

Soffer, A. (1978, February). The open editorial office. *Chest, 73*(2), 125.

Soffer, A. (1979, March). Identification of reviewers; a statement of policy. *Chest, 75*(3), 295-296.

Speck, B. W. (1993). *Publication peer review; an annotated bibliography* (Vol. 7). Westport, Connecticut: Greenwood Press.

Spodick, D. H. (1981, August). The peer review system and the editor's correspondence. *Archives of Internal Medicine, 141*(9), 1121.

Squires, B. P. (1987, July 1). Reviewing and editing: a shared responsibility. *Canadian Medical Association Journal, 137*(1), 16.

Squires, B. P. (1989, May 1a). Authors' rights 1. Knowing what to expect from *CMAJ. Canadian Medical Association Journal, 140*(9), 1003.

Squires, B. P. (1989, May 1b). Authors' rights: 1. knowing what to expect from the *CMAJ. Canadian Medical Association Journal, 140*(7), 1003.

Squires, B. P. (1989, July 1c). Biomedical manuscripts: what editors want from authors and peer reviewers. *Canadian Medical Association Journal, 141*(1), 17-19.

Squires, B. P. (1989, August 1d). Biomedical review articles: what editors want from authors and peer reviewers. *Canadian Medical Association Journal, 141*(3), 195-197.

Squires, B. P. (1989, October 1e). Editorials and platform articles: What editors want from authors and peer reviewers. *Canadian Medical Association Journal, 141*, 666-667.

Squires, B. P. (1995, June 1). A global network for medical journal editors. *Canadian Medical Association Journal, 152*(11), 1757-1759.

Stern, P. N. (1996, May-June). Putting the manuscript to bed: operationalizing the process. *Health Care for Women International, 17*(3), v-vii.

Stieg, M. F. (1983, February). Refereeing and the editorial process: the AHR and Webb. *Scholarly Publishing, 14*(2), 99-122.

Stull, G. R. (1989, April). Peer-review process is key to quality publication. *Ceramic Bulletin, 68*(4), 850-852.

Sussmann, L. (1966, November). Report of the editor of *Sociology of Education. American Sociologist, 1*(5), 284.

Swanson, E. A. & McCloskey, J. (1982, October). The manuscript review process of nursing journals. *Image, 14*(3), 72-76.

Talbott, J. H. (1969, July 28). Editorial responsibilities–editorial procedures. *JAMA, 209*(4), 552.

Talley, C. R. (1996, January 15). Selecting material for publication in *AJHP. American Journal of Health-System Pharmacy, 53*, 133-134.

Tregoning, S. (1993). Editorial. *Contemporary Nurse, 2*(3), 101.

Trigg, G. L. (1979, September 3). Communicating with authors. *Physical Review Letters, 43*(10), 651-652.

Vatner, S. F., Berk, B. C., Leinwand, L. A., Libby, P., Schwartz, K., & Strauss, H. C. (1996). A second term for the editors, status and goals for review process. *Circulation Research, 79*, 1-3.

Waeckerle, J. F. (1996, January). State of the *Journal. Annals of Emergency Medicine, 27*(1), 73-74.

Waeckerle, J. F. & Callaham, M. L. (1996, July). Medical journals and the science of peer review: raising the standard. *Annals of Emergency Medicine, 28*(1), 75-77.

Warren, R. (1973, May). Authors and editors meet. *Archives of Surgery, 106*(3), 360-362.

Weeks, R. A. & Kinser, D. L. (Eds.). (1994). *Editing the refereed scientific journal.* New York: IEEE Press.

Weick, K. E. (1983, June). From the editor, ASQ statistics. *Administrative Science Quarterly, 28*(2), 299.

Weiss-Lambrou, R. (1991, October). Peer review and journal publication. *Canadian Journal of Occupational Therapy, 58*(4), 167-170.

Weller, A. C. (1990a, March 9). Editorial peer review in U.S. medical journals. *JAMA, 263*(10), 1344-1347.

Weller, A. C. (1990b, July). Editorial peer review: methodology and data collection. *Bulletin of the Medical Library Association, 78*(3), 258-270.

Wessely, S. (1996). What do we know about peer review? *Psychological Methods, 26,* 883-886.

White, M. C. (1993, December). The peer review process of the *Journal. American Journal of Infection Control, 21*(6), 279-282.

Williams, E. S. & Lundberg, G. D. (1996, March 13). Information for readers, the JAMA 1995 editorial peer review audit. *JAMA, 275*(10), 804.

Wilson, J. (1974, October). The Journal of Clinical Investigation 1974. *Journal of Clinical Investigation, 54*(4), xv-xvii.

Winland, R. D. (1997, January). *General Dentistry*'s peer review process. *General Dentistry, 45*(1), 6.

Wise, P. S. Y. (1995, November/December). Giving thanks. *Journal of Continuing Education in Nursing, 26*(6), 243-244.

Yankauer, A. (1977, February). Editor's report. *American Journal of Public Health, 67*(2), 136-137.

Yankauer, A. (1978, March). Editor's report. *American Journal of Public Health, 68*(3), 220-221.

Yankauer, A. (1979, March). Editor's report: peer review. *American Journal of Public Health, 69*(3), 222-223.

Yankauer, A. (1982, March). Editor's report-peer review again. *American Journal of Public Health, 72*(3), 239-240.

Yankauer, A. (1983, March). Editor's report: LPU, the nation's health and other matters. *American Journal of Public Health, 73*(3), 247.

Yankauer, A. (1984, March). 1983: Editor's report. *American Journal of Public Health, 74*(3), 207-208.

Yankauer, A. (1986, July). Then and now, the *American Journal of Public Health*, 1911-85. *American Journal of Public Health, 76*(7), 809-815.

Yankauer, A. (1987, March). Editor's report—on decisions and authorships. *American Journal of Public Health, 77*(3), 271-272.

Yankauer, A. (1989, April). Editor's annual report—manuscript requirements. *American Journal of Public Health, 79*(4), 413-414.

Yankauer, A. (1990, April). Editor's report—scientific misconduct and the responsibility of journal editors. *American Journal of Public Health, 80*(4), 399-400.

Yankauer, A. (1990, March 9). Who are the reviewers and how much do they review? *JAMA, 263*(10), 1338-1340.

Zanna, M. (1992, April). My life as a dog (I mean editor). *Personality and Social Psychology Bulletin, 18*(4), 485-488.

Zetterman, R. K. (1996, December). Editorial review and the *American Journal of Gastroenterology. American Journal of Gastroenterology, 91*(12), 2459-2460.

Ziman, J. M. (1968). *Public knowledge: an essay concerning the social development of science*. London: Cambridge University Press.

Zuckerman, H. & Merton, R. K. (1971, January). Patterns of evaluation in science: institutionalisation, structure and functions of the referee system. *Minerva, 9*(1), 66-100.

# Chapter Two

# The Rejected Manuscript

*We all learn from our failures.*
(Frey, 1985, p. 3)

An underlying assumption in most of the literature on editorial peer review is that the most important journals in a field or discipline receive the most manuscripts. Therefore, the thinking continues, the journals that receive the most manuscripts can be the most selective, reject the most manuscripts and, as a result, publish the most important material in a field. Do data from studies of journal quality and manuscript rejection rates confirm this assumption? This chapter examines studies of rejected manuscripts and journal rejection rates to determine their influence on the scientific communication process and the publication of quality material.

The rejected manuscript not only affects the body of scientific knowledge, but it can also have a profound impact on the author. Garvey and colleagues conducted several studies in the late 1960s and early 1970s on scientific communication in the physical, social, and engineering sciences. Their investigation tracked the research-to-publication process of over 12,000 scientists. One of their more interesting findings was that a rejected manuscript was likely to change the career path of the author. They found that almost one-third of those authors who experienced a rejection had "abandoned the subject-matter area of their article" within a year (p. 214) (Garvey, Lin, & Tomita, 1972). In addition, those who continued to do research in the same area failed to progress at the same rate as colleagues who had not experienced a similar rejection. Do manuscripts rejected today still continue to have a similar impact on the authors? Were these manuscripts rightly rejected because the work was, indeed, scientifically flawed, unimportant, or uninteresting and, therefore, inappropriate for publication in the scientific literature? Did these rejected manuscripts ever become part of the literature?

The earliest study of the rejection rate of a journal was in the field of sociology. For several months in 1944 and 1945, Goodrich analyzed manuscripts received by the *American Sociological Review* (Goodrich, 1945). He reported that during this time the *American Sociological Review* rejected 37.5 percent of the manuscripts it received. This early study did not use the term "peer review," but the author discussed the "editorial responsibility to select from the total number of manuscripts received, about 60 percent for publication" (p. 720). One-third of the accepted manuscripts came from papers presented at the annual meeting of the American Sociological Society, and authors had a much higher chance of acceptance if they were members of the Society. The reason for this was simply stated: Goodrich maintained that those who were not members of the Society were most likely to "reflect the marginality of the subject matter to the field of sociology, or an elementary treatment of sociological materials" (p. 725). One criterion for accepting a manuscript was "relevance of the subject matter to the field of sociology" another "suggested" criterion was "membership of author in the American Sociological Society" (p. 720). Goodrich admitted that "manuscripts submitted by authors identified with major institutions are accepted in greater proportion than are those coming from authors with other affiliations" (p. 724), and yet he ascertained that this was not intentional: "no attempt was made on the part of the editors to accept a disproportionate number of manuscripts from persons in well-known institutions, nor to reject manuscripts of persons who were not affiliated with educational institutions" (p. 725).

Goodrich made no mention of "blind" reviewing, so one can assume that the reviewing editors knew who the authors were and if they were members of the American Sociological Association, came from a major educational institution, or had presented their work at the Association's annual meeting. The data are particularly interesting in that they point to the possibility of favoritism to well-known institutions and authors. The Goodrich study, with its assurance of impartiality juxtaposed with its preference for accepting manuscripts from society members, demonstrates a difficulty of analyzing rejection rates. One could, of course, assume that the rejected manuscripts were less important than the accepted ones. But one cannot help wondering about how the combined influences of author's prestige, institution, and societal membership affected the decision to publish or not to publish a particular work. Chapter Seven focuses on potential bias in the review process, bias that could result in the rejection of a manuscript for reasons other than its merits.

## Medical journals and the news media

One reason for rejection by some journals in the medical community is unrelated to the merits of the research. In 1969, Franz Ingelfinger, then editor of the *New England Journal of Medicine*, adopted a policy of never publishing a study if it had first been reported in either the news media or a limited-circulation journal (Ingelfinger, 1969). Two exceptions were made: abstracts published as part of a scientific meeting or press reports resulting from a presentation at a meeting. Ingelfinger took this action after the receipt of a manuscript had already been published in a journal with a limited circulation. He directed readers to the masthead of the *New England Journal of Medicine* that clearly stated: "articles are accepted for consideration with the understanding that they are contributed for publication solely to this journal" (p. 676). This policy has subsequently become known as the "Ingelfinger rule" and has been the subject of some disagreement and controversy. Grouse suggested that the *New England Journal of Medicine*'s policy would "adversely affect medical reporting of clinical research" (p. 375) (Grouse, 1981). The editor of *Annals of Internal Medicine*, Edward Huth, who disagreed with the Ingelfinger rule and had never applied it to the *Annals*, stated that "authors should be free to discuss important new findings with reporters before those findings reach print in journals" (p. 560) (Huth, 1983).

Arnold Relman continued to support the Ingelfinger rule when he assumed editorship of the *New England Journal of Medicine*, citing a study that showed "barely half of a group of randomly selected cardiology papers submitted to a national scientific meeting (and published in abstract form) have appeared as full-length articles in peer-reviewed journals" (p. 278) (Relman, 1980). Relman contended that papers presented at scientific meetings are often reports of new findings. The meetings themselves provide a forum for further discussion and debate and, thus, should not be considered ready for presentation to the public without the benefits of a formal peer review process. However, results of studies are likely to be reported to the public since members of the media attend scientific and medical conferences. Relman suggested that societies themselves ought to be prudent about encouraging members of the media to publish reports of preliminary findings. Relman's comment led the editors of *JAMA* to lament that "Dr. Relman apparently would have medical and surgical associations and government agencies close their doors to the press" (p. 374) (McBride, 1982).

In an editorial the next year, Relman assured readers and authors that the *Journal's* editors had always considered "material presented at open scientific meetings as in the public realm and have never rejected a manuscript merely because the work was presented at such a meeting and then reported in the press" (p. 824) (Relman, 1981). Two years later, he addressed the subject another editorial, telling authors they were "free to discuss important new findings with reporters before those findings reach print in journals, and we have never imposed the constraint on authors widely known as the Ingelfinger rule" (p. 560) (1983).

Relman raised the subject again, in 1988, by answering a number of questions concerning the Ingelfinger rule. No, if the full presentation has been published, the *Journal* will not publish the same material. Yes, presenters could talk to reporters after a presentation, but no, once a manuscript was accepted authors could not discuss particulars of the findings with reporters (Relman, 1988). Similarly, editors of journals of the American Medical Association (AMA) had a policy that stated "once a manuscript we have received is under peer review the AMA editors prefer that the information not be released to the public, except through presentation at scientific meetings, until the article appears in print" (p. 400) (Lundberg, Glass, & Joyce, 1991).

The editors of the *Annals of Internal Medicine* suggested the Ingelfinger rule protected both patients and physicians; and in 1991 they thought, in contrast to Huth, editor of the *Annals* in 1983, that "most major medical journals, including the *Annals*, now have similar policies" (p. 699) (Fletcher & Fletcher, 1991). The *New England Journal of Medicine*'s policy was clarified under the editorship of Jerome Kassirer, when it was decided that the embargo would continue with four exceptions that had evolved over the years (Angell & Kassirer, 1991):

- presentations at scientific meetings covered by the press,

- public health concerns of immediate implications,

- research results that had to be released because of governmental deliberations, and

- special arrangements made with the editor when findings were of urgent concern.

The second exception was cited in a 1997 editorial by Kassirer announcing the decision to publish a study that linked a combination of diet pills (fen-phen) with valvular heart disease (Kassirer & Angell, 1997). The researchers held a press conference to report their findings before the manuscript was published by the *New England Journal of Medicine* but after it had been accepted. Given the wide use of the drug combination the editor decided an immediate announcement before publication was in the best public interest.

Altman maintained that before enforcing the Ingelfinger rule with its main goal of subjecting a manuscript to peer review before publication, editors should prove that peer review improves the published article. "Editors contend that peer review has led to changes in, and even reversal of, conclusions of a study before publication. But editors have provided little data on how often peer review influences publication, or even how often it leads to important changes in a paper" (p.1385) (Altman, 1996).

## The rejection process

A manuscript can be rejected at any step in the review process: before review, after review, or after one or more revisions. Glenn, writing in the *American Sociologist*, suggested that any manuscript should be rejected without review if the editor thought the acceptance of that manuscript was "highly improbable" (p. 182) (Glenn, 1976). In fact, any number of editors listed in Table 1-2 have agreed with Glenn's view, and some have provided the percentage of articles their journal rejected without review.

Once a rejection decision has been made by the editor, the author must be informed of this decision, usually through a written rejection letter. Receiving a rejection letter is undoubtedly difficult for an author to accept. During his closing remarks as editor of the *Journal of Applied Psychology* Campbell claimed that "mild-mannered colleagues become enraged adversaries almost by return mail" upon receiving a rejection letter (p. 322) (Campbell, 1985).

Baue, past editor of *Archives of Surgery*, stated that all his rejection letters were the same:

> *Thank you for allowing us the privilege of reviewing your man-uscript. Unfortunately, the reviewers have not recommended your manuscript for publication* (p. 1310) (Baue, 1993).

Willis and Bobys were interested in learning about the type of rejection letters editors mail to authors and have conducted the only study of rejection letters. They wanted to understand the "communication-of-rejection process" and also to learn if the information contained in rejection letters might guide authors when rewriting their manuscripts. Willis and Bobys placed an announcement in the American Sociological Association's newsletter that asked recipients of rejection letters to send copies of the letters to them (Willis & Bobys, 1983). They received 350 copies of rejection letters that ranged in size from 24 words to 480 words (the above example from Baue has 21 words). Slightly over half (54 percent) of the rejection letters provided some justification for the rejection. The most frequent reason was that the manuscript was inappropriate for the journal (19 percent). Reviewers' comments had been included with 57 percent of the letters. Willis and Bobys considered this an "exploratory study…not intended as a test of any hypothesis" (p. 89). Since the reviewers' comments would be most helpful to the authors, it is noteworthy that only slightly over one-half of the rejected authors had received these comments with their rejection letters.

Relman admitted that it was impossible to give detailed reasons with each of the 3,000 rejection letters sent annually by the *New England Journal of Medicine* (Relman, Rennie, & Angell, 1980). Furthermore, he felt that detailed descriptions of the reasons would result in many rebuttals from authors. On the other hand, the editor of the *American Journal of Roentgenology* stated that their rejection letters explain their rationale and often included comments taken directly from the reviewers' reports (Chew, 1993).

In a thoughtful gesture to rejected authors, Ingelfinger expressed "extraordi-nary gratitude to the authors of unaccepted submissions" (p. 1301) (Ingelfinger, 1972). He explained that the editors were forced "to select the most desirable few among many eligible candidates, and to decide, in addition, to what extent a paper is worth a certain amount of limited page space" (p. 1301).

Archer's explanation to readers (and potential authors), at the time he was senior editor at *Journal of the American Medical Association* (*JAMA*), provided basic advice that any author could consider before sending a manuscript off to a journal:

> *A carelessly prepared manuscript may lead an editor to sus-pect that the author's investigation, observations, evaluation*

*of data, or formulation of concepts may have been equally careless. While such editorial judgments are subjective in part, they are legitimate influences, particularly in borderline decisions when many manuscripts are competing for scarce publication space* (p. 155) (Archer, 1975)

The editors of *British Medical Journal* (*BMJ*) outlined the reasons for rejecting some 4,000 manuscripts in 1979: "non-starters," case reports recorded elsewhere, oddities that are of interest only once, too preliminary findings, findings that do not affect clinicians, and rare clinical cases. They also had to consider the interest of their readers who were mostly medical generalists (1980). To keep the concept of the rejected manuscript in perspective, Johnson outlined the many reasons for rejection that may be unrelated to the merits of the research project. A manuscript may be inappropriate for the journal, it may be prepared carelessly, it may not be timely, there may not be space in the journal, or there may be an overriding need to maintain a balance of articles in the journal (Johnson, 1986).

A survey of a sample of members of the American Society of Agronomy determined authors experienced an average of 1.9 rejections over the course of their careers, "but nearly all were eventually able to publish their paper somewhere" (Mayland, Sojka, & Gbur, 1991). Another survey of 467 authors whose articles were indexed in *Current Contents: Social & Behavioral Sciences* revealed that 90.4 percent of them had experienced a rejection and the longer an author had been in a field, the more likely this experience (Rotton, Foos, Van Meek, & Levitt, 1995). A survey of prominent economists revealed that 85 percent of the respondents admitted to experiencing at least one rejection (Gans & Shepherd, 1994).

Several different approaches have been used in the examination of rejected manuscripts. Abstracts from meetings have been followed to find which ones were eventually published. Editors have been asked their reasons for rejecting manuscripts. Comparisons have been made of the quality and readability of accepted versus rejected manuscripts. Studies have been made of the citation patterns of manuscripts that were initially rejected but eventually published. Authors have been asked about their experience with rejection, and some editors have tracked the outcome of rejected manuscripts.

There have been a few studies that tracked either abstracts from presentations at meetings or outcomes of studies approved by institutional review boards. However, an abstract from a meeting or an investigation approved by an institutional review board may not have been completed or submitted to a journal. Several studies conducted over a number of years have each put the percentage of eventual publications from meeting presentations at about 50 percent: in science (Garvey, Lin, Nelson, & Tomita, 1972), in cardiology (Goldman & Loscalzo, 1980), in pediatrics (McCormick & Holmes, 1988), in ophthalmology (Scherer, Dickersin, & Langenberg, 1994), in biomedical research (Dirk, 1996), and in gastroenterology (Duchini & Genta, 1997). Goldman and Loscalzo pointed out that their findings supported the "policy of the *Uniform Requirements for Manuscripts Submitted to Biomedical Journals* that explicitly discourages authors from including abstracts in their reference lists" (p. 258) (Goldman & Loscalzo, 1980). In fact, two studies cited above, the one by Mayland, Sojka, and Gbur that asked about the number of rejections researchers experienced (Mayland et al., 1991) and the one by Duchini and Genta, were both located only in abstract form.

The findings from these studies seem to argue for journals not to publish regularly all proceedings from a meeting, since findings from a number of studies indicate that not all presentations pass the test of peer review and are published. In 1985, the *Archives of Surgery* had a tradition of publishing papers presented at some societies' annual meetings. The editor clarified that some review took place before presentation; however, the *Archives* still published about 90 percent of these presentations (Baue, 1985). Sponsored meetings are often published as supplements to journals. One study compared the quality of supplements to three medical journals, the *American Journal of Cardiology*, the *American Journal of Medicine*, and the *American Heart Journal*, with articles in the parent journal. Rochen and colleagues' findings supported the belief that supplements (often underwritten by pharmaceutical companies) provided material of less quality than standard peer-reviewed articles (Rochon, Gurwitz, Cheung, Hayes, & Chalmers, 1994). These investigators recommended that the same review process be used for supplements as for manuscripts submitted through usual channels. The implication of this study was, of course, that some of the material in the supplements would have been rejected had it undergone a formal editorial peer review.

Some presentations from scientific meetings and published in abstract form may eventually be incorporated into a separate manuscript and, therefore, become almost impossible to identify as a separate article, especially given the limited amount of information in an abstract. Some never published abstracts may have been rejected because they had negative results, that is, they did not support the hypothesis of the study (the null hypothesis is not rejected). The rejection of these studies is presumably based not on the quality of the research, but on the lack of a positive outcome. They are discussed in Chapter Eight, the statistical review of manuscripts.

## Reasons for manuscript rejection

To determine why editors reject manuscripts, nine investigators asked editors their reasons for rejection (Table 2-1). In each study responding editors were provided with a set of reasons a manuscript might be rejected and were asked to select or rank those reasons they were most likely to use.

These nine studies offer insight into the decision-making process of editors, yet they do not provide evidence that the stated reasons were the actual reason(s) for rejection of any one manuscript. Four of the studies originated from nursing, and each one asked a similar set of questions; three came from economics and business and likewise provided a nearly identical set of options for

| Editors' reasons for rejection | Economics[a] | Business[b] | Economics[c] | | Nursing[d] | Nursing-health[e] | | Psychology[f] | Nursing-health[g] | | Education[h] | Nursing[i] |
|---|---|---|---|---|---|---|---|---|---|---|---|---|
| | 1967 | 1968 | 1970 | 1975 | 1977 | 1982 | | 1985 | 1986 | | 1989 | 1991 |
| no new knowledge | 1 | 1 | 1 | 1 | | | | 2,5 | | | 6 | |
| too superficial | 2 | 2 | 2 | 4 | | | | | | | 2 | |
| inadequate research | 3 | 5 | 3 | 3 | 2 | 5 | 4 | 1,4,6 | 5 | 4 | | 2,5 |
| inappropriate subject matter | 4 | 3 | 5 | 2 | | | | | | | 4 | |
| poorly written | 5 | 4 | 4 | 5 | 3 | 1 | 3 | 3 | 7 | 6 | 3,7 | 1,4 |
| author's weak credentials | | 6 | 8 | | | | | | | | | |
| too speculative or esoteric | | 7,9 | 6,7 | | | | | | | | | |
| recently published on subject | | | | | 1 | 6,7 | 7,8 | | 8,9 | 8,9 | | 12,13 |
| too technical | | | | | 2 | 8 | 6 | | 10 | 10 | | 14 |
| inaccurate or undocumented | | | | | 2 | 2,3 | 2,5 | | 1,4 | 1,5 | | 6,7 |
| unimportant | | | | | 3 | 4 | 1 | | 3 | 3 | | 8 |
| not clinically applicable | | | | | | | | | 6 | 7 | | 9 |
| conclusions unwarranted by data | | | | | 3 | | | | 2 | 2 | | 3,11 |
| duplicate publication | | | | | 3 | | | | | | | |
| case history | | | | | 3 | | | | | | | |
| inaccurate statistics | | | | | | | | | | | 5 | 10 |
| author's guidelines not followed | | | | | | | | | | | 1 | |

| a-(Coe & Weinstock, 1967) | d-(McCloskey, 1977) | g-(Swanson & McCloskey, 1986) |
|---|---|---|
| b-(Coe & Weinstock, 1968) | e-(McCloskey & Swanson, 1982) | h-(Noble, 1989) |
| c-(Adams, 1977) | f-(Campbell, 1985) | i-(Swanson, McCloskey, & Bodensteiner, 1991) |

**Table 2-1: Editors' ranked reasons for rejecting manuscripts**

the editors. Each editor in these studies selected poor presentation or poor writing as one of the top 10 reasons for rejecting a manuscript; all but one cited inadequate research. The next most frequent reason was that the paper contributed no new knowledge for the discipline.

Several of the reasons for rejection are potentially correctable problems. The presentation of a manuscript, any undocumented information contained in the manuscript, inaccurate statistics, or unwarranted conclusions each have the potential for correction by the author. Other reasons for rejection might be valid for one journal, but not for another: timeliness of the subject, either the details or technical aspects of a manuscript, inappropriate subject matter, presence or absence of case histories, lack of clinical applicability, or insufficent attention to instructions to authors. Several reasons might suggest that publication is not possible in any peer-reviewed journal: inadequate, inaccurate, or unimportant research, or previous publication of the same study—a duplicate publication. Only two studies asked about the role an author's credentials played in the decision. This particular topic has been the subject of considerable debate and is discussed in Chapter Seven on Reviewers and Their Biases.

Kassirer speculated that there is a "rejection threshold ... a point at which the cumulative weight of a manuscript's faults tips the scales toward rejection" (p. 96) (Kassirer & Campion, 1994). He provides four general areas of manuscript deficiencies: design, presentation, interpretation, and importance of research. Indeed many of the reasons listed in Table 2-1 fall under these categories.

One study examined citation patterns of initially rejected manuscripts after they were published. From a set of 205 authors of highly cited articles, Campanario identified a subset of 22 authors who mentioned some difficulty in getting their manuscripts published (Campanario, 1996). According to the authors, "sometimes referees' negative evaluations can help improve the articles, in other instances referees and editors wrongly rejected the highly cited articles" (p. 302). In fact, three of the articles identified went on to become the most highly cited articles in each of the three journals in which they were eventually published.

*Question*

What is the evidence that the "best" science or scholarly material is published and the "worst" is rejected?

*Criteria for inclusion*

~ any studies that examine the quality of published articles versus the quality of rejected manuscripts.

*Comparable studies*

Three studies examined a group of manuscripts that were eventually either accepted or rejected and attempted to identify characteristics within the manuscripts that differentiated them. In an examination of 60 manuscripts submitted to a scholarly journal, Sigelman and Whicker used a six-point rating scale for judging overall quality and found accepted manuscripts were of a higher quality than rejected manuscripts (Sigelman & Whicker, 1987). The associate editors of *Psychology of Women Quarterly* were asked to evaluate characteristics of previously accepted or rejected manuscripts (Kahn, Presbury, Moore, & Driver, 1990). Reviewers judged the rejected manuscripts to contain more total problems than the accepted ones. Metoyer-Duran studied the readability of both accepted and rejected papers submitted to *College & Research Libraries*

| Reasons for rejection | Correctable or salvageable for rejecting journal? | Sociology[a] | Economy and political science[b] | Management[c] | Social studies of science[d] | Library science[e] | Library science[f] | Surgery[g] | Biomedical[h] | |
|---|---|---|---|---|---|---|---|---|---|---|
| Number of journals | | 1 | 3 | 2 | 1 | 1 | 1 | 1 | * | * |
| *Number of manuscripts* | | 1032 | 600 | 111 | 128 | 25 | 518 | 175 | 25** | 21*** |
| *inadequate theory or concepts* | no | 10.8% | 21.3% | 56.3% | 10.9% | 16.0% | 8.0% | | | |
| *poorly written/presented* | yes | 10.2% | 10.0% | 8.9% | 12.5% | 28.0% | 9.0% | 39.4% | 12.0% | |
| *methodological problems* | no | 8.8% | 26.0% | 8.5% | 8.6% | 24.0% | 10.0% | 37.8% | 12.0% | 24% |
| *data/conclusions poorly interpreted* | yes | 6.8% | | 2.3% | 12.5% | 12.0% | | 43.6% | | |
| *poor analysis* | yes | 6.7% | | | 24.2% | | 2.8% | | | |
| *unimportant* | no | 6.3% | 29.3% | | | | | | | |
| *statistics inadequate* | maybe | 6.2% | | | | | | 19.3% | | |
| *research poorly organized* | maybe | 5.5% | | 10.1% | | | 2.1% | | | |
| *duplicates other work/not new* | no | 5.2% | | | 11.7% | 48.0% | 27.6% | 28.6% | 25.0% | 10% |
| *out of scope for journal* | no | 5.0% | 9.6% | 7.7% | 4.7% | 16.0% | 14.1% | | | |
| *under review by other journal* | maybe | | 0.9% | | | | | | | |
| *cutting the data* | maybe | | | 1.9% | | | | | | |
| *inadequate literature review* | yes | | | | 11.7% | | 4.6% | | | |
| *not follow journal's policies* | yes | | | | | | 30.2% | | | |
| *low priority/no space* | no | | | | | | | | 29.0% | 19% |
| *other* | | 28.5% | 3.0% | 4.3% | 3.2% | 8.0% | 21.7% | | 25.0% | 48% |
| Total unsalvageable | | 36.1% | 86.2% | 72.5% | 35.9% | | 59.7% | | 66.0% | 53.0% |
| Total potentially salvageable | | 35.4% | 10.9% | 23.2% | 60.9% | | 18.5% | | 12.0% | 0.0% |
| Total percentages | | 100% | 100% | 100% | 100% | 152% | 100% | 199% | 103% | 101% |

a-(Smigel & Ross, 1970)

b-(Bonjean & Hullum, 1978)

c-(Daft, 1985)

d-(Chubin & Hackett, 1990)

e-(Landwirth, 1991)

f-(Hernon, Smith, & Croxen, 1993)

g-(Abby, Massey, Galandiuk, & Polk, 1994)

h-(Dirk, 1996)

\* papers written by faculty

\*\* eventually published

\*\*\* never published

**Table 2-2: Actual reasons for rejecting manuscripts**

(Metoyer-Duran, 1993). Using two measures, the Flesch-Kincaid and the Gunning's fog index, Metoyer-Duran determined that the scores from published papers were higher than the scores from rejected manuscripts. In each of these cases, the investigators found that a well-written manuscript is more likely to be accepted than a less well-written one.

To determine if the best manuscripts were accepted and the worst rejected, eight studies examined a set of rejected manuscripts and identified specific reasons for rejection (Table 2-2).

In two studies, percentages total more than 100 percent (Landwirth, 1991) (Abby et al., 1994). Both the Landwirth and Abby study provided multiple reasons for rejection; and, as pointed out by Kassirer (Kassirer & Campion, 1994), this is quite possible. Most studies in the table listed only the major or deciding factor in the rejection decision. Petruzzi claimed 52 percent of all papers were rejected from *Analytical Chemistry* because of such deficiencies as "insufficient new information, already published, lack of originality, and not relevant." Other reasons are insufficient supporting data (13 percent) and questions regarding the scientific merit and validity (Petruzzi, 1976). Since percentages were lumped together for over one-half of the major reasons, this study is not included in Table 2-2. The study by Dirk identified a group of rejected manuscripts authored by researchers who presented papers at a scientific meeting (Dirk, 1996). Rejection letters were analyzed to determine the reasons for rejection.

The actual reasons for a rejection decision provided in Table 2-2 are similar to the theoretical reasons listed in Table 2-1. As with the reasons listed in Table 2-1, some of the reasons for rejection should be correctable or salvageable, while others probably are not. Potentially correctable problems include: the presentation or writing style, the interpretation of the data or the conclusions, the analysis of the data, the literature review, and the degree to which the journal's policies are followed. The authors might be able to correct other problems, depending on the particular manuscript. These potentially correctable problems include statistical analysis or the organization of the research. Authors could circumvent some reasons for rejection by submitting a rejected manuscript to another journal with more appropriate subject coverage, a higher priority for a topic, or more space. Replication studies could be submitted to another journal as well, where an editor might be more sympathetic to this type of study. Submitting a manuscript for review to more than one journal at the same time is usually considered a breach of etiquette and, once identified, sufficient reason to reject a manuscript.

Finally, some problems are simply not correctable. An inadequate theory or concept or a methodological problem such as improper sampling techniques cannot be rectified with any amount of rewriting. If one considers only those manuscripts with noncorrectable problems, studies indicate that between 35.9 percent and 86.2 percent of manuscripts are simply not salvageable after rejection. Totals for both not salvageable and potentially salvageable reasons were not provided for the Landwirth and the Abbey studies since multiple reasons were given for rejecting any one manuscript, resulting in percentages adding up to more than 100 percent and rendering totals meaningless (Landwirth, 1991) (Abby et al., 1994).

In summary, both poor writing skills and methodological problems were identified by each study as primary reasons for rejection. Five of the eight studies each examined data from a single journal, the studies were from disparate disciplines, and they were conducted over a 25-year period. Both Table 2-1 and Table 2-2 provide a very similar list of manuscript deficiencies—one from a ranked list resulting from surveying editors and another from an analysis of rejected manuscripts. The studies originate from a number of different disciplines but identified similar reasons for rejection, implying that there are universal qualities essential for an acceptable manuscript.

## Rejection rates by disciplines

Since Goodrich collected data in 1945, many journal editors have undoubtedly examined their own journals in a similar manner and some of those studies that have been published have been cited in this work (Table 1-2). Although arranged by discipline, Table 1-2 provides little information on the rejection rates for particular disciplines, since each rejection rate is for one journal only. Some editors regularly publish rejection rates, others do it only occasionally, and still others never do it. Editors might divulge rejection rates as a way of acknowledging work of reviewers or editorial staff, or of illustrating to the readership how selective the journal is.

Information on rejection rates can be found in discipline-specific monographs designed to help authors decide where to submit their manuscripts. In the social and behavioral sciences, Mullins included a list of over 500 journal titles in which 117 titles included information on rejection rates—which ranged from 56 percent to 94 percent (Mullins, 1977). A series of similar monographs exists for business administration and economics (Cabell, 1981). Cabell's 1981 directory included information on over 250 journal titles. In addition to information on rejection rates, this directory also included information on the review process of each journal and the percentage of invited articles that the journal editor solicited. In sociology, the author's guide to journals profiles 350 scholarly journals (Sussman, 1978). In social work, an author's guide profiles about 200 journals and provides peer review information on such items as the type of peer review, the time to review, the acceptance rate, as well as information on communication with authors and publication timelines (Beebe, 1997). Some journals have not provided detailed information and the publication provides no summary information about social work journals in general. Fraley and Via identified 91 library and information science journals, providing information on editorial practices, including individual journal rejection rates (Fraley & Via, 1982). These and similar publications, while undoubtedly very helpful to authors searching for a publication outlet, tell little about the relative importance of any one journal title to a field. They tend to include all journals in a field and usually offer no or little analysis or means to differentiate between journals.

*Question*

Are rejection rates discipline dependent, discipline independent, or related solely to the quality of the journal?

*Criteria for inclusion*

~ any study of rejection rates of a defined group of journals either within one discipline or among disciplines, particularly if rejection rates are linked to journal quality.

Single-journal studies were excluded for the simple reason that information from a single journal cannot be generalized, and therefore such studies do not add any insight to the behavior of a particular discipline.

*Comparable studies*

Thirty-four studies of rejection rates of groups of journals were identified. Seven were excluded from this analysis because in each journal selection was limited to a "convenience sample," a sample that was not reproducible, was ill defined, or simply not explained. These seven studies of rejection rates and reasons for exclusion follow:

Juhasz and colleagues selected journal titles from the holdings of a science and technology library. The selected titles were "assumed to be peer refereed" (p. 178) (Juhasz, Calvert, Jackson, Kronick, & Shipman, 1975). The authors did not try to analyze data by discipline, but grouped all journals together for the analysis. The 10 recommendations for editors on how to improve the peer review process were not based on any data analysis.

Gordon interviewed editors residing in London "covering a broad spectrum of disciplines" (p. 139) (Gordon, 1978). Those editors represented a convenience sample. Gordon also did not conduct any discipline-specific analysis.

A section of an additional study by Gordon listed a set of research journals from the United Kingdom with no description of the selection process. The data from another section of this study that provided information on the journals published by the Institute of Physics are included in this analysis (Gordon, 1979).

Hargens conducted a longitudinal study of 30 journals that "tend to be among the most prestigious in their field," and were "similar" to the ones studies by Zuckerman and Merton (p. 140) (Hargens, 1988). His sample was rather skewed. Ten (one-third) of the titles were from chemistry; the remaining 20 titles included one or two from a wide range of disciplines. Hargens made no discipline-specific comparisons. An additional study by Hargens compared differences from three titles: one each from astrophysics, zoology, and sociology (Hargens, 1990).

Sen and Chakraborty used a combination of questionnaires and interviews to study journals originating from Calcutta (Sen & Chakraborty, 1993). These investigators included 26 journal titles from a variety of scientific disciplines and their analysis contained no discipline-specific differentiation.

Yamazaki surveyed editors of 28 journals in which Japanese life scientists "preferred to publish their papers" (p. 124) (Yamazaki, 1995). He did not further

| Discipline | Journal section criteria | # of journals | Rejection rate mean | Rejection rate range | Year | References |
|---|---|---|---|---|---|---|
| Anthropology | leading journals | 2 | 48% | | 1967 | (Zuckerman & Merton, 1971) |
| Art | random selection | 19 | 65% | | 1981 | (Miller & Serzan, 1984) |
| Biology | leading journals | 12 | 29% | | 1967 | (Zuckerman & Merton, 1971) |
| | random selection | 19 | 41% | | 1981 | (Miller & Serzan, 1984) |
| Chemistry | leading journals | 5 | 31% | | 1967 | (Zuckerman & Merton, 1971) |
| | top journals | 10 | 29% | | 1978 | (Beyer, 1978) |
| Computer science | author survey | | 38% | | 1977 | (King, McDonald, & Roderer, 1981) |
| Dentistry | journals/circulation | 69 | | 0%-80% | 1984 | (Federico, Lee, Boozer, & Diaz, 1984) |
| Economic | major journals | 39 | 62% | 10%-95% | 1966 | (Coe & Weinstock, 1967) |
| | leading journals | 4 | 69% | | 1967 | (Zuckerman & Merton, 1971) |
| | selected | 20 | | 35%-91% | 1969 | (Coe & Weinstock, 1983) |
| | selected | 72 | 67% | 10%-93% | 1970 | (Adams, 1977) |
| | selected | 72 | 77% | 40%-98% | 1975 | (Adams, 1977) |
| | random selection | 12 | 79% | | 1981 | (Miller & Serzan, 1984) |
| | selected | 20 | | 50%-90% | 1982 | (Coe & Weinstock, 1983) |
| Education | random selection | 22 | 70% | | 1981 | (Miller & Serzan, 1984) |
| | prominent journals | 49 | 72% | 30%-98% | 1988 | (Henson, 1988) |
| Geography | leading journals | 2 | 30% | | 1967 | (Zuckerman & Merton, 1971) |
| Geology | leading journals | 2 | 22% | | 1967 | (Zuckerman & Merton, 1971) |
| | random selection | 18 | 35% | | 1981 | (Miller & Serzan, 1984) |
| + environmental | author survey | | 19% | | 1977 | (King et al., 1981) |
| History | leading journals | 3 | 90% | | 1967 | (Zuckerman & Merton, 1971) |
| | random selection | 24 | 62% | | | (Miller & Serzan, 1984) |
| Language | MLA, inclusive | 166 | | 0%-90% | 1961 | (Lavelle, 1966) |
| | | | | 17%-95% | 1965 | (Lavelle, 1966) |
| | leading journals | 5 | 86% | | 1967 | (Zuckerman & Merton, 1971) |
| | random selection | 21 | 74% | | 1981 | (Miller & Serzan, 1984) |
| Life sciences | author survey | | 48% | | 1977 | (King et al., 1981) |
| Library science | selected journals | 33 | 66% | 0%-97% | 1976 | (O'Connor & Van Orden, 1978) |
| | selected journals | 48 | | 0%-95% | 1988 | (Budd, 1988) |
| | status of journal | 34 | | 25%-75% | 1992 | (Haas, Milton, & Quinn, 1996) |
| | indexed, selected | 68 | | 0%-93% | 1996 | (Via, 1996) |
| Management | major journals | 37 | 71% | 25%-93% | 1968 | (Coe & Weinstock, 1968) |
| | selected journals | 16 | | 45%-90% | 1968 | (Coe, 1984) |
| | selected journals | 16 | | 55%-90% | 1982 | (Coe, 1984) |
| Mathematics | leading journals | 5 | 50% | | 1967 | (Zuckerman & Merton, 1971) |
| | random selection | 12 | 47% | | 1981 | (Miller & Serzan, 1984) |
| + engineering | author survey | | 35% | | 1977 | (King et al., 1981) |
| Medicine | random selection | 22 | 52% | | 1981 | (Miller & Serzan, 1984) |
| | met 5 criteria | 16 | 67% | | 1990 | (Weller, 1990) |
| | indexed | 86 | 48% | | 1990 | (Weller, 1990) |
| Nursing | indexed | 65 | | 10%-95% | 1975 | (McCloskey, 1977) |
| | Indexed | 100 | 59% | 7%-94% | 1982 | (McCloskey & Swanson, 1982) |
| | indexed | 139 | 61% | 0%-97% | 1984 | (Swanson & McCloskey, 1986) |
| | indexed | 92 | 59% | 0%-96% | 1990 | (Swanson et al., 1991) |
| Philosophy | leading journals | 5 | 85% | | 1967 | (Zuckerman & Merton, 1971) |
| Physics | top journals | 12 | 24% | | 1967 | (Zuckerman & Merton, 1971) |
| | author survey | | 19% | | 1977 | (King et al., 1981) |

Table 2-3: Journal rejection rates by discipline

| Discipline | Journal section criteria | # of journals | Rejection rate mean | Rejection rate range | Year | References |
|---|---|---|---|---|---|---|
| Physics | top journals | 10 | 35% | | 1978 | (Beyer, 1978) |
| | IOP journals* | 7 | | 17%-35% | 1978 | (Gordon, 1979) |
| Political science | leading journals | 2 | 84% | | 1967 | (Zuckerman & Merton, 1971) |
| | top journals | 10 | 87% | | 1978 | (Beyer, 1978) |
| Psychology | APA journals* | | | 50%-88% | 1964 | (Newman, 1986) |
| | APA journals | 17 | 77% | 55%-87% | 1978 | (Webb, 1979) |
| | leading non-experimental journals | 7 | 70% | | 1967 | (Zuckerman & Merton, 1971) |
| | leading experimental | 2 | 51% | | 1967 | (Zuckerman & Merton, 1971) |
| | author survey | | 71% | | 1977 | (King et al., 1981) |
| | journals | 99 | | 5%-90% | 1981 | (Buffardi & Nichols, 1981) |
| | top cited | 10 | 79% | 51%-90% | 1981 | (Buffardi & Nichols, 1981) |
| | published by the AACD* | 15 | 59% | 25%-50% | 1983 | (Seligman, 1986) |
| | top journals in subspecialties | 57 | | 45%-90% | 1993 | (Rotton, Levitt, & Foos, 1993) |
| + psychiatry | random selection | 15 | 69% | | 1981 | (Miller & Serzan, 1984) |
| Sociology | leading journals | 14 | 78% | | 1967 | (Zuckerman & Merton, 1971) |
| | author survey | | 59% | | 1977 | (King et al., 1981) |
| | top journals | 10 | 87% | | 1978 | (Beyer, 1978) |
| | random selection | 19 | 69% | | 1981 | (Miller & Serzan, 1984) |

* IOP: Institute of Physics
  APA: American Psychological Association
  AACD: American Association of Counseling and Development

**Table 2-3: Journal rejection rates by discipline (continued)**

elaborate on how the titles were selected, nor did he differentiate by discipline in the discussion or conclusions or verify if Japanese authors preferred to publish in foreign journals.

The remaining 27 studies investigated discipline-specific rejection rates for a defined group of journals. Table 2-3 summarizes data from these studies by discipline and within each discipline chronologically. Generalizations from these studies are difficult to make for several reasons, including differences in journal selection techniques, in the definition of a discipline, in the wide range of rejection rates with each study, and in the differences of sample sizes.

*Journal selection*

Dissimilar selection techniques were used. Even within one discipline, most of the studies attempted to define a set of the "best" or "top" or "selected" or "leading" journals within that discipline. The number of titles per discipline in these studies ranged from two to 166. Different techniques were used to include journal titles within a discipline:

- In 13 studies, journals were selected from a list of indexed journals, from a directory, or from a previously published list of selected titles.

  Four nursing studies evaluated journals indexed in *Cumulative Index to Nursing and Allied Health* (*CINAHL*) (McCloskey, 1977), (McCloskey & Swanson, 1982), (Swanson & McCloskey, 1986), and (Swanson et al., 1991).

One economic study identified titles indexed in the *Journal of Economic Abstracts* in which at least 50 percent of the published articles were from unsolicited manuscripts (Coe & Weinstock, 1967).

A study of business titles included journals indexed in *Business Periodical Index* and received a substantial portion of articles from authors at large (Coe & Weinstock, 1968).

One study identified titles selected from *Library Literature* (O'Connor & Van Orden, 1978).

Four studies used a previous list of recommended journal titles (Zuckerman & Merton, 1971), (Budd, 1988), (Rotton et al., 1993), and (Via, 1996).

Two studies used a random number table to select a percentage of journals, Miller from the *Directory of Publishing Opportunities in Journals and Periodicals* (Miller & Serzan, 1984) and Weller from *Index Medicus* (Weller, 1990).

- Four studies used a group of journals published by the American Psychological Association (Webb, 1979) (Newman, 1986), the Institute of Physics (Gordon, 1979), and the American Association of Counseling and Development (Seligman, 1986). In addition, one study of library science titles included publication of journals by library associations as a criterion (Haas et al., 1996).

- In three studies, academicians were asked to identify the leading journals in a field (Coe & Weinstock, 1983), (Coe, 1984), (Beyer, 1978). In both of the Coe studies respondents themselves were asked to name the best journals in a field. Beyer used a slightly different approach, asking respondents to vote on the best titles from a list of journals named in the survey. Respondents had the option of adding any leading titles not provided by Beyer. There was a wide disparity in the number of votes received for titles in each group. The top10 physics titles received the widest range: from 269 for the title with the most votes to 15 for the title with the least. Chemistry journals received from 139 to 25 votes; sociology journals received between 177 and nine votes; and political science journals received between 173 and 12 votes. These ranges make it clear that even within the top 10 titles for each discipline, some titles rose much more solidly to the top than others. It is also clear from the tallied list of votes per title that there was more consensus for the titles that came out on the very top than those at the bottom of each list. The two studies by Coe and colleagues did not provide vote tallies.

- One study examined the most frequently cited journals in psychology (Buffardi & Nichols, 1981).

- One study used dental journals with a circulation of over 1,000 (Federico et al., 1984).

- One study of medical journals used a combination of citations to the journals, circulation and indexing information (Weller, 1990).

- One study surveyed authors. Information the authors supplied was then used to estimate the rejection rates in the life sciences (p. 67). However, journals were not named in this study (King, McDonald, & Roderer, 1981).

- Three studies used a less defined group of journals without clarifying the exact criteria used: from a survey of 231 economic and business journals, Adams identified 72 nonregional economic journals (Adams, 1977). Henson surveyed editors of prominent education journals (Henson, 1988). Haas, Milton, and Quinn selected recognized journals in the field of library science, journals published by learned societies, and "the target audience" (p. 233) (Haas et al., 1996).

### Definitions of disciplines

The definitions of disciplines were not specific enough to compare different studies of the same discipline. For example, one study listed a discipline as geology (Zuckerman & Merton, 1971) and another listed what could be a similar set of journals as "earth, environment, and physical sciences" (Miller & Serzan, 1984). Zuckerman and Merton included the top five chemistry journals, while Beyer listed the top 10 titles in chemistry (Beyer, 1978). Zuckerman and Merton used only the top two political science titles; Beyer listed 10 leading titles in that field. Zuckerman and Merton did not name any journal titles, so any overlap of titles was impossible to determine. The rubric of "life sciences" as used by King could include titles from either biology or medicine (King et al., 1981).

### Range of rejection rates

Twenty-three studies found such a wide range of rejection rates within a discipline that this information alone provided no insight into either the discipline's rejection rate or the influence of the editorial peer review process on the rejection rates. For 13 of these studies, the range of rejection rates was greater than 70 percent for the disciplines.

Mean rejection rates are included in Table 2-3 only when provided by the author of the study. The study by O'Connor and Van Orden (O'Connor & Van Orden, 1978) illustrates the difficulty with calculating a mean rejection rate. O'Connor and Van Orden studied journals published in the field of library science. The rejection rates for individual titles ranged from 0 percent to 93 percent, with a mean rejection rate of 77.3 percent. The authors viewed this percentage as a "high manuscript rejection rate" (p. 389). However, 30 percent of the titles studied had a rejection rate of less than 50 percent. The mean is misleading because the range was so great. The mean rejection rate of a set of journals that is inadequately defined does not provide a discipline's overall rejection rate and gives little insight into editorial peer review practices.

Weller divided the discipline of medicine into two levels of journals. One group of journals included journal titles that met a strict set of criteria (recommended lists of journals, indexed in *Index Medicus*, number of citations the journal received, and size of circulation), while a second group of titles met only one criterion (randomly selected titles from journals indexed in *Index Medicus*). The mean rejection rate for the more selected journals was significantly higher than the rejection rates for the less selective set of titles (67.2 percent vs. 48.2 percent) (Weller, 1990). This study indicates that generalizations within a discipline cannot be made without taking into account some evaluative characteristics of the journals that were analyzed.

*Sample size*

Sample sizes were so small in some cases that the validity of any conclusion about discipline-dependent averages of rejection rates is questionable. Beyer studied only 10 titles from each discipline. The Zuckerman and Merton study in particular used a very small number of journal titles from each discipline: in 12 of the 16 disciplines they studied five journal titles or fewer were included in the sample. One discipline, linguistics, only included one journal title and was, therefore, excluded from Table 2-3.

## Rejection rates over time

Data from the studies cited above have been collected over a period of almost 30 years. Several studies were from the late 1960s and early 1970s, and some used data from several years prior to the publication date.

*Question*

How have rejection rates changed over a period of time?

*Criteria for inclusion*

~ any study that examined the same group of journals over a period of time.

*Comparable studies*

Each study that examined this question tracked individual journal titles.

A 1973 editorial in *The Sociological Quarterly* (McCartney, 1973) stated that rejection rates for both the *American Sociological Review* and the *American Journal of Sociology* had "passed the 90 percent rejection rate and the rates of other sociology journals are near that figure. The mean rejection rate for seven prominent sociology journals in 1972 was 86 percent" (p. 600). The citation to this information was not provided.

Three studies in Table 2-3 compared rejection rates of a group of journals for two different years: Lavelle in literature and language for 1961 and 1965 (Lavelle, 1966), Adams in economics for 1970 and 1975 (Adams, 1977), and Coe and Weinstock in management for 1968 and 1982 (Coe, 1984). In each of these studies, the lowest rejection rate for any journal was in the earlier date studied. These data need a little closer scrutiny. In the Coe and Weinstock study, for three of the 16 journals the earlier rejection rates were not available, for another three there was no change or a decrease in the rejection rate, and for five titles the change in rejection rate was 15 percent or less. In the Adams study, the mean rejection rate increased by 10 percent for the time period, but for 43 of the 72 titles (59.7 percent) data were available only for one date.

Coe and Weinstock asked educators to estimate the rejection rates for 20 financial journal titles (Coe & Weinstock, 1983). Coe and Weinstock then compared the estimates with the actual rejection rate for each journal and discovered that educators' perceived acceptance rates of journals in finance did not correlate with the actual rejection rates. The authors noted a tendency of faculty to overestimate acceptance rates for the years studied—1968 and 1982. For nine of the 20 titles studied there were data on rejection rates for both dates. For two titles, the rejection rates were the same for both time periods. Six of the remaining seven had a higher rejection rate in 1982 than in 1968; the increases ranged from 5 percent to 30 percent.

Two studies examined changes in rejection rates for a group of journals over time. Hargens estimated rejection rates for a group of journals between the late 1960s and the early 1980s (Hargens, 1988). He estimated the rejection rates by dividing the number of articles published by the number of submissions. He concluded that rejection rates for these 30 journals remained "very stable over time and are largely unaffected by changes in submissions" (p. 139). He did not group titles by discipline, but examined titles independently, and he did identify some variances. For example, *Physical Review* had rejection rates of 17 percent and 21 percent for the late 1960s and early 1980s, respectively. *Physical Review Letters* also remained fairly constant although the rejection rates of 52 percent and 56 percent were much higher for the same time period (p.150). These two titles were the top two vote getters for physics journal titles in Beyer's list. The rejection rates of some journals did not remain as constant as the two physics journals. The rejection rate of the *Journal of Abnormal Psychology* rose from 60 percent to 82 percent during this period; *American Anthropology* experienced a similar increase of from 69 percent to 85 percent. The rejection rate of the *Journal of Applied Psychology* also increased from 66 percent to 83 percent. The rejection rate of each of these increased by about 20 percentage points during these 20 years. Did the 20 percent increase reflect a growing importance of these journals, an increase in productivity of authors in these fields, stricter editorial guidelines, or a move toward smaller journals? Hargens did not explore the reasons for these changes in rejection rates.

Several of the editors of journals listed in Table 1-2 regularly published information on rejection rates of their journals. The *American Journal of Public Health*, the *Canadian Medical Association Journal*, *JAMA*, and the *New England Journal of Medicine* all published at least six editorials on their review process over a period of 15 years and each provided data on rejection rates. The three U. S. journals had a rather consistent rejection rate—ranging from 80 percent to 90 percent, while the *Canadian Medical Association Journal's* rejection rate remained constant at about 50 percent. The *American Political Science Review* published rejection rates over a period of 20 years; the rejection rate in 1977 was 94.6 percent and in 1997 it was 93.5 percent (Jones, 1977) (Finifter, 1997).

These studies and isolated examples provide little evidence to support a theory that rejection rates have steadily increased or changed, but, more important, neither do they refute this theory. There are very little data on very few journals, and some methodological problems with a number of those few studies, and so it is difficult to reach any conclusions about some disciplines experiencing a higher rejection rate than others. Any study of this nature needs to take the particular ranking of a journal or the selection criteria into account before reaching conclusions. Any conclusions must be qualified in terms of the original criteria for inclusion in the study, and data must not be extrapolated to include all journals in a discipline.

## Authors' responses to rejected manuscripts

Journal editors worry that reviewers have a more difficult time with new (brilliant) ideas than with run-of-the-mill ideas. In a humorous commentary on the reasons why Christopher Columbus' idea to sail west to reach India would not have passed peer review, a fictitious reviewer has a plausible explanation for recommending the proposed trip be rejected: "I have to state that it is not comprehensible to the general astronomer ... I am highly skeptical about the value of this paper" (p. 13) (Azbel, 1993).

In a more serious investigation into the rejection of novel ideas, Campanario (Campanario, 1995) focused his commentary on eight authors who eventually won Nobel prizes after their prize-winning ideas were initially rejected by reviewers and editors. Campanario suggested that referees may have failed to understand the importance of the subject. The fact that the articles reported unexpected results might also have led the referees to question the results. In a similar attempt to identify examples of the rejection of innovative ideas, Gans and Shepherd (Gans & Shepherd, 1994) asked all economists who had either won the Nobel Prize or the John Bates Clark Medal about rejection of any of their manuscripts. From the responses, the authors compiled a list of 28 articles published between 1931 and 1991 that were initially rejected. Respondents also reported that most of their initially rejected manuscripts were published after some delay.

But ideas that eventually win Nobel prizes are original and often at odds with current thinking. Perhaps the rejection of a manuscript with a radical idea alone is not too much of a condemnation on the process. Or is it? The world has numerous examples of the rejection of new ideas: from Copernicus' revolutionary idea that the earth moved around the sun to Darwin's theory that all species have evolved through a natural selection process. Society has interesting ways of dealing with ideas it finds unacceptable. Galileo was jailed for teaching Copernican theory, while Darwin's theory was accepted quickly in most scientific circles, but since it was inconsistent with a literal interpretation of the book of Genesis it caused a theological controversy that continues to resurface regularly (http://www.eb.com:180/cgi-bin/g?DocF=macro/5001/68.html).

Some editors and scholarly societies have a formal policy on any appeals process; others have suggested that such policies should exist. The American Psychological Association's Council of Editors asked authors of rejected manuscripts not to increase the editors' workload with an appeal (American Psychological Association, 1975). The Council went on to state that "an article is not rejected if the editor believes it can be made more acceptable by suitable revisions" (p. 711). Finally authors were encouraged to resubmit the rejected manuscript to another journal. The editors of *JAMA* informed readers that appeals "can be successful, but only rarely" (p. 13) (Durso, 1997).

Several authors have encouraged editors who do not have a formal appeals policy to institute one. Pullen suggested that an appeals board be established to reconsider rejected manuscripts in engineering (Pullen, 1977). Writing on the publication process in the social sciences, Lindsey recommended that all journals establish a formal appeals process (Lindsey, 1978). During a discussion after a presentation by Armstrong about the review process for management journals, Ayres suggested that journals establish a rejection review board that would review all rejection recommendations and report to the editor (Armstrong, 1982). In chemistry, Rockwood argued that authors should be able to appeal criticism by reviewers (Rockwood, 1985). Hartley suggested several items in a proposed code of practice for editors; one of them was to institute a formal appeals process (Hartley, 1988). Epstein developed a similar list with a similar recommendation that the editor provide a "meaningful" (p. 884) appeals process (Epstein, 1995).

There have been a few examples of editors who have written about their appeals process, including the 5.2 percent of editors of the 134 journals listed in Table 1-2 who mentioned an appeals process. Relman in response to a complaint about a rejection decision encouraged rejected authors to submit their own rebuttal (Relman, 1970). Soffer, at the time he was editor of *Chest*, as a response to authors who frequently claimed that editorial boards were "arbitrary and capricious in judgment," ran an "open editorial office" in which he encouraged authors to discuss rejected manuscripts with him. He believed that "an author should have recourse to further consideration if he believes that his paper has been misjudged" (p. 125) (Soffer, 1978). Soffer's 1978 editorial included an example of a manuscript he initially rejected. He received a critique from the rejected authors and gave the reviewers the opportunity to reply to the authors' rebuttal. The reviewers stuck with their original recommendations. However, Soffer subsequently accepted the manuscript. The reviewers then thanked the editor for sending the authors' rebuttal and providing a forum to sort out answers to scientific questions. Christiansen asked 26 editors of IEEE journals about their procedures for an appeal of a rejection decision (Christiansen, 1981). Three editors had no appeals procedure; others had established some type of appeals process, often informal. The editors of *Social Work* instituted a policy permitting any author of a rejected manuscript to rewrite and resubmit the work (Beaver, Gottlieb, & Rosenblatt, 1983).

Lazarus, editor of *Physical Review Letters* in 1980, pointed out that authors who wished to "appeal adverse publication decisions" (p. 1528) could do so (Lazarus, 1980). He referred readers to the *Bulletin of the American Physical Society* for the most recent statement on their formal appeals procedure. The editor of *Diabetes Care* informed authors who felt "that the action taken by the editors was wrong should feel free to rebut; we will be glad to reconsider our decision and obtain additional reviews, if appropriate" (p. 209) (Service, 1983).

The editors of the *Canadian Medical Association Journal* provided three reasons in which an appeal would be considered: "the paper has national significance and should be published in a Canadian journal; the reviewers' and editors' objections can be overcome by revision; and an inequitably unfavorable decision has been delivered because a reviewer misinterpreted the paper" (p. 302) (Bolster & Morgan, 1986).

Gordon asked a group of biochemists what they would do if their manuscripts were rejected (Gordon, 1984). Only 5 percent maintained they would definitely not resubmit the manuscript to another journal. Over one-half, 58 percent, of the biochemists stated that they would certainly resubmit their rejected manuscripts, and another 36 percent said that perhaps they would resubmit. This was an opinion survey so behavior might actually be somewhat different. But it does provide a clue to authors' interest in pursuing publication, even after a rejection.

In addition to these examples of editors providing a statement or establishing a written formal policy on an appeals process, what is known about authors' follow-up to rejected manuscripts?

*Question*

What steps is an author likely to take once a manuscript has been rejected?

*Criteria for inclusion*

~ any study that tracked rejected manuscripts to their final disposition.

*Comparable studies*

Several editors conducted studies of their own journals to determine if manuscripts they rejected were ever published or if manuscripts they accepted for publication had been previously rejected by another journal. The first section of Table 2-4 lists 17 studies in which editors determined the outcome of manuscripts that they rejected; several editors also asked accepted authors about previous rejections. Between 27.7 percent and 85 percent of the rejected manuscripts, an average of 51.4 percent, were eventually published elsewhere. Editors waited a few years, somewhere between two and nine years, after they had rejected the manuscripts before attempting to locate it in another journal. Many of these editors pointed out the shortcomings of this approach. First, the editors had to determine if a published article was in fact the same manuscript that they had rejected. The editors might not have been able to identify a rejected manuscript whose contents were incorporated into another article. Second, depending on the thoroughness of a particular search, the editors might not be able to locate the rejected manuscript as a published article. Third, the article might have been published, but not yet indexed. Most editors qualified their findings by acknowledging that they might not have located all published manuscripts they had rejected and that their figures were most likely a minimal percentage of those articles that were subsequently published.

A second approach to tracking rejected manuscripts is to query authors about how they have dealt with rejection decisions. The second section of Table 2-4 lists six studies that asked authors about any rejected manuscripts; four studies from the first section of Table 2-4 also asked about previous rejections. These studies found that an average of 21.6 percent, from 12 percent to 35 percent, of the accepted manuscripts were previously rejected. One phase of the large study conducted by Garvey and colleagues asked about prior rejection of manuscripts. Approximately 12 percent of 3,676 articles had received a previous rejection (Garvey et al., 1972). Nine out of 10 (90 percent) of the rejected and subsequently published manuscripts were accepted by the second journal (p. 213-4). The remaining manuscripts were submitted to two or more journals. Six manuscripts, 1.3 percent, were submitted to four or more journals before they were accepted. Each rejection added about three months to the publication time. Weller asked a random sample of authors who had published articles identified in the survey about the review process of the article. This study found a similar percentage, between 15.7 percent and 20.8 percent (depending on the group of journals that had published the article) of manuscripts had been rejected prior to acceptance (Weller, 1996).

As discussed above, the author of a rejected manuscript has the option of appealing the decision. However, many authors may not be aware of this opportunity or for a variety of reasons may choose not take this step. There is only limited information on the success of an appeal after a rejection decision. Mitchell determined that about 20 percent of those authors receiving a rejection letter in organization behavior wrote the editor (Mitchell, Beach, & Smith, 1985). This study did not collect data on the outcome, either positive or negative, of these letters of inquiry. The investigators did note, however, that the study did show that 75 percent of manuscripts in this field were published, while rejection rates for the field ranged from 50 percent to 95 percent, leading to speculation as to "how these two sets of figures can both be true" (p. 256). Brysbaert discussed how authors "negotiated the acceptance" of papers after rejection and felt that editors should in all fairness, rather than wait for an appeal by the authors to renegotiate a rejection, try to evaluate each submitted manuscript and not routinely reject manuscripts (Brysbaert, 1996).

Only one study asked editors about the success of appeals by authors (Simon, Bakanic, & McPhail, 1986) and found that for the *American Sociological Review*,

| Journal titles/Subject | % of published articles previously rejected | % of rejected published in another journal | # of years after rejection | % resubmitted after rejection | % accepted after appeal of the rejection decision | References |
|---|---|---|---|---|---|---|
| **Individual journals** | | | | | | |
| American Historical Review | | 50% | | | | (Stieg, 1983) |
| American Journal of Public Health | 25%<br>35%<br>33% | 50%<br><br><br>72% | 3 | | | (Yankauer, 1982)<br>(Yankauer, 1985)<br>(Yankauer, 1986)<br>(Koch-Weser &<br>Yankauer, 1993) |
| American Journal of Roentgenology | | 64% | 4.5 | | | (Chew, 1990) |
| American Journal of Surgery | | 28% | 3 | | | (Abby et al., 1994) |
| American Sociological Review | | | | | 13% | (Simon, Bakanic,<br>& McPhail, 1986) |
| Angewandte Chemie | | 71% | | | | (Daniel, 1993) |
| Archives of Surgery | | 30% | | | | (Warren, 1973) |
| British Journal of Surgery | | 32% | 5 or 6 | | | (Farndon, Murie,<br>Johnson, Earnshaw,<br>& Guillou, 1997) |
| British Medical Journal | | 68% | | | | (Lock, 1985) |
| College and Research Libraries | | 42% | | | | (Hernon et al., 1993) |
| Journal of Clinical Investigation | | 85% | 6 | | | (Wilson, 1978) |
| Journal of Documentation | | 27.7% | 2 to 9 | | | (Cronin &<br>McKenzie, 1992) |
| Mayo Clinic Proceedings | 15% | | | | | (Roland &<br>Kirkpatrick, 1975) |
| New England Journal of Medicine | | 85% | | | | (Relman, 1978) |
| **Groups of authors** | | | | | | |
| psychology | 20.0% | | | | | (Garvey &<br>Griffith, 1971) |
| scientists and engineers | 12.0% | | | | | (Garvey et al., 1972) |
| science fields | | | | 28.0% | | (King et al., 1981) |
| social and behavioral sciences | 19.4% | | | 83.3% | | (Rotton et al., 1995) |
| medical researchers in top journals | 20.8% | | | | | (Weller, 1996) |
| medical researchers in indexed journals | 15.7% | | | | | (Weller, 1996) |
| biomedical | | 35.6% | | | | (Dirk, 1996) |
| **Groups of journals** | | | | | | |
| Astronomy: Publication of the Astronomical Society of the Pacific, Astronomical Journal, and Astrophysical Journal | | 31.3% | 3 | | | (Abt, 1988) |
| Family medicine: nine titles | 20.1% | | | | | (Whitman<br>& Eyre, 1985) |
| **Average** | 21.6% | 51.4% | | 55.7% | 13.0% | |

**Table 2-4: Final publication outcome of rejected manuscripts**

13 percent of the rejected authors successfully appealed the rejection. Rotton (Rotton et al., 1995) asked authors from *Current Contents: Social & Behavioral Sciences* about any rejected manuscripts. A total of 83.3 percent had sent their most recent rejected manuscript to a different journal. The investigators did not determine what percentages of these were eventually published. However, 19.2 percent of the most recently published articles had been previously rejected.

The peer review process that results in a rejected manuscript might and probably does provide the authors with a valuable critique, and, therefore, the revised manuscript might be a more likely candidate for acceptance once resubmitted. There are little data on the reworking of manuscripts before resubmission to another journal. Wilson examined articles initially rejected by the *Journal of Clinical Investigation*. Only one-sixth of the articles had undergone additional work before resubmission (Wilson, 1978). Yankauer followed a set of previously rejected manuscripts published in the *American Journal of Public Health* and determined that just over half of 61 manuscripts had been "moderately or substantially revised" (p. 7) before they were sent to a second journal (Yankauer, 1985). Bakanic and McPhail determined sociologists were more likely to have an initially rejected manuscript accepted if they revised it prior to resubmission (Bakanic, McPhail, & Simon, 1987).

A survey by Linder investigating authors' and readers' evaluations of *Personality and Social Psychology Bulletin* found recipients of rejection letters were not deterred from considering the same journal for future submissions (Linder, 1977).

All these studies indicate that there is strong motivation on authors' part to see their material in print and these studies indicate that a rejection is often no real deterrent for authors. In answer to an author's complaint that a rejection can be an easy way out of an editorial dilemma (Neufeld, 1970), the editor-in-chief of the publications of the American Physical Society, whose work on the atomic nucleus was rejected in 1937 because "there cannot be much left of individual particle states and even less of shells," stated that a rejection "merely means that the paper will be printed elsewhere" (p. 10) (Goudsmit, 1970).

## Quality of journals that accepted rejected manuscripts

Steig, in a study of the *American Historical Review*, pointed out that as the most frequently cited history journal, any other publication outlet selected by an author after rejection would have a lower impact factor (Stieg, 1983). Fye ascertained that "a rejected manuscript is usually submitted to another journal, lower in prestige perhaps, but more in need of material" (p 320). (Fye, 1990). This section examines this widely held assumption.

The previous section provided some data on the percentage of rejected manuscripts that were eventually published. Over 20 percent of articles published were previously rejected and over 50 percent of rejected manuscripts were eventually published. The stated assumption at the beginning of the chapter was

that the best journals publish the best material. Does it follow that those journals that accepted previously rejected manuscripts were of a lower quality then
the journals that initially rejected the manuscripts?

Five studies traced rejected manuscripts to final publication to try to determine the quality of journals that accepted previously rejected manuscripts.
Chew discovered that 13 percent of the manuscripts rejected by the *American
Journal of Roentgenology* and subsequently published by another journal were
published in journals with a higher impact factor and 19 percent in journals
with a larger circulation (Chew, 1990). *Radiology* published 9.8 percent of the
rejected manuscripts and has both a higher impact factor and a larger circulation. Cronin and McKenzie found similar results with manuscripts rejected
from the *Journal of Documentation*—relatively few of subsequently published
rejected manuscripts, 17.6 percent, were published in journals with a higher
impact factor (Cronin & McKenzie, 1992).

Three additional studies in biomedicine reached different conclusions. In a
study of eight medical journals regularly read by family practitioners, Whitman
and Eyre found that two-thirds of published, previously rejected manuscripts
had first been rejected by one of those same eight major family practice journals
under investigation (Whitman & Eyre, 1985). Weller also found that authors do
not necessarily move from "leading" journals to less prestigious journals after a
rejection. Authors appeared willing to submit a manuscript to a more prestigious
journal than the one that had rejected it and were apparently unhampered by a
perceived prestige of particular journals even after a manuscript had been
rejected. Close to one-half, 44.4 percent, of the manuscripts that had been
rejected by a journal in the more selected group of journals were accepted by
another journal in the same set of journals (Weller, 1996). Only 20.6 percent of
those rejected by one of the more selected set of journals were published in a less
select group of journals. A similar study of biochemists tracked 10 manuscripts
that had initially been rejected; seven of the 10 (70 percent) had been submitted
to and accepted by journals of a higher rank (p. 39) (Gordon, 1984).

*Limitations of studies*

- Although there are similar reasons for rejecting manuscripts across
  disciplines, these studies have shed little light on the process of how
  editorial peer review improves a manuscript. Indeed the little data there
  are on the follow up of rejected manuscripts indicates that editorial peer
  review may have little impact on the overall changes in manuscripts.
  This question will be explored further in the chapter on author's
  experience with editorial peer review.

- There are relatively few studies of rejection rates by discipline in any
  one discipline. Studies have not used the same journal selection criteria
  so comparisons are rather difficult and probably not very meaningful. For
  example, all four nursing journals used similar criteria, but all included

a different number of journals. Yet the average rejection rate, which was computed in three studies, is remarkably similar being between 59 percent and 61 percent.

- In the journals within any one study the range of rejection rates is very large, making the significance of the average rejection rate rather dubious and comparisons among disciplines problematic.

- For the same reasons, looking at rejection rates for any one discipline over time neither confirms nor refutes the assertion that rejection rates for some journals are rising. There has been a steady increase in the number of journals and these may serve to keep any one journal's relative rejection rate rather stable. Those very few studies that found an increase in rejection rates over time had problematic data.

- A shortcoming of many of these studies is a lack of a definition of how particular journals were selected for the sample. A large variety of techniques were used to identify a group of journals and, once identified, the group varied in size considerably. Since so many different techniques were used for journal selection, any results or conclusions tend not to be generalizable.

- Two major studies, the Zuckerman-Merton study in 1971 and the Beyer study in 1978, which are frequently cited, are quite old. Current well-designed studies are needed in this area. Journal publications have changed considerably since these older studies were conducted. Certainly both studies need to be redone with careful attention to study design to determine if these results are still valid.

### Recommendation

It is sometimes difficult or impossible to determine whether or not a publication has been peer reviewed. One of the findings of a number of studies is that only about half of the papers presented at professional meetings are eventually published. Findings also indicate that groups of papers published as supplements to journals or as symposia are either not subjected to the same level of peer review, are sponsored by a for-profit venture, or are printed as a separate series. A reader who happens upon a reference through a database search has little way of knowing that an article from one of these sources is less likely to be peer reviewed than an article published in the main body of a journal issue. Material from Chapter One also indicated that most journals publish some material that is not peer reviewed.

- Editors should inform readers of the level of peer review for each item in a journal. A subtitle attached to each published article would easily clarify its peer review status. The subtitle would then be incorporated into the title and would become part of the information about the article in any database.

Databases now include information on such factors as editorials and news items. As indexing and abstracting services and journal publishing move to an electronic environment, a few additional words on each title or subtitle would not add to the burden of journal or database producers.

• Studies should be designed to determine if indeed the best science and scholarship is published, while the worst or unacceptable is rejected.

## Conclusions about rejected manuscripts

The chapter began with the question of whether rejected manuscripts became part of the literature and what role the rejected manuscript plays in the scientific communication process. Studies have shown that indeed, a good percentage of rejected manuscripts do become a part of the published literature. What studies have not shown is the degree to which the best is published and the worst is rejected.

Do Garvey and his colleagues' conclusions still hold? Does a rejected manuscript really change the career path of the author? Since so many manuscripts are rejected and subsequently published, it would suggest that rejected manuscripts no longer have profound impacts on careers of the authors.

There are a variety of measures used to rank journals within a discipline, including impact factor, circulation, and index status; another factor is the journal's rejection rate. The unreplicative ability of some of the journal selection criteria, the small size of the studies, and the age of a number of the important studies all suggest that more data are needed to determine if there are differences among disciplines regarding rejection rates. Some new, solid research is needed in this area and some of the earlier studies that are frequently quoted certainly should be redone to test the current validity of the conclusion. Any new study should define all parameters of the journal selection and the study design to avoid the shortcomings of the early studies. Journal ranking within any one discipline is an important component of any study in this area.

Data suggest that there are the same criteria for rejection across disciplines, both in theory and in practice. Data also suggest that a large percentage of rejected manuscripts become a part of the literature. It is noteworthy to compare the rather high percentage of manuscripts with unsalvageable problems (18.1 percent to 64.8 percent) to data that indicate between 30 percent and 85 percent of rejected manuscripts were eventually published. These numbers indicate a persistence on the part of authors to see their work through to publication. There is some evidence that authors' use a rather fluid view of journals and do not necessarily select a lower rated journal after rejection, but use other criteria when deciding where to resubmit. These numbers also indicate that undoubtedly a certain percentage of manuscripts (or ideas) disappear once rejected. But the degree to which this happens and the impact of these rejections on the scientific knowledge base are unknown. There may be inconsistencies between the reasons for rejection communicated to the author and the apparent ease with which a rejected manuscript gets published. Based on these data, the stated reasons for rejection, and the eventual publication of rejected manuscripts, one could conclude that what is regarded as an unsalvageable problem by one journal might be viewed as salvageable by another journal. More study is needed to examine these issues.

Has this chapter shown that those journals that reject the most manuscripts publish the most important material in a field? The studies simply do not answer this question. These studies examined specific material received and rejected by certain journals. The studies did not analyze the broader and perhaps more important question—is the best science published? On the one hand, editors were able to give substantial reasons for rejecting a manuscript and, on the other hand, it appears that these reasons did not prevent another journal from publishing the rejected manuscript.

Finally, the relationship between rejection rates and the importance of a journal has not been established. What has been established is merely that the more selective the criteria for including a journal in a study, the higher the rejection rate is for that journal. Almost every study discussed in this chapter has supported this finding, regardless of discipline. Each discipline has a set of journals with both high and low rejection rates; how these are translated into journal quality needs to be further investigated. While rejection rates are one important aspect of editorial peer review, they are only one factor in the whole process.

## References

(1980, February 23). The editor regrets. *British Medical Journal*, 508.

(1983, October). Medical journals and urgent medical news. *Annals of Internal Medicine, 99*(4), 559-561.

Abby, M., Massey, M. D., Galandiuk, S., & Polk, H. C., Jr. (1994, July 13). Peer review is an effective screening process to evaluate medical manuscripts. *JAMA, 272*(2), 105-107.

Abt, H. (1988, April). What happens to rejected astronomical papers? *Publications of the Astronomical Society of the Pacific, 100*, 506-508.

Adams, J. E. (1977, Spring). The challenge and response of economics journal policies: a comparative survey. *Collegiate News and Views, 30*(3), 25-27.

Altman, L. K. (1996, May 18). The Ingelfinger rule, embargoes, and the journal peer review—part 1. *Lancet, 347*, 1382-1386.

American Psychological Association. (1975, September). Publication in APA journals: advice from the editors. Council of editors. *American Psychologist, 20*(9), 711-712.

Angell, M., & Kassirer, J. P. (1991, November 7). The Ingelfinger rule revisited. *New England Journal of Medicine, 325*(19), 1371-1373.

Archer, J. D. (1975, April 14). Attributes of a rejected manuscript. *JAMA, 232*(2), 165.

Armstrong, J. S. (1982). The ombudsman: is review by peers as fair as it appears? *Interfaces, 12*(5), 62-74.

Azbel, M. (1993, June). Could Columbus have passed peer review? *Physics Today,* *46*(6), 13, 15.

Bakanic, V., McPhail, C., & Simon, R. J. (1987, October). The manuscript review and decision-making process. *American Sociological Review, 52*(5), 631.

Baue, A. E. (1985, August). Peer and/or peerless review. Some vagaries of the editorial process. *Archives of Surgery, 120*(8), 885-888.

Baue, A. E. (1993, December). Reflections of a former editor. *Archives of Surgery, 128*(12), 1305-1314.

Beaver, M., Gottlieb, N., & Rosenblatt, A. (1983, July-August). Dilemmas in manuscript evaluations. *Social Work, 28*(4), 326.

Beebe, L. (1997). *An author's guide to social work journals.* Washington, DC: NASW Press.

Beyer, J. M. (1978, Winter). Editorial policies and practices among leading journals in four scientific fields. *Sociological Quarterly, 19,* 68-88.

Bolster, A. & Morgan, P. P. (1986, February 15). How CMAJ controls the quality of its scientific articles. *Canadian Medical Association Journal, 134*(4), 301-303.

Bonjean, C. M., & Hullum, J. (1978, Fall). Reasons for journal rejection: an analysis of 600 manuscripts. *PS, 11*(4), 480-483.

Brysbaert, M. (1996, November). Improving the journal review process and the risk of making the poor poorer. *American Psychologist, 51*(11), 1193.

Budd, J. (1988, September 1). Publication in library and information science: the state of the literature. *Library Journal, 113*(14), 125-131.

Buffardi, L. C. & Nichols, J. A. (1981, November). Citation impact, acceptance rate, and APA journals. *American Psychologist, 36*(11), 1453-1456.

Cabell, D. W. E. (1981). *Cabell's directory of publishing opportunities in business, administration and economics* (2nd ed.). Beaumont, Texas: Lamar University.

Campanario, J. M. (1995, March). On influential books and journal articles initially rejected because of negative referee's evaluation. *Science Communication, 16*(3), 304-325.

Campanario, J. M. (1996, April). Have referees rejected some of the most-cited articles of all times. *Journal of the American Society for Information Science, 47*(4), 302-310.

Campbell, J. P. (1985). Editorial: some remarks from an outgoing editor. In L. L. Cummings & P. J. Frost (Eds.), *Publishing in the organizational sciences* (pp. 321-333). Homewood, IL: Richard D. Irwin, Inc.

Chew, F. S. (1990, March). Fate of manuscripts rejected for publication in the ARJ. *American Journal of Roentgenology, 156*(3), 627-632.

Chew, F. S. (1993, February). Manuscript peer review: general concepts and the *AJR* process. *American Journal of Roentgenology, 160*(2), 409-411.

Christiansen, D. (1981, August). Peer review reviewed. *IEEE Spectrum, 18*(8), 21.

Chubin, D. E. & Hackett, E. J. (1990). Peer review and the printed word, *Peerless Science, Peer review and U.S. science policy* (pp. 83-123): State University of New York Press.

Coe, R. K. (1984, September). Evaluating the management journals: a second look. *Academy of Management Journal, 27*(3), 660-666.

Coe, R. K. & Weinstock, I. (1967, Winter). Editorial policies of major economic journals. *Quarterly Review of Economics and Business, 7*(4), 37-43.

Coe, R. K. & Weinstock, I. (1968, January). Publication policies in major business periodicals. *Southern Journal of Business,* 1-10.

Coe, R. K. & Weinstock, I. (1983, Winter). Evaluating the finance journals: the department chairperson's perspective. *Journal of Financial Research, 6*(4), 345-349.

Cronin, B., & McKenzie, G. (1992, September). The trajectory of rejection. *Journal of Documentation, 48*(3), 310-317.

Daft, R. L. (1985). Why I recommended that your manuscript be rejected and what you can do about it. In L. L. Cummings & P. J. Frost (Eds.), *Publishing in the organizational sciences* (pp. 193-209). Homewood, IL: Richard D. Irwin, Inc.

Daniel, H-D. (1993). An evaluation of the peer review process at *Angewandte Chemie*. *Angewandte Chemie, 32*(2), 234-238.

Dirk, L. (1996, September). From laboratory to scientific literature. *Science Communication, 18*(1), 3-28.

Duchini, A. & Genta, R. M. (1997, April). From abstract to peer-reviewed article: the fate of abstracts submitted to the DDW. *Gastroenterology, 112*(4), A12.

Durso, T. W. (1997, September 15). Editors' advice to rejected authors: just try, try again. *The Scientist, 11*(18), 13.

Epstein, S. (1995, October). What can be done to improve the journal review process. *American Psychologist, 50*(9), 883-885.

Farndon, J. R., Murie, J. A., Johnson, C. D., Earnshaw, J. J., & Guillou, P. J. (1997, July). The referee process of *The British Journal of Surgery*. *British Journal of Surgery, 84*(7), 901-903.

Federico, J., Lee, M. M., Boozer, C. H., & Diaz, D. (1984, March). Report of a survey comparing sixty-nine journals in the dental profession. *Educational Directions in Dental Hygiene, 9,* 9-18.

Finifter, A. W. (1997, December). Report of the editor of the *American Political Science Review*, 1996-97. *PS, 30*(4), 783-791.

Fletcher, S. W. & Fletcher, R. H. (1991, April 15). Early release of research results. *Annals of Internal Medicine, 114*(8), 698-700.

Fraley, R. & Via, B. J. (1982). Survey of library & information science journal publishers. In B-C. Sellen (Ed.), *Librarian/author; a practical guide on how to get published* (pp. 117-224). New York: Neal-Schuman Publishers, Inc.

Frey, J. J. (1985, January/February). Peer review and the fate of manuscripts. *Family Medicine, 17*(1), 3.

Fye, W. B. (1990, August 15). Medical authorship, traditions, trends, and tribulations. *Annals of Internal Medicine, 113*(4), 317-325.

Gans, J. S., & Shepherd, G. B. (1994, Winter). How are the mighty fallen: rejected classic articles by leading economists. *Journal of Economic Perspectives, 8*(1), 165-179.

Garvey, W. D. & Griffith, B. C. (1971, April). Scientific communication: its role in the conduct of research and creation of knowledge. *American Psychologist, 26*(4), 349-362.

Garvey, W. D., Lin, N., Nelson, C. E., & Tomita, K. (1972, August). Research studies in patterns of scientific communication: II. The role of national meetings in scientific and technical communication. *Information Storage and Retrieval, 8*(4), 159-169.

Garvey, W. D., Lin, N., & Tomita, K. (1972, October). Research studies in patterns of scientific communication: III. Information-exchange processes associated with the production of journal articles. *Information Storage and Retrieval, 8*(5), 207-211.

Glenn, N. D. (1976, August). The journal article review process: Some proposals for change. *American Sociologist, 11*(3), 179-185.

Goldman, L., & Loscalzo, A. (1980, July 31). Fate of cardiology research originally published in abstract form. *New England Journal of Medicine, 303*(5), 255-259.

Goodrich, D. W. (1945, December). An analysis of manuscripts received by the editors of the *American Sociological Review* from May 1, 1944 to September 1, 1945. *American Sociological Review, 10*(6), 716-725.

Gordon, M. D. (1978). Disciplinary differences, editorial practices and the patterning of rejection rates. *Journal of Research Communication Studies, 1*, 139-159.

Gordon, M. D. (1979, March). Peer review in physics. *Physics Bulletin, 30*, 112-113.

Gordon, M. D. (1984, February). How authors select journals: a test of the reward maximization model of submission behavior. *Social Studies of Science, 14*(1), 27-43.

Goudsmit, S. A. (1970, April). To amend refereeing. *Physics Today, 23*(4), 10.

Grouse, L. D. (1981, January 23/30). The Ingelfinger rule. *JAMA, 245*(4), 375-376.

Haas, L., Milton, S., & Quinn, A. (1996, Winter). Surviving the publishing process: a beginner's guide. *RQ, 36*(2), 230-246.

Hargens, L. L. (1988). Scholarly consensus and journal rejection rates. *American Sociological Review, 53*(1), 139-151.

Hargens, L. L. (1990, March 9). Variations in journal peer review systems. Possible causes and consequences. *JAMA, 263*(10), 1348-1352.

Hartley, J. (1988, November). Editorial practices in psychology journals. *Psychologist, 1*(11), 428-430.

Henson, K. T. (1988, June). Writing for education journals. *Phi Delta Kappa, 69*(10), 752-754.

Hernon, P., Smith, A., & Croxen, M. B. (1993, July). Publications in *College & Research Libraries*: accepted rejected, and published papers, 1980-1991. *College and Research Libraries, 54*(4), 303-321.

Huth, E. J. (1983, October). Medical journals and urgent medical news. *Annals of Internal Medicine, 99*(4), 559-561.

Ingelfinger, F. J. (1969, September 18). Definition of "sole contribution". *New England Journal of Medicine, 281*(12), 676-677.

Ingelfinger, F. J. (1972, December 21). Season's greetings. *New England Journal of Medicine, 287*(25), 1301.

Johnson, B. (1986, Fall). The rejected manuscript: role of the editor. *CBE Views, 9*(3), 84-85.

Jones, C. (1977, Fall). Report of the managing editor of the *American Political Science Review*, 1976-77. *PS, 10*(4), 448-453.

Juhasz, S., Calvert, E., Jackson, T., Kronick, D. A., & Shipman, J. (1975, September). Acceptance and rejection of manuscripts. *IEEE Transactions on Professional Communication, 18*(3), 177-185.

Kahn, A. S., Presbury, J. H., Moore, H. B., & Driver, J. D. (1990). Characteristics of accepted versus rejected manuscripts. *Psychology of Women Quarterly, 14*, 7-14.

Kassirer, J. P. & Angell, M. (1997, December 11). Prepublication release of journal articles. *New England Journal of Medicine, 337*(24), 1762-1763.

Kassirer, J. P. & Campion, E. W. (1994, July 13). Peer review, crude and understudied, but indispensable. *JAMA, 272*(2), 96-97.

King, D., McDonald, D. D., & Roderer, N. K. (1981). *Scientific journals in the United States: their production, use and economics*. Stroudsburg, Pennsylvania: Hutchinson Ross Publishing Company.

Koch-Weser, D. & Yankauer, A. (1993, November). The authorship and fate of international health papers submitted to the American Journal of Public Health. *American Journal of Public Health, 83*(11), 1618-1620.

Landwirth, T. K. (1991, July). Why authors fail. *Bulletin of the Medical Library Association, 79*(3), 337-338.

Lavelle, J. (1966, November). Facts of journal publishing, IV. *Publications of the Modern Language Association of America, 81*(6), 3-12.

Lazarus, D. (1980, November 10). Authors, editors and referees. *Physical Review Letters, 45*(19), 1527-1528.

Linder, D. E. (1977). Evaluation of the *Personality and Social Psychology Bulletin* by its readers and authors. *Personality and Social Psychology Bulletin, 3*, 583-591.

Lindsey, D. (1978). *The scientific publication system in social science*. San Francisco: Jossey-Bass Publishers.

Lock, S. (1985). *A difficult balance. Editorial peer reviewed in medicine*. Philadelphia: ISI Press.

Lundberg, G. D., Glass, R. M., & Joyce, L. E. (1991, January 16). Policy of AMA journals regarding release of information to the public. *JAMA, 265*(3), 400.

Mayland, H. F., Sojka, R. E., & Gbur, E. E. (1991). The peer-review process under review. *Journal of Animal Science, 69*(Supplement 1), 228.

McBride, G. (1982, January 23/30). Now for the latest news. *JAMA, 245*(4), 374-375.

McCartney, J. L. (1973, Autumn). Publish or perish. *Sociological Quarterly, 14*, 450, 600.

McCloskey, J. (1977, July-August). Publishing opportunities for nurses: a comparison of 65 journals. *Nurse Educator, 2*(4), 4-13.

McCloskey, J. & Swanson, E. A. (1982, June). Publishing opportunities for nurses: a comparison of 100 journals. *Image, 14*(2), 50-56.

McCormick, M. C. & Holmes, J. H. (1988, February). Publication of research presented at pediatric meetings. *American Journal of Diseases of Children, 139*(2), 122-126.

Metoyer-Duran, C. (1993, November). The readability of published, accepted, and rejected papers appearing in *College & Research Libraries. College and Research Libraries, 54*(6), 517-526.

Miller, A. C., & Serzan, S. L. (1984, November/December). Criteria for identifying a refereed journal. *Journal of Higher Education, 55*(6), 673-699.

Mitchell, T. R., Beach, L. R., & Smith, K. G. (1985). Some data on publishing from the authors' and reviewers' perspective. In L. L. Cummings & P. J. Frost (Eds.), *Publishing in the organizational sciences* (pp. 248-264). Homewood, IL: Richard D. Irwin, Inc.

Mullins, C. J. (1977). *A guide to writing and publishing in the social and behavioral sciences.* New York: John Wiley & Sons.

Neufeld, J. (1970, April). To amend refereeing. *Physics Today, 23*(4), 9-10.

Newman, S. H. (1986, October). Improving the evaluation of submitted manuscripts. Importance of improving evaluations. *American Psychologist, 21*(10), 980-981.

Noble, K. A. (1989). Publish or perish: what 23 journal editors have to say. *Studies in Higher Education, 14*(1), 97-102.

O'Connor, D. & Van Orden, P. (1978, September). Getting into print. *College and Research Libraries, 39*(5), 389-396.

Petruzzi, J. M. (1976, September). Peer review in *Analytical Chemistry. Analytical Chemistry, 48*(11), 875A.

Pullen, K. A., Jr. (1977, January). Reviewing the reviewers. *IEEE Spectrum, 14*(1), 16, 18.

Relman, A. S. (1970, May 14). Anonymous authors and reviewers. *New England Journal of Medicine*, 1160.

Relman, A. S. (1978, July 27). Are we a filter or a sponge? *New England Journal of Medicine, 299*(4), 197.

Relman, A. S. (1980, July 31). News reports of medical meetings: how reliable are abstracts? *New England Journal of Medicine, 303*(5), 277-278.

Relman, A. S. (1981, October 1). The Ingelfinger rule. *New England Journal of Medicine, 305*(14), 824-826.

Relman, A. S. (1988, April 28). More on the Ingelfinger rule. *New England Journal of Medicine, 318*(17), 1125-1126.

Relman, A. S., Rennie, D., & Angell, M. (1980, December 25). Greetings - with regrets. *New England Journal of Medicine, 303*(26), 1527-1528.

Rochon, P. A., Gurwitz, J. H., Cheung, M., Hayes, J. A., & Chalmers, T. C. (1994, July 13). Evaluating the quality of articles published in journal supplements compared with the quality of those published in the parent journal. *JAMA, 272*(2), 108-113.

Rockwood, A. L. (1985, February 4). The peer review system. *Chemical and Engineering News, 63*(5), 5.

Roland, C. G. & Kirkpatrick, R. A. (1975, June 12). Time lapse between hypothesis and publication in the medical sciences. *New England Journal of Medicine, 292*(24), 1273-1276.

Rotton, J., Foos, P., Van Meek, L., & Levitt, M. (1995). Publication practices and the file drawer problem: a survey of published authors. *Journal of Social Behavior and Personality, 10*(1), 1-13.

Rotton, J., Levitt, M., & Foos, P. (1993, August). Citation impact, rejection rates, and journal value. *American Psychologist, 48*(8), 911-912.

Scherer, R. W., Dickersin, K., & Langenberg, P. (1994, July 13). Full publication of results initially presented in abstracts. *JAMA, 272*(2), 158-162.

Seligman, L. (1986, December). The manuscript evaluation process used by AACD journals. *Journal of Counseling and Development, 65*, 189-192.

Sen, S. K. & Chakraborty, S. K. (1993, March). Quality control in Indian science: a study on refereeing systems of twenty-six Indian journals. *Journal of Scientific & Industrial Research, 52*(3), 133-150.

Service, F. J. (1983, March-April). Manuscript review. *Diabetes Care, 6*(2), 208-209.

Sigelman, L. & Whicker, M. L. (1987, September). Some implications of bias in peer review: a simulation-based analysis. *Social Science Quarterly, 68*(3), 494-509.

Simon, R. J., Bakanic, V., & McPhail, C. (1986). Who complains to journal editors and what happens. *Sociological Inquiry, 56*(2), 259-271.

Smigel, E. O., & Ross, H. L. (1970, February). Factors in the editorial decision. *American Sociologist, 5*(1), 19-21.

Soffer, A. (1978, February). The open editorial office. *Chest, 73*(2), 125.

Stieg, M. F. (1983, February). Refereeing and the editorial process: the AHR and Webb. *Scholarly Publishing, 14*(2), 99-122.

Sussman, M. B. (1978). *Author's guide to journals in sociology and related fields* (Ed.). New York: The Haworth Press.

Swanson, E. A. & McCloskey, J. (1986, September/October). Publishing opportunities for nurses. *Nursing Outlook, 34*(5), 227-235.

Swanson, E. A., McCloskey, J., & Bodensteiner, A. (1991, Spring). Publishing opportunities for nurses: a comparison of 92 U.S. journals. *Image: Journal of Nursing Scholarship, 23*(1), 33-38.

Via, B. J. (1996, July). Publishing in the journal literature of library and information science: a survey of manuscript review process and acceptance. *College and Research Libraries, 57*(4), 365-376.

Warren, R. (1973, May). Authors and editors meet. *Archives of Surgery, 106*(3), 360-362.

Webb, W. B. (1979, February). Continuing education: refereeing journal articles. *Teaching of Psychology, 6*(1), 59-60.

Weller, A. C. (1990, March 9). Editorial peer review in U.S. medical journals. *JAMA, 263*(10), 1344-1347.

Weller, A. C. (1996, July). Editorial peer review: a comparison of authors publishing in two groups of U.S. medical journals. *Bulletin of the Medical Library Association, 84*(3), 359-366.

Whitman, N. & Eyre, S. (1985, January/February). The pattern of publishing previously rejected articles in selected journals. *Family Medicine, 17*(1), 26-28.

Willis, C. L. & Bobys, R. S. (1983, Spring/Summer). Perishing in publishing: an analysis of manuscript rejection letters. *Wisconsin Sociologist, 20*(2-3), 84-91.

Wilson, J. (1978). Peer review and publication. *Journal of Clinical Investigation, 61*, 1697-1701.

Yamazaki, S. (1995). Refereeing system of 29 life science journals preferred by Japanese scientists. *Scientometrics, 33*(1), 123-129.

Yankauer, A. (1982, March). Editor's report—peer review again. *American Journal of Public Health, 72*(3), 239-240.

Yankauer, A. (1985, Summer). Peering at peer review. *CBE Views, 8*(2), 7-10.

Yankauer, A. (1986, July). Then and now, the *American Journal of Public Health*, 1911-1985. *American Journal of Public Health, 76*(7), 809-815.

Zuckerman, H. & Merton, R. K. (1971, January). Patterns of evaluation in science: institutionalisation, structure and functions of the referee system. *Minerva, 9*(1), 66-100.

# Chapter Three

# Editors and Editorial Boards: Who They Are and What They Do

*The stars in a field may prefer to let this load fall on a less competent but still qualified group who are willing to shoulder the work.*

(Crandall, 1977, p. 579)

*The stars in a field may prefer to let this load fall on the shoulders of people with less scientific status.*

(Bakker & Rigter, 1985, p. 18)

Any way one states it, the question is: where do editors rank professionally in their discipline? Are they experts in editorial peer review, coming to the job prepared for the tasks associated with scholarly publishing, or does their expertise reside within their own disciplines?

In a 1951 editorial in the *Journal Lancet*, Hewitt described a part-time medical editor: "Commonly, such an editor is eminent in some field of medicine or surgery. He is likely to know authors personally who are writing in his field, to be aware of the soundness or unsoundness of these authors, and to be acquainted with what has been done and what remains to be done in the field. Consequently, he is in a position to solicit papers from desirable authors and to pass judgment on the soundness of purpose of a manuscript" (p. 147-148) (Hewitt, 1951). Hewitt also characterized a professional full-time editor: "He has wide acquaintance among potential authors and solicits from them some of the material he prints. He reads nearly everything submitted to, or prepared for inclusion in, his publication" (p. 145). Hewitt made no mention of editorial peer review. The purpose of citing Hewitt is to illustrate the role of editors at that time, especially with respect to soliciting and selecting manuscripts for publication. The driving force in selecting manuscripts seemed to be some knowledge of an author's previous work or a personal knowledge of an author's professional status. Hewitt's comments have the sound of an "old boys" ring, but it was one that was undoubtedly the norm at the time and would probably not have appeared in the least bit inappropriate or prejudicial to the reader at that time.

Hewitt was probably the first person to present a detailed description of the duties of a modern editor. As for his own job as editor, Hewitt acknowledged that it was the "hardest, most confining, most fatiguing" and "satisfying" work he had ever done (p. 148). He went on to describe in detail the many aspects of editing and copyediting in the publication process.

As described in Chapter One, during the post-World War II period, editorial peer review was adopted as an integral component of the scholarly communication process. How have editors shaped the editorial peer review process and editorial guidelines, thereby influencing the content of their journals? What factors affect the selection of editors? What bias do they bring to the process? To what extent do editors rely on the guidance of editorial boards and reviewers? What evidence is there that editors have scientifically analyzed their practice and engaged in a "best practice" of editorial peer review? Has the literature defined a best practice? This chapter examines these questions.

## Role of editors

Borysewicz summed up the role of editor with these thoughts (Borysewicz, 1977):

> *The primary role of an editor, specifically as the proprietor of a scientific journal, is not to be creative but to be self-effacing. An editor must function as an intermediary between author and audience. The editor must provide a network of review, scientific and editorial, for the author; clarification of the message for the audience; and massage for both by sensitive handling of the peer review process and by maintaining a sense of common purpose and balance through the various and crucial aspects of publication (p. 261).*

Gaston claimed that editors "who maintain the integrity of the [editorial peer review] process have a limited amount of freedom" (p. 789) (Gaston, 1979). By the time the manuscript has been received in the editorial office, the study has been completed, the methodology unalterable, and conclusions determined. Editors are put in the position of reconciling a number of interests, including that of the authors, the readers, the publishers, the printers, in addition to their own prestige as editors and scientists as well as the prestige of the journal and the discipline (Munters, 1981). Angell outlined a similar set of "competing claims" (p. 67) for editors of medical journals: editors serve the public, readers, authors, and owners (Angell, 1991).

A number of writers have pointed to broad responsibilities of editors:

- Guard against incompetent and poorly done reviews (Einhorn, 1971)

- Shape the direction their discipline takes (Rodman & Mancini, 1977)

- Maintain confidentiality and impartiality, and remain courteous (Schiedermayer & Siegler, 1986)

- Guide new authors (Kole, 1989)

- Clarify if the reviewer's primary obligation is to the author (offer helpful suggestions) or to the editor (recommend acceptance or rejection) (Bornstein, 1991)

- Resign from any editorial board memberships, in order to avoid a real or perceived conflict of interest (Baue, 1993)

- Sustain integrity in research, publish guidelines, follow-up all allegations of misconduct, publish corrections and retractions (Caelleigh, 1993)

- Furnish an important mentoring role (Saidman, 1995)

Lavelle identified a lack of time and support staff as the primary concerns of editors (Lavelle, 1966). Rodman surveyed editors of 33 sociology journals to shed light on some of the day-to-day issues of editors (he did not state how he determined which editors to use in this study) (Rodman & Mancini, 1977). The four major problems that editors encountered were the time needed to edit the journal, the availability of enough good articles, the quality of writing, and the time reviewers took to return manuscripts. Those issues that caused fewest problems for editors included organizing editorial procedures, rejecting colleagues' manuscripts, maintaining editorial files, and dealing with rejected authors. Editors did not view the editorship post as contributing to their careers. The opportunity to make acquaintances with others in the field was viewed positively as was the opportunity to influence the discipline and to remain current in it.

## Role of appointed editorial boards

The editorial board members appointed by editors have three primary functions, depending on a particular journal: 1) review manuscripts; 2) provide input to journal policy; and 3) positively influence a journal in a number of ways, i.e., manuscript submissions, circulation, and prestige. Some editors used editorial board members primarily as reviewers (Baue, 1993). In order to review manuscripts, DeBakey believed that board members should be knowledgeable in their scientific fields, but that editors also needed a mechanism to rotate board membership (DeBakey, 1976). Meadows suggested that "an editorial board with restricted membership may ... be almost as efficient as a complex refereeing system" (p. 792) (Meadows, 1977). He however, has a serious objection to his own suggestion: "... it cuts down the interaction within the scientific community" (p. 793). (See Chapter Five for the role and performance of editorial board members when they serve as reviewers.)

A panel discussion held at the 1980 annual meeting of the Council of Biology Editors, while agreeing that most journals had editorial boards, asked if editorial boards were necessary (Fuccillo & Holmes, 1980). Panelists agreed that boards were very important for a number of reasons and had different functions for different journals:

- Editorial board members have different roles depending on the needs of the journal or the editor.

- There is the assumption that editorial board members are selected because of the prestige they bring to the journal and the disciplines they represent.

- Editorial board members are usually appointed by the editor and may be appointed to fill the role of a section editor or serve as individual reviewers.

- The presence of prestigious board members may be "essential to the starting and continuation of some commercial-type journals not representing any scientific-technical society but simply a discipline" (p. 18-19).

- Diligent reviewers are sometimes given board membership to recognize their efforts.

- Editorial board members are usually given a term of service, thus making removal of an ineffective board member relatively easy.

- Editorial board members are viewed as supporters of the journal.

A group of scientists discussed the length of time editorial board members should serve and raised a number of additional topics. Editorial board members might undertake a number of tasks including, "policy making, refereeing, arbitration, dealing with problems of ethics, attending Board meetings, encouraging papers to be published in the journal, and arranging for referees" (p. 402) (Shelley, 1981/1982). This discussion group, led by Shelley, thought a limited term was appropriate for board members. Morris also felt editorial board members should be given rotating terms to make it easier to replace an unsuitable one (Morris, 1985).

Using what may be a fairly typical view in any discipline, in the field of library and information science, Steffens and Robbins summarized the role of the editorial boards. Boards must work with the editor in "determining the development of and changes to the scope and policies of the journal; and developing the review process of both submitted and solicited manuscripts" (p. 198) (Steffens & Robbins, 1991).

## Editorial appointments

A study of editors and editorial boards in psychiatry found that both editors and editorial boards had a preponderance of male members (Benedek, 1976); in psychology, Over determined that women were well-represented on editorial boards (Over, 1981). An investigation into the gender of editors of the 100 clinical medicine journals with the highest impact factor identified 92 males and four females as editors (Hatfield, Ostbye, & Sori, 1995). The remaining four journals appeared to have no primary editor. None of these investigations attempted to identify the percentage of women in any of the specialties studied. While they provide raw data on gender differences, they do not provide data on the relative differences of their representation in the specialties, if any. (See Chapter Seven for gender issues as they relate to the editorial peer review process.)

### Editors

A survey of editors of education journals revealed that an editor was most likely to be selected by the previous editor, the president or executive board of a professional association, the commercial publisher, or a publication committee of a professional association (Silverman, 1976). On an international scale, in a given discipline, the most productive countries produce the most editors (Bakker & Rigter, 1985).

In what may be similar to many scholarly associations, the stated policy of the American Psychological Association is to use the Publication and Communications Board to select editors (Eichorn & VandenBos, 1985). The board then appoints a search committee who seeks well-qualified individuals to serve in the post.

In an opinion survey, Beyer asked editors of the 10 most prestigious journals in physics, chemistry, sociology, and political science which criteria they considered the most important in selecting editors (Beyer, 1978). Criteria included previous publication in that journal, institutional affiliation (usually a university), prestige within a discipline or subspecialty, personal knowledge of the individual, and position in a professional association. Although opinions varied among the different disciplines, generally prestige within a discipline or subspecialty ranked the highest in each discipline, while publication in the journal or affiliation with a professional association ranked lowest. Since this was an opinion survey of those already serving as editor, it is not known if any of these criteria do, in fact, play a role in editorial appointments.

### Editorial Boards

Silverman asked editors of education journals what criteria they considered important in selecting members to the editorial board (Silverman, 1978). The top five criteria were (p. 17):

• Representation of the divergent interests of the readers,

• Knowledge of literature and field,

- Specialization in an area,

- Evidence of scholarly ability, and

- Interest in working for the journal.

In Beyer's study discussed above, she also asked about criteria for editorial board appointments. Important characteristics included prestige either in a discipline or subspecialty (Beyer, 1978). Taking a more pragmatic view, Michel believed that most physics journals appointed editorial boards for a "decorative role" (p. 9), and that board members' time would be better served if their subject expertise was tapped for use in the role of referee (Michel, 1982). Steffens and Robbins thought criteria for selecting board membership should include such factors as subject and methodology expertise, institutional focus, individual interest, and geographic distribution (Steffens & Robbins, 1991). For the most part, editors selected for board membership comprise a group of scholars who represent the readership of the journal.

Lindsey thought the process of selecting editorial boards placed "overwhelming emphasis on a record of scientific accomplishment ... if criteria other than scientific accomplishments are used, they need to be clearly understood and relevant to the task of the editor. In addition, the criteria should be objective" (p. 520) (Lindsey, 1992). Baue, editor of *Archives of Surgery*, looked for "distinguished chairs and chairmen, chiefs, clinic leaders, and respected clinicians and investigators"; in addition, board members should be "good, considerate and capable" (p. 1307), which could be determined by first using them as reviewers (Baue, 1993). While not exploring reasons for editorial appointments, *JAMA* editors looked at gender issues within the editorial staff of the *Journal* (Gilbert, Williams, & Lundberg, 1994). Not surprisingly, the investigators "found that male editors handling research articles submitted to *JAMA* in 1991 were older, were employed full-time, and had more years of experience, yet carried a lighter manuscript caseload than the female editors" (p. 141). These statistically significant differences led to "no apparent effect on the final outcome of the peer review process acceptance for publication" (p. 139).

Pferrer and colleagues tested the theory that the impact of institutional representation on editorial boards would be greatest for those disciplines with a less developed scientific paradigm (Pfeffer, Leong, & Strehl, 1977). Three disciplines were compared: chemistry, sociology, and political science. "As expected, the estimated effect of institutional representation on editorial boards was strongest in political science with the least developed scientific paradigm, while there was no apparent editorial board effect in chemistry, the discipline with the most developed paradigm" (p. 938).

A study of 49 international chemistry journals indicated that if any members of the editorial staff excelled in their field, they were more likely to be editorial board members than editors-in-chief (Zsindely, Schubert, & Braun, 1982a).

*Questions*

What criteria are used to select editors and editorial board members? Is their selection related to professional status?

*Criteria for inclusion*

~ any study that compares the professional or academic standing of editors or editorial boards in the same discipline.

*Comparable studies*

Twenty-one studies provide data on the achievements or professional status of editors and editorial board members (Table 3-1). Table 3-1 is arranged by discipline; for studies that investigated more than one discipline, there is a separate entry under each discipline.

These studies originate from economics, education, medicine, nursing, political science, psychology, the natural sciences, the social sciences, and statistics. They have used a number of different measures to determine professional status or reputation of editors and editorial board members, including academic affiliation, institutions from which they received an advanced degree, number of publications, citation patterns to their work, and professional standing within the scientific community.

## Social Sciences and Psychology

Eight studies of the professional status of editors and editorial board members have been conducted in the social sciences and psychology. These disciplines have been grouped together because several studies compared data among them.

Crane conducted the first study that provided comparative data on the academic affiliation of editors of major social and economic journals (Crane, 1967). Crane used standard tools for identifying major universities but did not name any universities. Between 1956 and 1965, 55 percent of the editors for *American Economic Review* were affiliated with major universities. Between 1946 and 1955, 23 percent of the editors for the *American Sociological Review* came from major universities. This percentage increased to 34 percent between 1956 and 1965. Between 1946-55, 56 percent of editors for the *American Sociological Review* received doctorates from major universities, between 1956-1965 the percentage increased to 66 percent, while 71 percent of editors of the *American Economic Review* had obtained doctorates from major universities. Crane's data points out the increase in the percentage of editors coming from major universities for these journals from the 1940s through the 1960s.

Using a different technique—that of identifying institutions from which editors received their doctoral degrees—Yoels established that 61.2 percent of all editors of the *American Sociological Review* between 1948-1968 came from three universities: Chicago, Columbia, and Harvard (Yoels, 1971). Yoels also investigated editorial appointments of the eight major journals from seven learned societies: physics,

| Discipline | # of editors & editorial board | # of journals | Editors' institutional affiliation | Editors' academic degrees | Professional accomplishments of editors | Years covered | References |
|---|---|---|---|---|---|---|---|
| Biology | 192 | 2 | | 36.9% from top 3 or 4 universities | | 1948-68 | (Yoels, 1974) |
| Chemistry | 59 | 1 | | 39% from top 3 universities | | 1948-68 | (Yoels, 1974) |
| | | 49 | | | editors less cited than editorial boards | 1980 | (Zsindely et al., 1982a) |
| | | 27 | | | correlation between number of gatekeepers and citation rate; 10 countries produce 75% of new results | 1978 | (Braun & Bujdoso, 1983) |
| Economic | 31 | 1 | 55% from major universities | 71% from major universities | | 1956-65 | (Crane, 1967) |
| | | 1 | | 51.1% from top 3 universities | | 1948-68 | (Yoels, 1974) |
| | | 25 | 39% from top 6 schools | | | 1988 | (Gibbons & Fish, 1991) |
| Education | | 130 | | 46% from research I universities | 65% not published in past 3 years | | (Silverman, 1976) |
| Medicine | | 1168 | | | editors productive and eminent scientists; scientifically productive countries provide most editors | | (Bakker & Rigter, 1985) |
| | 894 | 769 | | | editors less cited than articles in their journals | 1981-85 | (Zsindely & Schubert, 1989) |
| | 78 | 1 | | | board members serve on a median of 3 boards each | 1989 | (Reideberg & Reidenberg, 1991) |
| Nursing | 58 | 58 | | 66% M.A. or Ph.D. | | 1980 | (Binger, 1982) |
| | 9 | 9 | | | editors selected for their publication experience | 1993 | (Fondiller, 1994) |
| Physics | 37 | 1 | | 35.1% from top 3 universities | | 1948-68 | (Yoels, 1974) |
| Political Science | 41 | 1 | | 51.3% from top 3 universities | | 1948-68 | (Yoels, 1974) |
| Psychology | 63 | 1 | | 36.5% from top 3 universities | | 1948-68 | (Yoels, 1974) |
| | 101 | 5 | | 100% Ph.D. | production index: 21; corrected quality ratio: 50.1 | 1953-74 | (Lindsey, 1976) |
| | 101 | 5 | | 100% Ph.D. | production index: 15; corrected quality ration: 64.6 | 1965-74 | (Lindsey, 1978) |
| | 165 | 5 | | | mean citation count 39.2 | 1990 | (Pardeck et al., 1991a) |
| | 165 | 5 | | | 50% of editors cited 16+ times | 1990 | (Pardeck, 1992) |
| Science | | 252 | | | editors come from countries where science is valued | 1980 | (Zsindely, Schubert, & Braun, 1982b) |
| Social Work | 108 | 7 | | 54% Ph.D. | production index: 2.0; corrected quality ration: .54 | 1965-74 | (Lindsey, 1976) |
| | not given | 1 | | | production index: 8.3 | 1974-75 | (Gilbert, 1977) |

**Table 3-1: Professional status of editors and editorial boards**

| Discipline | # of editors & editorial board | # of journals | Editors' institutional affiliation | Editors' academic degrees | Professional accomplishments of editors | Years covered | References |
|---|---|---|---|---|---|---|---|
| Social Work | | | 7 | 54% Ph.D. | production index: 1.5; corrected quality ration: .64 | 1965-74 | (Lindsey, 1978) |
| | 69 | 5 | | | mean citation count: 15.6 | 1990 | (Pardeck et al., 1991a) |
| | 69 | 5 | | | 14% of editors cited 16+ times | 1990 | (Pardeck, 1992) |
| | 363 | 18 | | | correlation between impact factor of journal and achievement of editorial board | | (Lindsey, 1992) |
| Sociology | 34 | 1 | 23% from major universities | 56% from major universities | | 1946-55 | (Crane, 1967) |
| | 67 | 1 | 34% from major universities | 66% from major universities | | 1956-65 | (Crane, 1967) |
| | 284 | 2 | | 61.2% from 3 universities | | 1948-68 | (Yoels, 1971) |
| | 98 | 1 | | 59.2% from top 3 universities | | 1948-68 | (Yoels, 1974) |
| | 114 | 6 | | 100% Ph.D. | production index: 14; corrected quality ration: 31.1 | 1953-74 | (Lindsey, 1976) |
| | 114 | 6 | | 100% Ph.D. | production index: 11.5; corrected quality ration: 37.0 | 1965-74 | (Lindsey, 1978) |
| | 27 | 4 | 96% academic affiliation | 55.6% Ph.D. | | 1980 | (Munters, 1981) |
| Statistics | 267 | 14 | 23 institutions represented | | | 1988 | (Gibbons, 1990) |

**Table 3-1: Professional status of editors and editorial boards (continued)**

chemistry, biology, economics, psychology, political science, and sociology; he employed the same methodology as his previous study (Yoels, 1974). The top three or four universities granting doctorates in each discipline (different academic institutions were represented for different disciplines) contributed from between 35.1 percent and 59.2 percent of the total number of editors in each discipline. Yoels thought that both Crane's and his studies provided "evidence of 'extra-scientific' influences upon the selection of journal editors in the social sciences" (p. 265). Both studies, Yoels maintained, uncovered evidence of a "vicious circle" in which graduates of the top schools had an advantage: they received editorial appointments and then accepted manuscripts from authors at these same schools (p. 274).

In the one study from the Netherlands, the academic standing of the editorial boards of four journals in sociology was compared to the population of sociologists (Munters, 1981). Munters concluded that the editorial boards were far from representative of all sociologists. All but one editor came from academic affiliations, while over 75 percent of the Dutch sociologists were not affiliated with an academic institution.

Lindsey conducted a study of editorial board members' distinctions and achievements by investigating the standing of editorial board members in the fields of psychology, social work, and sociology (Lindsey, 1976). Journal titles for this study were selected from previous lists of important journals in these fields. Lindsey measured the productivity of editorial board members, the number of citations to their publications, and the highest degrees they had received. Lindsey concluded that editorial board members in psychology were the most productive and received a higher number of citations to their publications than those working in the field who were not editorial board members. He developed a "corrected quality ratio," which was "a measure of the combined quality of performance of the editorial board members in terms of citations to productivity" (p. 801). Psychology had the highest corrected quality ratio of 50.1, followed by sociology at 31.1, and then social work at .54. According to Lindsey, "social work journal editorial boards are consistently composed of individuals who, in comparison to the editors in sociology and psychology, are not distinguished by the excellence or volume of their own contribution to the knowledge base of the field" (p. 802).

Lindsey's conclusions proved to be controversial. Gilbert, on the editorial board of *Social Work*, one of the journals studied by Lindsey, thought Lindsey's reliance on the number of publications as the sole measure of distinction was too narrow a view. Gilbert maintained that distinction could also be measured by professional practice. He described what he considered a more serious methodological problem with Lindsey's study: articles were identified from an index of sociology and psychology journals that covered a 19-year period, while the index used for social work journals covered a nine-year period (Gilbert, 1977). Gilbert conducted his own survey of editorial board members of *Social Work* for a one-year period and found both a higher adjusted total articles index (7.5 versus Lindsey's 2.9) and a higher production index (8.3 versus Lindsey's 4.4). Lindsey countered that Gilbert had not used the same sample of editorial board members as his study, which provided "all the information needed for replicating the study" (p. 1113) (Lindsey, 1977b). Lindsey repeated his conclusion that "social work journal editorial boards are consistently composed of individuals who, in comparison to editors in sociology and psychology, are not distinguished by the excellence or volume of their contribution to the knowledge base in the field" (p. 1114).

Crandall also questioned Lindsey's approach, claiming Lindsey had not taken into account that different disciplines might have different standards of publication. Nor did Lindsey compare editorial board members with other researchers within the disciplines of psychology, sociology, or social work (Crandall, 1977). Crandall emphasized that editors might not be at the top of their fields and that editorships require a commitment of time that would take one out of the research arena. In a response to the comments by Crandall, Lindsey qualified his original conclusions. "Psychology appears to appoint individuals who are characterized by superior scientific achievement for purposes more concerned with enhancing the prestige of their journal than with attaining assistance in the manuscript review process. Sociology boards do not appear to have adopted this approach" (p. 585) (Lindsey, 1977a).

Lindsey then conducted a follow-up study of psychology, sociology, and social work computing data for the years 1965-74 for all three disciplines. Results of this study are almost identical to his 1976 study (Lindsey, 1978).

Interest in the professionalism of editorial boards in psychology and social work resurfaced again in 1991 when Pardeck and colleagues conducted a study of board members in social work and psychology journals using journal titles similar to those used by Lindsey (Pardeck et al., 1991a). (A second publication by Pardeck and the same list of six coauthors is a very similar article (Pardeck et al., 1991b).) Pardeck and colleagues studied citation counts of editorial board members from both groups of journals. They concluded that editorial boards of psychology journals were more likely than boards of social work journals to be cited. They also claimed that "editorial board members of psychology journals have higher levels of distinction and achievement in their discipline than do editorial board members of social work journals" (p. 523). Pardeck reanalyzed the data, after he determined they were "more appropriately analyzed using the median scores and the Kruskal-Wallis one-way analysis of variance statistic" (p. 489) (Pardeck, 1992). He concluded: "social work journals have a very limited impact on the social work, social science, and behavioral sciences literature." (p. 493).

Lindsey ascertained that Pardeck's analysis (from the study reanalyzed by Pardeck) focused "too much on a comparison of the accomplishments of social work editorial members relative to psychology editorial board members and draws inferences from those comparisons that are not warranted by the data" (p. 515) (Lindsey, 1992). To test his point, Lindsey "rank ordered social work journals on the median measures of impact factor and median citation counts of editorial board members" (p. 520). To this he applied a Spearman rank order correlation and determined there was a "strong association between the distinction and achievements of editorial board members and the impact of the journal" (p. 520).

This is all rather messy. A reasonable alternate approach might be *not* to compare editors and editorial boards among disciplines, but rather to accept the premise that each discipline has its own standards of professionalism and publication patterns. The social sciences incorporate a number of practice-based specialties, and much of the controversy arises in the practice-based specialties that are comprised of professionals who might be less likely to publish than professionals in other specialties.

## Nursing

Two publications focusing on editors of nursing journals (both the study by Copp and the study by Blank and McElmurry) were excluded from Table 3-1. Copp praised a group 12 editors of prominent nursing journals, highlighting their professional status, accomplishments, ties to professional associations, writing ability, and scholarly contributions (Copp, 1997). While bestowing a warm tribute on these editors, Copp included no data. Blank and McElmurry wanted to learn how editors were selected for nursing journals (Blank & McElmurry, 1988).

They surveyed a "convenience" sample of nine editors. They did find that these nursing editors thought they had been selected for the editorship for their previous experience with the publication process.

Two studies of nursing journals are in Table 3-1. Binger's study of 58 editors of nursing journals (Binger, 1982) showed that editors held higher degrees than the average nurse. Three-quarters of the editors also held a professional position and devoted less than 40 percent of their time carrying out editorship responsibilities. Building on Binger's work, Fondiller surveyed editors of 80 U.S. nursing journals and learned that almost half of the editors had had previous experience with newsletters, editorial review boards, and the like, while 13.2 percent had some training in journalism. A total of 71.7 percent of the nursing journal editors had worked with either the content of a journal or had some type of editorial experience prior to taking an editorship appointment (Fondiller, 1994).

## Medicine and the Sciences

Four studies have investigated international patterns of professional standings of editors and editorial boards in medicine and the sciences. Zsindely and colleagues (Zsindely et al., 1982b) compared the number of science journal editors from different countries to the number of scientists from these same countries. They concluded, "country-by-country distribution of the editors of international journals may characterize the scientific research activity of the countries" (p. 67). But the investigators also pointed out that international relationships enhanced by countries with a more open communication policy may make scientists from these countries more " 'visible' and as a result receive relatively more invitations to participate in the editorial boards of international journals" (p. 67). In a study of international chemistry journals, the same group of researchers looked for a correlation between the number of times editors of chemistry journals were cited and the impact factor of those journals (Zsindely et al., 1982a). Zsindely and Schubert found a significant correlation between these two factors. The correlation was weaker when data from editors-in-chief were correlated with citation patterns. In an international comparison of editors in the field of analytical chemistry, Braun and Bujdoso found a correlation between the number of gatekeepers (editorial board members) in a country and their citation rate and their publication productivity as well as a correlation between the number of gatekeepers and the number of publications from a country (Braun & Bujdoso, 1983).

In a large international study of membership of editorial boards for 1,168 medical journals, Bakker and Rigter were interested in determining if international appointments originated from countries with large research programs (Bakker & Rigter, 1985). Particularly, the authors wanted to learn the strengths and weaknesses of the Dutch medical research output. Thirty-four percent of all Dutch editorial boards came from the U.S. and 32 percent of all editors-in-chief came from the U.S. Americans dominated the boards of the top 25 percent of all journals. The top journals were those with the highest impact factor. Dutch scientists mentioned as prominent by their foreign counterparts were more likely to hold editorships. Bakker and Rigter concluded that editors of influential medical journals were productive and eminent scientists.

Zsindely and Schubert examined citation patterns of editors of 769 medical journals identified by using subject fields from *Science Citation Index* (Zsindely & Schubert, 1989). They formed two indexes: an index of editor expertise (the ratio of the editor's mean citation rate per cited paper to that of the editor's own journal) and an index of editor authority (the ratio of the editor's percentage of in-journal citations to that of the editor's journal). According to these indexes, editors did not have a higher-than-average citation rate. Editors were considered authorities but not experts in their fields.

A few additional studies examined the professional ranking and activities of editorial boards. In a nonscientific discipline—education—Silverman determined that 65 percent of editors had not published in the past three years (Silverman, 1976). Forty-six percent of the editors of scholarly journals, 19 percent of editors of professional journals, and 13 percent of editors of association journals had previous experience with board membership of the journals they edited. Reideberg wanted to know the likelihood that editorial board members served on more than one board. A survey of 78 board members and associate editors of the journal *Clinical Pharmacology & Therapeutics* found that these board members served on editorial boards of 97 journals (Reideberg & Reidenberg, 1991). The survey also revealed that in the two years prior to the survey two-thirds of board members had published in *Clinical Pharmacology & Therapeutics*. In a study of editorial board members of statistics journals, Gibbons determined the institutional affiliations of 267 board members of 14 U. S. statistics journals (Gibbons, 1990). No one person served on more than three editorial boards. Board members came from 82 different institutions, representing 71 percent of all institutions with an undergraduate major or concentration in statistics in the United States. Gibbons concluded that there is "no select group of individuals, institutions, or geographical areas in the U.S. that dominates decisions about manuscripts submitted to these 14 journals" (p. 211).

Using a number of different measures, these studies determined editors' and editorial board members' relative importance in a field. Studies in economics found that editors graduated from the schools with the best economics programs and, while serving as editors, were affiliated with these same schools. Studies in science found editors graduated from prestigious universities, but had inconsistent findings when citation patterns of editors and board members were compared to other scientists. Some studies found a positive correlation and others did not. Studies in nursing concluded editors had earned higher degrees and had more publication experience than the average practitioner. Studies in sociology and psychology looked at publication patterns and other measures of productivity and the researchers became embroiled in a discussion about differences among specialties within these disciplines. One study in medicine found editors to be productive and eminent scientists, another one found medical editors to be less cited than other authors. In education, editors were more likely to be connected with a journal prior to an editorial appointment. In pharmacy, it was determined that editorial board members served on a number of different boards simultaneously. In statistics, those on editorial boards proved to represent a large proportion of institutions in the United States. Studies of editors from the 1940s through 1970s indicate that most came from prominent institutions. Some more recent studies indicate that institutional influences might not be as strong today. Internationally the most scientifically productive countries produce the most editors.

Each of these studies identified a group of editors or editorial boards and examined ways they are distinguished in their respective fields. These studies indicate that by a number of measures, editors and editorial board members, while maybe not "stars" in their fields, have certainly obtained some level of professional recognition. The studies do seem to confirm the extra scientific influence on the choice of editors and editorial boards referred to by Yoels (Yoels, 1974).

## Editors' publication criteria

Once appointed, editors establish their own publication criteria. After manuscripts have been reviewed and comments returned by the reviewers, editors have the option of either agreeing or disagreeing with the reviewers and deciding to accept the manuscript, to ask for revisions, or to reject it. What criteria or standards have they established for manuscript evaluation?

Noble asked a group of editors of higher education journals which type of manuscripts held an "appeal" for them (Noble, 1989). The top five characteristics of manuscripts that had an immediate appeal to the editors were its professional appearance, its new or novel treatment of a subject, its thoroughness, the author's writing style and clarity, and the author's ability to follow journal guidelines.

Chase asked professors from 16 departments in the natural and social sciences from big 10 universities, which criteria they used to evaluate scientific writing (Chase, 1970). In a set of 10 criteria developed by Chase, scientists were asked to rate each criterion as essential, important, or somewhat important for scientific writing in their field. She was interested in knowing if there were normative criteria for publication and if different disciplines used different criteria. She did identify disciplinary differences: "the harder and natural sciences stress precise mathematical and technical criteria, whereas the softer social sciences emphasize less-defined logico-theoretical standards" (p. 264-5).

Can one assume that these normative publication criteria, with certain disciplinary differences, are the criteria editors use to reach a decision about a manuscript? Or, does the manuscript that carries some "appeal"—factors unrelated for the most part to the scientific merits of a work—also enter into an editorial decision?

*Question*

What publication criteria do editors use when deciding to accept or reject a manuscript? Do normative publication criteria exist?

*Criteria for inclusion*

~ any study that asks a group of editors about their criteria for making publication decisions.

*Comparable studies*

Eleven studies examined publication criteria from an editor's perspective (Table 3-2). The ranking of Chase's criteria by scientists have been added to this table for comparison. Other than Chase's study each of these studies surveyed a group of editors or members of editorial boards about the criteria they apply to acceptance decisions. All studies presented editors or editorial board members with a list of publication criteria and asked editors to rank them. Because some descriptions of publication criteria were very detailed, some criteria in Table 3-2 have more than one ranked number. For example, Silverman and Collins included three characteristics that fit under the general term "topic selection": timeliness of topic, professional controversial topic, and position paper (Silverman & Collins, 1975). Each of these has been given the number of their ranked order under topic selection in Table 3-2.

In the field of personnel, Frantz surveyed 79 members of the editorial boards of six journals (Frantz, 1968). He found clear agreement among respondents for the top criterion: the study must contribute to the knowledge base of the discipline. Wolff queried 132 editors from journals in the field of clinical psychology and asked them to rank in order of importance from a set of 15 publication criteria (Wolff, 1970). The top three criteria were contribution to knowledge, research design, and objectivity in reporting.

Smigel and Ross tracked the reasons that manuscripts were or were not accepted by the journal *Social Problems* (Smigel & Ross, 1970). The reasons for accepting 258 manuscripts are identified in Table 3-2. Lindsey asked 323 journal editors from sociology, psychology, and social work to rate the value of 12 criteria developed by Chase and Smigel and Ross (Lindsey & Lindsey, 1978), (Chase, 1970, August), (Smigel & Ross, 1970).

Silverman and Collins studied the publication process of authors and editors associated with education associations and education journals (Silverman & Collins, 1975). They asked respondents about the rationale for using publication criteria for selecting a journal for manuscript submission, authors' relationship with journals, journal standards, and criteria for manuscript acceptance. An additional study by Silverman, using criteria similar to Chase's and adapted for the field of education, surveyed 248 journal editors who represented research, professional, scholarly and association journals in education (Silverman, 1978). Silverman divided the criteria into content criteria and process criteria. Lacy and Busch asked 103 editors of agricultural journals to rate 13 publication criteria (Lacy & Busch, 1982). In this study, scientists were also asked to rate the same criteria, and their responses have also been included in Table 3-2. There are some minor differences, but Lacy and Busch found relative agreement between editors and scientists.

| Criteria \ Discipline | natural and social sciences[a] | personnel guidance[b] | psychology[c] | sociology[d] | education[e] | management sociology[f] | physics[g] | chemistry[g] | sociology[g] | political sci[g] | sociology social work psychology[h] | education[i] | agriculture[j] | agriculture[k] | radiology[l] |
|---|---|---|---|---|---|---|---|---|---|---|---|---|---|---|---|
| Logical rigor | 1 | | | | | | 4 | 2 | 1 | 1 | | | | | |
| Contribution to knowledge | | 1 | 1 | 9 | 6 | 6,9 | 1 | 5 | 2 | 5 | 1 | 4,7 | 1 | 1 | |
| Research design, methodology | 9 | 2 | 2 | 5,8-11 | 7,8 | | | | | | 2,7 | 16 | 3 | 6 | 5 |
| Objectivity | | 3 | 3 | | | | | | | | | 14,17,18, 20,23 | 8 | 9 | |
| Topic selection | | 4 | 7 | 1,6 | 2,9,10 | 4,5,7,8 | 2 | 7 | 5 | 6 | 8 | 3,5,6,10,15,19 | 2 | 2 | |
| Writing style, organization | 3 | 5 | 5 | 3,6 | | | 3 | 6 | 4 | 3 | | | | | 4 |
| Creativity | | | | | | | | | | | 5 | | 6 | 3 | 2 |
| Practical implications | 10 | 6 | 11 | 4 | 4 | | | | | | 10 | 2,12 | 11 | 8 | 3 |
| Original evidence, findings | 4 | | | | 3 | | 9 | 9 | 9 | 9 | 6 | | 4 | 4 | |
| Mathematical precision, rigor | 5 | | | | | | 5 | 3 | 7 | 2 | | | | | |
| Statistical analysis | | 7 | 4 | | | 1,2,3 | | | | | | | | | |
| Theoretical model, significance | 8 | 8 | 6 | 2 | | | 8 | 8 | 3 | 4 | 3 | 22 | 7 | 7 | |
| Good taste | | | | | | | | | | | 8 | | | | |
| Literature review, scholarship | 6 | 9 | 8 | | | | 6 | 4 | 8 | 8 | 4 | | 5 | 5 | 1 |
| Suggestions for future research | | | 9 | | | | | | | | | | | | |
| Ethically acceptable | 7 | | | | | | | | | | 9 | | 9 | 10 | |
| Value of article to readership | | | | | 1 | | | | | | | 1,21 | 10 | 11 | |
| Depth, breadth, long-term value | | | | | 5 | | | | | | | 9,11,13 | | | |
| Clarity of tables | | 10 | 10 | | | | | | | | | | | | |
| Manuscript length | | 11 | 12 | | | | | | | | | | | | |
| Entertainment quality | | | | | | | | | | | 11 | | 13 | 13 | |
| Punctuation, journal's style | | 12 | 14 | | | | | | | | | | | | |
| Replicability | 2 | | | | | | 7 | 1 | 6 | 7 | | | | | |
| Author's status and reputation | | 13 | 13 | | | 10 | | | | | | 12 | 12 | 12 | |
| Institutional affiliation | | 14 | 15 | | | | | | | | | | | | |
| Review article | | | | | | | | | | | | | | | 6 |
| **Total number of criteria** | 10 | 14 | 15 | 11 | 19 | 37 | 9 | 9 | 9 | 9 | 12 | 23 | 13 | 13 | 6 |

a. Scientists studied (Chase, 1970)
b. Editorial boards studied (Frantz, 1968)
c. Editors and advisors studied (Wolff, 1970)
d. Editors studied (Smigel & Ross, 1970)
e. Editors studied (Silverman & Collins, 1975)

f. Editors and advisors studied (Kerr, Tolliver, & Petree, 1977)
g. Editors studied (Beyer, 1978)
h. Editorial boards studied (Lindsey & Lindsey, 1978)

i. Editors studied (Silverman, 1978)
j. Editors studied (Lacy & Busch, 1982,)
k. Scientists studied (Lacy & Busch, 1982)
l. Editorial boards studied (Siegelman, 1989)

**Table 3-2: Ranking of publication criteria**

Kerr and colleagues queried editors and advisory boards of 19 leading management and social sciences journals. They asked respondents to rate 37 characteristics and decide if each would count toward, against, or not influence the decision to accept a particular manuscript (Kerr et al., 1977). The top 10 characteristics that would lead to an acceptance have been included in Table 3-2. They did find that an author's reputation, the successful tests of a new theory, and a new or innovative idea were characteristics that would increase the likelihood of a manuscript's acceptance. Characteristics of manuscripts that respondents thought should be rejected included: studies that had statistically insignificant results, were replications, were outside the mainstream, or had been published as proceedings.

Beyer asked editors of the leading journals in four disciplines—physics, chemistry, social science, and political science—about publication criteria (Beyer, 1978). Table 3-2 lists responses for each of the four disciplines. For most responses there was fairly general agreement among disciplines. One exception was for chemistry; a high value was placed on replication studies, which was ranked much lower for the other disciplines. It is interesting to note that replication studies were ranked second by the scientists Chase studied. In the field of radiology, Siegelman received responses from 219 board members who rated desirable qualities of manuscripts (Siegelman, 1989). Radiologists' most desirable qualities were good documentation, innovation, and practicality.

Gottfredson conducted a study that has not been included in Table 3-2 in which he asked editors and editorial board members from nine psychology journals to react to 83 statements describing manuscript characteristics (Gottfredson, 1978). He did find substantial agreement on the desirability of specific characteristics but did not rank them. Gottfredson thought his results showed that "prescriptive norms for scientific evaluation exist and transcend subdisciplinary bounds" (p. 924). Examples of manuscript characteristics that he used include that the manuscript attempts to unify the field, it deals with an important topic, it has excellent generalizability, it is exciting to read, and other characteristics related to clarity of writing style, logical thought, and interest.

Each of Chase's 10 criteria is identified as an important characteristic in at least one of these studies. Differences in types of research or scholarly publication of particular disciplines are probably the reasons for the differences between some of the findings. A number of criteria identified have little scientific meaning, particularly the criteria of "good taste" and "entertainment quality." Some criteria may overlap to some extent: "mathematical precision or rigor" could be very similar to "statistical analysis." In all but two studies there was agreement that one of the top criteria for publication was that a manuscript must make a contribution to knowledge. In every case that editors were asked about the importance of authors' status or institutional affiliation, these were ranked among the least important reasons for accepting a manuscript.

McCartney reviewed data from some of the studies of publication criteria and wondered how close these criteria were to the real ways in which manuscripts were accepted or rejected (McCartney, 1979). McCartney suggested they were "unreliable as accounts of how board members evaluate manuscripts" (p. 814).

Some insight about the applicability of these criteria can be gained from a comparison of Table 3-2 (rank of publication criteria) with Table 2-2 (reasons for rejection). The two sets of studies have similar findings. For example, one of the primary reasons for rejecting manuscripts was its inadequate theory or concept; this was one of the top five reasons given for rejection in each study. One of the major criteria for acceptance was that the manuscript should contribute to knowledge; this was ranked among the top six criteria in nine of the 10 studies. The two sets of studies then have similar findings, as a manuscript with inadequate theory or concept would not contribute to knowledge. All of the studies in Table 2-2 identified poor writing as one of the top six reasons for rejecting a manuscript; in studies on criteria for acceptance, writing style was considered an important criterion in each study in which that question was asked. Similarly, methodological problems were a common reason for rejection, and correspondingly research design or theoretical model was highly ranked as a publication criterion in all but one study. While pairing corresponding acceptance criteria with rejection criteria may be intuitive, the exercise points to an agreement between the theoretical reasons or normative publication criteria for acceptance and a lack of this attribute as a reason for rejection.

## Bias of editors

Once an editor has been selected and has developed a theoretical or practical framework for the editorial peer review process, the editor must face his or her own set of personal biases that are brought to the situation and cannot help be a factor in the decision making process.

The editor of the *Archives of Surgery* listed a number of factors that would prejudice him against a manuscript (Warren, 1978). These included such obvious issues as a disregard for the instructions to authors, a manuscript still in a "draft" form, or the improper use of English. Warren added a number of surgical topics that he admitted he has a hard time "stifling prejudice" against (which are not listed here as they are very technical, for example, a prejudice against "arterial steals"). However, writing many years later and in a different discipline, Riggio deplored the prospect of an editor's rejecting a manuscript simply because of a disagreement with the author's orientation or conclusions (Riggio, 1990).

Neuliep and Crandall asked editors of social and behavioral sciences journals about their view of replication studies. Ninety-four percent of the respondents said that replication studies were not "examples of research encouraged for submission in the editorial policy of their journals" (p. 87) (Neuliep & Crandall, 1990). Some other types of editorial bias include arguments for or against certain topics, for or against the orthodox or unconventional, for or against certain individuals or institutions, or against negative studies (p. 1391) (Sharp, 1990).

Feinstein articulated a number of factors that identify editorial bias (Feinstein, 1991).

> *An editorial policy is biased if it depends on doctrinaire, ideologic, or political beliefs about science, rather than the scientific quality of the research itself. For example, a bias is obviously present (or created) if editors refuse to publish "negative reports," or results of therapeutic comparisons done without randomization, or research that raises skeptical questions about well-established, "sacred cow" beliefs. The editorial process is also biased if approval is affected not by a work's contents, but by its source: the authors, institution, or auspices responsible for the research* (p. 339).

Gove saw several forces at work and offered some insights and guidance for editors to help counter bias (Gove, 1979):

- The review process is a political process.

- There is a significant amount of arbitrariness in the publication process.

- Once accepted, a manuscript should be published.

- Special consideration should be given to theoretically controversial papers or replication studies.

- Manuscripts should not be restricted to a limited format.

To investigate a related issue, Von Glinow and Novelli administered a questionnaire to 315 individuals in the field of organizational behavior (Von Glinow & Novelli, 1982). Respondents were asked whether a list of 54 items presented ethical dilemmas. Some of their questions touched more on bias-related issues rather than ethical issues. For example, 75 percent of respondents agreed that it was improper "for a reviewer to take an editor or chairperson's particular biases into account" (p. 425) while reviewing a manuscript. Respondents questioned editors' ability to reject a manuscript without further review, their ability to override the recommendation of all reviewers, or their tendency not to forward all reviewers' comments. Each of these examples illustrates that the line between ethics and bias is not always clear. In these examples there could be reasonable explanations for the editors' actions that have nothing to do with ethical behavior. In fact, an editor could easily decide to use reviewers only for potentially publishable manuscripts by immediately rejecting a poorly written, relatively uninteresting manuscript on a subject of marginal interest to the journal's readership. An editor could override all reviewers' recommendations to accept a particular manuscript if the editor uncovered a major flaw within it that had not been identified by reviewers. Or, the editor may be protecting the author by not forwarding an overly harsh or inappropriate review.

Vaisrub maintained that editors should use their judgment on the types of manuscripts they send for peer review. He asserted that "the nature of the cargo rather than the pier at which it docks should determine a manuscript's course for a peer or a peerless review" (Vaisrub, 1978) (p. 197).

A few studies have tried to analyze the degree or impact of any bias on the part of the editor and determine if these biases are in anyway measurable.

*Question*

Have studies identified any measurable biases of editors that affect editorial decisions?

*Criteria for inclusion*

~ any study of the editorial decision-making process that examines the role of editorial biases in the decision-making process.

*Comparable studies*

One potential source of editorial bias is the presence of a relationship between the editor and the author. In fact all the studies that have addressed this question have looked for an editor-author relationship. Ten studies have approached the question of trying to identify a measurable editorial bias by investigating any editor-author relationship. There is the generally held belief that regardless of editors' publication criteria, they are likely to accept manuscripts from colleagues or former graduate students.

Schaeffer was the earliest researcher to examine any potential editorial bias (Schaeffer, 1970). He undertook an investigation after a complaint from psychologists who claimed that: "APA [American Psychological Association] journals practice a form of professional discrimination such that one must be a member of the 'in group' (i.e., an editor, his friend, student, or ex-student) in order to have one's papers—regardless of quality—published in these journals" (p. 362). Schaeffer paired a group of APA journals with non-APA journals. Each article for the study period of 1967 was placed in one of three categories: (1) at least one author was a journal editor, (2) at least one author was affiliated with the same institution of the editor, or (3) none of the authors was an editor or affiliated with the same institution as an editor of the journal. Schaeffer did not uncover evidence of bias attributable to any authors' or editors' institutional connections. Both APA and non-APA journals "devote less than one-tenth of their articles to their editors' contributions, up to one-third to contributions from their immediate colleagues, and the remainder (one-half to nine-tenths) to sources outside their immediate affiliation" (p. 364).

Rodman and Mancini cautioned editors about using "inside track submissions" (p. 371). Their study of 31 journals of higher education found that 89 percent of 28 responding editors had published articles written by departmental colleagues, 85 percent by associate or advisory editors, 56 percent by an official of a sponsoring organization, and 34 percent had published their own article (Rodman & Mancini, 1977). They thought their study raised questions about professional conflict of interest.

Laband compared differences in article length with author-editor connections in economics (Laband, 1985). Laband concluded that there is "unmistakable and highly significant evidence that the average length of articles published by authors from the same school as the editor exceeds that of articles published by unaffiliated authors" (p. 510).

A group of 37 well-known astrophysicists published 242 articles in the *Astrophysical Journal* over a 10-year period (Abt, 1987). To determine if these articles had been treated any differently from those of less-known astrophysicists these 242 articles were compared to another set of 242 articles written by less well-known astrophysicists. Abt compared the editorial peer review process of both sets of manuscripts and concluded that there was no evidence of preferential treatment given to papers by well-known astrophysicists. However, their papers were accepted at a higher rate than those of less well-known authors, indicating that in Abt's view, papers of well-known authors are justifiably accepted at a higher rate.

Willis and McNamee examined the impact of editor-author networks within sociology journals (Willis & McNamee, 1990). They suggested that the "fluctuations in academic labor markets have weakened this network, resulting in a reduction in the strength of the institutional connections in journal publications" (p. 363) and as a result a weakening of the structure of invisible colleges.

Laband and Piette examined a set of 1,051 articles published in 28 economics journals in 1984 and identified any personal ties between the authors and editors (Laband & Piette, 1994). About 25 percent of the articles had some author-editor connection. A comparison of citation patterns revealed that citations to those articles with "an author/editor connection were more than twice as great as citations of articles without such connections" (p. 200). Laband and Piette concluded that "this implies that a practice interpreted as 'favoritism' by many scholars in fact serves to enhance efficiency in the market for scientific knowledge" (p. 194). An additional study by Smith and Laband investigated potential editorial bias by examining citation patterns from a group of accounting research journals (Smith & Laband, 1995). Their study of 292 papers published in 15 top accounting journals found strong evidence that editors were able to use their professional connections to "capture" high-impact manuscripts and publish them (p. 21).

Campanario looked for any journal-related author influences in 18 educational psychology journals (Campanario, 1996). He uncovered a wide range of journal-related authors, from 1.28 percent to 33.33 percent, depending on the particular journal. He found "a positive relationship between the use of journals by journal-related authors and impact factor of the journal" (p. 184). Similar to Laband, Campanario found that for three journals, articles with editor-author or referee-author influences were significantly longer than other articles in the journals.

Using a different approach, Houlihan and colleagues surveyed editors and associate editors of 13 primary APA journals to determine the frequency with which editors and editorial board members publish in their own journals (Houlihan, Hofschulte, Sachau, & Patten, 1992). Since the authors asked only about articles, there is an assumption that editorials were excluded from this inquiry. Over 60 percent of the editors and associate editors had published at least one article in their own journals while serving in the editorial posts. Furthermore, 41 percent of the editors and 20 percent of the associate editors thought their position aided them in the publication process. In a similar study, Weller found that between 4.8 percent and 6.2 percent of randomly selected authors in medicine served on the editorial boards of the publishing journal (Weller, 1996). Approximately 30 percent of authors queried served on at least one editorial board of a different journal.

Rodman provides data on editor-author connections, but does not provide corresponding data to determine if editors come from the most productive departments or institutions. Editors and board members do continue to publish in their own journals after editorial appointments, but they publish in other journals as well. One of the more curious findings of two studies was the correlation between the length of the article and an editor-author connection (Laband & Piette, 1994) (Campanario, 1996).

These 10 investigators tested the claim that editors practice a form of professional favoritism. While a degree of author-editor connections is present, these very papers are eventually cited more frequently than other articles from the same journal and, therefore, indicate that the author-editor relationship has a positive impact on the scholarly communication process. These few studies provide little evidence of strong editorial bias from editor-author relationships. Citation data indicate that even if there is some degree of an editor-author relationship, editors are able to capture manuscripts likely to be cited. These studies are limited in that they examine editor behavior independent of any interaction with reviewers or the reviewer process. The area of editorial bias and editor-author connections is an area that has received relatively little attention and is ripe for more research.

## Editorial peer review process

A publication committee of the American Physical Society reviewed the editorial peer review process of physics journals and tried to assess the attitude of the physics community to the review process (Dehmer, 1982). The committee then met with editors of *Physical Review* and *Physical Review Letters* to inquire about standard procedures for handling manuscripts, choosing reviewers, time spent on a manuscript, number of times reviewers were used, form letters, etc. The committee also wanted to know about prospects for double-blind reviewing and any appeals process used by the editors. The committee decided that there was no "typical" manuscript and the process of acquiring the kind of information they were seeking required much more time than they had originally envisioned.

*Question*

Is there a standard editorial peer review process?

*Criteria for inclusion*

~ any study that examines a defined group of editors to document the editorial peer review process they have established.

*Comparable studies*

Twenty-seven studies investigated the editorial peer review process of a defined group of editors who were asked about some aspect or aspects of their editorial peer review process (Table 3-3). When editors were queried about rejection rates, these data have been included in Table 2-1 and are not repeated here. Similarly, data on anonymity and blind review are supplied in Chapter Seven. The response rate for these 27 surveys ranged from 47 percent to 100 percent with an average response rate of 78 percent. The relatively high response rate for this survey research might indicate a desire on the part of the editors to share information about their processes, to assist in the understanding of editorial peer review, or to learn more about the process themselves. Three of the 27 studies did not provide response rate information (Coe & Weinstock, 1968; Glen & Konigsson, 1976; Christiansen, 1981).

The studies in Table 3-3 covered a range of editorial activity and often had a purpose different from documenting the editorial peer review process. For example, several of the studies in nursing were directed at nurses, informing them about the publication process and offering pointers to help with the publication process. Topics covered in the surveys are listed in Table 3-3.

Table 3-3 includes information on the percentage of journals that were peer reviewed and the degree to which a journal solicited manuscripts, when provided by the study. If available, the method used to identify journals within any one group is included in the table. For many of the studies, limited information is provided about study design, making replication or generalizability difficult.

Two studies of the review process are not included in Table 3-3 (Gordon, 1978) (Juhasz, Calvert, Jackson, Kronick, & Shipman, 1975). Gordon asked a convenience sample of editors about their peer review process (Gordon, 1978). Editors from a variety of research fields with London addresses were interviewed. While the author offered insights into the reviewing process, the study included journals from a number of disciplines but with no differentiation among disciplines, and it is not included in Table 3-3. Similarly, Juhasz and colleagues surveyed a convenience sample of journal editors, yet made no distinction in responses by discipline (Juhasz et al., 1975).

| Discipline | Journal selection criteria | Respondents # | Respondents % | Percentage of journals peer reviewed | Journals that solicit manuscripts | Topics and policies covered in surveys* | References |
|---|---|---|---|---|---|---|---|
| Dentistry | circulation, 1,000+ | 69 | 97% | 52% | majority; range: 0%-80.6% | advice to authors | (Federico, Lee, Boozer, & Diaz, 1984) |
| Earth sciences | all European editors in field | 156 | not given | 68% review all manuscripts | | reviewer selection process, reviewing procedures; information for editors provided | (Glen & K., 1976) |
| Economics | major, indexed | 39 | 54% | more than 50% of all manuscripts reviewed | | editorial policies, evaluation of manuscripts, reasons for rejection, advice to authors | (Coe & Weinstock, 1967) |
| | major | 37 | not given | 100% implied | | publication policies, advice to authors | (Coe & Weinstock, 1968) |
| Education | central to field | 14 | 78% | | | advice to authors | (Silverman & Collins, 1975) |
| Engineering | IEEE journals | 26 | not given | 100% implied | | variation in review process by different journals; editors satisfied with process | (Christiansen, 1974) (Christiansen, 1981) |
| Library science | selected, indexed | 33 | 100% | | 32% of all articles solicited | publication policies, critique of rejected manuscripts | (O'Connor & Van Orden, 1978) |
| | selected | 48 | 90% | 42% | yes | reviewer selection process, process for unsolicited manuscripts | (Budd, 1988) |
| | selected, indexed | 68 | 80% | 50% | 44% of all journals | journal quality; review process | (Via, 1996) |
| | recognized, indexed | 34 | 67% | 62% | | | (Haas, Milton, & Quinn, 1996) |
| Medicine | core | 75 | 54% | | | policies for ethical review | (Brackbill & Hellegers, 1980) |
| | 5 selection criteria | 16 | 100% | 100% | 94% of all journals | review process, statistical review, reviewer agreement, editorial policies | (Weller, 1990) |
| | random from index | 86 | 70% | 100% | 75% of all journals | review process, statistical review, reviewer agreement, editorial policies | (Weller, 1990) |
| | indexed, high priority | 221 | 82% | 98% | | policies, practices, and attitudes of editors | (Wilkes & Kravitz, 1995) |
| (economics) | major | 12 | 80% | 100% implied | | policies for ethical review, reviewer training | (Schulman, Sulmasy, & Roney, 1994) |
| | indexed, subject | 214 | 73% | 56%-65% of articles reviewed | | editorial policies on degree of peer review | (Colaianni, 1994) |
| (economics) | indexed & selected | 70 | 47% | | | policies for review of economic manuscripts | (Jefferson & Demicheli, 1995) |
| Nursing | indexed | 65 | 77% | | discussed | review process, advice to authors, reasons for rejection | (McCloskey, 1977) |
| | indexed & library holdings | 64 | 73% | 81% | 90% of all journals | review process | (McElmurry, Newcomb, Barnfather, & Lynch, 1981) |
| | indexed | 100 | 89% | | 73% of all journals | review process | (McCloskey & Swanson, 1982) |
| | indexed | 100 | 89% | 75% | | review process, review board, definition of peer review | (Swanson & McCloskey, 1982) |

**Table 3-3: Editorial peer review process: Surveys of editors by discipline**

| Discipline | Journal selection criteria | Respondents # | Respondents % | Percentage of journals peer reviewed | Journals that solicit manuscripts | Topics and policies covered in surveys* | References |
|---|---|---|---|---|---|---|---|
| Nursing | indexed | 139 | 79% | 87% | discussed | review process, reasons for rejection, guidelines for authors | (Swanson & McCloskey, 1986) |
| | indexed | 92 | 87% | 94% | discussed | reasons for rejection, advice to authors | (Swanson, McCloskey, & Bodensteiner, 1991) |
| | U. S. | 80 | 66% | | 54% of all journals | policies and standard procedures | (Fondiller, 1994) |
| Psychology | association | 31 | 97% | | | editorial policies | (Hartley, 1988) |
| Social science | published guide | 32 | 75% | | | review process | (Whitley, 1970) |
| Multi-discipline | top 10 in each discipline | | | | | editorial policies and practices | (Beyer, 1978) |
| | randomly selected from directory | 251 | 79% | | | recommendations for review procedures | (Miller & Serzan, 1984) |
| Average | | | 78% | | | | |

**Table 3-3: Editorial peer review process: Surveys of editors by discipline (continued)**

The following studies had well-defined journal sets:

- A study of the social sciences used journals listed in a published guide (Whitley, 1970).

- A study of electrical engineering used all *Transactions* of the Institute of Electrical and Electronics Engineers (Christiansen, 1981).

- A study of earth sciences surveyed all European editors in the field (Glen, J.W. & Konigsson, K.L., 1976).

- A study of medicine used all journals on a list of recommended journals for a small medical library (Brackbill & Hellegers, 1980).

- A study of dentistry used journals with a circulation of over 1,000 (Federico et al., 1984).

- A study of all psychology journals published by the British Psychology Association and the American Psychology Association (Hartley, 1988).

- A study of medicine used a combination of circulation, citations, ranking on lists, and randomly selected journals (Weller, 1990).

- A study of medicine used all U.S. journals with a high indexing priority from the National Library of Medicine (Wilkes & Kravitz, 1995).

Several studies identified journals covered in an indexing service but did not use all the journals in the index:

- Two studies of nursing journals included all nursing journals indexed in the *Cumulative Index to Nursing and Literature* except newsletter, bulletins, and journals published by state nurses associations (McCloskey, 1977), (Swanson & McCloskey, 1982), and (Swanson & McCloskey, 1986).

- Another study of nursing journals included those indexed journals for which at least 50 percent of the readership were nurses (Swanson et al., 1991).

- A study of library science titles by Via (Via, 1996) built on two previous lists (O'Connor & Van Orden, 1978) (Budd, 1988). O'Connor's original list was comprised of selected titles from "national library journals" (p. 389).

The studies cited above provide enough details of the journal selection criteria for replication; the remaining studies used somewhat ambiguous criteria and would be less easy to replicate. Authors explained their selection criteria with such terms as top, major, central, high priority, or indexed. (There is the commonly held notion that those researchers and scholars working in a particular discipline know which journals are the best.)

Several of the surveys did not ask the editors if their journal was peer reviewed; however, it was often clear from the questions asked that the investigators assumed journals were peer reviewed. Table 3-3 only includes the statement "implied" peer review if there is a strong indication within the article that a journal was peer reviewed. For example, if the study included a table in which editors provided the number of reviewers per manuscript, it can be logically concluded that the journal was peer reviewed.

Surveys often included questions about processing and publication issues, such as journal circulation, publication frequency, publication time lag (both to review and to publish after completion of review), length of articles, number of articles published, payment of referees, and language of publication. (Rejection rates, reviewer selection, anonymity and blind review, and the number of reviewers per manuscript are discussed elsewhere in this monograph.) There are some issues of interest that were seldom addressed in these surveys: level of review of solicited manuscripts and the type of material in a journal that does not undergo the peer review process.

Differences in study design make generalizations difficult:

- Some studies had a narrow focus. For example, one study examined the use of economic reviewers in medical journals (Schulman et al., 1994); another looked for any policies on ethical reviewing in medical journals (Brackbill & Hellegers, 1980).

- Several studies named each journal in a table and included information about that journal but did not summarize or average the information provided in the tables (Coe & Weinstock, 1967), (McCloskey, 1977), (Swanson & McCloskey, 1982), (Federico et al., 1984), (Hartley, 1988), (Budd, 1988), (Haas et al., 1996), and (Via, 1996).

- Some studies discussed summary information without providing the actual data; for example, "the majority of the editors were satisfied with the

review process" (p. 21) (Christiansen, 1974), or "editors who do have
a regular referee panel usually also have specific reasons for rejection"
(p. 173) (Whitley, 1970).

Even in the studies of editorial peer review it is often unclear which journals
included in the study were peer reviewed. Figure 1-1 illustrates steps in the editorial peer review process. This fundamental process was probably assumed to
be in place when the surveys were designed. Different studies asked different
questions regarding journal policies. However, not all journals were peer
reviewed. When investigators asked about journal content, it was also clear that
not all material in a peer reviewed journal underwent peer review. As can be
seen from several studies of nursing journals, not all journals in a discipline are
peer reviewed. In fact, even after asking editors if their journals were peer
reviewed, McElmurry decided that she would not state "unequivocally" (p.
140) which journals were peer reviewed (McElmurry et al., 1981). Colaianni,
in a study of *Index Medicus* titles, determined that for four clinical subjects
between 56 percent and 65 percent of all published articles were actually subjected to peer review (Colaianni, 1994).

Solicited manuscripts may not be peer reviewed at the same level as unsolicited manuscripts. When data are available, between 44 percent and 94 percent
of journals solicited manuscripts; however, these percentages were available for
only one-third of the studies. A few studies asked if manuscripts were solicited
but did not probe for additional information on how solicited manuscripts are
handled. One study of dentistry found that journals contained anywhere from
zero percent to 80.6 percent solicited manuscripts (Federico et al., 1984). A
study of medicine inquired about the review process for solicited manuscripts
and, depending on the group of journals, found between 40 percent and 73.8 percent of the editors usually or always used the same review process for solicited
and unsolicited manuscripts (Weller, 1990). It is clear that solicited manuscripts
may comprise a significant portion of content for many journals. More study is
needed to determine the editorial peer review process for solicited manuscripts.

Recommendations, when made by investigators, were usually not made as a
result of data analysis. These studies, while describing how editors in different disciplines have implemented the editorial peer review process, have not identified an
established or generally accepted code of practice or set of guidelines that editors
can use in making operational decisions, nor have these studies attempted to
demonstrate or prove that one method of practice works better than the others.
What the publications committee of the American Physical Society discovered
proved to be correct: it is hard to document the review process and even more difficult to use that information to recommend or establish standards (Dehmer, 1982).

## Editorial guidelines

The most common place for information about a journal's procedures and
guidelines is in the instructions to authors. A few studies have examined the

| Guidelines / Discipline | psychology[1] | science[2] | science[3] | sociology[4] | medicine[5] | business[6] | multi-discipline[7] | science[8] | psychology[9] | business[10] | psychology[11] |
|---|---|---|---|---|---|---|---|---|---|---|---|
| Editors have every manuscript reviewed. | | x | | | | | | | | | |
| Editors reject inappropriate manuscripts. | | | | x | | | | | | | |
| Two or more editors conduct initial screening. | | | | | | | x | | | | |
| Reviewers appointed by the editor. | | x | | | | | | | | | |
| Reviewers appointed by editor and one more. | | | | | | | x | | | | |
| Reviewers should be experts/non-biased. | x | | | | | | | | | | |
| Reviewers should not be board members. | | | | | | | x | | | | |
| Review done by two or more. | x | | x | x | | | x | | | | |
| Editors blind referee to author. | x | x | | | | x | x | | x | x | |
| Editors blind author to referee. | | | | | | | | | | x | |
| Editors use open review. | | | | | | x | | | | | |
| Editors disclose reviewers' names in the end. | x | | | | | | | | | x | |
| Editors publish guidelines regularly. | | | x | | | | x | | | | |
| Editors publish style requirements regularly. | | | x | | | | x | | | | x |
| Editors send reviewers' reports to authors. | | | | | | | x | | x | | |
| Editors filter out bad reports. | | | | | x | | | | | | |
| Editors evaluate reviewers' reports. | x | | | | | | | | | x | |
| Authors evaluate reviewers' reports. | | | | | | | | | | | x |
| Reviewers maintain confidentiality. | | | x | x | | | | | | | |
| Reviewers sign reports. | | | | | | | | | x | | |
| If reviewers sign reports, editor should forward to authors. | | | | | | | x | | | | |
| Reviewers make a publication recommendation. | | x | | | | | | | | | |
| Rejection needs agreement of more than one editor. | | x | | | | | | | | | |
| Editors read each rejected manuscript. | | | | | x | | | | | | |
| Reviewer disagreement needs more review. | | x | x | | | | | | | | |
| Time limit for referees to review. | x | | x | | | | | x | | | |
| Time limit for editorial decisions. | | x | | | | | | x | | | |
| Time limit on all appointments. | x | | | | | | | | | x | |
| Editors handle limited number of manuscripts. | | | | | | | | x | | | |
| Reviewers receive standard guidelines. | | | x | | | x | | x | x | x | x |
| Reviewers should understand material. | x | | | | | | | | | | |
| Reviewers' critiques should be helpful. | x | | | | | | | | | | |
| Reviewers' critiques should be written. | | | | | x | | | | | | |
| Editors send reviewers' reports to all reviewers. | | | | | | | | | x | | |
| Editors inform reviewers of outcome. | | | x | | | | | | | | |
| Editors establish appeals process. | | | | | | | | | x | x | x |

Table 3-4: Suggested editorial guidelines

| Guidelines \ Discipline | psychology[1] | science[2] | science[3] | sociology[4] | medicine[5] | business[6] | multi-discipline[7] | science[8] | psychology[9] | business[10] | psychology[11] |
|---|---|---|---|---|---|---|---|---|---|---|---|
| Editors have code of ethics. | | | | | X | | | | X | | |
| Editors state which articles refereed. | | X | | | | | | | | | |
| Editors and referees should apply for job. | | | | | | | | | | X | |
| Editors publish more brief reports. | X | | | | | | | | | | |
| Editors provide peer review information. | | | | | | | | X | | | |
| Editors publish reports on peer review. | | | | | | | | X | | | |
| Editors train reviewers. | | | | | | | | X | | | |
| Editors have enough associate editors. | | | | | | | | X | | | |
| Authors nominate reviewers. | | | | | | | X | | | | |
| Authors send explanatory note to reviewers. | | | | | | | X | | | | |
| Authors can respond to reviewers' reports. | | | | | X | | | | | | |
| Authors supply guarantee of no prior publication. | | | | X | | | | | | | |
| **Number of proposed guidelines** | 10 | 8 | 10 | 3 | 4 | 5 | 10 | 7 | 6 | 9 | 4 |

1. (Brackbill & Korten, 1975)
2. (Ziman, 1975)
3. (Juhasz et al., 1975)
4. (Glenn, 1976)
5. (Horrobin, 1981/1982)
6. (Armstrong, 1982)
7. (Miller & Serzan, 1984)
8. (Crandall, 1986)
9. (Hartley, 1987), (Hartley, 1988)
10. (Carland, Carland, & Aby, 1992)
11. (Epstein, 1995)

**Table 3-4: Suggested editorial guidelines (continued)**

information on guidelines contained in journals. A set of 88 biomedical journals was identified from a list of faculty publications from a school of medicine (Anderson & Goldstein, 1981). Anderson and Goldstein found "clear descriptions" (p. 103) of the editorial peer review process in 26 percent of the journals, and less than 10 percent contained objective measures for manuscript acceptance and rejection. Weller concluded that the higher the rank of a medical journals the more likely it was to have a statement about its editorial peer review process, ranging from 18.7 percent for non-indexed titles to 53.3 percent for the highest ranked titles (Weller, 1987).

A few journals have published codes of practice for their journals. For example, *Protein Science's* code of practice includes specific responsibilities for authors, reviewers, and editors (1994). The code states that editors must ensure scientific integrity, assure that all editorial decisions are based on objectivity, maintain confidentiality, and exercise judicious use of editorial authority.

Eleven authors have outlined recommended codes of practice or guidelines for editors. These codes are summarized in Table 3-4 and arranged in chronological order.

Ziman reported on the guidelines established by the Scientific Information Committee of the Royal Society (Ziman, 1975). An editorial in *Nature* also referred to Ziman's guidelines, mentioning three in particular: every manuscript should be reviewed; no manuscript should be rejected because of a single, negative review; and each manuscript should be reviewed within a stated time period (1975). The editorial concluded with an outline of a new, tight timetable for handling manuscripts and a new internal review procedure by which an associate editor would review each manuscript. Juhasz concluded a survey of science journal editors with a set of 10 recommendations (Juhasz et al., 1975). In a study designed to define the characteristics of a peer-reviewed journal, Miller and Serzan developed a list of "recommendations for improving the reviewing practices of academic and professional journals" (p. 676). These recommendations then became their criteria for defining a peer-reviewed journal. Their study found that few journals followed these criteria (Miller & Serzan, 1984). Miller and Serzan concluded "consensually agreed-upon, well-defined standards do not exist for reviewing procedures of academic and professional journals" (p. 692). Crandall supported Miller and Serzan's recommendations and added a few of his own, including such criteria as placing time limits on reviewers and editors, limiting the number of manuscripts sent to reviewers, and training reviewers (Crandall, 1986). Hartley suggested a set of six practices for psychology journals, surveyed editors of 30 psychology journals, determined how his recommendations matched current practices, and concluded that current practices were not far from his suggestions (Hartley, 1988).

Weller also compared published recommendations with actual data on practices of journal editors and concluded (Weller, 1994):

> *Using published recommendations as an argument for modifying procedures presents difficulties. The recommendations covered a wide range of topics with little overlap among them.... Authors offered no explanation as to why some procedures were recommended while others were not. Some recommendations were inconsistent with others. Recommendations were almost never based on data. No data were supplied to suggest that there would be a change in outcome if certain recommendations were followed or what change in outcome would be desirable"* (p. 23-24).

Carland and colleagues developed a set of recommended ethical guidelines for researchers, referees, and editors with a corresponding set of recommendations for improving the review process (Carland et al., 1992). The authors suggested that all journals should adopt and publish codes of practice that are aimed at providing prompt, ethical, unprejudiced, competent, and courteous behavior on the part of editors, authors, and reviewers.

Brackbill and Korten questioned psychologists about their most recent editorial peer review experience. The 10 most frequently mentioned suggestions are in Table 3-4 (Brackbill & Korten, 1975). Glenn thought that referees' reports were often based on "hasty, careless, biased, and/or incompetent refereeing" (p. 179) and proposed recommendations to offset that tendency (Glenn, 1976). Horrobin was interested in establishing rules to assure that an editor would not reject a manuscript that "finally demonstrated the cause of cancer" (p. 330) or some other equally innovative idea (Horrobin, 1981/1982). Some of his guidelines, while interesting, do not fit the format of Table 3-4 and are not included in it. These include: "The editor must beware of reports which could not be shown in full to an author" or from a "brilliant but unsound" author, and editors "must be prepared to take risks." (p. 330-331).

The guidelines and recommendations in Table 3-4 cover many aspects of the editorial peer review process. There is little consensus among these recommendations, and together they have the appearance of a "laundry list" of suggestions. Almost 70 percent of the 47 suggestions are mentioned only once. Only one recommendation is mentioned by more than one-half of those making recommendations (blind the reviewer to the author). Some sound obvious (e.g., reviewers should be experts/not biased and editors should appoint good reviewers to the board). Some conflict with each other (e.g., editors review each manuscript versus editors reject inappropriate manuscripts). Some are of uncertain value (e.g., a requirement that a certain the number of editors initially evaluate a manuscript and a requirement of the number of reviewers per manuscript). Some are probably of value, but almost impossible to fulfill all the time (e.g., time limits for reviewers or editors). Many are probably used to some degree by most editors (e.g., reviewers make publication recommendations, reviewers maintain confidentiality, reviewers receive standard guidelines).

The recommendation to blind the reviewer to the author is mentioned frequently. Carland and colleagues add a caveat to this recommendation; they suggest that the information on the identity of authors and reviewers should be available after the review process is complete. The chapter on reviewer bias discusses many of these recommendations.

*Limitations of studies of editors*

- The qualities that make an effective editor have not been identified.

- Some of the studies of the professional status of editors were controversial at the time of their publication. Particularly cross-disciplinary comparisons serve little purpose, as demonstrated with the studies of the productivity of editors in sociology, psychology, and social work. The different scholarly publication patterns in different fields make cross-disciplinary comparisons of productivity of editors problematic. While some studies indicated editors had a higher professional status than others in the same discipline, these studies did not prove that this status affected their performance as an editor. Nor did they provide a process for judging or evaluating editors within a discipline or provide a rationale for thinking that editors should be the most productive, highest cited, or most notable in a field. Studies of comparative data on editors within a discipline that address these issues would be more meaningful than comparisons between fields.

- Studies that ranked publication criteria, while identifying important manuscript characteristics, probably provide little assistance for editors when making acceptance or rejection decisions. Editors were often asked to respond to a theoretical question rather than examine their actual practice.

- Studies of the editorial peer review process of journals did not always describe fully how journals were selected, making any generalizations difficult. Some did not ask if the journal was peer reviewed or to define peer review. What any one journal submits to peer review, including treatment of solicited manuscripts, needs more investigation.

- Chapter One summarized recommendations made by the International Committee of Medical Journal Editors (ICMJE). This group has been careful not to place too many restrictions, requirements, or guidelines on the process, and has limited their definition to the requirement that an outside reviewer evaluate manuscripts. Data are needed to confirm which recommendations from the ICMJE would or could result in a better peer review process.

- The studies of suggested editorial guidelines provided little consensus. Recommendations were not based on data, so it is unclear which ones might help in designing a "good" editorial peer review process.

- Studies have tended to concentrate on process issues, not qualitative measures.

*Recommendations*
- In any study of editors or board members, careful consideration needs to be given to journal selection. When survey instruments are used, established survey research techniques must be employed. Editors should be asked specific questions and results reported systematically. Items that have great impact on a journal should be investigated, including solicited manuscripts and the role they play in the total contents of a journal or the degree to which manuscripts are rejected without review.

- In addition to the regular publication of instructions to authors, editors should publish their editorial peer review guidelines and provide details of the process, including their policies on the type of recommendations listed in Table 3-4.

## Conclusions from studies of editors and editorial board members

This chapter began by asking if studies had identified evidence of a "best practice" for the editorial peer review process. Most studies have not addressed that question but have looked at aspects of it: the process, the guidelines, the publication criteria, etc. The studies of editors and editorial board members have examined editorial practices and shown that there are a variety of practices. The next area for investigation is to examine which practices might prove to be the most beneficial. Some of these will be explored in subsequent chapters.

Studies of editors and the editorial peer review process still need more investigation. The studies analyzed in this chapter, even with their limitations, provide clues or guidelines as to how to design a study and what questions to ask to identify which practices are of value to editorial peer review.

Some general conclusions can be drawn about editors and their roles:

- Editors generally employ a basic editorial peer review process and within that basic process many variations exist.

- Editors' roles can be viewed either as complex, politically centered roles or as straightforward, process-centered roles, depending on the perspective of the writer.

- Editors and editorial board members possess a number of characteristics associated with prestige. Almost every study indicated that within a field or discipline editors and editorial board members have a higher degree of professional exposure than others in the field, and that editors are selected for their educational background, scholarly contributions, or publication experience.

- Disciplines have their own publication standards; therefore, any comparisons of the professional status of editors and editorial boards should focus on only one discipline.

- Editors bring some degree of bias into the editorial peer review process, not necessarily a negative bias, but a bias that appears to help them identify important publications.

- There appears to be a concordance between publication criteria and reasons for rejection.

It is estimated that today there are eight to 10 million scientific and technical documents published annually (Arndt, 1992). This addition of 7,000 articles to the scientific literature daily greatly increases the workload of editors who handle all these manuscripts. Editors themselves would not be committed to this additional work without recognizing the need for and value of this process. However, of this total body of scholarly work, what is and what is not peer reviewed needs more investigation.

## References

(1975, November 6). Do scientific journals need code of practice? *Nature, 258*(5530), 1.

(1994, January). The *Protein Science* code of ethics. *Protein Science, 3*(1), xi.

Abt, H. (1987, May). Are papers by well-known astronomers accepted for publication more readily than other papers? *Publications of the Astronomical Society of the Pacific, 99*, 439-441.

Anderson, P. J. & Goldstein, R. K. (1981). Criteria of journal quality. *Journal of Research Communication Studies, 3*, 99-110.

Angell, M. (1991). Whom do journal editors serve? In S. Lock (Ed.), *The future of medical journals: in commemoration of 150 years of the British Medical Journal* (pp. 67-73). London: British Medical Journal.

Armstrong, J. S. (1982). The ombudsman: is review by peers as fair as it appears? *Interfaces, 12*(5), 62-74.

Arndt, K. A. (1992, September). Information excess in medicine. *Archives of Dermatology, 128*, 1249-1256.

Bakker, P. & Rigter, H. (1985, January). Editors of medical journals: who and from where. *Scientometrics, 7*(1-2), 11-22.

Baue, A. E. (1993, December). Reflections of a former editor. *Archives of Surgery, 128*(12), 1305-1314.

Benedek, E. P. (1976, January). Editorial practices of psychiatric and related journals: implications for women. *American Journal of Psychiatry, 133*(1), 89-92.

Beyer, J. M. (1978, Winter). Editorial policies and practices among leading journals in four scientific fields. *Sociological Quarterly, 19*, 68-88.

Binger, J. L. (1982, April). Nursing journal editors. *Nursing Outlook, 30*(4), 260-264.

Blank, J. J. & McElmurry, B. J. (1988, July/August). Editors of nursing journals; Who are they and how were they selected? *Nursing Outlook, 36*(4), 179-181.

Bornstein, R. F. (1991, Autumn). An adversay model of manuscript review: further comments. *Journal of Mind and Behavior, 12*(4), 479-485.

Borysewicz, M. L. (1977). *The creative role and function of editors.* Paper presented at the First International Conference of Scientific Editors, Jerusalem.

Brackbill, Y. & Hellegers, A. E. (1980, April). Ethics and editors. *Hastings Center Report, 10*(2), 20-22.

Brackbill, Y. & Korten, F. (1975, October). Journal reviewing practices: Authors' and APA members' suggestions for revision. *American Psychologist, 25*(10), 937-940.

Braun, T. & Bujdoso, E. (1983, March). Gatekeeping patterns in the publication of analytical chemistry research. *Talanta, 30*(3), 161-167.

Budd, J. (1988, September 1). Publication in library and information science: the state of the literature. *Library Journal, 113*(14), 125-131.

Caelleigh, A. S. (1993, September). Role of the journal editor in sustaining integrity in research. *Academic Medicine, 68*(9, Supplement), S23-S29.

Campanario, J. M. (1996, March). The competition for journal space among referees, editors, and other authors and its influence on journals' impact factors. *Journal of the American Society for Information Science, 47*(3), 184-182.

Carland, J. A., Carland, J. W., & Aby, C. D., Jr. (1992). Proposed codification of ethicacy in the publication process. *Journal of Business Ethics, 11*, 95-104.

Chase, J. M. (1970, August). Normative criteria for scientific publication. *American Sociologist, 5*(3), 263-265.

Christiansen, D. (1974, July). Who gets published? *IEEE Spectrum, 11*(7), 33.

Christiansen, D. (1974, August). Who gets published? Part II: transactions. *IEEE Spectrum, 11*(8), 31.

Christiansen, D. (1981, August). Peer review reviewed. *IEEE Spectrum, 18*(8), 21.

Coe, R. K. & Weinstock, I. (1967, Winter). Editorial policies of major economic journals. *Quarterly Review of Economics and Business, 7*(4), 37-43.

Coe, R. K. & Weinstock, I. (1968, January). Publication policies in major business periodicals. *Southern Journal of Business*, 1-10.

Colaianni, L. A. (1994, July 13). Peer review in journals indexed in *Index Medicus. JAMA, 272*(2), 156-158.

Copp, L. A. (1997, September-October). Contributions by nursing editors to the profession. *Journal of Professional Nursing, 13*(5), 275-276.

Crandall, R. (1977, July). How qualified are editors? *American Psychologist, 32*(7), 578-579.

Crandall, R. (1986, October). Peer review: improving editorial procedures. *BioScience, 36*(9), 607-609.

Crane, D. (1967, November). The gatekeepers of science: Some factors affecting the selection of articles for scientific journals. *American Sociologist, 2*(4), 195-201.

DeBakey, L. (1976). *The scientific journal, editorial policies and practices. Guidelines for editors, reviewers, and authors*. St. Louis: C.V. Mosby Company.

Dehmer, P. (1982, February). APS reviews refereeing procedures. *Physics Today, 35*(2), 9, 95.

Eichorn, D. H. & VandenBos, G. R. (1985, December). Dissemination of scientific and professional knowledge. Journal publication within the APA. *American Psychologist, 40*(12), 1309-1312.

Einhorn, H. J. (1971, June). Responsibility of journal editors and referees. *American Psychologist, 26*(6), 600-601.

Epstein, S. (1995, October). What can be done to improve the journal review process. *American Psychologist, 50*(9), 883-885.

Federico, J., Lee, M. M., Boozer, C. H., & Diaz, D. (1984, March). Report of a survey comparing sixty-nine journals in the dental profession. *Educational Directions in Dental Hygiene, 9*, 9-18.

Feinstein, A. R. (1991). Construction, consent, and condemnation in research on peer review. *Journal of Clinical Epidemiology, 44*(4/5), 339-341.

Fondiller, S. H. (1994, March). Is nursing at risk? *Nursing & Health Care, 15*(3), 142-148.

Frantz, T. T. (1968, December). Criteria for publishable manuscripts. *Personnel and Guidance Journal, 47*(4), 384-386.

Fuccillo, D. A. & Holmes, S. (1980). Are editorial boards necessary? *CBE Views, 3*(4), 18-19.

Gaston, J. (1979, November). The big three and the status of sociology. *Contemporary Sociology, 8*(6), 789-793.

Gibbons, J. D. (1990, August). U.S. institutional representation on editorial boards of U.S. statistics journals. *American Statistician, 44*(3), 210-213.

Gibbons, J. D. & Fish, M. (1991, Fall). Ranking of economics faculties and representation on editorial boards of top journals. *Journal of Economic Education, 22*(4), 361-372.

Gilbert, J. R., Williams, E. S., & Lundberg, G. D. (1994, July 13). Is there a gender bias in JAMA's peer review process? *JAMA, 272*(2), 139-142.

Gilbert, N. (1977, December). Editorial board membership. *American Psychologist, 32*(12), 1109-1110.

Glen, J. W., & Konigsson, K. L. (1976). Refereeing in earth-science journals. *Earth Science Editing, 3*, 11-13.

Glenn, N. D. (1976, August). The journal article review process: Some proposals for change. *American Sociologist, 11*(3), 179-185.

Gordon, M. D. (1978). Disciplinary differences, editorial practices and the patterning of rejection rates. *Journal of Research Communication Studies, 1*, 139-159.

Gottfredson, S. D. (1978, October). Evaluating psychological research reports; dimensions, reliability, and correlates of quality judgments. *American Psychologist, 33*(10), 920-934.

Gove, W. R. (1979, November). The review process and its consequences in the major sociology journal. *Contemporary Sociology, 8*(6), 799-804.

Haas, L., Milton, S., & Quinn, A. (1996, Winter). Surviving the publishing process: a beginner's guide. *RQ, 36*(2), 230-246.

Hartley, J. (1987, October). A code of practice for refereeing journal articles. *American Psychologist, 42*(10), 959.

Hartley, J. (1988, November). Editorial practices in psychology journals. *Psychologist, 1*(11), 428-430.

Hatfield, C., Ostbye, T., & Sori, C. (1995, March 11). Sex of editor in medical journals. *Lancet, 345*(8950), 662.

Hewitt, R. M. (1951, March). Medical editors and their work. *Journal Lancet, 72*(3), 145-149.

Horrobin, D. (1981/1982). Peer review: is the good the enemy of the best? *Journal of Research Communication Studies, 3*, 327-334.

Houlihan, D., Hofschulte, L., Sachau, D., & Patten, C. (1992, December). Critiquing the peer review process: examining a potential dual role conflict. *American Psychologist, 47*(12), 1679-1681.

Jefferson, T., & Demicheli, V. (1995, February 28). Are guidelines for peer-reviewing economic evaluations necessary? A survey of current editorial practices. *Health Economics, 4*, 383-388.

Juhasz, S., Calvert, E., Jackson, T., Kronick, D. A., & Shipman, J. (1975, September). Acceptance and rejection of manuscripts. *IEEE Transactions on Professional Communication, 18*(3), 177-185.

Kerr, S., Tolliver, J., & Petree, D. (1977). Manuscript characteristics which influence acceptance for management and social science journals. *Academy of Management Journal, 20*(1), 132-141.

Kole, L. A. (1989, May/June). Between hammer and anvil. *Journal of the American Academy of Physician Assistants, 2*(3), 162-163.

Laband, D. N. (1985, October). Publishing favoritism: a critique of departmental rankings based on quantitative publishing performance. *Southern Economic Journal, 52*(2), 510-515.

Laband, D. N. & Piette, M. J. (1994, February). Favoritism versus search for good papers: empirical evidence regarding the behavior of journal editors. *Journal of Political Economy, 102*(1), 194-302.

Lacy, W. B. & Busch, L. (1982, Fall). Guardians of sciences: journals and journal editors in the agricultural sciences. *Rural Sociology, 47*(3), 429-448.

Lavelle, J. (1966, November). Facts of journal publishing, IV. *Publications of the Modern Language Association of America, 81*(6), 3-12.

Lindsey, D. (1976, November). Distinction, achievement, and editorial board membership. *American Psychologist, 31*(11), 799-804.

Lindsey, D. (1977a, July). Participation and influence in publication review proceedings: a reply. *American Psychologist, 32*(7), 579-586.

Lindsey, D. (1977b, December). The processing of self-criticism by social work editorial boards. *American Psychologist, 32*(12), 1110-1115.

Lindsey, D. (1978). The operation of professional journals in social work. *Journal of Sociology and Social Welfare, 5*(2), 273-298.

Lindsey, D. (1992, October). Improving the quality of social work journals. *Research on Social Work Practice, 2*(4), 515-524.

Lindsey, D. & Lindsey, T. (1978). The outlook of journal editors and referees on the normative criteria of scientific craftsmanship. Viewpoints from psychology, social work and sociology. *Quality and Quantity, 12,* 45-62.

McCartney, J. L. (1979, November). Behind the editorial curtain. *Contemporary Sociology, 8*(6), 814-816.

McCloskey, J. (1977, July-August). Publishing opportunities for nurses: a comparison of 65 journals. *Nurse Educator, 2*(4), 4-13.

McCloskey, J. & Swanson, E. A. (1982, June). Publishing opportunities for nurses: a comparison of 100 journals. *Image, 14*(2), 50-56.

McElmurry, B. J., Newcomb, B. J., Barnfather, J., & Lynch, M. S. (1981). The manuscript review process in nursing publications. *Current Issues in Nursing,* 129-143.

Meadows, A. J. (1977). The problem of refereeing. *Scientia, 112*, 788-794.

Michel, F. C. (1982, December). Solving the problem of refereeing. *Physics Today, 35*(12), 9, 82.

Miller, A. C. & Serzan, S. L. (1984, November/December). Criteria for identifying a refereed journal. *Journal of Higher Education, 55*(6), 673-699.

Morris, N. (1985, January). Editorial boards. *Earth & Life Science Editing* (24), 15.

Munters, Q. J. (1981). The social science editor as gatekeeper. *Journal of Research Communication Studies, 3*, 37-45.

Neuliep, J. W. & Crandall, R. (1990). Editorial bias against replication research. *Journal of Social Behavior and Personality, 5*(4), 85-90.

Noble, K. A. (1989). Publish or perish: what 23 journal editors have to say. *Studies in Higher Education, 14*(1), 97-102.

O'Connor, D. & Van Orden, P. (1978, September). Getting into print. *College and Research Libraries, 39*(5), 389-396.

Over, R. (1981, August). Representation of women on the editorial boards of psychology journals. *American Psychologist, 36*(8), 885-891.

Pardeck, J. T. (1992, October). Are social work journal editorial boards competent? Some disquieting data with implications for *Research on Social Work Practice. Research on Social Work Practice, 2*(4), 487-496.

Pardeck, J. T., Arndt, B. J., Light, D. B., Mosley, G. F., Thomas, S. D., Werner, M. A., & Wilson, K. E. (1991a). Distinction and achievement levels of editorial board members of psychology and social work journals. *Psychological Reports, 68*, 523-527.

Pardeck, J. T., Arndt, B. J., Light, D. B., Mosley, G. F., Thomas, S. D., Werner, M. A., & Wilson, K. E. (1991b, June). An exploration of editorial boards of psychology and social work journals: implications for child welfare practice. *Early Child Development and Care, 71*, 89-96.

Pfeffer, J., Leong, A., & Strehl, K. (1977, June). Paradigm development and particularism: journal publication in three scientific disciplines. *Social Forces, 55*(4), 938-951.

Reideberg, J. W. & Reidenberg, M. M. (1991, July). Report of a survey of some aspects of editorial board peer review at *Clinical Pharmacology & Therapeutics. Clinical Pharmacology and Therapeutics, 50*(1), 1-3.

Riggio, R. E. (1990). Biases in editorial decisions and the blocking issue. *Journal of Social Behavior and Personality, 5*(6), 503-504.

Rodman, H. & Mancini, J. (1977). Editors, manuscripts, and equal treatment. *Research in Higher Education, 7*(4), 369-374.

Rodman, H., & Mancini, J. (1977, April). Problems and satisfactions of journal editors. *Scholarly Publishing, 8*(3), 239-245.

Saidman, L. J. (1995, July). What I have learned from 9 years and 9,000 papers. *Anesthesiology, 83*(1), 191-197.

Schaeffer, D. L. (1970, April). Do APA journals play professional favorites? *American Psychologist, 25*(4), 362-365.

Schiedermayer, D. L., & Siegler, M. (1986, October). Believing what you read, responsibilities of medical authors and editors. *Archives of Internal Medicine, 146*(10), 2043-2044.

Schulman, K., Sulmasy, D. P., & Roney, D. (1994, July 13). Ethics, economics, and the publication policies of major medical journals. *JAMA, 272*(2), 154-156.

Sharp, D. W. (1990, March 9). What can and should be done to reduce publication bias? *JAMA, 263*(10), 1390-1391.

Shelley, I. J. (1981/1982). Term of office for members of editorial boards. *Journal of Research Communication Studies, 3*, 401-404.

Siegelman, S. S. (1989, November). Desirable qualities of manuscripts. *Radiology, 173*(2), 467-468.

Silverman, R. J. (1976, November). The education journal editor: a portrait. *Journal of Education, 158*(4), 39-68.

Silverman, R. J. (1978, April). Diffusion of educational knowledge through journals: gatekeepers' selection criteria. *Viewpoints in Teaching and Learning, 54*, 1-22.

Silverman, R. J., & Collins, E. L. (1975). Publishing relationships in higher education. *Research in Higher Education, 3*, 365-382.

Smigel, E. O. & Ross, H. L. (1970, February). Factors in the editorial decision. *American Sociologist, 5*(1), 19-21.

Smith, K. J. & Laband, D. N. (1995). The role of editors' professional connections in determining which papers get published: evidence from accounting research. *Accounting Perspectives, 1*, 21-30.

Steffens, D. L. & Robbins, J. B. (1991). The role of editors and editorial boards in journal publishing. In C. R. McClure & P. Hernon (Eds.), *Library and information science research; perspectives and strategies for improvement.*

Swanson, E. A. & McCloskey, J. (1982, October). The manuscript review process of nursing journals. *Image, 14*(3), 72-76.

Swanson, E. A. & McCloskey, J. (1986, September/October). Publishing opportunities for nurses. *Nursing Outlook, 34*(5), 227-235.

Swanson, E. A., McCloskey, J., & Bodensteiner, A. (1991, Spring). Publishing opportunities for nurses: a comparison of 92 U.S. journals. *Image: Journal of Nursing Scholarship, 23*(1), 33-38.

Vaisrub, S. (1978, February). Peer review; a view from another pier. *Archives of Internal Medicine, 138*(2), 197.

Via, B. J. (1996, July). Publishing in the journal literature of library and information science: a survey of manuscript review process and acceptance. *College and Research Libraries, 57*(4), 365-376.

Von Glinow, M. A., & Novelli, L., Jr. (1982, June). Ethical standards within organizational behaviour. *Academy of Management Journal, 25*(2), 417-437.

Warren, R. (1978, January). Power and prejudice. *Archives of Surgery, 113*(1), 13-14.

Weller, A. C. (1987, October). Editorial policy and the assessment of quality among medical journals. *Bulletin of the Medical Library Association, 75*(4), 310-316.

Weller, A. C. (1990, March 9). Editorial peer review in U.S. medical journals. *JAMA, 263*(10), 1344-1347.

Weller, A. C. (1994). Guidelines for editorial peer review: comparison of recommendations with current practices of medical journals. In R. A. Weeks & D. L. Kinser (Eds.), *Editing the refereed scientific journal* (pp. 17-25). New York: IEEE Press.

Weller, A. C. (1996, July). Editorial peer review: a comparison of authors publishing in two groups of U.S. medical journals. *Bulletin of the Medical Library Association, 84*(3), 359-366.

Whitley, R. D. (1970, September). The formal communication system of science: a study of the organisation of British social science journals. In P. Halmos (Ed.), *The sociology of sociology* (Vol. 16, pp. 163-179). Keele, Straffordshire, Great Britain.

Wilkes, M. S. & Kravitz, R. L. (1995, August). Policies, practices, and attitudes of North American medical journal editors. *Journal of General Internal Medicine, 10*(8), 443-450.

Willis, C. L. & McNamee, S. J. (1990, June). Social networks of science and patterns of publication in leading sociology journals, 1960-85. *Knowledge: Creation, Diffusion, and Utilization, 11*(4), 363-381.

Wolff, W. M. (1970, July). A study of criteria for journal manuscripts. *American Psychologist, 25*(7), 636-639.

Yoels, W. C. (1971, May). Destiny or dynasty: doctoral origins and appointments patterns of editors of the American Sociological Review, 1948-68. *American Sociologist, 6*(2), 134-139.

Yoels, W. C. (1974, Spring). The structure of scientific fields and the allocation of editorships on scientific journals: some observations on the politics of knowledge. *Sociological Quarterly, 15*(2), 264-276.

Ziman, J. (1975, November). Journal guidelines. *Nature, 258*(5533), 284.

Zsindely, S. & Schubert, A. (1989, October). Editors-in-chief of medical journals: are they experts, authorities, both, or neither? *Communication Research, 16*(5), 695-700.

Zsindely, S., Schubert, A., & Braun, T. (1982a). Citation patterns of editorial gatekeepers in international chemistry journals. *Scientometrics, 4*(1), 69-76.

Zsindely, S., Schubert, A., & Braun, T. (1982b). Editorial gatekeeping patterns in international science journals. A new science indicator. *Scientometrics, 4*(1), 57-68.

# Chapter Four

# The Authorship Problem

*It is time to abandon authorship.*
(Horton, 1997, p. 6)

The scientific community can be slow to accept radically new scientific theories, even when presented with data supporting the theory. Some argue that this alone is proof that editorial peer review does not work. Others take a more pragmatic approach and say the tendency to reject new theories is not surprising; innovative ideas are frequently initially rejected and new theories must be conclusively proven before they will be accepted. Indeed, the chapter on rejected manuscripts described several examples of initially rejected, innovative ideas whose discoverers eventually were awarded a Nobel prize.

Authors themselves succumb to the fear of publishing new ideas. Comroe (Comroe, 1976) cites three classic examples of author-initiated delays in publication caused by authors' concerns about opposition to their findings. Copernicus waited 31 years to publish his theory of a sun-centered universe. Harvey delayed publication of his discovery of circulation of the blood for 12 years. Darwin waited 23 years to publish the *Origin of Species*. There are other lesser-known examples. Long administered anesthesia to a patient in 1842, but he delayed trying to get this information published. Among his reasons: he needed more patients, he was busy, and "physicians high in authority" (p. 563) had a different view of what might work to relieve pain in surgery. Gley sealed for 17 years results of his experiments on dogs that identified the link between insulin and diabetes because more research was needed that "required a great number of experimental animals" (p. 564). Comroe ended his description of these cases of delayed publication of important findings by asserting that today any scientist can get work published if he or she is willing to forego a prestigious journal.

While career productivity of scholars is not a subject of this monograph, clearly the editorial peer review process touches huge numbers of researchers and scholars throughout the course of their careers. Anyone who has authored a scholarly or scientific journal article has more than likely come in contact with the editorial peer review process. A survey administered by the American

Council of Learned Societies of a stratified sample of 3,835 members in seven disciplines found that 79 percent of academic respondents said they had published in refereed journals (Morton & Price, 1986). The percentage increased to 88 percent by the time academicians reached mid-to-late careers.

This chapter examines the process from the author's perspective, covering those issues that the author has some control over. Who claims authorship? How do authors select a journal to which to submit their manuscripts? What is the value of the review process to authors? Trends in coauthorship and contributions of coauthors to manuscripts, both of which have implications for the editorial peer review process, are also discussed.

Once a scholar or researcher has completed a project, a decision must be made whether or not to publish the results or the idea. At times, a potential author decides not to prepare a manuscript for submission to a journal. This phenomenon has been referred to as the "file drawer problem." Rosenthal estimated that 95 percent of studies with nonsignificant results have been relegated to the "file drawer" (Rosenthal, 1979). One part of a survey of 740 authors asked researchers about studies in which a manuscript had never been prepared. About 15 percent, decided not to submit manuscripts to journals. The most frequent excuse was that the findings did not produce statistically significant results (Rotton, Foos, Van Meek, & Levitt, 1995). The phenomenon of only submitting reports of studies with statistically significant results is discussed in the chapter on statistical review of manuscripts.

## Coauthorship

On the surface, responsibilities of authorship appear to be straightforward. Except in cases of outright fraud or plagiarism, questions of authorship responsibility can, of course, only be raised in coauthored works. There is no need to question who authored a single-authored paper or who has responsibility for its content. During this century there has been a steady increase in the number of authors per article, especially in the sciences and medicine. In 1953, Alexander complained that the trend away from individual research endeavors and toward teamwork has "a tendency to degrade authorship into a form of menial patronage." He suggested editors "lay down rigid rules restricting the maximum number of authors which would be tolerated, except in unusual circumstances" (p. 283) (Alexander, 1953).

Several cases of fraud in the early 1980s increased the medical community's sensitivity to the issue of defining authorship and of assuring that all authors accept responsibility for a published work (Huth, 1984). Huth suggested that authorship responsibility should be decided on by team members at the beginning of a research project. Researchers who are asked to come into a project as coauthor after it has begun, should be careful to ask enough questions to make sure they truly understand the project (Huth, 1983). In a discussion of the responsibilities of authorship, Schiedermayer and Siegler emphasized that authors must maintain ethical standards in designing and conducting research studies, they must adhere to an intellectual honesty, and they must publicly accept responsibility for the whole work (Schiedermayer & Siegler, 1986).

When an author's name appears far down on a list of coauthors, it can reflect negatively on that author and diminish recognition, even if the person had made substantial contributions to a lengthy clinical trial that took years and involved multiple sites (Oliver, 1995). Notwithstanding, Horton and Smith claimed in many cases coauthorship is rampant: "physicists do it by the hundred; scientists do it in groups" (p. 723) (Horton & Smith, 1996b).

Data support the observation that there is an ever-increasing rise in the number of authors per article. Fourteen studies in medicine have collected data on the degree of coauthorship over several decades (Table 4-1). These studies range from an examination of data from only one journal to a large study of *Index Medicus* titles. Findings from each study are averaged for each decade from the 1930s to the 1990s. Increases in the average number of authors per article for each decade is illustrated in Figure 4-1. Each decade has seen a

| Specialty—Titles | 1930s | 1940s | 1950s | 1960s | 1970s | 1980s | 1990s | Number of journals | References |
|---|---|---|---|---|---|---|---|---|---|
| medicine—Lancet | 1.3 | | | | 4.3 | | | 1 | (Strub & Black, 1976) |
| medicine—NEJM | 1.2 | | | | 4.2 | | | 1 | (Strub & Black, 1976) |
| medicine—Obstet & Gynec | | | 1.9 | | 3.4 | | | 1 | (Dardik, 1977) |
| medicine—NEJM | | 2.0 | 2.6 | 2.8 | 4.9 | | | 1 | (Fletcher & Fletcher, 1979) |
| medicine—Ann Intern Med | 1.3 | | | 3.2 | 4.7 | | | 1 | (Burman, 1982) |
| medicine—NEJM | 1.2 | | | 3.8 | 5.2 | | | 1 | (Burman, 1982) |
| pediatrics—J Pediatrics | 1.5 | 2.0 | | 2.6 | | 4.0 | | 1 | (Hayden & Saulsbury, 1982) |
| medicine—NEJM | | | | | 4.0 | 5.9 | | 1 | (Alvarez-Dardet, Gascon, Mur, & Nolasco, 1985) |
| cardiology | | | | 2.9 | 3.7 | 5.2 | | 7 | (Friesinger, 1986) |
| radiology | | | | 2.2 | | 4.4 | | 16 | (Chew, 1986) |
| radiology | | | 2.0 | 2.3 | 3.1 | 4.4 | | 2 | (Chew, 1986) |
| medicine | | | | | | 4.3 | | 8 | (Satyanarayana & Ratnakar, 1989) |
| Index Medicus titles | | | | | 3.9 | 6.4 | | | (Sobal & Ferentz, 1990) |
| medicine—Br J Neurosurg | | | | | 2.8 | | 4.3 | 1 | (Mylonas, 1992) |
| radiology | | | | 2.2 | | | 4.4 | 12 | (Mussurakis, 1993) |
| medicine | | | | | | 4.0 | 5.1 | 8 | (Epstein, 1993) |
| medicine | 1.8 | 2.6 | 2.8 | | 4.7 | 4.7 | | 4 | (Onwude, Staines, & Lilford, 1993) |
| **Averages** | 1.4 | 2.2 | 2.3 | 2.8 | 4.1 | 4.8 | 4.6 | | |

**Table 4-1: Changes in the average number of authors in medical articles over time**

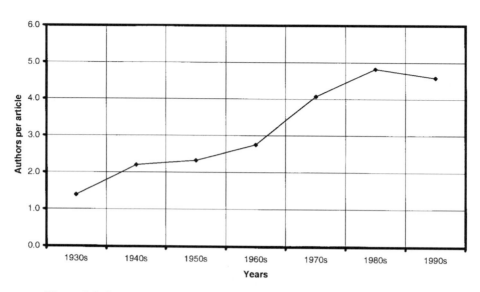

**Figure 4-1: Average number of authors per article in medicine**

steady increase in the average number of authors per article with one exception: from the 1980s to the 1990s, there is a very slight decrease, from an average of 4.8 to 4.6 authors per article. Of course, data from the 1990s only represent a portion of the decade, but these data could also indicate that the
average number of authors per article may have peaked or at least leveled out.

Epstein examined authorship trends from 1982 to 1993 in eight biomedical
journals; data from all journals have been averaged in Table 4-1 (Epstein, 1993).
From the years 1982 to 1993, all but two journals showed a trend toward increasing the numbers of authors per article. For example, during this time period
*Lancet*'s average number of authors per article increased from three to six, the
*Journal of Clinical Oncology* increased from four to seven, and the *Proceedings
of the National Academy of Science* increased from two to four. Epstein selected
the eight journal titles because they covered a "broad spectrum of biomedical research" (p. 765). He was also interested in knowing if this increase was a factor
in the National Library of Medicine's decision to index only the first six authors
of any article covered by *Index Medicus*. Epstein did find that two medical journals (*Lancet* and the *New England Journal of Medicine*) published more six-au-
thored than seven-authored articles. He was not able to document that newer research technologies demand more collaboration.

Studies from other disciplines have followed similar patterns. Journals published by the American Psychological Association have shown steady increases in the number of authors per article: from 1.47 in 1949 to 1.72 in 1959,
1.88 in 1969, and 2.19 in 1979 (Over, 1982). From the early to the late 1970s,
in all scientific disciplines the number of authors per article, based on *Science*

*Citation Index* data, increased from 2.01 to 2.50 (Burman, 1982). A study of articles published in chemistry showed the same trends. The number of authors per article increased from 2.1 in 1960 to 3.7 in 1985 (McNamee & Willis, 1994). Over this same time period, McNamee and Willis found less dramatic increases in coauthorship patterns in economics (from 1.1 to 1.4), in sociology (from 1.2 to 1.5), and in philosophy (from 1.0 to 1.1).

Trends in coauthorship have also been tracked by examining changes in the percentage of single-authored articles over time. Price predicted in 1963 that the single-authored paper would be extinct by 1980 (Price, 1963). While single-authored articles still continue to be published, there is an undeniable increase in collaboration studies, as shown by these additional examples:

- The percentage of single-authored papers decreased from 90 percent in the 1920s to about 30 percent in the 1980s in the *American Journal of Public Health* (Yankauer, 1986).

- The percentage of single-authored articles decreased from 78.4 percent in 1928 to 41.8 percent in 1948, and to 3.1 percent in 1968 in the *New England Journal of Medicine* (Diamond, 1969).

- In another study of the *New England Journal of Medicine*, the percentage of single-authored articles decreased from 9 percent to 3 percent from 1983 to 1989 (Sobal & Ferentz, 1990). Almost 10 percent of all articles carried the designation "et al," which is *Index Medicus'* designation for more than six authors on an article. These two studies of the *New England Journal of Medicine*—one finding 3.1 percent of all articles single authored in 1968 and the other finding 9 percent of all articles single authored in 1983—might indicate some annual fluctuation in the number of authors per article, a difference in definition of what constitutes an article, or an actual decrease in the percentage of single-authored articles from 1968 to 1983. The final option is unlikely, given all the data on trends in the number of authors per article.

- The percentage of single-authored articles written by academic chemists decreased from 16.8 percent in 1962 and 1963 to 5.2 percent in 1984 and 1985 (Bayer & Smart, 1991). Team research efforts (defined as three or more authors) continued to increase, comprising over one-half of all academic chemists who published in the years from 1979 to 1985.

- The percentages of single-authored articles decreased from a range of 50 percent to 85 percent in the 1920s in five science journals to a range of 1 percent to 29 percent for the same five journals in 1989 (Benson, 1991).

- The percentage of coauthored papers in five internationally known information systems journals increased from 59 percent in 1989 to 75 percent by 1995 (Cunningham & Dillon, 1997).

Onwulde and colleagues compared the number of authors per article of the 400 most cited articles from *Science Citation Index* with 100 of the most cited articles from four leading medical journals (Onwude, Staines, & Lilford, 1993). As in medicine, the numbers of authors per article in science has increased. In 1935, there was an average of 1.78 and 1.174 authors per article for medicine and science, respectively. This increased to an average of 4.74 and 2.99 authors per article for medicine and science respectively for the period 1960 to 1990.

Physics (Sampson, 1995) has also undergone dramatic increases in the number of coauthored articles. In 1951, the *Physical Review* published 142 articles: 45.1 percent had one author, 40.8 percent had two authors, and the remaining 14.1 percent had three, four, or five authors. By 1991, this journal had been divided several times, eventually forming five publications: *The Physical Review A, B, C,* and *D,* and *Physical Review Letters.* These five publications together have come close to doubling the number of articles five times in four decades (from 142 articles in 1951 to 4,392 articles in 1991). In 1991, 54.6 percent of the articles had three or more authors and 47 (1.0 percent) had over 20 authors. Three articles actually had over 200 authors.

These studies illustrate increases in the percentage of coauthored articles in several disciplines. This constantly increasing percentage of multi-authored articles raises a question about any potential impact the number of authors might have on the editorial peer review process. In fact, in a study that tried to correlate prestige of authors to acceptance rates in the *Physical Review,* Zuckerman and Merton eliminated all coauthored papers because these were accepted at a rate of about 95 percent (Zuckerman & Merton, 1971). This study was from one discipline—physics—and conducted many years ago. Since that time, as described above by Sampson, multi-authored articles have become quite commonplace in physics. A large analysis of multiple authorship conducted by Harsanyi concluded: "collaborative research is increasing in many disciplines, resulting in many questions involving funding, productivity, ... formal and informal communication, and even the idea of what constitutes authorship" (p. 430) (Harsanyi, 1993). Harsanyi suggested that this is an area where research is needed.

Benson reflected on four reasons usually given for the rise in collaboration: the professionalization of science has created a structure for collaborative research; the trend for interdisciplinary research has increased; the development of "big science" has created large teams of researchers; and, the nature of federal funding, which also encourages increased collaboration (Benson, 1991). Benson admitted that these reasons might only be partially responsible and maintained the real cause lies in the transformation of publications from "tools for communication" to "tools of commerce" (p. 329). He decried that for a scientist worth is now equated with length of curriculum vitae.

The implications of coauthorship encompass a number of areas related to editorial peer review, including the increased likelihood that a reviewer might know one of the authors if the manuscript is not blinded to the reviewer. An author might want to add a well-known person as a coauthor to give the manuscript more credibility or "weight." A head of a laboratory might insist that his or her name be added as an author as a way of recognizing that the project generated from a particular laboratory or from a particular group.

In 1983, Moulopoulos and colleagues developed a model that estimated the relative contribution of each coauthor by assuming that each author's contribution to a manuscript was related to the order of authorship (Moulopoulos, Sideris, & Georgilis, 1983). Using a sample of four authors who had written from 70 to 364 articles over the course of their careers, a corrected number of articles was calculated by estimating an author's fractional contribution to each article. The recalculation suggested that from 31 to 94 full articles were written by these researchers, depending on the formula used. The authors decided that "no accurate conclusions can be drawn as to the relative research activity of an author compared with that of his coauthors or as to the individual mainly responsible for the quality of the paper" (p. 1610). They also suggested that editors require a statement of specific contributions from each author in coauthored works.

In a letter to the editor in the *British Medical Journal* (*BMJ*), in 1986, Mould asked if any studies had asked authors very specific questions about their contributions to coauthored articles (Mould, 1986). He suggested that for each author there would be an indication of their contribution to the work, such as: idea, science, technical help, administrative role, any data collection, statistical analysis, graphics, and writing.

Any multi-authored work requires that the authors decide how to order their names. Trying to take a practical approach by assisting a group of authors on how to decide authorship order, a number of authors developed a scoring system. For example, Schmidt divided a research endeavor into five parts: conception, design, data collection, data analysis, and manuscript preparation (Schmidt, 1987). Total contribution for each one of the five parts equal 100 percent. Each researcher's relative contribution is assigned in each of the five parts and all values are totaled; authorship order is based on the ranking of the scores. In another example, Ahmed and colleagues recommended that each coauthor decide if the contribution was minimal, some, or significant for each of seven categories: conceiving the idea; designing the study; implementing the project; analyzing and interpreting the data; drafting the article; revising and reviewing the article; and accepting public responsibility for it (Ahmed, Maurana, Engle, Uddin, & Glaus, 1997). These authors then demonstrated the practical application of the scale with their own decision on ordering their five names.

*Question*

Have any studies assessed the contribution of individual authors in coauthored works?

*Criteria for inclusion*

~ any study that analyzed a group of published coauthored articles to determine specific contributions of each author.

*Comparable studies*

No study has approached this question with the detail suggested by Mould. Three studies have attempted to shed some light on this question; each asked first authors of a set of articles about their contributions to the work.

Shapiro and colleagues administered a survey to the first authors of 200 articles with four or more authors in five leading basic science journals and five leading medical journals. First authors were asked to rate contributions made by their coauthors. According to the first author, 21 percent of the basic science coauthors made no contribution to the "more intellectual tasks of research (conception, design, analysis and interpretation, and writing or revision)" (p. 441). Thirty percent of the coauthors of clinical papers had similarly made no substantial contributions according to the first author (Shapiro, Wenger, & Shapiro, 1994). In an accompanying editorial, Rennie and Flanagin recognized that many of those listed as authors had made important contributions but had done so in their roles of "multicenter collaborators, supporters, recruiters, committee members, and study monitors" (p. 471). Therefore, the editorial suggested that these contributors only needed to be thanked in the acknowledgments with a statement of their contributions (Rennie & Flanagin, 1994). The editorial maintained that "true authorship and its conferred responsibility are lost in a group byline" (p. 471). However, even acknowledgments can be problematic. The editor of the *New England Journal of Medicine* described a manuscript they accepted with an acknowledgment section that listed 63 institutions and 155 physicians (Kassirer & Angell, 1991).

In the second study that surveyed first authors, Goodman selected 14 multi-authored papers from a "peer reviewed general medical journal." Goodman asked the authors to identify the types of contributions made by coauthors. A list of 16 criteria for authorship was provided (the table in the article listed only 15 criteria). Contributions that qualify satisfactory for authorship include: a person had the original idea, designed the study, authored either first or later drafts, or approved final draft. Contributions that did not fulfill authorship requirements were: obtained grant, held a position of department head, referred patients, examined patients, collected samples, gave technical help, gave statistical help, and provided help with presentation. Contributions that *might* fulfill authorship responsibility were supervised data collection and analyzed data. Goodman, similar to Shapiro and colleagues, found that about one-third of the coauthors had not made a "'substantial contribution' to the intellectual content of the papers" (p. 1482) (Goodman, 1994). In 50 percent of the articles, the department head was listed as author and had fulfilled none of the criteria for authorship.

In the third survey, Slone mailed the first authors of 275 articles published in the *American Journal of Roentgenology* in 1992 and 1993 a questionnaire designed to establish the contributions of coauthors (Slone, 1996). According to the results, after the first author, each coauthor had a decreasing level of contribution to the work. Ninety-nine percent of first authors, 75 percent of second authors, 47 percent of third authors, 31 percent of fourth authors and 25 percent of fifth through tenth authors contributed to at least three of four categories: research design, data collection, data analysis, and manuscript preparation. The author admitted that since he asked only first authors for responses, their own contributions might have been overestimated, and other coauthors might have a different opinion. It is interesting to note that the percentages of contributions follow the same order assumed by Moulopoulos and colleagues: the first author contributed the most. Questions on individual contributions directed to each author in a coauthored work might produce different results.

Slone also asked first authors about undeserved or "gift authorship," a term used to describe the practice of listing a person as an author for a variety of reasons, none of which are related to actual contributions to the article. Responses indicated that, as the number of authors on an article increases, the number of gift authorship increases proportionately. Articles with three authors had a gift authorship rate of about 9 percent while articles with six or more authors had a gift authorship rate of about 30 percent. Reasons for conferring gift authorship included "out of a sense of obligation, out of fear of offending a colleague, or for merely referring cases" (p. 577). One in eight of the gift authors was a section chief or department head.

The practice of listing department chairs as authors was studied by Shulkin and colleagues (Shulkin, Goin, & Rennie, 1993). They tracked publications of 233 persons who were chairs of departments of medicine in U.S. medical schools for at least one year from 1979 to 1990. During these years, "there was no statistically significant decrease in the average number of articles per year for which the chairmen were last authors, and there was a significant increase in the average number of coauthors per year on published articles" (p. 688). The authors of the study admitted that they were "not able to determine the degree to which honorary authorship is still existent and functional," (p. 692) but hoped that this study would provide baseline data for future studies.

In a different slant on the issue of gift authorship, Eastwood questioned post-doctoral fellows. Of 1,005 mailed surveys, only 324 (32 percent) were returned. Of the 324 respondents almost one-half (48 percent) believed that being a laboratory head was sufficient qualification for being listed as an author. Slightly fewer (44 percent) thought that those who obtained funding should be listed as authors (Eastwood, Derish, Leash, & Orday, 1996). The viewpoint of these post-doctoral fellows seems to indicate that there is certainly ambiguity as to who can legitimately be given authorship credit, especially by those at the beginning their careers.

Smith wrote an editorial in the *BMJ* decrying the trend of adding the names of laboratory or department heads and highlighting a recent scandal in London. In this example a department head, in response to the discovery of a published, fraudulent piece of research he coauthored, dismissed himself from any personal responsibility by claiming: "The head of the department's name is always put on reports out of politeness. I was not part of this work." (p. 1456) (Smith, 1994).

Might coauthors, particularly gift authors, influence the outcome of the editorial peer review process? Is there a relationship between number of authors and acceptance rate? On one hand, several people contributing to a manuscript might produce a positive impact on the quality of the submitted manuscript. On the other hand, a single author might feel a personal responsibility to produce an acceptable manuscript, a responsibility not felt to the same degree by a group of coauthors.

*Question*

What is the impact of the number of authors per manuscript on the acceptance rate or quality of manuscript?

*Specific criteria*

~ any study that has examined a correlation between the number of authors per manuscript and its subsequent acceptance.

*Comparable studies*

In addition to the comment made by Zuckerman and Merton that 95 percent of coauthored manuscripts were accepted, two studies found a correlation between the number of authors per manuscript and its likelihood of acceptance (Gordon, 1980), (Presser, 1980). Gordon analyzed 1,859 submissions to a leading astronomy journal from 1968 to 1974. There was a significant relationship between the number of authors on a manuscript and its subsequent acceptance. Single-authored manuscripts had a 63 percent chance of acceptance; manuscripts with six or more authors had a 100 percent chance of acceptance.

Presser tested the hypothesis that researchers who collaborated produced a higher quality of research. Presser reviewed editorial decisions on all manuscripts submitted to *Sociometry* during 1976 and 1977. He divided the submissions into three disciplines: psychology, sociology, and other. For each group, a single-authored manuscript was more likely to be rejected than a manuscript with two or more authors. Presser concluded: "Authors who work with others are more likely to write higher quality papers, regardless of discipline" (p. 97). Presser equated acceptance with quality but did not test the articles for quality. Presser found a higher acceptance rate with coauthored manuscripts but did not take into account a possible reviewer bias in favor of multiple authorship. He assumed (possibly correctly and possibly incorrectly) that an accepted manuscript was *de facto* evidence of a higher quality manuscript.

A commonly accepted measure of an article's importance is the degree to which it is cited. Four studies have compared citation patterns of coauthored articles with single-authored articles (Oromaner, 1975), (Bayer, 1982), (Smart & Bayer, 1986), and (Bridgstock, 1991). Oromaner studied articles in three prominent sociology journals—*American Journal of Sociology*, *American Sociological Review*, and *Social Forces*—to trace any correlation between the number of authors and subsequent citation patterns. After 10 years, 42 percent of all articles had not been cited. Single-authored articles were less likely to be cited than multi-authored articles: 54

percent versus 62 percent. Each single-authored article received a mean of 2.3 citations, while the multi-authored articles received a mean of 2.6 citations in a 10-year period. While Bayer (Bayer, 1982, August) found that in the literature of marriage and the family eminent authors receive more citations than their lesser-known colleagues, there was no relationship between the number of authors on an article and any subsequent citation counts (p. 531).

Smart and Bayer address this same question with an analysis of 10-year citation patterns in the leading specialty journal in three fields representative of the applied sciences—clinical psychology, management science, and educational measurements (Smart & Bayer, 1986). All self-citations were excluded to eliminate the compounding influence of self-citations in coauthored works. There were consistently fewer citations for single-authored than for coauthored publications. In the 15 years since the randomly selected articles had been published, the coauthored articles had, depending on the journal, from 18 percent to 64 percent more citations than the single-authored articles. Bridgstock tested the hypothesis that published articles with more than one author are of a higher quality; higher quality was measured by citation analysis. Bridgstock analyzed 656 articles from four Australian journals and concluded, "it is hard to see a clear-cut case for believing that published papers with multiple authors are of a higher quality than papers with only a single author" (p. 43) (Bridgstock, 1991).

In a study that examined citation patterns within a group of researchers, Chubin and Studer determined that "individuals within laboratories project very similar citation profiles ... It is difficult to differentiate an individual from a laboratory ... This does not mean that citations cannot be used profitably for analysis, but rather they must be manipulated and interpreted with caution" (p. 180-181) (Chubin & Studer, 1979).

Two studies showed that coauthored works were more likely to be accepted than single-authored works. The authors did assume a correlation between the quality of a work and its acceptance. Studies found mixed results when they tried to determine if a coauthored article was of a higher quality than a single-authored article: two of four studies showed no correlation between the quality of an article as measured by citations to it and the number of coauthors. The Oromaner study did find more citations for the multi-authored articles but did not test this finding against single-authored articles for any statistically significant differences.

## Selecting journals for manuscript submission

After all authorship decisions have been made, particularly the number and order of coauthors, and the manuscript has been prepared for submission, a decision must be made as to where to submit the manuscript.

After a study of journal publication outlets of four departments in a medical school, Kochen and Tagliacozzo saw a need for a mathematical model to assist authors in selecting journals to submit their papers to (Kochen & Tagliacozzo,

1974). Authors from these four departments published in a variety of different journals over a four-year period—from six different journals for the authors in one department to 69 different journals for the authors in another department. The journal selection model was based on journal characteristics that included relevance, acceptance rate, circulation, prestige, and publication time lag. Kochen and Tagliacozzo viewed their work as the first step in developing "an author-journal matching service" (p. 209). However, they have apparently not published a follow-up study that tested this model or described if it had a practical application. Indeed, this particular article had not received any citation in *ISI's* citation databases through 1998.

Ludbrook offered advice to surgeons who were looking for a journal publication outlet that could be applied to almost any aspiring author: gain maximum exposure by selecting a journal that is covered by the major index in a field, choose a journal with an appropriate readership, and pick a journal that covers the subject matter of the manuscript (p. 329) (Ludbrook, 1991). Doering had similar advice for pharmacists: target the manuscript to a journal geared towards the readership you want, select a journal with "the best reputation and the highest standards, but one for which there is a realistic chance of their accepting the paper," (p. 8) and, finally, if the manuscript is rejected, select a journal with less prestige (Doering, 1991).

*Questions*

How do authors select a journal to which they want to submit a manuscript? Is there any evidence that the editorial peer review process is a deciding factor?

*Criteria*

~ any study that asks a group of authors what criteria they used to select a particular journal.

*Comparable studies*

Rotton and colleagues surveyed authors listed in the psychology section of 11 consecutive issues of *Current Contents: Social & Behavioral Sciences*, from October 1984 to January 1985 (Rotton et al., 1995). Almost all respondents (96.1 percent) reported that their last publication outlet was a refereed journal. This was the only journal selection criteria question asked by Rotton and, therefore, it is not included in the following discussion. By the type of questions asked in the following studies, it was clear that the authors assumed the journals they were asking about were refereed.

Six studies asked authors their reasons for selecting a particular journal (Table 4-2). Each supplied a list of criteria for the respondents to select from or rank.

Silverman queried members of the American Association of Higher Education (AAHE) and the Association of Professors of Higher Education (APHE) about their publication process (Silverman & Collins, 1975). Silverman found fairly high agreement, a Kendall Coefficient of Concordance of 0.82, among authors on their criteria for journal selection. He also found that most authors decided where to submit a manuscript before it was written: only 27 percent of APHE and 43 percent of AAHE members waited until after the manuscript was written before deciding where to submit it.

| Criteria \ Discipline | education[a*] | biomedical scientists[b] | organizational behavior[c] | biochemistry[d] | medical faculty[e] | medicine[f] | only one investigator listed criteria |
|---|---|---|---|---|---|---|---|
| journal's readership | 1,3 | 2 | 2 | 1 | 2 | 2 | |
| publication policies | 2,2 | | | 11,13 | | | |
| journal's prestige | 3,1 | 3 | 1 | | 1 | 3 | |
| subject coverage of journal | 4,5 | 1 | | 3 | 3 | 1 | |
| professional association publication | 5,6 | ** | | | | | |
| publication speed | 6,4 | ** | | 5 | 6 | 6 | |
| likelihood of acceptance | 7,8 | | 3 | 4 | 4 | | |
| solicited | 8,9 | | | | | | x |
| quality of review | 9,7 | | 4 | 2 | 8,11 | | |
| refereed journal | 10,10 | | | | 12 | | |
| know editorial board | | | | 12 | | | x |
| length of review process | | | 5 | 7 | | | |
| page charges | | ** | | 8 | | | |
| career benefit | | | | 9 | | | x |
| presentation of material | | | | 6,10 | | 4 | |
| circulation size | | | | | 5 | | x |
| quality of editorial staff | | | | | 7 | 5 | |
| prior publication | | | | | 9 | | x |
| recommendation of colleague | | | | | 10 | 7 | |
| likelihood of media coverage | | | | | 13 | | x |
| **Number of criteria** | 10 | 6 | 5 | 13 | 13 | 7 | |

a. (Silverman & Collins, 1975)
b. (Levitan, 1979)
c. (Mitchell, Beach, & Smith, 1985)
d. (Gordon, 1984)
e. (Frank, 1994)
f. (Weller, 1996)
* authors from two associations were queried;
** not considered important criteria

**Table 4-2: Ranking of journal selection criteria by authors**

Levitan asked a stratified sample of biomedical scientists one question about journal selection in a study about the importance of professional societies to them (Levitan, 1979). In her article, Levitan supplied only the authors' top three reasons for selecting a journal to publish in: readership, prestige, and subject of journal. Levitan found that authors did not consider a journal's connection with a learned society, speed of publication, or page charges as important journal-selection criteria. Mitchell and colleagues surveyed 357 members of professional societies affiliated with organizational behavior (Academy of Management, the Industrial/Organizational Division of the American Psychological Association, fellows of the American Psychological Association, and the Society of Organizational Behavior) and asked them to rank five journal-selection criteria (Mitchell, Beach, & Smith, 1985). Two hundred and three (57 percent) returned completed surveys. Gordon surveyed biochemists to determine which factors led to authors' decisions to select a particular journal (Gordon, 1984). The opinion that the journal's "refereeing of the scientific content ... would be competent and fair" (p. 35) was the second most frequently cited reason, just under the importance of journal readership, which ranked first. Frank asked all active clinical and research faculty from Stanford University School of Medicine about their journal selection criteria (Frank, 1994). The three most important criteria were the journal's prestige, readership, and subject coverage. Weller asked authors who had published in medical journals why they had selected a journal for an article that was identified within the survey instrument (Weller, 1996). Respondents in the Weller survey selected the same three most important criteria as in the Levitan and Frank studies, but in yet another order: subject coverage was first, followed by readership and then prestige.

Journal readership was one of the top three journal selection criteria in each of the six studies, all but one study found the journal's prestige was one of the top three criteria, and all but two listed subject coverage as one of the top three criteria. Speed of publication was mentioned in all but one study; however, one study found it not to be an important factor. The estimated likelihood of acceptance tended to rank about the middle of most studies. Those criteria ranked lower were such items as a personal knowledge of the editorial board, the way the material is presented in the journal, recommendations of colleagues, or the media attention the journal receives. Responses might be different, of course, if respondents were given a different set of criteria. It should be noted that many of the criteria that ranked rather low were only listed as criteria in one study. Criteria measured by only one investigation have been identified in Table 4-2 with an "x" the last column.

The authors' perception of the importance of the review process received mixed ratings: in one study it was ranked second out of 13 criteria, in another at the bottom of five criteria, and in two other studies near the bottom. The responses might indicate either the authors' lack of specific knowledge about the review process for a given journal or their ambiguous feelings about the review process as a criterion for journal selection.

## Value of the editorial peer review process to authors

Once a journal has been selected, how do authors view the resulting editorial peer review process? Do they consider it editorial advice that will help tighten up their manuscripts, or do they view it as essential in identifying or correcting potentially embarrassing errors, misinterpretation of data, or incorrect conclusions?

Certainly some authors feel frustrated with the editorial peer review process. Individual examples are in the literature, often in the form of letters to the editor, from authors who were unhappy with some aspect of the editorial peer review process. Some of these letters complain that manuscripts were rejected or harshly criticized for minor issues. A couple of examples of this occurrence from both an author and editor offer some insight into the problems. In a fairly typical commentary, one author complained that his manuscripts had been rejected and returned with only one of the two reviewers' reports. The returned report was generally positive; the editor refused to return the negative review (Evans, 1986). In this case, the author was left not knowing why the manuscript had been rejected. In another example, an editor pointed out that it is extremely difficult to know if an author has indeed made the suggested manuscript revisions. The editor complained that authors often submit a "curt letter with the revised manuscript saying that all the changes have been carried out" (p. 1328) (Morgan, 1986).

Bakanic, McPhail, and Simon suggested authors would derive more value from the review process if they understood it for a particular journal, if they considered how their manuscript matched with the journal, and if, when revising, they paid close attention to the reviewers' comments (Bakanic, McPhail, & Simon, 1990).

Several commentaries have suggested that authors be given the opportunity to provide a written feedback to editors about the reviews themselves (Hall, 1979) (Epstein, 1995) (Fine, 1996), particularly if a review is negative (Finke, 1990). Authors could also inform editors when they feel an inappropriate reviewer has been selected (Smith, 1977). Engaging the author in the evaluation of the reviews would provide valuable feedback to the editors.

Ruegg tested for overall quality of published articles and concluded that "experts are generally satisfied with the quality of the peer reviewed papers, but would like research articles to be more thoroughly treated from a statistical point of view" (p. 776) (Ruegg, 1996). But this study provided no comparative data on whether peer review had improved the articles.

*Questions*

Is there a measurable value of the review process from the perspective of the author?

*Specific criteria*

~ any study that identifies any measurable impact of value or importance of the editorial peer review process from the author's perspective.

*Comparable studies*

Ten studies were identified that asked authors about their experience with the review process. Each study used a survey instrument; each asked somewhat different questions. Information from these studies has been summarized in Table 4-3.

Bradley (Bradley, 1981) asked authors who belonged to the American Psychological Association, Psychonomic Society, or the American Statistical Association about their most recent "compulsorily revised" article. Almost three-quarters of respondents to each of three questions felt that some changes requested by the reviewers were the result of a "whim, bias, or personal preference," that changes were requested to make the author conform to the "strictly subjective preferences of the editors and/or referees," or that comments both trivial and important were incorrect (p. 32). However, 72 percent of these same respondents believed that the review process improved the quality of their manuscript, but the survey did not asked for details on how manuscripts were improved from the authors' perspective. Similarly, 87 percent of members of the Psychonomic Society thought that the quality of editorial revisions requested justified the time needed to make the changes (p. 33). The Bradley study asked questions in a particularly negative way, which may account for some of the negative attitudes of the authors. A question like "Have you ever felt that referees try to find something to object to just to convince the editor that they have done a conscientious job?" (p. 33) might by making the suggestion elicit agreement (which it did 65 percent of the time).

Mitchell found that 50 percent of authors publishing in organizational behavior journals did not need to make any revisions to their articles prior to publication, and if they did, the revisions were only minor (Mitchell et al., 1985). One in four papers from "fellows," who were presumably the more senior members of the group, had undergone major revisions prior to acceptance while the proportion was significantly more for nonfellows—two out of three. The vast majority of authors favored blind review. However, fellows preferred to have the option of having a blind review while nonfellows preferred all manuscripts be blinded. This later result suggests the lesser-known researchers might have felt more comfortable with reviewers not knowing who they were.

Cofer identified a direct relationship between manuscript acceptance and ultimate satisfaction with the review process (Cofer, 1985). He asked the editors of 17 American Psychological Association journals to provide the names of the 15 most recently accepted and the 15 most recently rejected manuscripts. Eighty percent of the authors were satisfied with the process if their manuscript had been accepted. On the other hand, only about half that percentage (39 percent) were satisfied with the process if their manuscript had been rejected.

Cowen and colleagues surveyed authors who had revised manuscripts prior to their acceptance by American Psychological Association journals. Cowen was able to determine when an article had been revised by the presence of two sets

| Discipline of authors studied | Number | Satisfied with process | Process improved quality of article | Revisions | Conclusions | References |
|---|---|---|---|---|---|---|
| *psychology & statistics* | 411 | 64% | 72% | all | Respondents had overwhelming support for the peer review system. | (Bradley, 1981) |
| *organizational behavior* | 203 | | 25% had major revisions | 50% | Respondents viewed review process as subjective and lacking reliable judgments. | (Mitchell et al., 1985) |
| *psychology* | 1,020 | 80% when accepted; 39% when rejected | 87% | | Respondents found reviewers' and editors' comments helpful. | (Cofer, 1985) |
| *psychology* | 483 | editorial process viewed favorably | moderately | took ~20 hours | Respondents thought it was hard to judge the extent of article improvement. | (Cowen, Spinell, Hightower, & Lotyczewski, 1987) |
| *pediatrics* | 90 | accepted evaluate reviews more favorably | 60-70% | | Authors of accepted manuscripts more likely to respond to survey. Authors of rejected manuscripts found reviews helpful. | (Garfunkel, Lawson, Hamrick, & Ulshen, 1990) |
| *communication* | 215 | | | | Respondents had more satisfaction with communication than outcome. Quality or value of reviews viewed as moderately helpful. | (Leslie, 1990) |
| *economics* | 87 | relationship between helpful comments and subsequent citations | | | Study found articles with longer reviewers' reports cited more. | (Laband, 1990) |
| *agronomy* | | most had positive experience | improves quality | | Respondents thought better journals had a better review process. | (Mayland, Sojka, & Gbur, 1991) |
| *anesthesiology* | 95 | accepted viewed process more favorably | | | Respondents of rejected manuscripts found reviewers comments helpful. | (Sweitzer & Cullen, 1994) |
| *medicine* | 479 | 60% | 51-56% | averaged from 1.1 to 1.2 times | Respondents thought peer review had the greatest impact on the presentation of the manuscript. | (Weller, 1996) |

**Table 4-3: Value of the editorial peer review process to authors**

of dates on the published article (Cowen, Spinell, Hightower, & Lotyczewski, 1987). The report provided little data from the survey, but the results did make Cowen wonder if the "net gain for the field resulting from manuscript revision always exceeds the net cost" (p. 404).

Garfunkel and colleagues also found that authors of accepted manuscripts viewed the review process more favorably than authors of rejected manuscripts

(Garfunkel, Lawson, Hamrick, & Ulshen, 1990). Leslie asked a random sample of members of the Association for Education in Journalism and Mass Communication about the manuscript submission and editorial peer review process (Leslie, 1990). The process viewed most positively was the relatively minor step of acknowledging receipt of the manuscript. Two elements viewed least positively were the time the review process took and the reasons the editor gave for rejection.

One study used an interesting methodology: Laband received copies of reviewers' reports and correlated the length of the review with subsequent citations to the articles. He found "referees' comments demonstrate a positive impact on subsequent citation of papers, while comments made by editors showed no such impact" (p. 341) (Laband, 1990).

Mayland and colleagues surveyed a sample of members of the American Society of Agronomy on their experience with the peer review process (Mayland, Sojka, & Gbur, 1991). Data from the study were not available, but according to the researchers, in agronomy few authors had negative experiences with editorial peer review and most of their time with the process was spent revising manuscripts.

Sweitzer and Cullen asked authors who had submitted manuscripts to the *Journal of Clinical Anesthesia* specific questions about their experience with editorial peer review (Sweitzer & Cullen, 1994). More authors of accepted manuscripts responded and these authors were also more satisfied with the process than those who had been rejected. In a random sample of authors who had published in two groups of medical journals, Weller found that more than 60 percent of all authors felt that reviewers understood the manuscript, about 50 percent felt reviews offered constructive suggestions, about 35 percent thought the review improved the content of the manuscript, and about 20 percent felt the review clarified conclusions in the article (Weller, 1996). Only 2 percent to 3 percent of the respondents said that conclusions had actually been changed, and 6 percent to 10 percent considered the statistical analysis improved. Authors had very similar opinions regardless of whether the manuscript had first been rejected.

Except for the Cofer and the Sweitzer and Cullen studies, all studies examined authors of published articles; this group of respondents might to be kinder in their replies than authors of unpublished manuscripts. Authors readily admit that the review process improves the quality of their manuscript and that is the goal of peer review. But the degree of any substantive improvement was less clear.

## Authorship guidelines and definition

In 1953, Alexander defined authorship as "the contribution of creative thinking to the achievement of science" (p. 281) (Alexander, 1953). Has this lofty definition been replaced by a prescriptive one? Silverman maintained that the major contributor to a project should be the first author (Silverman & Collins, 1975). In 1982, the *New Zealand Journal of Medicine* had a policy that required each manuscript be accompanied by "a statement in writing from all authors that they had read and agreed to its publication" (p. 498) (Robinson, 1982). Huth suggested that there should be "wide and public acceptance among all scientific disciplines of clearly defined and specific criteria for authorship" (p. 258) (Huth, 1986b). Friesinger, concerned that journals did not have "a policy that judges the legitimacy of authorship" (p. 1241), developed a set of three requirements for authorship (Friesinger, 1986):

• One who provides critical suggestions and guidelines for the total project

• One who provides critical help with data collection

• One who provides critical help with data analysis and writing (p. 1241)

In 1986, Huth (Figure 4-2) published five principles of authorship (Huth, 1986a). These have been discussed and reworked by the International Committee of Medical Journal Editors (ICMJE), which now has a similar definition. Professional associations often publish manuals designed to help authors who desire to publish in their journals. Two examples also in Figure 4-2 are from the American Psychological Association and the American Chemical Society (American Psychological Association, 1994) (American Chemical Society, 1997).

The Council of Biology Editors advised researchers to decide who will be an author early in a project and provided a basic requirement for authorship: "an author should be able to take public responsibility for the content of the paper," (p. 593) including responding to any letters to the editors (Fotion & Conrad, 1984). Fotion emphasized that this approach to authorship meant that each author had a two-fold responsibility, both to participate and to understand any research project.

Nehring and Durham developed a set of 14 guidelines for authors contemplating collaboration (Nehring & Durham, 1986). Most suggestions focused on decision and communication issues in a joint project. Those particularly related to joint authorship include: establish criteria for participation; decide on order of credit (i.e., order of authorship); determine who will prepare drafts and rewrites; and, decide who will correspond with the editor. Houk and Thacker listed eight principles of authorship: origin of ideas; design; data collection; leadership; analysis and interpretation of the data; writing; review of final manuscript; and ability to defend the article publicly (Houk & Thacker, 1991). The *Journal of the American Medical Association* (*JAMA*) stated it simply: "It is first essential to decide who is an author and who is not" (p. 1857) and the first author is the person who contributed the most (Riesenberg & Lundberg, 1990).

In a set of 16 recommendations made by the Institute of Medicine in *The Responsible Conduct of Research in the Health Sciences*, one recommendation was directed at journals: "scientific journals should develop policies to promote responsible authorship practices" (p. 46) (Hollander, 1990).

The National Psychosis Research Framework established guidelines for authorship in multicenter collaborations (Barker & Powell, 1997). The first guideline

## Huth's principles

*Principle 1:*
Each author should have participated sufficiently in the work represented by the article to take public responsibility for the content.

*Principle 2:*
Participation must include three steps: (1) conception or design of the work represented by the article, or analysis and interpretation of the data, or both; (2) drafting the article or revising it for critically important content; and (3) final approval of the version to be published.

*Principle 3:*
Participation solely in the collection of data (or other evidence) does not justify authorship.

*Principle 4:*
Each part of the content of an article critical to its main conclusions and each step in the work that led to its publication (steps 1, 2, and 3 in Principle 2) must be attributable to at least one author.

*Principle 5:*
Persons who had contributed intellectually to the article but whose contributions do not justify authorship may be named and their contribution described—for example, "advice," "critical review of study proposal," "data collection," "participation in clinical trial." Such persons must have given their permission to be named. Technical help must be acknowledged in a separate paragraph (p. 269) (Huth, 1986a)

## International Committee of Medical Journal Editors' principles

Each author should have participated sufficiently in the work to take public responsibility for the content. Authorship credit should be based only on substantial contributions to (a) either the conception and design or the analysis and interpretation of the data and to (b) drafting the article or revising it critically for important intellectual content and on (c) final approval of the version to be published. All three conditions must be met. Participation solely in the acquisition of funding or the collection of data does not justify authorship. General supervision of a research group is not sufficient for authorship ... Editors may ask authors to describe what each contributed; this information may be published (p. 272) (International Committee of Medical Journal Editors, 1997).

## The American Psychological Association's definition

Authorship is reserved for persons who make a primary contribution to and hold primary responsibility for the data, concepts, and interpretation of results of a published work. Authorship encompasses not only those who do the actual writing but also those who have made substantial scientific contributions to a study (p. 4) (American Psychological Association, 1994).

## The American Chemical Society's definition of coauthorship
### #11 in a set of 12 ethical guidelines of an author

The co-authors of a paper should be all those persons who have made significant contributions to the work reported and who share responsibility and accountability for the results. Other contributions should be indicated in a footnote or an "Acknowledgments" section. An administrative relationship to the investigation does not of itself qualify a person for co-authorship (but occasionally it may be appropriate to acknowledge major administrative assistance) ... The author who submits a manuscript for publication accepts the responsibility of having included as co-authors all persons appropriate and none inappropriate. The submitting author should have sent each living co-author a draft copy of the manuscript and have obtained the co-author's assent to co-authorship of it (p. 421) (American Chemical Society, 1997).

**Figure 4-2: Principles and definitions of authorship**

is to decide on allocation of authorship early in a project. The order of authorship should reflect relative contributions, the final draft must be circulated to all authors at all sites, collaborating authors must be acknowledged in each presentation, and papers with data from more than one site should acknowledge that fact.

The *New England Journal of Medicine* instituted "fairly liberal" guidelines for ascribing responsibility of authorship and acknowledgments (Kassirer & Angell, 1991). These guidelines included: authorship by a group is not acceptable; if there are more than eight authors (or 12 from a multicenter trial), each author must sign an authorship statement; and space for acknowledgments is limited.

In addition to a published set of guidelines, Lundberg and Flanagin, editors of *JAMA*, announced in a 1989 editorial that all authors were required to sign a statement validating authorship and ensuring that they (p. 2003-2004) (Lundberg & Flanagin, 1989):

- certify sufficient participation in the work to take public responsibility for it.

- vouch for the validity of the work.

- have reviewed and approved of the final version of the manuscript.

- ensure that the information has not been previously and will not be subsequently published elsewhere without permission of the editor.

- are able to produce data on which the manuscript is based for examination if requested by the editors.

These requirements were then added to the journal's instructions to authors. Lundberg and Flanagin took this step for a number of reasons:

> *Pressures to publish, increased competition in the research and academic communities, and inadequate education of researchers and authors have allowed naïve authors to unknowingly transgress the ill-defined boundaries of publication and authorial ethics, and a lack of formal policies (or enforcement thereof) has allowed dishonest authors to intentionally deceive* (p. 2003).

In a policy slightly different from the *New England Journal of Medicine*, *JAMA* required that when authorship is attributed to a collaborative group, each member of the group must meet full authorship requirements (Glass, 1992). By 1996, *JAMA's* editors further codified authorship responsibility by requiring each author to sign the following very precise statement (Lundberg & Glass, 1996):

> *I have participated sufficiently in the conception and design of this work and the analysis of the data (when applicable) as well as the writing of the manuscript, to take public responsibility for it. I believe the manuscript represents valid work. I have reviewed the final version of the manuscript and approve*

*it for publication. Neither this manuscript nor one with sub-*
*stantially similar content under my authorship has been pub-*
*lished or is being considered for publication elsewhere, except*
*as described in an attachment. If requested, I shall produce*
*the data upon which the manuscript is based for examination*
*by the editors or their assignees (p. 75).*

*JAMA's* editors questioned the appropriateness of the ICMJE's definition
(Figure 4-2) because of "incomplete application of this definition, the proliferation of multiple authorship, and other concerns" (p. 75). They invited the *JAMA's*
readership to share their views on the usefulness of the ICMJE statement.

A meeting was convened in Nottingham in 1996 with representatives from the
ICMJE and other editors and researchers interested in considering the need for a
new definition of authorship (Horton & Smith, 1996a). One outcome of this meeting was the suggestion that "authorship" be replaced by a set of credits similar to
those used in film credits. The use of such terms as "contributor, department head"
or "statistician" would make the role of each contributor clear (Godlee, 1996). Previously several members of the medical statistics department at the University of
Southampton had offered the opinion that merely acknowledging a statistician
does "not guarantee that appropriate statistical analysis has been done or its interpretation published" (p. 869). They wanted statisticians' work to be recognized by
permitting them to be coauthors (Mullee, Lampe, Pickering, & Julious, 1995).

A new version of the *Uniform Requirements for Manuscripts Submitted to
Biomedical Journals* was published by the International Committee of Medical
Journal Editors in 1997 with a revised definition of authorship (Figure 4-2) (International Committee of Medical Journal Editors, 1997). In August of 1997,
*JAMA* published a special communication that summarized the recent discourse
on authorship responsibility. Rennie, Yank, and Emanuel proposed "a radical
conceptual and systematic change, to reflect the realities of multiple authorship
and to buttress accountability" (p. 579) (Rennie, Yank, & Emanuel, 1997).
Rather than use the term "author," Rennie, Yank, and Emanuel supported using
the term "contributor" for the person who was "fully responsible for the por-
tions of the work they performed and have some obligation to hold one another
to standards of integrity" (p 582). They also defined "guarantors" as "those who
have contributed substantially but who also have made added efforts to ensure
the integrity of the entire project. They organize, oversee, double-check, and
must be prepared to be accountable for all parts of the completed manuscript,
before and after publication" (p. 582). The Rennie, Yank, and Emanuel editorial in *JAMA* also pointed out that the *Uniform Requirements* have added a sen-
tence to their statement: "Editors may require authors to justify the assignment
of authorship" (p. 581).

The *BMJ* began using a set of definitions similar to *JAMA*'s. The *BMJ*
thought authors should experiment with using the designations of contributors
and guarantors, when appropriate, and were also willing to engage in a debate

on this topic (Smith, 1997a). Smith stated that *BMJ* would, when authors wanted it, publish a list of contributors and guarantors (Smith, 1997b). Also in 1997, Horton announced that *Lancet* would publish at the end of each article a list of "contributors" and their respective roles (Horton, 1997).

Some editors in the medical community have questioned the appropriateness of the term author. Time will tell if the suggestion to "abandon authorship" becomes a reality, has an impact on authorship responsibility, or reverses the trend toward increased coauthorship.

## *Limitations of studies on authorship*

- Results of the studies on authors' criteria for selecting journals to submit to provide limited insight into the place of the editorial peer review process in journal selection.

- There has not been a study like the one Mould suggested: to determine the contributions of each author in a group of coauthored articles.

- In the three studies of the contributions of coauthors, only first authors were asked to respond. Other coauthors might have a perspective different from the first author concerning each one's relative contribution. Real reasons may be difficult to identify or verify.

- Studies of the value of peer review from an author's perspective were few and had very limited findings.

- There has been little written about "salami science," or publication of the "least publishable unit." This practice obtains multiple publications from one study. This issue probably needs to be addressed by the groups and organizations that have tried to tighten the definition of authorship (Huth, 1992).

## *Recommendations*

- The role of individual authors in collaboration studies needs more study. Studies need a design that does not limit the investigation to the first author's perspective. Each investigator that studied this question seemed to assume that the first author did indeed make the largest contribution to the work. This assumption needs to be tested.

- A study on authors' attitudes towards receiving "credits" similar to the film industry in lieu of authorship is worth exploring.

## Conclusions about authors

From this discussion, it is clear that authorship credit is not a straightforward issued. From these studies, it is also clear that the trend toward an increasing number of authors per article continues; in fact most articles now are coauthored. At the same time some editors, particularly in medicine, are paying a great deal of attention to authorship responsibility and definitions. Data on whether coauthorship influences the editorial peer review process are limited. While editors are working on new definitions of authorship, there is little evidence that these definitions have had a measurable influence on trends in coauthorship or gift authorship.

Some argue that those who secured a grant have the right to be listed as an author on an article resulting from the funding. Others argue that a department head should be considered a legitimate "author" if he or she provides not only space, consultation, supplies, and personnel, but also input that generates the ideas for a research project.

If the editorial peer review process were blinded, the reviewers would of course also not know the number of authors or if an author was a department head. See Chapter Seven for more on blind review.

The degree or value of peer review from an author's perspective appears to be linked to the acceptance or rejection of a manuscript. But it is interesting to note that even after a manuscript has initially been reject, once it has been accepted, the author favorably views the review process.

It is possible that single-authored manuscripts are rejected at a higher rate than coauthored manuscripts because they are not as well written, the science is not as important, or the analysis is not as thorough as in a coauthored article. A few studies that compared the quality of single-authored versus coauthored articles had mixed results.

Authorship questions have received a lot of attention in the medical journal community. Even with the attention, not all those in medicine are aware of the ongoing discussions. Bhopal and colleagues queried 66 researchers about their awareness of the criteria for authorship as defined by the ICMJE (Bhopal et al., 1997). While 50 percent had heard of the ICMJE, only 24 percent were aware of the authorship criteria. And only 62 percent believed that ICMJE criteria for authorship were needed. Bhopal and colleagues suggested that "future criteria should be agreed by researchers and editors and should give weight to important practical contributions to research" (p. 1012). The same sentiment was expressed by Shulkin after a study of publication patterns of department chairs: "Changes in the definition of authorship by medical journal editors did not seem to be important influences on the authorship patterns of chairman" (p. 688) (Shulkin et al., 1993).

Huth proposed that editors might have to take responsibility for some of the issues surrounding the "authorship problem." "Unfortunately editors have not always translated their views into exact statements in their "information for authors" pages on what they see as responsible and irresponsible authorship. But even if more did, how many authors would follow the rules? Experienced editors see all too often plenty of evidence that their information pages are unseen or ignored. What is needed is the right ethos." (p. 1063) (Huth, 1992). Horton and Smith lamented that the ICMJE's definition of authorship is "commonly ignored" and, if nothing else, shows that "the ideas of researchers and editors on authorship differ substantially" (p. 723) (Horton & Smith, 1996b). Many of the recommendations may be made in an attempt to promote ethical behavior. It is difficult to mandate ethics.

Perhaps Benson summed up the authorship problem best with his assertion that editors' measures included "attempts to provide novel definitions for authorship, requirements to sign statements of authorial responsibility, numerical rankings devised to list authors according to the level of contribution, multiple categories of authorship to recognize the expansion of the notion of a scientific author, and the simple expedient of alphabetizing all the contributing authors. But all these only recognize that a problem exists and offer alternatives to regulate the symptom rather than calling for a cure" (p. 329-330) (Benson, 1991). The cure: "only persons who conduct and write the research should be allowed to be listed as author" (p. 330). Of course, deciding on who those persons actually are is the heart of the problem.

The authorship problem has provided many editorial comments and very few studies, particularly regarding its relationship to the editorial peer review process. While the attempts by editors to control the proliferation of coauthorship may be well-meant and perhaps worthy, factors such as an author's need to publish for continued funding of research projects, the publication requirements of academic institutions, and the complexity of research projects will all work to keep the authorship problem unresolved for the present.

## References

Ahmed, S. M., Maurana, C. A., Engle, J. A., Uddin, D. E., & Glaus, K. D. (1997, January). A method of assigning authorship in multiauthored publications. *Family Medicine, 29*(1), 42-44.

Alexander, R. S. (1953, July). Trends in authorship. *Circulation Research, 1*(4), 281-283.

Alvarez-Dardet, C., Gascon, E., Mur, P., & Nolasco, A. (1985, June 6). 10-year trends in the Journal's publication. *New England Journal of Medicine, 312*(23), 1521-1522.

American Chemical Society. (1997). *The ACS style guide.* (2nd ed.). Washington, DC: American Chemical Society.

American Psychological Association. (1994). *Publication manual of the American Psychological Association.* (4th ed.). Washington DC: American Psychological Association.

Bakanic, V., McPhail, C., & Simon, R. J. (1990, Winter). If at first you don't succeed: review procedures for revised and resubmitted manuscripts. *American Sociologist, 21*(4), 373-391.

Barker, A. & Powell, R. A. (1997, April 5). Authorship: guidelines exist on ownership of data and authorship in multicentre collaborations. *British Medical Journal, 314*(7086), 1046.

Bayer, A. E. (1982, August). A bibliometric analysis of marriage and family literature. *Journal of Marriage and the Family, 44*(3), 527-538.

Bayer, A. E. & Smart, J. C. (1991, November/December). Career publication patterns and collaborative "styles" in American academic science. *Journal of Higher Education, 62*(6), 613-636.

Benson, K. R. (1991). Science and the single author: historical reflections on the problem of authorship. *Cancer Bulletin, 43*(4), 324-331.

Bhopal, R., Rankin, J., McColl, E., Thomas, L., Kaner, E., Stacy, R., Pearson, P., Vernon, B., & Rodgers, H. (1997, April 5). The vexed question of authorship: views of researchers in a British medical faculty. *British Medical Journal, 314*(7086), 1009-1012.

Bradley, J. V. (1981, January). Pernicious publication practices. *Bulletin of the Psychonomic Society, 18*(1), 31-34.

Bridgstock, M. (1991, September). The quality of single and multiple authored papers; an unresolved problem. *Scientometrics, 21*(1), 37-48.

Burman, K. D. (1982, October). "Hanging from the masthead": reflections on authorship. *Annals of Internal Medicine, 97*(4), 602-605.

Chew, F. S. (1986, November). The scientific literature in diagnostic radiology for American readers: a survey and analysis of journals, papers, and authors. *American Journal of Roentgenology, 147*, 1055-1061.

Chubin, D. E. & Studer, K. E. (1979). Knowledge and structures of scientific growth. *Scientometrics, 1*(2), 171-193.

Cofer, C. N. (1985). Some reactions to manuscript review from a questionnaire study. *Behavioral and Brain Sciences, 8*(4), 745-746.

Comroe, J. H., Jr. (1976). Publish and/or perish. *American Review of Respiratory Disease, 113*, 561-565.

Cowen, E. L., Spinell, A., Hightower, A. D., & Lotyczewski, B. S. (1987, April). Author reaction to the manuscript review process. *American Psychologist, 42*(4), 403-405.

Cunningham, S. J. & Dillon, S. M. (1997). Authorship patterns in information systems. *Scientometrics, 39*(1), 19-27.

Dardik, H. (1977, September). Multiple authorship. *Surgery, Gynecology, and Obstetrics, 145*, 418.

Diamond, D. (1969, June 26). Multi-authorship explosion. *New England Journal of Medicine, 280*(26), 1484-1485.

Doering, P. L. (1991, September). Writing & reviewing for pharmacy journals. *Florida Pharmacy Today, 55*, 7-11.

Eastwood, S., Derish, P., Leash, E., & Orday, S. (1996). Ethical issues in biomedical research: perceptions and practices of post-doctoral research fellows responding to a survey. *Science and Engineering Ethics, 2*, 89-114.

Epstein, R. J. (1993, March 20). Six authors in search of a citation: villains or victims of the Vancouver convention? *British Medical Journal, 306*(6880), 765-767.

Epstein, S. (1995, October). What can be done to improve the journal review process. *American Psychologist, 50*(9), 883-885.

Evans, R. W. (1986, January 18). Disclosure of journal referees' reports. *Lancet, 1*(8473), 158.

Fine, M. A. (1996, November). Reflections on enhancing accountability in the peer review process. *American Psychologist, 51*(11), 1190-1191.

Finke, R. A. (1990, May). Recommendations for contemporary editorial practices. *American Psychologist, 45*(5), 669-670.

Fletcher, R. H., & Fletcher, S. W. (1979, July 26). Clinical research in general medical journals. *New England Journal of Medicine, 301*(4), 180-183.

Fotion, N., & Conrad, C. C. (1984). Authorship and other credits. *Annals of Internal Medicine, 100*, 592-594.

Frank, E. (1994, July 13). Authors' criteria for selecting journals. *JAMA, 272*(2), 163-164.

Friesinger, G. C. (1986, November). Who should be author? *Journal of the American College of Cardiology, 8*(5), 1240-1243.

Garfunkel, J. M., Lawson, E. E., Hamrick, H. J., & Ulshen, M. H. (1990, March 9). Effect of acceptance or rejection on the author's evaluation of peer review of manuscripts. *JAMA, 263*(10), 1376-1378.

Glass, R. M. (1992, July 1). New information for authors and readers: grouped authorship, acknowledgments, and rejected manuscripts. *JAMA, 268*(1), 99.

Godlee, F. (1996, June 15). Definition of "authorship" may be changed. *British Medical Journal, 312*(7045), 1501-1502.

Goodman, N. W. (1994, December 3). Survey of fulfillment of criteria for authorship in published medical journals. *British Medical Journal, 309*(6967), 1482.

Gordon, M. D. (1980). A critical assessment of inferred relations between multiple authors, scientific collaboration, the production of papers and their acceptance for publication. *Scientometrics, 2*(3), 193-201.

Gordon, M. D. (1984, February). How authors select journals: a test of the reward maximization model of submission behavior. *Social Studies of Science, 14*(1), 27-43.

Hall, J. A. (1979, September). Author review of reviewers. *American Psychologist, 34*(9), 798.

Harsanyi, M. A. (1993). Multiple authors, multiple problems—bibliometrics and the study of scholarly collaboration: a literature review. *Library and Information Science Research, 15*, 325-354.

Hayden, G. F. & Saulsbury, F. T. (1982, July). A review of the *Journal of Pediatrics*: the first 50 years. *Journal of Pediatrics, 101*(1), 5-11.

Hollander, R. D. (1990, Winter). Journals have obligations, too: commentary on "confirmational response bias." *Science, Technology, & Human Values, 15*(1), 46-49.

Horton, R. (1997, June 5). The signature of responsibility. *Lancet, 350*(9070), 5-6.

Horton, R. & Smith, R. (1996, March 23a). Signing up for authorship. *Lancet, 347*(9004), 780.

Horton, R. & Smith, R. (1996, March 23b). Time to redefine authorship. *British Medical Journal, 312*(7033), 723.

Houk, V. N. & Thacker, S. B. (1991, October). The responsibilities of scientific authorship. *Scholarly Publishing, 23*(1), 51-55.

Huth, E. J. (1983, August). Responsibility of coauthorship. *Annals of Internal Medicine, 99*(2), 266-267.

Huth, E. J. (1984, January). Abuses of authorship. *Annals of Internal Medicine, 100*(1), 147-148.

Huth, E. J. (1986, February-a). Guidelines on authorship of medical papers. *Annals of Internal Medicine, 104*(2), 269-274.

Huth, E. J. (1986, February-b). Irresponsible authorship and wasteful publications. *Annals of Internal Medicine, 104*(2), 257-259.

Huth, E. J. (1992, August). Journals and authors; rules, principles, and ethos. *Diabetes Care, 15*(8), 1062-1064.

International Committee of Medical Journal Editors. (1997, January 15). Uniform requirements for manuscripts submitted to biomedical journals. *Canadian Medical Association Journal, 156*(2), 270-277.

Kassirer, J. P. & Angell, M. (1991, November 21). On authorship and acknowledgments. *New England Journal of Medicine, 325*(21), 1510-1512.

Kochen, M. & Tagliacozzo, R. (1974, May/June). Matching authors and readers of scientific papers. *Information Storage and Retrieval, 10*(5/6), 197-210.

Laband, D. N. (1990, May). Is there value-added from the review process in economics? Preliminary evidence from authors. *Quarterly Journal of Economics, 105*(2), 341-352.

Leslie, L. Z. (1990, April). Peer practices of mass communication scholarly journals. *Education Review, 14*(2), 151-165.

Levitan, K. B. (1979). Scientific societies and their journals: Biomedical scientists assess the relationship. *Social Studies of Science, 9*(3), 393-400.

Ludbrook, J. (1991). Where should I submit my surgical manuscript. *Australian and New Zealand Journal of Surgery, 61*, 329-331.

Lundberg, G. D., & Flanagin, A. (1989, October 13). New requirements for authors: signed statements of authorship responsibility and financial disclosure. *JAMA, 262*(14), 2003-2004.

Lundberg, G. D. & Glass, R. M. (1996, July 3). What does authorship mean in a peer-reviewed medical journal. *JAMA, 276*(1), 75.

Mayland, H. F., Sojka, R. E., & Gbur, E. E. (1991). The peer-review process under review. *Journal of Animal Science, 69*(Supplement 1), 228.

McNamee, S. J. & Willis, C. L. (1994, June). Stratification in science. *Knowledge: Creation, Diffusion, and Utilization, 15*(4), 396-416.

Mitchell, T. R., Beach, L. R., & Smith, K. G. (1985). Some data on publishing from the authors' and reviewers' perspective. In L. L. Cummings & P. J. Frost (Eds.), *Publishing in the organizational sciences* (pp. 248-264). Homewood, IL: Richard D. Irwin, Inc.

Morgan, P. P. (1986, June 15). The joys of revising a manuscript. *Canadian Medical Association Journal, 134*, 1328.

Morton, H. C. & Price, A. J. (1986, Summer). The ACLS survey of scholars. Views on publications, computers, libraries. *Scholarly Communication, 5*(1-16).

Mould, S. M. (1986, April 12). Analysis of authorship. *British Medical Journal, 292*, 1017.

Moulopoulos, S. D., Sideris, D. A., & Georgilis, K. A. (1983, November 26). Individual contributions to multiauthor papers. *British Medical Journal, 287*, 1608-1609.

Mullee, M. A., Lampe, F. C., Pickering, R. M., & Julious, S. A. (1995, April 1). Statisticians should be coauthors. *British Medical Journal, 310*, 869.

Mussurakis, S. (1993). Coauthorship trends in the leading radiological journals. *Acta Radiologica, 34*(4), 316-320.

Mylonas, C. (1992). Research in neurosurgical journals. *British Journal of Neurosurgery, 6*(1), 41-46.

Nehring, W. & Durham, J. D. (1986, January-February). Multiple authorship and professional advancement. *Dimensions of Critical Care Nursing, 5*(1), 58-62.

Oliver, M. F. (1995, March 18). AI, or the anonymity of authorship. *Lancet, 345*(8951), 668.

Onwude, J. L., Staines, A., & Lilford, R. J. (1993, May 15). Multiple author trend worst in medicine. *British Medical Journal, 306*, 1345.

Oromaner, M. (1975, January). Collaboration and impact: the career of multi-authored publications. *Social Science Information, 14*(1), 147-155.

Over, R. (1982, September). Collaborative research and publication in psychology. *American Psychologist, 37*(9), 996-1001.

Presser, S. (1980, February). Collaboration and the quality of research. *Social Studies of Science, 10*(1), 95-101.

Price, D. J. D. S. (1963). *Little science, big science*. New York: Columbia University Press.

Rennie, D. & Flanagin, A. (1994, February 9). Authorship! Authorship! Guests, ghosts, grafters, and the two-sided coin. *JAMA, 271*(6), 469-471.

Rennie, D., Yank, V., & Emanuel, L. (1997, August 20). When authorship fails, a proposal to make contributions accountable. *JAMA, 278*(7), 579-585.

Riesenberg, D. & Lundberg, G. D. (1990, October 10). The order of authorship: who's on first. *JAMA, 264*(14), 1857.

Robinson, R. G. (1982, July 28). The manuscript 1982. *New Zealand Medical Journal, 95*(712), 498.

Rosenthal, R. (1979, May). The "file drawer problem" and tolerance for null results. *Psychological Bulletin, 86*(3), 638-641.

Rotton, J., Foos, P., Van Meek, L., & Levitt, M. (1995). Publication practices and the file drawer problem: a survey of published authors. *Journal of Social Behavior and Personality, 10*(1), 1-13.

Ruegg, M. W. (1996). Study on the quality of peer reviewed articles published in *'lwt'*. *Lebensm.-Wiss. u.-Technol (Food and Science Technology), 29*(8), 776-780.

Sampson, Z. J. (1995). Authorship counts: forty years of the *Physical Review* and *Physical Review Letters. Scientometrics, 32*(2), 219-226.

Satyanarayana, K. & Ratnakar, K. V. (1989, September). Authorship patterns in life sciences, preclinical basic and clinical research papers. *Scientometrics, 17*(3-4), 363-371.

Schiedermayer, D. L. & Siegler, M. (1986, October). Believing what you read, responsibilities of medical authors and editors. *Archives of Internal Medicine, 146*(10), 2043-2044.

Schmidt, R. H. (1987). A worksheet for authorship of scientific articles. *Bulletin of the Ecological Society of America, 68*, 8-10.

Shapiro, D. W., Wenger, N. S., & Shapiro, M. F. (1994, February 9). The contributions of authors to multiauthored biomedical research papers. *JAMA, 271*(6), 438-442.

Shulkin, D. J., Goin, J. E., & Rennie, D. (1993, September). Pattern of authorship among chairman of departments of medicine. *Academic Medicine, 9*, 688-692.

Silverman, R. J. & Collins, E. L. (1975). Publishing relationships in higher education. *Research in Higher Education, 3*, 365-382.

Slone, R. M. (1996, September). Coauthors' contributions to major papers published in the *AJR*: frequency of undeserved coauthorship. *American Journal of Radiology, 167*, 571-579.

Smart, J. C. & Bayer, A. E. (1986). Author collaboration and impact: a note on citation rates of single and multiple authored articles. *Scientometrics, 10*(5-6), 297-305.

Smith, J. (1994, December 3). Gift authorship: a poisoned chalice? *British Medical Journal, 309*(6967), 2456-2457.

Smith, K. C. (1977). Peer review defended. *The Sciences, 17*, 5.

Smith, R. (1997a, April 5). Authorship: time for a paradigm shift?: The authorship system is broken and may need a radical solution. *British Medical Journal, 314*(7086), 992.

Smith, R. (1997b, September 20). Authorship is dying: long live contributorship: The *BMJ* will publish lists of contributors and guarantors to original articles. *British Medical Journal, 315*(7110), 696.

Sobal, J. & Ferentz, K. S. (1990, August 16). Abstract creep and author inflation. *New England Journal of Medicine, 323*(7), 488-489.

Strub, R. L. & Black, F. W. (1976, November 13). Multiple authorship. *Lancet, 2*(7994), 1090-1091.

Sweitzer, B. J. & Cullen, D. J. (1994, July, 13). How well does a journal's peer review process function? A survey of authors' opinions. *JAMA, 272*(2), 152-153.

Weller, A. C. (1996, July). Editorial peer review: a comparison of authors publishing in two groups of U.S. medical journals. *Bulletin of the Medical Library Association, 84*(3), 359-366.

Yankauer, A. (1986, July). Then and now, the *American Journal of Public Health*, 1911-1985. *American Journal of Public Health, 76*(7), 809-815.

Zuckerman, H. & Merton, R. K. (1971, July). Sociology of refereeing. *Physics Today, 24*(7), 28-33.

# Chapter Five

# The Role of Reviewers

*Golden rule: Referee manuscripts as you would like to have your own papers treated.*

(Siegelman, 1988, p. 360)

Most manuscripts received in an editorial office are evaluated by outside reviewers selected by the editor. A reviewer reads a manuscript, makes some suggestions for revisions, and usually recommends that the manuscript be accepted, rejected, or accepted with revisions, either minor or major. In spite of this rather straightforward role, complexities exist at every step of the process. This chapter analyzes the role of the reviewers. Reviewer agreement, potential bias, and statistical review are important issues and each is covered in a separate chapter.

Manheim offered his view of the reviewer's role: a reviewer judges the quality, priority and novelty of the work, recommends changes, takes "the heat off editors by absorbing the responsibility of unfavorable decisions" (p. 191), and lends a professional weight to the acceptance of a publication (Manheim, 1975). Most editors would, I believe, disagree with the third point and would consider "taking the heat" for a rejection decision as clearly their own responsibility, not the reviewer's.

In 1978, the American Psychological Association (APA) estimated that if each manuscript received by APA journals were read by two reviewers, these reviewers would read 14,750 manuscripts (Webb, 1979). Also, in 1978, Relman estimated that the review process for the *New England Journal of Medicine* alone required a total of six to seven person-years of peer review (Relman, 1981).

Given the time and energy that reviewing requires of reviewers, why do they do it? Probably echoing the opinion of many researchers and scholars, a chemist considered reviewing a duty and added that it is a *quid pro quo* payment in kind for those who review his manuscripts (Bauer, 1984). Bauer learned from reviewing, and at the same time it boosted his morale. He also articulated more sinister motives: to learn from the competition, to delay publication, or to plagiarize. Markland addressed the positive aspect of reviewing and concluded "a good job of refereeing must be a reward in itself and the reviewer has to receive major satisfaction from the pride of a job well done" (p. ix-x) (Markland, 1989). Markland did suggest to editors some tangible rewards that might encourage researchers and scholars to review: pay reviewers, reduce their journal subscription rate, or select them for editorial board membership.

Topics on the role of reviewers are arranged sequentially by reviewer selection, professional attributes of reviewers, reviewer guidelines, and the value of reviewers' reports and their impact on the quality of published articles.

## Reviewer selection

The selection of a reviewer may influence the outcome of a manuscript. Bishop speculated that the "choice of referees for a paper is the single, most important decision that editors make in dealing with submitted manuscripts" (p. 53) (Bishop, 1984). Bardach also agreed that the "selection of reviewers is the most important factor in peer review" (p 517) (Bardach, 1988). And according to Laband "the most valuable function performed by an editor may be efficient matching of manuscripts with reviewers" (p. 349) (Laband, 1990).

However, good reviewers can be overused. Harrison complained that as a reviewer for eight different physics journals he had received on the average one manuscript every eleven days for two years. He had reservations about a referee's power: "The referee constitutes a one-man tribunal in which he acts anonymously as the expert witness, the prosecutor, the judge and the jury" (p. 86) (Harrison, 1977).

Kochen and Perkel developed a mathematical model "to maximize the chance that manuscripts will be evaluated by the most competent referees" (p. 203) (Kochen & Perkel, 1977). The four steps of the model included methods of expanding the pool of referees, selecting from that pool, soliciting judgments from them, and combining referee judgments for points of consensus to assist the editor. The *Journal of the Association for Computing Machines* experimented with this model for five years and found that "implementation of some aspects of these procedures help to improve the quality of accepted papers" (p. 203). Quality was defined as subsequent citations to an article. However, the only time Kochen and Perkel's article has been cited in *ISI's* citation database, *Web of Science*, was when Bakanic cited it as an example of publications that criticize reviewers' reports (Bakanic, McPhail, & Simon, 1989).

Each editor probably maintains a list of potential reviewers. Editors may use names from a previous editor, editorial boards, names cited in a manuscript, or names from a literature search. They may know researchers or scholars personally. Editors have successfully employed other methods to compile a list of reviewers:

• asking authors to make recommendations (Manheim, 1973) (Kochen & Perkel, 1977)

• printing a list of subject topics of interest to the journal and asking readers (potential reviewers) to select areas of their expertise (Kittredge, 1984) (Talley, 1991)

- using a regular committee of reviewers and asking committee members to suggest a second reviewer for each manuscript (Arnell, 1986)

- mailing questionnaires to potential reviewers (Carney & Lundberg, 1987)

- asking readers to complete an experience profile (Lehr, 1991)

- seeking advice from current reviewers (Chew, 1993)

- inviting interested readers to volunteer in writing (Saracevic, 1986), (Harter, 1993)

- using scholars and researchers who have contacted them directly (Polak, 1995)

- publishing a reviewer interest form (Franken, 1997)

While admitting that there were no data to show that review selection criteria had any influence on review performance, Polak suggested editors develop strict criteria before selecting reviewers. He recommended criteria such as primary authorship on five papers or knowledge of statistics or experimental design (Polak, 1995). Fine, editor of *Family Relations*, kept a note on which reviewers gave constructive comments and continued to use only those who wrote helpful reviews (Fine, 1996).

Researchers and scholars can take an active role in securing a place for themselves as reviewers, if they are interested. Those interested in reviewing are encouraged to become professionally active, write a paper, and meet editors (Smith, 1990). Of course, the potential reviewers editors identify are often already very busy with their own research endeavors and might have little time to devote to a manuscript (Finke, 1990).

To point out the need for care in selecting reviewers, Kapp addressed the need for specialized reviewers in medicine with a study to determine the degree to which attorneys were used to review law-related medical manuscripts (Kapp, 1988). He surveyed 75 refereed and nonrefereed "significant medical journals" (p. 318) and received a 69.3 percent response rate. He found that the procedures for the review of legal material ranged from none at all to extensive. The contradiction of asking editors of nonrefereed journal about their reviewing practices or the question of whether a nonrefereed medical journal could also be "significant" were not addressed in the article. However, the author did add that his report "makes no pretense to scientific rigor or statistical precision" (p. 318).

As early as 1972, computer software was viewed as a potential help to editors both with the reviewer selection process and the administrative and management functions of a journal (Bernard, 1979/1980). In 1983, Bertsch and Fleming described a software program used by the 11 journals published by the American Chemical Society (Bertsch & Fleming, 1983). The program had modules for reviewer selection and journal administration. By 1987, the *Journal of the American Medical Association* (*JAMA*) announced that it had a "customized fully electronic reviewer file using a hierarchical data-base management system" (p. 87)

(Carney & Lundberg, 1987). In 1990, Weller found that large medical journals were more likely than small ones to have an automated reviewer system: 81.3 percent of a set of large medical journals compared to 35.5 percent of a set of small, specialized journals used automated reviewer selection software (Weller, 1990). Talley was happy to dispense with a set of file cards—"dog-eared from years of heavy use" (p. 950)—when the *American Journal of Hospital Pharmacy* moved to an electronic reviewer database (Talley, 1991). The database matched potential reviewers with the topic of a manuscript. Friedman evaluated reviewers' reports and maintained comments on the evaluations in a computerized database, using the information for future reviewer selection (Friedman, 1995). Weller found that, indeed, from 50 percent to 56 percent (depending on the journal category) of editors of medical journals indexed in *Index Medicus* evaluated reviewers' reports and kept a record of them for future reference (Weller, 1990).

Salasche provided a list of six qualities of a peer reviewer, admitting that there is no such thing as a "pool of ideal peers" (p. 423) (Salasche, 1997). A reviewer:

- has expertise on the subject under scrutiny,

- is not necessarily the "expert,"

- is willing to spend time to be thorough,

- is willing to make the paper better,

- can render an informed, unbiased decision, and

- has no conflict of interest with authors, subject, or product (p. 424).

Through a series of interviews, Gordon attempted to establish a profile of a good reviewer. Gordon found that, in general, editors thought that younger reviewers took their job more seriously than older, more eminent reviewers (Gordon, 1980). However, some editors thought that the younger reviewers were too concerned with details and failed to see the "purpose and significance" of a study (p. 269). These comments suggest that age or experience might play a role in reviewers' performance.

Two types of studies examine the reviewers themselves. Quantitative studies ask a group of reviewers about their practices, such as the amount of time they spend reviewing, the number of journals they review for, and the number of manuscripts they review in a given time period. Qualitative studies seek to evaluate the contents of the reviews and relate that to reviewer characteristics, particularly reviewers' professional status. Each of these types of studies is reviewed in the following discussion.

## Reviewer characteristics

*Question*

What is known about reviewer characteristics, in particular, the time spent by reviewers or their professional status?

*Criteria for inclusion*

~ any study that provided comparative data on reviewers' workload or their professional status.

*Comparable studies*

Seventeen studies identified a group of reviewers or potential reviewers and enumerated their quantitative contributions (Table 5-1).

Several studies provided data on the number of weeks reviewers took to return a manuscript. Rodman found that board members returned manuscripts quicker than nonboard members for a sociology journal (Rodman, 1970a). For board members, 71 percent of manuscripts were returned in three weeks, while only 52 percent of the nonboard members had returned manuscripts in three weeks. In economics, Mason determined that the average manuscript was returned in 20 weeks (Mason, Steagall, & Fabritius, 1992). Another study in economics found that 75 percent of all manuscripts were returned in 10 weeks (Hamermesh, 1994). A study of one medical journal, the *American Journal of Roentgenology,* found that its reviewers took an average of 4.5 weeks to return a manuscript (Polak, 1995). In both library science and biology, over 90 percent of manuscripts were returned in four weeks (Glogoff, 1988) (Gidez, 1990).

Another group of studies determined the number of journals a reviewer was likely to review for. A study of a medical journal revealed that 67 percent of reviewers review for more than one journal (Pigg, 1987). In journalism, Endres and Weardem found a similar percentage of reviewers (70 percent) reviewed for more than one journal (Endres & Wearden, 1990). Endres and Weardem developed a profile of reviewers in journalism and mass communication that included such characteristics as age, gender, academic degree, degree-granting institution, areas of expertise, but offered no comparative data on specialists in these fields who did not serve as reviewers. The authors were surprised to find that the reviewers were a homogenous group (white males with Ph.D.s in their 40s).

Five studies in medicine examined the length of time reviewers spent reviewing a manuscript. In the first study, a group of 265 reviewers for the *American Journal of Public Health* spent an average of 2.7 hours reviewing a manuscript. These reviewers also reviewed for a total of 274 other journals averaging about 3.6 additional journals for each reviewer; only 13 percent reviewed solely for the *American Journal of Public Health* (Yankauer, 1990). In the second study, editors of the *British Medical Journal* (*BMJ*) conducted a prospective study that compared reviewers of pediatric and psychiatric manuscripts (Lock & Smith, 1990). Lock and Smith compiled data for a nine-month period. They found that the median for this time period was six manuscripts per reviewer and that reviewers spent less than two hours per manuscript. The authors were "surprised" (p. 1343) by the small amount of time spent on reviews. The reviewers who were most frequently asked to review by the *BMJ* were those most likely to review for other journals as well. Reviewers were "male, academic, and predominately from

| Discipline studied | Reviewers | | Time to review | | Mean hours per manuscript | # of manuscripts reviewed | # of journals review for | Findings & Conclusions | References |
|---|---|---|---|---|---|---|---|---|---|
| | # | % | weeks | % | | | | | |
| sociology, board members | 384 | | 3 | 71% | | | | Editorial board members more prompt than outside referees. | (Rodman, 1970) |
| sociology, outside referees | 154 | | 3 | 52% | | | | | |
| scientists | | | | | 6 | | | 15 minutes longer for an acceptance recommendation. | (King, McDonald, & Roderer, 1981) |
| medicine, one journal | 150 | | | | | | 67% more than one | Editors prepared new packet to help reviewers. | (Pigg, 1987) |
| library science, 31 journals | 110 | 55% | 2 4 | 49% 94% | | 82% at least 1; 19% over 10 per year | | Reviewers are academics and they regularly publish. | (Glogoff, 1988) |
| management, two journals | 73 | 75% | | | 5.4 | | 5.7 | Reviewers are professionals who commit time to reviewing. | (Jauch & Wall, 1989) |
| journalism | 230 | 47% | | | | | 70% more than one | Reviewers are a homogeneous group. | (Endres & Wearden, 1990) |
| biology, association members | 900 | 45% | 2 4 | 51% 93% | 4.2 | 81% at least 1 per 1.5 years | 3.4 | | (Gidez, 1990) |
| medicine, one journal | 265 | 96% | | | 2.7 | 11.2 per year | 3.6 | Reviewers are experts, members of reviewing network, and devote appreciable time. | (Yankauer, 1990) |
| medicine, one journal | 301 | 88% | | | 1.35 | 6 per .75 years | 5 | Reviewers review in their own specialty. | (Lock, 1990) |
| medicine, one journal | 254 | | | | 3 | | | Time to review is similar for blind and nonblind review. | (McNutt, Evans, Fletcher, & Fletcher, 1990) |
| medicine, one journal | 65 | 83% | 4 | 70% | 3 | 19 per year | | Board members perceive peer review works well. | (Reideberg & Reidenberg, 1991) |
| economics, society members | 304 | 9% | 20 | | | | | Economists found both a perceived and actual problem with reviewing time. | (Mason, Steagall, & Fabritius, 1992) |
| social science, six journals | 80 | 41% | | | | 22 per year | 6.4 | Reviewers had reviewed for an average of 15 years. | (Neuliep & Crandall, 1993) |
| economics | 269 | 78% | 6 10 | 50% 75% | | | | Editors can reach a decision on most papers in a few months. | (Hamermesh, 1994) |
| medicine, one journal | 156 | | | | 1.6 | men: 12.9 per year; women: 6.8 | 4.3 | Those with more experience spent less time reviewing. | (Nylenna, Riis, & Karlson, 1994) |
| radiology, one journal | 759 | | | | | 13.9 per 1.5 years | | Data support continued use of two reviewers per manuscript. | (Friedman, 1995) |
| medicine, one journal | 90 | | 4.5 | | | | | Reviewers spend more time on complex studies. | (Polak, 1995) |
| Average | | 62% | | | 3.4 | | 4.7 | | |

**Table 5-1: Reviewers' workload**

London and university cities" (p. 1343). In the third study, NcNutt and colleagues tracked the difference in reviewing time between blinded and non-blinded manuscripts (McNutt, Evans, Fletcher, & Fletcher, 1990). Reviewers spent about three hours per manuscript for both types of manuscripts. In the fourth study, reviewers for *Clinical Pharmacology & Therapeutics* reported that they spent about three hours over a two-day period for the last manuscript they reviewed (Reideberg & Reidenberg, 1991). In the fifth study, Nylenna and colleagues' results were similar to Lock and Smith's. Scandinavian reviewers spent about 1.6 hours per manuscript (Nylenna, Riis, & Karlson, 1994).

In addition to the medical studies, King, McDonald, and Roderer in science, Jauch and Wall in management, and Gidez in biology each asked reviewers to estimate the amount of time they spent reviewing a manuscript. (King, McDonald, & Roderer, 1981) (Jauch & Wall, 1989) (Gidez, 1990). The Jauch and Wall study and the Gidez study each found that scientists spent more time per manuscript than any of the studies in medicine. Both of these were retrospective surveys that inquired about the "typical" amount of time the respondents spent per manuscript. King and colleagues provided summary data only from their 1977 study, which found reviewers of scientific manuscripts spent about 6 hours reviewing a manuscript when they recommended rejection and about 15 minutes longer when they recommended acceptance (p. 112). These data were cited again in 1995 by King and Griffins (King & Griffins, 1995). As pointed out by Yankauer, King and colleagues did not provide details of how their data were obtained (Yankauer, 1990). The King study was conducted in the late 1970s in the sciences, while most of the studies in Table 5-1 were conducted in the late 1980s and 1990s in medicine. Time spent on reviewing manuscripts may be discipline-specific.

There could well be differences between estimated time and actual time spent by reviewers per manuscript. Three of the medicine studies asked reviewers to keep track of the actual time they spent reviewing a particular manuscript (Lock, 1990) (McNutt et al., 1990) (Nylenna et al., 1994). Reviewers in these three studies averaged 1.98 hours per manuscript. For the other two studies in medicine, reviewers were asked to estimate the time they spent on a manuscript (Yankauer, 1990) (Reideberg & Reidenberg, 1991). Reviewers estimated they spent an average of 2.8 hours per manuscript in these two studies. Nonetheless, reviewers in medicine seem to spend less time per manuscript than reviewers in the sciences. However, the differences in study design make it impossible to draw any conclusions about differences in time spent on reviewing manuscripts based on disciplines.

In the field of library science, Glogoff asked editorial board members from a core list of 31 library science titles about their refereeing experience (Glogoff, 1988). Eighty-two percent of board members reviewed manuscripts during a one-year period. Forty percent reviewed from one to three manuscripts, while 8 percent reviewed over 15 manuscripts. This was a retrospective survey and given the way their data were grouped, it was not possible to calculate the average number of manuscripts a board member reviewed during the year. Seventy-five percent of those responding never found out the final disposition of the manuscripts they reviewed.

These studies, although examining the general rubric of reviewers' workload, took a number of different approaches. Seven studies examined the number of weeks a reviewer took to return a manuscript. Eight studies provided data on the number of hours a reviewer spent reviewing a manuscript. Eleven studies investigated the total commitment reviewers made by examining either the number of journals each reviewed for or the total number of manuscripts reviewed each year. A number of studies elicited data in more than one of these categories. These studies indicate that there may indeed be a "profile" of an average reviewer. A reviewer reviews for a number of different journals (averaging about 4.7 journals), spends from slightly over an hour to about six hours per manuscript (averaging about 3.4 hours), and reviews a relatively large number of manuscripts each year. Data for the last category use a number of different measures, making averaging impossible. Also, the time to return a manuscript may vary among disciplines. The use of same reviewers by more than one editor indicates that editors may look for similar characteristics in reviewers. Good reviewers may have some universal qualities that are independent of particular needs of one journal.

## Reviewers' reports

*Question*

What is known about the overall quality of reviewers' reports?

*Criteria for inclusion*

~ any study that provides qualitative data on the contents of reviewers' reports.

*Comparative studies*

This group of studies of reviewers looked for any relationship between reviewers' professional or other qualitative characteristics and the quality of reviews (Table 5-2). Four of the six studies examined a consecutive set of manuscripts received by one journal (Stossel, 1985) (Evans, McNutt, Fletcher, & Fletcher, 1993) (Murphy & Utts, 1994) (Friedman, 1995). Stossel, while he was editor of the *Journal of Clinical Investigation*, rated a group of reviewers as having high, medium, or low status depending on their academic rank, reputation, or length of time in a field (Stossel, 1985). He found that high status reviewers disproportionately refused to review. While nearly two-thirds of all reviews were good, the low-status reviewers were the most likely group to provide a good review.

Evans and colleagues studied a group of reviewers for the *Journal of General Internal Medicine* to determine if they reviewed differently when they knew the author and the institutional affiliation (Evans et al., 1993). They found that reviewers were more likely to provide good reviews if they were blinded to the authors. (See Chapter Eight on reviewer biases for a discussion of this finding.)

| Discipline studied | Question or purpose | Reviewers | Reviewers' status defined by | Findings | References |
|---|---|---|---|---|---|
| medicine, one journal | Do eminent investigators review? | 1600 | academic rank, reputation, years in field | low status reviewers produced the highest proportion of good reviews | (Stossel, 1985) |
| medicine, one journal | To determine characteristics of good reviewers | 226 | age, academic rank, degrees, administrator | best reviewers: (1) younger, (2) from prestigious institutions, (3) known to the editor, (4) blinded to authors | (Evans, McNutt, Fletcher, & Fletcher, 1993) |
| botany, one journal | To provide baseline information about reviewers | 134 | academic rank and affiliation, age, publications | no significant differences between different categories of reviewers, except those experienced gave better reviews | (Murphy & Utts, 1994) |
| economics, seven journals | To provide baseline information about reviewers | 343 | academic degree and affiliation, publications | reviewers asked to review at peak of career; editors select authors from their journals as reviewers, better journals use higher-quality reviewers | (Hamermesh, 1994) |
| medicine, fabricated manuscript | To determine referee characteristics and manuscript assessment | 180 | specialty, country, age, gender, experience | experienced and young reviewers gave a "stricter" assessment | (Nylenna et al., 1994) |
| radiology, one journal | To assess quality of review process | 759 | editor's own rating scale | prolific and experienced reviewers among the best, and received the most manuscripts | (Friedman, 1995) |

**Table 5-2: Relation of status of reviewers to quality of reviews**

Another aspect of this study compared the quality of the reviews to a number of reviewer characteristics. The authors observed a trend in which the better reviews came from academics who were assistant professors rather than associate or full professors. Reviewers who were younger and from prestigious institutions were more likely to produce better reviews.

Murphy and Utts analyzed 138 reviewers of 93 manuscripts for the journal *Physiologia Plantarum* (Murphy & Utts, 1994). They found no differences in quality of reviews for different academic ranks of reviewers. The lack of differences might be attributed to the fact that, for the most part, senior reviewers were used: 83 percent of the reviewers were professors, associate professors or equivalent. Murphy and Utts felt their study showed "none of the subgroups ... produced reviews that differed significantly from those of the whole set of respondents" (p. 542) for depth of review, tone of review, constructive suggestions, and the recommendation to accept or reject. However, the authors suggested that the subjective element of the review cannot be removed. They referred to the studies by Stossel and Evans in medicine both of which found younger, less-experienced reviewers performed better than older, more-experienced ones (Stossel, 1985) (Evans et al., 1993). Murphy and Utts thought their results might show discipline differences between medicine and the sciences.

Overall, Murphy and Utts concluded that none of these studies have helped editors with the reviewer selection process.

The *American Journal of Roentgenology* analyzed reviewers' reports over seven and one-half years from 1986 to 1994 (Friedman, 1995). Just over 70 percent of reviewers processed between 10 and 30 manuscripts. All reviews were rated by the editor or associate editor using a four-point scale (four for the highest rating and one the lowest). Not surprising, those reviewers who received the highest grades were most likely to receive more manuscripts. Of the seven reviewers who had evaluated 40 or more manuscripts, none had received a score of three or below for any manuscript, while 41 percent of those who had received between one and five manuscripts had received a score of three or below.

Hamermesh asked editors of 11 (unnamed) economic journals to keep data on reviews for 50 consecutive manuscripts; seven editors agreed to (Hamermesh, 1994). Hamermesh rated both reviewers and journals by the frequency with which they were cited. Hamermesh concluded: "papers sent to better journals are refereed by higher-quality scholars, and, one would hope, obtain more useful comments from them" (p. 156). The latter observation was not documented.

Nylenna, Riis, and Karlson asked Scandinavian reviewers to review one of two "nonauthentic, but realistic, short manuscripts with a number of common methodological flaws" (p. 149) (Nylenna et al., 1994). The younger, experienced reviewers performed better than older, less-experienced reviewers. The investigators found no influence of such factors as gender, specialty, or nationality (Norwegian, Swedish, or Danish).

Rodman suggested signed agreements between editors and reviewers would assure that editors limit the number of manuscripts they give reviewers and that reviewers return the completed reviews promptly (Rodman, 1970b). This suggestion seems not to have been implemented and was probably not realistic since reviewers volunteer their time and might be reluctant to agree to work within certain prescribed parameters.

No studies were identified that scientifically investigated the reviewer selection process and there was no clear indication that editors' reviewer selection criteria have an impact on the quality of the review. The investigators used different measures for reviewer status: academic rank, age, citations to work, institutional affiliation. There were mixed findings on whether a novice or an experienced reviewer performed better.

## Guidelines for reviewers

It is assumed that most editors provide some type of guidelines for reviewers when they send a manuscript. At the very least editors must explain to reviewers why they have received a particular manuscript and explain how the reviewer is expected to handle it. One study asked reviewers which type of instructions they preferred. An understandably high percentage of reviewers— 89 percent of 156 referees in this case—preferred a structured form as opposed to brief or very limited guidelines (Nylenna, Riis, & Karlson, 1995). Almost all

(97.5 percent) inexperienced reviewers preferred a structured form. These same data were reported in an additional publication by the same authors (Nylenna et al., 1994). A study by Lock and Smith that evaluated a structured reviewer's form found that 90 percent of the referees felt that editors had explained to them exactly what was expected in the review (Lock & Smith, 1990).

Several editorials have focused on the nonscientific and nonscholarly aspects of review, pointing out the need for reviewers to behave in a responsible manner and to use common courtesy. Pyke, writing in the *BMJ*, outlined a set of "simple rules" that covered 11 points: do not lose the manuscript; be prompt; answer the questions the editor asks; if in doubt favor publication; do not nit-pick; do not be overawed by authors or ask them silly questions; do not get bogged down in details; make clear to the editor any comments that should not be passed on to the authors; do not be impressed by references to reviewer's work; and do not contact the author (Pyke, 1976). These seem rather basic but probably generate from some degree of frustration felt by at least one editor. Futhermore, in 1993, Baue, editor of *Archives of Surgery*, reiterated most of Pyke's recommendations and added several more: read the manuscript, do not ask questions that are answered in it, and do not ask for more work unless it can be done with available data (Baue, 1993). Then in 1995, Humphries, in a statement of policies of *Pediatric Neurosurgery*, repeated Baue's rules (Humphreys, Reigel, & Epstein, 1995).

In the guidelines for the *American Journal of Hospital Pharmacy*, Zellmer suggested reviewers be prompt, objective, specific, and avoid acrimony (Zellmer, 1977).

In nursing, Alspach provided a similar list of suggestions for reviewers for *Critical Care Nurse*, including several do's and don'ts: do be prompt, objective, specific, constructive, and legible; don't focus on mechanics, rewrite paper, be acrimonious, reveal one's identity, or violate confidence (Alspach, 1994).

Reviewers of *Physics Today* were reminded that the quality of a journal hinged on the quality of their reports and that the task of the reviewer is to assist the editor and the author. Reviewers' reports should be informative and explicit with a detailed report to the author and should not be "caustic" (p. 92) (Sommers, 1983).

Similar to those outlined by Pyke for the *BMJ*, Baines laid out a set of attitudes that a reviewer of the *Canadian Medical Association Journal* should take pains to avoid: the reviewer as author, as ignoramus, as zealot, as idée-fixé, as provocateur, as hurried, as editor, as competitor, as prima donna, and as obstacle (Baines, 1987). Also, in the *Canadian Medical Association Journal*, Huston listed 12 attributes of an excellent medical reviewer that (with the exception of the one directly relevant to medicine) would be appropriate for any discipline (Huston, 1994). Reviewers should "determine their appropriateness as reviewer, maintain confidentiality, rule out bias, avoid conflict of interest, meet deadlines, cultivate open-mindedness, know the structure of scientific papers, draw upon medical acumen, employ critical appraisal skills, screen for misconduct, use tact, and eschew triviality" (p. 1212). Also in medicine, Frank suggested editors should maintain confidentiality, disclose conflict of interest, be objective, be specific, respond quickly, and describe areas of expertise (Frank, 1996).

In the journal *Biometrics*, Finney made a number of recommendations to reviewers based on the need for ethical reviewing practices. The referee should not be a friend of one of the authors (a suggestion that implies nonblind review), should complete the review on time, should not use ideas from the manuscript, should keep information in the manuscript confidential, should not communicate with the author, and should return all material to the editor (Finney, 1997).

Reviewers commonly receive the same manuscript twice (after having recommended rejection on the first review). Meile believed that under such circumstances it is unethical for a reviewer to consider the manuscript a second time, claiming this is a "double jeopardy" for the author, and the reviewer should decline to review (Meile, 1977).

The qualities suggested for reviewers at times sound like a laundry list of correct behavior and are thus hard to regulate, but through these suggestions editors have attempted to assist reviewers in conducting a constructive and professional review. In addition to these behavioral guidelines, a number of editors published reviewer guidelines to help reviewers with the more practical aspect of evaluating manuscripts. Twenty-four sets of published guidelines were identified and each is summarized in Table 5-3. Some editors include a copy of the exact form they mail to reviewers; others listed the set of questions they ask reviewers to answer.

These guidelines illustrate the complexity of the task of the reviewer. One would expect that questions asked of reviewers would be related to editors' publication criteria. Indeed, many criteria presented in Table 5-3 are similar to publication criteria in Table 3-2. However, there is little overlap in the references between these two tables. Siegelman, editor of *Radiology*, is the only author cited in both tables. Table 3-2 summarizes the results of Seigelman's survey of editorial board and leading reviewer's ratings of seven publication criteria (Siegelman, 1989) and Table 5-3 cites a 12-item checklist that Seigelman developed for reviewers (Siegelman, 1988). Seigelman's editorial is the only medical publication in Table 3-2, while 12 of the 24 (50.0 percent) sets of guidelines summarized in Table 5-3 originate from some area of medicine. One checklist for reviewers, arrived at using the Delphi method, asked reviewers to name criteria they use when evaluating a manuscript. This method identified 246 criteria reviewers should use when evaluating manuscripts (Campion, 1993).

Forscher published the first "rules for referees" in 1965. He suggested that a reviewer should judge a manuscript on its newness, its bibliography, the reliability of its methods, the presence of any internal contradictions, the appropriateness of tables and illustrations. Reviewers should also look for clarity in writing, validity of the argument, proper interpretations of results, and any "loopholes" in thinking (p. 320) (Forscher, 1965).

In 1976, Mahoney argued that peer review should be reformed by "drastically" (p. 104) altering the role of the referee (Mahoney, 1976). He recommended that graduate students would make better reviewers than "peers." He also recommended that "manuscripts should be evaluated solely on the basis of their relevance and their methodology" (p. 105). His suggestion to use graduate students

| Discipline of journal studied | Type of guidelines | Type of questions on guidelines | Form asks for decision to accept or reject? | Purpose or conclusions of study | References |
|---|---|---|---|---|---|
| psychology | proposed checklist | on presentation, value, importance, significance, methodology, and contribution | yes | to foster discussion | (Wolff, 1973) |
| sociology | 3 questions on form | on presentation, content, and appropriateness | yes | peer review with its "perils, problems, and slowness will continue" (p. 9) | (Bealer, 1974) |
| nursing | 15 questions | on content, contribution, hypothesis, literature review, definitions, assumptions and limitations, methodology, sample, findings, results, conclusions | no | to explain process | (Carnegie, 1975) |
| psychology | 50 questions | on topic, style, introduction, method, design, statistics, figures and tables, discussion, conclusion | no | provided in response to requests for it | (Maher, 1978) |
| physiotherapy | guidelines for evaluation | on importance, originality, design, conclusions, discussion, writing, references | yes | to explain process | (Cleather, 1981) |
| engineering | 55 questions | on writing style, grammar, organization, definition, persuasive or effective thinking | if yes to all | to help reviewers make positive contributions | (Haness, 1983) |
| medicine | 7 questions | on originality, importance, validity, statistical analysis, conclusions, writing, general interest | no | part of reinstating the practice of acknowledging reviewers | (Lundberg, 1984) |
| statistics | 4 questions | on interest, building on work of others, methods, clarity | no | referees should receive tangible rewards: monetary, subscription discounts, or editorial board appointments | (Gleser, 1986) |
| library science | 7 criteria | on scope, objectives, organization, methodology, inferences, conclusions, style | yes | peer review is universally used and improves quality | (Crawford, 1988) |
| radiology | 12-point checklist | on abstract, keywords, purpose, objectives, methodology, discussion, clarity of writing | yes; 9 options | to explain review process | (Siegelman, 1988) |
| ceramics | 10 questions | on acceptability, revision, literature review, title, abstract, methodology, conclusions, writing, illustrations, topic | yes | to explain review process | (Stull, 1989) |
| medicine | 26[1] and 30[2] questions on the form | on abstract, introduction, methods, results, discussion, references | no | to foster discussion and be a learning tool for reviewers | 1 - (Squires, 1989); 2 - updated (Huston, 1994) |
| medicine | 9 questions | on description, development and logic of argument, resolution to issues | no | to explain that editorials and platform articles need a different type of review | (Squires, 1989) |
| computers | 6 questions | on errors, relevance, definitions, technically complete, and organization | yes | guidelines should be useful as a training tool | (Smith, 1990) |
| ophthalmology | 14 questions | on subject, organization, quality, | no | acceptance or rejection depends on many factors | (Newell, 1990) |
| pharmacy | 19 questions | on purpose, objectives, methods, relevance, abstract, and acceptable | yes | to provide a brief overview of process | (Doering, 1991) |
| environment | 5 questions | on length, tables, figures, need for re-review, and need for reviewer anonymity | yes | editor uses a form to communicate outcome to authors | (Lehr, 1991) |

**Table 5-3: Reviewer guidelines**

| Discipline of journal studied | Type of guidelines | Type of questions on guidelines | Form asks for decision to accept or reject? | Purpose or conclusions of study | References |
|---|---|---|---|---|---|
| *psychology* | 14 questions | on contribution to knowledge, content, theory, rigor, results, length, statistics, writing style | no | guidelines do not solve problem of low reliability and low validity | (Eysenck & Eysenck, 1992) |
| *library science* | 9 questions | on study design, originality, literature review, methodology, conclusions, findings, organization, interest | yes | to explain review process | (Harter, 1993) |
| *medicine* | list of 17 potential flaws | on originality, follow up, sample size, controls, methodology, design, jargon, interest | no | standards of review needed | (Cotton, 1993) |
| *psychology* | 246 criteria in 16 categories | on topic, literature review, concept, sampling, justification, measures, design, procedures, data analysis, results, discussion, conclusions, presentation, contribution | no | to provide a checklist to aid reviewers | (Campion, 1993) |
| *nursing* | areas for review | on accuracy, appeal, clarity, depth, figures, organization, references | no | to inform reviewers of process | (Alspach, 1994) |
| *medicine* | checklist, numerical score for each category | on contents and presentation | no | research on best type of form needed | (Nylenna et al., 1995) |
| *medicine* | ideal list of editor-review communication | on quality, importance, scientific rigor, novelty, clarity, ethics, accompanying editorial, appropriateness | no | ethical issues should be addressed by all editors | (Frank, 1996) |

**Table 5-3: Reviewer guidelines (continued)**

as reviewers does not appear to have moved forward and would undoubtedly be met with some resistance, while his second suggestion has been addressed by a number of the editors in Table 5-3.

Only one study was identified that asked specific questions about the use of editorial guidelines. Frank studied the peer review system by surveying editors of the 71 most frequently cited U.S. journals in *ISI*'s citation frequency index and attempted to identify ways in which reviewers' opinions were elicited (Frank, 1996). The response rate was a remarkable 97.3 percent. Almost all (95.5 percent) editors responding asked reviewers to make an acceptance or rejection recommendation. There was considerable variation in the other categories of information requested of reviewers: 71.6 percent of the editors asked reviewers to rank novelty or originality, 68.7 percent wanted to know if the manuscript was clear, and 50.7 percent requested an opinion on whether the conclusions were reasonable and appropriate. Most editors (92.5 percent) used a reviewer form, but only 25.4 percent sent extensive instructions. Frank concluded her report with a set of recommendations for the types of information editors should ask of reviewers. Most were taken from the Council of Biology Editors' *Style Manual* and covered such topics as quality, importance, scientific rigor, novelty, clarity, ethics, appropriateness, and the need for an accompanying editorial.

Squires, editor of the *Canadian Medical Association Journal*, used two separate sets of questions for reviewers: one for reports of original research or clinical and community studies (Squires, 1989a), and one for editorials and platform articles (Squires, 1989b).

Even while using guidelines provided by the editors, reviewers approach the review of a manuscript with their own style. Salasche (Salasche, 1997) suggested eight steps each reviewer should take while reviewing any manuscript:

- familiarize oneself with the material with a run-through read of manuscript,

- identify the author's main objective or hypothesis,

- identify the type of article and place it in a category,

- reread the manuscript as often as necessary,

- determine if the main objective was satisfied or the hypothesis proven,

- determine if new or valid information was provided or if older material was successfully assimilated and clarified,

- decide whether to recommend acceptance or rejection, and

- determine ways in which the manuscript could be improved if recommending acceptance (p. 424).

Bowen and colleagues in 1972 suggested that a "standardized evaluation system" (p. 224) be used in which manuscripts would be subjected to an "operational, structured scoring system to guide the rater" (p. 223) (Bowen, Perloff, & Jacoby, 1972). Such a scoring system was recently developed by Cho and Bero, who tested its validity by assessing published drug studies (Cho & Bero, 1994). Points (between two and zero) were assigned to each of 24 manuscript characteristics (study design, appropriate subjects, random selection of subjects, statistics, and other characteristics similar to those listed in Table 5-3). A score of two was assigned if the study positively met a criterion, one if it partially met a criterion, and zero if either it did not meet a criterion or the particular criterion was not applicable for this study. This study was done in a controlled setting by evaluating published articles. Conditions were similar to those of a reviewer judging a manuscript, leading Cho and Bero to conclude that it could easily be implemented for standard manuscript review.

Mitchell and colleagues sent members of the review boards of five organizational behavior journals a survey to determine how reviewers approach the review process. Subjects were interviewed, and from the information gathered a set of characteristics of a good manuscript was developed. Similar to the Cho and Bero study, these items closely resemble many of the guidelines summarized in Table 5-3: the importance of the work, including its contribution, readership interest, and breadth; the methodology of the work including its design, measurement, and analysis; the logical considerations of the work in the introduction, method, results, discussion, and conclusion sections; and the presentation including writing, figures and tables and level of presentation (p. 259) (Mitchell, Beach, & Smith, 1985).

In 1986, Kochar suggested that in order to cut down on the "extremely wasteful and time consuming" (p. 148) elements of peer review that "major medical journals establish a consortium to receive and review scientific articles. Authors would submit their work directly to the consortium, along with a list of journals in which they would prefer to see it published" (p. 148) (Kochar, 1986). He went on to suggest some implementation steps, including suggesting the International Committee of Medical Journal Editors (ICMJE) as the best forum for discussion of this proposal. Kochar's commentary has not been cited in *ISI's* citation database, *Web of Science*. Nylenna and colleagues have also suggested that the ICMJE take a look at minimum requirements for a standardized reviewer's evaluation form (Nylenna et al., 1995).

In several of the articles cited in Table 5-3 it was clear that the author's (who was usually an editor) purpose was to foster discussion about reviewer guidelines, in fact, several editors used those very words. Editors appeared not only to be describing their process but they were also asking for suggestions on how to improve the guidelines and thereby help reviewers to do a better job. It was also clear from this discussion that editors were aware of the tremendous role the reviewers play and that editors understood the goodwill provided by the reviewers and probably viewed communicating with reviewers in the public forum as a way to garner buy-in and assistance.

In summary, the guidelines in Table 5-3 ranged from very detailed forms to a very brief letter asking for reviewer's comments. Some asked for detailed commentaries, others asked only a few questions, and some had a rating scale for each criterion. Some editors asked very specific questions about each section of a manuscript: introduction, methodology, analysis, discussion, etc. Some asked about writing style and the presence or absence of certain elements in the manuscript. Some asked global questions about the manuscript's contribution to knowledge. Many of the forms did not specifically ask for a recommendation to accept, reject, or revise. This may be so fundamental that editors assumed reviewers would automatically be asked to make such a recommendation. Editors had a number of purposes: to explain the process, to foster discussion, to help reviewers, to acknowledge reviewers, to improve review, to train reviewers, and to improve their own process.

## Value of reviewers' reports

Has the groundwork of providing guidelines for reviewers and communicating their positions paid off for editors? Are reviewers' reports valuable to editors? An informal review of section editors for the *Archives of Disease in Childhood* found that on a scale of zero (worst) to five (best), 25 percent of the reviewers' reports scored a two or less (McKenzie, 1995). McKenzie recommended that editors develop guidelines for structured reviewers' reports. The previous section illustrated that a number of editors have provided guidelines, but not necessarily structured reports. Are there other measures of the value of reviewers' reports to the editors? Table 4-3 (Chapter Four) examined the value of reviewers' reports from an author's perspective; this section examines the value of the reviewers' reports from the editor's perspective.

In a letter to *Physics Today*, Galam asked physicist authors to send him some of their "more interesting" reviewers' reports (Galam, 1984). Galam was not only interested in publishing a "representative sample of referees' reports" (p.11), but also in receiving information from authors about ways in which reviewers' reports were instrumental in their revising their manuscripts before publication. That same issue of *Physics Today* carried a similar letter by Arrott who asked for any "anecdotal material from those who believe they have had their opportunities in physics restricted by irresponsible peer review" (Arrott, 1984). A search of several databases, including *ISI's*, failed to identify any publication as a result of either of these two requests.

Reviewers for journals of the Canadian Psychological Association were asked about how they made acceptance or rejection decisions (Rowney & Zenisek, 1980). Two manuscript characteristics considered to have the most positive influence for almost one-half of reviewers were either a new theory was tested or the reviewers knew the author. Three characteristics viewed as having the most negative influence were the control group was absent, the manuscript had been presented at a meeting that published full proceedings, or the study was a replication of a previous study.

*Questions*

Have any studies examined the reviewers' reports for content? Have any studies linked the value of the reviewers' reports to the value of the published article?

*Criteria for inclusion*

~ any study that evaluated a set of reviewers' reports for content or tried to measure the value or the influence of the reviewers' report on the revised document.

*Comparable studies*

The quality of a review can be judged from different perspectives: the author's, an independent judge's, or the editor's. There have been studies of each perspective. Authors' opinions of how the review process influences the manuscript are covered in Chapter Four. This section summarizes studies of the other perspectives. Eleven studies use some quantifiable method to investigate the content of reviewers' reports and then judge the quality of the revised document. Table 5-4 summarizes those studies that used someone other than the author to judge the value of the reviewers' reports.

Spencer and colleagues were interested in learning if reviewers' reports could be analyzed objectively and asked editors to provide sample reviews for

| Discipline | # of journals | # of reviews | Qualities examined | Findings | Conclusions | References |
|---|---|---|---|---|---|---|
| psychology | 31 | 529 | psycholinguistical analysis of reviews | 40% of sample had more than 25% emotional persuasion and unanchored comments | both accepted and rejected manuscripts contain similar comments | (Spencer, Hartnett, & Mahoney, 1986) |
| sociology | 1 | 755 | analysis of positive and negative comments of reviewers | ration of negative to positive comments 3 to 1 for rejected manuscripts; 1.5 to 1 for accepted | referees always critical, but more positive comments for accepted manuscripts | (Bakanic et al., 1989) |
| education | | 216 | tone of reviews | developed four reviewer profiles: critic, conciliator, competitor, procrastinator | accepted manuscripts had more constructive suggestions | (Fagan, 1990) |
| economics | several | 89 | length of review and subsequent citations to article | longer referees' comments had a positive impact on number of citations | editors' comments had no such influence | (Laband, 1990) |
| radiology | 1 | 17,978 | categorize reviewers' by scores they assigned to manuscripts | identified reviewers who deviated from the mean | editors should recognize and control for variation | (Siegelman, 1991) |
| medicine | 1 | 101* | readability before and after review | both Gunning fog index and the Flesch reading ease scores improved after review | improvement in readability, but both articles and abstracts difficult to read | (Roberts, Fletcher, & Fletcher, 1994) |
| medicine | 1 | 111* | quality of manuscript before and after review | influenced improvements in discussion of study limitations, generalizations, use of confidence interval, and tone of conclusion | peer review improves the quality of reports on medical research | (Goodman, Berlin, Fletcher, & Fletcher, 1994) |
| management | 1 | 400 | influence of four characteristics of review | constructive tone of reviewers led to acceptance | did not find that biases in review process favored one type of research over another | (Beyer, Chanove, & Fox, 1995) |
| nursing | 1 | 56* | readability before and after review | significant improvement for both the Flesch and Gunning indexes | peer review accomplished aim | (Biddle & Aker, 1996) |
| medicine | 1 | 98 | article improvement after review | 14 of 23 questions showed quality significantly improved after review | peer review valuable and possible biases have a negligible effect | (Pierie, Walvoort, & Overbeke, 1996) |
| psychology | 1 | 823 | consistency of reviewers' evaluation of manuscripts | little evidence of social particularism or content particularism | reviewers focus on empirical research | (Gilliland & Cortina, 1997) |

\* number of manuscripts

**Table 5-4: Value of reviewers' reports**

the study (Spencer et al., 1986). In the 500 plus reviewers' reports received, "over 40 percent of the sample (276 reviews of accepted manuscripts and 253 of rejected manuscripts) had more than 25 percent emotional persuasion and unanchored comment [sic], which indicates intrusion of bias and prejudices in the review process" (p. 21).

Bakanic, McPhail, and Simon examined reviewers' comments from a sample of manuscripts received by the *American Sociological Review* (Bakanic et al., 1989). They had access to comments directed to both the editor and the authors from accepted and from rejected manuscripts. Overall there were more negative comments than positive ones in all the reviews, but the negative comments outweighed the positive ones for rejected manuscripts at a ratio of three to one. The corresponding ratio for accepted manuscripts was 1.5 to one. Since editors may receive comments not intended for authors, they, of course, receive more information about a manuscript than authors receive in the reviewers' reports. The investigators learned that editors received more negative comments on the private reports than on the reports intended for the authors only.

Fagan asked authors who had submitted manuscripts to education journals to share copies of their reviewers' reports with him (Fagan, 1990). As with the two letters by physicists cited above, Fagan's request was posted in a nationally read journal. He received copies of 216 reviewers' reports from 108 manuscripts (46 accepted, and 62 rejected). From these, Fagan developed a reviewer profile comprised of four types of reviewers: conciliator (all recommended acceptance), critic (pointed out both strengths and weakness of a manuscript), competitor (mostly negative statements), and procrastinator (took longer and only contained negative comments). If a manuscript was accepted the author was more likely to have constructive, helpful comments, whereas if the manuscript was rejected the comments tended to be only negative. Fagan offered his study as a way for both authors and editors to better understand the reviewer.

Laband asked 731 authors of 1,062 articles in several economics journals to send him copies of reviewers' reports they had received (Laband, 1990). He received usable responses from only 87 (11.9 percent) authors for 89 (8.4 percent) published articles. He correlated length of review with subsequent citations and found that "The length of referees reports, ... demonstrates a marginally significant, positive impact on subsequent citations of a paper. There also appears to be a positive relationship between referee comments that are self-reported [by the authors] as being helpful and subsequent citations of a paper" (p. 348). But he also found another correlation that might confound his conclusion: longer articles also received more citations. He did not investigate the possibility that longer articles might produce longer reviewers' reports. The relationship between article length and its value proves to be interesting. Two studies discussed in Chapter Three also found a correlation between the length of an article and subsequent citations to it (Laband & Piette, 1994) and (Campanario, 1996).

Siegelman, editor of *Radiology*, scored a set of reviewers' reports and identified a group of reports that deviated from the mean (Siegelman, 1991). Two categories of reports had the greatest deviation: those with ratings consistently higher than the norm and those with ratings consistently lower than the norm. Reviewers who regularly rated manuscripts high comprised from 5 percent to 13.9 percent of all reviewers, and those who rated manuscripts consistently low comprised from 4.3 percent to 12.7 percent of all reviewers. Siegelman pointed out that "failure to recognize and control for reviewer variation may be unfair to authors" (p. 637). As editor, Siegelman continually monitors reviewers' ratings to identify those reviewers at the far ends of the normal distribution chart and suggested that the "always positive" and the "always negative" reviewers should not regularly receive either the best or the worst manuscripts.

Roberts and colleagues used the Gunning Fog Index and the Flesch scores to identify any changes in readability to a group of manuscripts received by the *Annals of Internal Medicine* after editorial peer review (Roberts, Fletcher, & Fletcher, 1994). Their results showed that "peer review and editorial processes slightly improved readability of original articles" (p. 119). Similar results were found in a study of a nursing journal, the *Journal of the American Association of Nurse Anesthetists*. (Biddle & Aker, 1996). Scores for both the Flesch scores and the Gunning Fox Index were higher after manuscripts had undergone changes suggested by peer review.

Beyer and colleagues examined reviews from the *Academy of Management Journal* carried out from 1984 to 1987 (Beyer, Chanove, & Fox, 1995). They evaluated reviews using four perspectives: gatekeeping (criteria applied to decision making), particularism (decision based on knowledge of person as opposed to scientific merits), accumulated advantage (demographic characteristics of the authors), and reviewer style (degree to which developmental feedback to authors is provided). The investigators did find some advantage to the particularism and accumulated advantage perspectives. A constructive tone of reviewers' reports assisted in the editor's decision to publish a manuscript.

Applying Beyer and colleagues' methodology to the *Journal of Applied Psychology*, Gilliland and Cortina studied 823 original submissions. They found support for the gatekeeping functions "in that reviewers and editors appeared to pay particular attention to the adequacy of the research design, operationalization of constructs, and theoretical development.... Little evidence was found for social particularism ... or content particularism" (p. 427) (Gilliland & Cortina, 1997). They concluded that "reviewers and editors are focussing [sic] their attention on factors that most researchers agree are critical features of empirical research and that they are affected little, if at all, by features of the research or author that might reflect a 'bias' of some type" (p. 452). See Chapter Seven for a discussion of reviewer bias.

Two studies compared the quality of manuscripts both before and after review.

Pierie, Walvoort, and Overbeke asked readers to evaluate manuscripts as submitted, accepted, and published (Pierie, Walvoort, & Overbeke, 1996). Evaluators received identically typeset manuscripts, so they were not aware of where in the process each manuscript was at the time of the evaluation. After review, 14 of the 23 areas of evaluation (61 percent) significantly improved in quality in the accepted over the submitted manuscripts, while 11 of 16 (69 percent) showed improvement in the published over the accepted manuscripts. The areas in the manuscript that showed least improvement were the objectives, methods, and conclusions.

Goodman and colleagues examined manuscript quality from the *Annals of Internal Medicine* by rating each manuscript using 34 criteria both before and after review; the investigators determined that peer review improved 33 of the 34 criteria. Different reviewers were used to evaluate each version of the manuscripts. Goodman and colleagues found the greatest improvements in the "discussion of study limitations, generalizations, use of confidence intervals, and tone of conclusions" (p. 11) (Goodman, Berlin, Fletcher, & Fletcher, 1994).

In summary, several studies using a number of different approaches, characterized reviewers' reports in a number of ways and made conclusions about the review process. Reviews of accepted manuscripts had a more positive tone and fewer negative phrases than reviews of rejected manuscripts. Another group of studies tested the readability of a manuscript before and after review and found manuscripts more readable after review. An education study of a scoring system for manuscripts recommended that to ensure fairness editors monitor reviewers who deviate from the norm. Studies have shown that review does improve manuscripts, but the degree of improvement is hard to pinpoint. None of these studies provided strong evidence that reviewers' reports result in manuscripts that are drastically different from the one that was submitted. The two studies that examined manuscripts before and after review found improvements in the revised manuscript, particularly in the conclusions and in defining the statistical limitations of the study.

## Limitations

- No study showed a best or most successful method of selecting reviewers. There is an element of "who the editor knows" as being a deciding factor. There is little study in this area.

- A number of the studies of reviewers' time were retrospective; reviewers were asked to estimate the time it took to review, which they might not remember accurately. Prospective studies would be much more enlightening. In fact, the studies that found the most time spent by reviewers per manuscript were estimated times for "typical" manuscripts.

- Editors and investigators have published guidelines to assist reviewers with the review process. Although intuitively one would assume that published guidelines help reviewers produce a better review, no study has compared the details or content of the guidelines with the quality of the review in those journals that publish guidelines.

- A variety of different methodologies was used to test the value of the reviewers' reports, making comparisons difficult and providing little basis for generalizations beyond the impression that review does improve the final published article.

*Recommendations*

- A few studies have documented alterations to manuscripts before and after review to measure the value of the review process. These studies provide a good beginning by supplying baseline data, and employing methodologies that could be replicated in future studies, and offer several methods of analysis. More studies are needed to build on the few that have already been conducted.

- Published guidelines for reviewers are very helpful to the understanding of the review process. Authors can gain insight into how to construct a good manuscript and be informed about how their manuscripts will be reviewed. Editors of scholarly and scientific journals can use published guidelines to construct their own guidelines. Reviewers learn the rationale for the guidelines they receive. Journal readers who understand the review process have a solid basis for understanding articles in a journal. The continued refinement of these guidelines might lead to standardized guidelines as suggested by a number of authors. Overall, the careful structuring and publishing of reviewers' guidelines by editors can only result in a more careful review of manuscripts and more careful attention to the review process. It is recommended that editors regularly publish such guidelines and these might lead to the adoption of standard guidelines.

## Conclusions about role of reviewers

This chapter examined editors' selection of reviewers, the reviewers' workload, the relationship between the quality of their work and their professional standing, the guidelines they receive, and the value of their work for the published article. A group of studies have examined the review process from the reviewer's perspective: how much time they spend per manuscript, how many journals they review for, how many manuscripts they review per year. Studies have shown that reviewers spend several weeks to return a manuscript, but relatively few total hours reviewing a manuscript. Since reviewers may spend time digesting the information presented in a manuscript, it may be difficult for them to pinpoint the exact number of hours they actually spend on a review. Because reviewers are frequently used by more than one journal, it seems that editors must be adept at ferreting out good reviewers. Good reviewing characteristics are probably rather universal, although from the studies that have been undertaken little data exist that might identify exactly what these characteristics are. Studies that compared experience of the reviewers to the quality or value of the review had mixed results. If the selection of a reviewer is the most important component of the review process, as suggested at the beginning of the chapter, it is also the least understood.

There is also little information on how reviewers compare in professional status to their nonreviewing colleagues. One reason for the lack of studies in this area may be that reviewers as a group are difficult to study. Much of the data about reviewers are in reviewers' files in editorial offices. Given the confidential nature of information about reviewers, editors may be reluctant to share this information with anyone outside the editorial office.

The guidelines cited in Table 5-3 suggest that there are standard elements in a manuscript that editors of almost any discipline could earmark as points reviewers should examine. The guidelines range from a few general questions to upwards of 250 items for the reviewer to consider. These guidelines should lay the groundwork for future studies. Some published guidelines were arranged similar to the sections of a manuscript: introduction, methodology, data collection, findings, discussion, and conclusions. Others focus more on the value of the manuscript—its significance or importance. Still others focus on writing style. What is clear is that in the eyes of the editor the role of the reviewer is very important and very complex.

The few studies that looked at the value of the review process from the authors' perspective found that authors felt that review did not result in substantive changes, but that it did help with structuring conclusions, clarifying data, and writing style. Goodman and colleagues (Goodman et al., 1994) found improvement in all but one of 34 manuscript characteristics. The value of the reviewer process from the analysis of manuscripts before and after review is similar to the value of the process as articulated by authors.

## References

Alspach, G. (1994, December). What journal editors would like from reviewers. *Critical Care Nurse, 14*(6), 13-16.

Arnell, P. (1986, November). Communication through publication: the role of reviewers. *Physiotherapy, 72*(11), 530-533.

Arrott, A. (1984, December). Peer reviews. *Physics Today, 37*(12), 92-93.

Baines, C. J. (1987, July 1). Reviewing the reviewers. *Canadian Medical Association Journal, 137*(1), 15.

Bakanic, V., McPhail, C., & Simon, R. J. (1989, Winter). Mixed messages: referees' comments on the manuscripts they review. *Sociological Quarterly, 30*(4), 639-654.

Bardach, J. (1988, September). The case for peer review. *Plastic and Reconstructive Surgery, 82*(3), 516-517.

Baue, A. E. (1993, December). Reflections of a former editor. *Archives of Surgery, 128*(12), 1305-1314.

Bauer, S. H. (1984, December 24). Ethics (or lack thereof) of refereeing. *Chemical and Engineering News, 62*(52), 2, 33.

Bealer, R. C. (1974, Spring). On journal reviewing procedures: a statement. *Rural Sociology, 39*(1), 6-11.

Bernard, H. R. (1979/1980). CARS: computer assisted referee selection. *Journal of Research Communication Studies, 2,* 149-157.

Bertsch, C. R. & Fleming, J. L. (1983, May 15-20). *Computer assisted reviewer selection and manuscript administration: a critical review.* Paper presented at the Scholarly communication around the world, Philadelphia, PA.

Beyer, J. M., Chanove, R. G., & Fox, W. B. (1995, October). The review process and the fates of manuscripts submitted to *AMJ. Academy of Management Journal, 38*(5), 1219-1260.

Biddle, C., & Aker, J. (1996, February). How does the peer review process influence AANA Journal article readability? *AANA Journal, 64*(1), 65-68.

Bishop, C. T. (1984). *How to edit a scientific journal.* Philadelphia: ISI Press.

Bowen, D. D., Perloff, R., & Jacoby, J. (1972, May). Improving manuscript evaluation procedures. *American Psychologist, 27*(3), 221-225.

Campanario, J. M. (1996, March). The competition for journal space among referees, editors, and other authors and its influence on journals' impact factors. *Journal of the American Society for Information Science, 47*(3), 184-192.

Campion, M. A. (1993). Article review checklist: a criterion checklist for reviewing research articles in applied psychology. *Personnel Psychology, 46*(3), 705-718.

Carnegie, M. E. (1975, July-August). The referee system. *Nursing Research, 24*(4), 243.

Carney, M. J., & Lundberg, G. D. (1987, July 3). We've come a long way—thanks to peer review. *JAMA, 258*(1), 87.

Chew, F. S. (1993, February). Manuscript peer review: general concepts and the *AJR* process. *American Journal of Roetngenology, 160*(2), 409-411.

Cho, M. K., & Bero, L. A. (1994, July 13). Instruments for assessing the quality of drug studies published in the medical literature. *JAMA, 272*(2), 101-104.

Cleather, J. (1981, September/October). Manuscript review and the editing process. *Physiotherapy Canada, 33*(5), 283-286.

Cotton, P. (1993, December 15). Flaws documented, reforms debated at congress on journal peer review. *JAMA, 270*(23), 2775-2778.

Crawford, S. (1988, January). Peer review and the evaluation of manuscripts. *Bulletin of the Medical Library Association, 76*(1), 75-77.

Doering, P. L. (1991, September). Writing & reviewing for pharmacy journals. *Florida Pharmacy Today, 55,* 7-11.

Endres, F. F., & Wearden, S. T. (1990, Summer). Demographic portrait of journal reviewers. *Educator, 45*(2), 45-52.

Evans, A. T., McNutt, R. A., Fletcher, S. W., & Fletcher, R. H. (1993, August). The characteristics of peer reviewers who produce good-quality reviews. *Journal of General Internal Medicine, 8*(8), 422-428.

Eysenck, H. J. & Eysenck, S. B. G. (1992, April). Peer review: advice to referees and contributors. *Personality and Individual Differences, 13*(4), 393-399.

Fagan, W. T. (1990, August). To accept or reject: peer review. *Journal of Educational Thought, 24*(2), 103-113.

Fine, M. A. (1996, November). Reflections on enhancing accountability in the peer review process. *American Psychologist, 51*(11), 1190-1191.

Finney, D. J. (1997, June). The responsible referee. *Biometrics, 53*, 715-719.

Finke, R. A. (1990, May). Recommendations for contemporary editorial practices. *American Psychologist, 45*(5), 669-670. Forscher, B. K. (1965, October 15). Rules for referees: The duties of the editorial referee are examined to establish efficient and uniform practices. *Science, 150*(3694), 319-321.

Frank, E. (1996, March/April). Editors' requests of reviewers: a study and a proposal. *Preventive Medicine, 25*(2), 102-104.

Franken, E. A., Jr. (1997, October). Peer review and *Academic Radiology. Academic Radiology, 4*(10), 663-664.

Friedman, D. P. (1995, April). Manuscript peer review at the *AJR*: facts, figures, and quality assessment. *American Journal of Roentgenology, 164*(4), 1007-1009.

Galam, S. (1984, December). Impact of referees' reports. *Physics Today, 37*(12), 11.

Gidez, L. I. (1990, 1991). *The peer review process: strengths and weaknesses—a survey of attitudes, perceptions, and expectations.* Paper presented at the Serials Librarian, St. Catharines, Ontario.

Gilliland, S. W. & Cortina, J. M. (1997, Summer). Reviewer and editor decision making in the journal review process. *Personnel Psychology, 50*(2), 427-452.

Gleser, L. J. (1986). Some notes on refereeing. *American Statistician, 40*(4), 310-312.

Glogoff, S. (1988, November). Reviewing the gatekeepers: A survey of referees of library journals. *Journal of the American Society for Information Science, 39*(6), 400-407.

Goodman, S. N., Berlin, J. A., Fletcher, S. W., & Fletcher, R. H. (1994, July 1). Manuscript quality before and after peer review and editing at the Annals of Internal Medicine. *Annals of Internal Medicine, 121*(1), 11-21.

Gordon, M. D. (1980). The role of referees in scientific communication. In J. Hartley (Ed.), *The psychology of written communication, selected readings* (pp. 263-275). New York: Nichols Publishing Co.

Hamermesh, D. S. (1994, Winter). Facts and myths about refereeing. *Journal of Economic Perspectives, 8*(1), 153-163.

Haness, J. (1983, March). How to critique a document. *IEEE Transactions on Professional Communication, PC-26*(1), 15-17.

Harrison, E. R. (1977, January). A referee's plea. *Physics Today, 30*(1), 85-87.

Harter, S. P. (1993, July). The peer review process. *Library Quarterly, 63*(3), v-vi.

Humphreys, R. P., Reigel, D. H., & Epstein, F. J. (1995, May). The editor's labours: separating the wheat from the chaff. *Pediatric Neurosurgery, 22*(5), 23-27.

Huston, P. (1994, April 15). Information for peer reviewers. *Canadian Medical Association Journal, 150*(8), 1211-1216.

Jauch, L. R. & Wall, J. L. (1989, March). What they do when they get your manuscript: a survey of *Academy of Management* reviewer practices. *Academy of Management Journal, 32*(1), 157-173.

Kapp, M. B. (1988). Legal discussions in medical literature: is there adequate peer review? *Medicine and Law, 7*, 317-321.

King, D., McDonald, D. D., & Roderer, N. K. (1981). *Scientific journals in the United States: their production, use and economics*. Stroudsburg, Pennsylvania: Hutchinson Ross Publishing Company.

King, D. W. & Griffins, J-M. (1995, Spring). Economic issues concerning electronic publishing and distribution of scholarly articles. *Library Trends, 43*(4), 713-740.

Kittredge, P. (1984, October). Wanted: a word from the wise. *Respiratory Care, 29*(10), 991-993.

Kochar, M. S. (1986). The peer review of manuscripts—in need for improvement. *Journal of Chronic Diseases, 39*(2), 147-149.

Kochen, M. & Perkel, B. (1977). *Improving referee-selection and manuscript evaluation*. Paper presented at the First International Congress on Scientific Editors, Dordrect, Holland.

Laband, D. N. (1990, May). Is there value-added from the review process in economics? Preliminary evidence from authors. *Quarterly Journal of Economics, 105*(2), 341-352.

Laband, D. N. & Piette, M. J. (1994, February). Favoritism versus search for good papers: empirical evidence regarding the behavior of journal editors. *Journal of Political Economy, 102*(1), 194-302.

Lehr, J. H. (1991, March/April). The peer review system according to *Ground Water*. *Ground Water, 29*(2), 167-168.

Lock, S. & Smith, J. (1990, March 9). What do peer reviewers do? *JAMA, 263*(10), 1341-1343.

Lundberg, G. D. (1984, February 10). Appreciation to our peer reviewers. *JAMA, 251*(6), 758.

Maher, B. A. (1978, August). A reader's, writer's, and reviewer's guide to assessing research reports in clinical psychology. *Journal of Consulting and Clinical Psychology, 46*(4), 835-838.

Mahoney, M. J. (1976). The endless quest. In M. J. Mahoney (Ed.), *Scientist as subject: the psychological imperative* (pp. 79-107). Cambridge, Massachusetts: Ballinger Publishing Company.

Manheim, F. T. (1973, May). Referees and the publication crisis. *EOS Transactions of the American Geophysical Union, 54*(5), 532-537.

Manheim, F. T. (1975, September). The scientific referee. *IEEE Transactions on Professional Communication, 18*(3), 190-195.

Markland, R. E. (1989, Fall). Musings of a well-travelled editor. *Decision Sciences, 20*(4), vii-xiii.

Mason, P. M., Steagall, J. W., & Fabritius, M. M. (1992, August). Publication delays in articles in economics what to do about them. *Applied Economics, 24*(8), 859-874.

McKenzie, S. (1995, June). Reviewing scientific papers. *Archives of Disease in Childhood, 72*(6), 539-540.

McNutt, R. A., Evans, A. T., Fletcher, R. H., & Fletcher, S. W. (1990, March 9). The effects of blinding on the quality of review. *JAMA, 263*(10), 1371-1376.

Meile, R. L. (1977, February). The case against double jeopardy. *American Sociologist, 12*(1), 532.

Mitchell, T. R., Beach, L. R., & Smith, K. G. (1985). Some data on publishing from the authors' and reviewers' perspective. In L. L. Cummings & P. J. Frost (Eds.), *Publishing in the organizational sciences* (pp. 248-264). Homewood, IL: Richard D. Irwin, Inc.

Murphy, T. M. & Utts, J. M. (1994, November). A retrospective analysis of peer review at Physiolgia Plantarum. *Physiologia Plantarum, 92*(3), 535-542.

Neuliep, J. W. & Crandall, R. (1993). Reviewer bias against replication research. *Journal of Social Behavior and Personality, 8*(6), 21-29.

Newell, F. W. (1990, February 15). Peer review. *American Journal of Ophthalmology, 109*(2), 221-223.

Nylenna, M., Riis, P., & Karlson, Y. (1994, July 13). Multiple blinded reviews of the same two manuscripts; effects of referee characteristics and publication language. *JAMA, 272*(2), 149-151.

Nylenna, M., Riis, P., & Karlson, Y. (1995, June). Are refereeing forms helpful? A study among medical referees in Denmark, Norway and Sweden. *European Science Editing* (55), 3-5.

Pierie, J-P. N. E., Walvoort, H. C., & Overbeke, A. J. P. M. (1996, November 30). Readers' evaluation of effect of peer review and editing on quality of articles in the Nederlands Tijdschrift voor Geneeskunde. *Lancet, 348*(9040), 1480-1483.

Pigg, R. M. (1987, January). Comments on the *Journal* peer review system. *Journal of School Health, 57*(1), 5-7.

Polak, J. F. (1995, September). The role of the manuscript reviewer in the peer review process. *American Journal of Radiology, 165*(3), 685-688.

Pyke, D. A. (1976, November 6). How I referee. *British Medical Journal, 2*(6044), 1117-1118.

Reideberg, J. W. & Reidenberg, M. M. (1991, July). Report of a survey of some aspects of editorial board peer review at *Clinical Pharmacology & Therapeutics*. *Clinical Pharmacology and Therapeutics, 50*(1), 1-3.

Relman, A. S. (1981). Journals. In K. S. Warren (Ed.), *Coping with the biomedical literature*: Praeger Special Studies.

Roberts, J. C., Fletcher, R. H., & Fletcher, S. W. (1994, July 13). Effects of peer review and editing on the readability of articles published in Annals of Internal Medicine. *JAMA, 272*(2), 119-121.

Rodman, H. (1970, March-a). Notes to an incoming journal editor. *American Psychologist, 25*(3), 269-273.

Rodman, H. (1970, November-b). The moral responsibility of journal editors and referees. *American Sociologist, 5*(4), 351-357.

Rowney, J. A. & Zenisek, T. J. (1980, January). Manuscript characteristics influencing reviewers' decisions. *Canadian Psychology, 21*(1), 17-21.

Salasche, S. J. (1997, June). How to "peer review" a medical journal manuscript. *Dermatologic Surgery, 23*(6), 423-428.

Saracevic, T. (1986). The refereeing process at *Information Processing & Management*. *Information Processing & Management, 22*(1), 1-3.

Siegelman, S. S. (1988). Guidelines for reviewers of *Radiology*. *Radiology, 166*(2), 360.

Siegelman, S. S. (1989, November). Desirable qualities of manuscripts. *Radiology, 173*(2), 467-468.

Siegelman, S. S. (1991, March). Assassins and zealots: variations in peer review; special report. *Radiology, 178*(3), 637-642.

Smith, A. J. (1990, April). The task of the referee. *Computer, 23*(4), 65-71.

Sommers, H. S., Jr. (1983, April). Improving refereeing. *Physics Today, 36*(4), 92-93.

Spencer, N. J., Hartnett, J., & Mahoney, J. (1986, January). Problems with reviews in the standard editorial practice. *Journal of Social Behavior and Personality, 1*(1), 21-36.

Squires, B. P. (1989, July 1a). Biomedical manuscripts: what editors want from authors and peer reviewers. *Canadian Medical Association Journal, 141*(1), 17-19.

Squires, B. P. (1989, October 1b). Editorials and platform articles: What editors want from authors and peer reviewers. *Canadian Medical Association Journal, 141*, 666-667.

Stossel, T. P. (1985, March 7). Reviewer status and review quality. *New England Journal of Medicine, 312*(10), 658-659.

Stull, G. R. (1989, April). Peer-review process is key to quality publication. *Ceramic Bulletin, 68*(4), 850-852.

Talley, C. R. (1991, May). Tracking manuscripts and reviewers electronically. *American Journal of Hospital Pharmacy, 48*(5), 950.

Webb, W. B. (1979, February). Continuing education: refereeing journal articles. *Teaching of Psychology, 6*(1), 59-60.

Weller, A. C. (1990, March 9). Editorial peer review in U.S. medical journals. *JAMA, 263*(10), 1344-1347.

Wolff, W. M. (1973, March). Publication problems in psychology and an explicit evaluation schema for manuscripts. *American Psychologist, 28*(3), 257-261.

Yankauer, A. (1990, March 9). Who are the reviewers and how much do they review? *JAMA, 263*(10), 1338-1340.

Zellmer, W. A. (1977, August). What editors expect of reviewers. *American Journal of Hospital Pharmacy, 34*(8), 819.

# Chapter Six

# Reviewer Agreement

Nurse, editor: *Conflicting reviewers' comments are inherent in the review system.*

(Johnson, 1996, p. 1)

Physician, editor: *Reviewer disagreement may be a good thing; it is in fact to be expected.*

(Morgan & Yankauer, 1987, p. 79)

If a set of reviewers independently evaluate the merits of a manuscript and agree with each other, the job of the editor is presumably made relatively easy—the editor will (should, might, ought to?) agree with the consensus of the reviewers and act accordingly. If a manuscript is well thought out and well written with logical conclusions based on solid methodology, data collection, and data analysis, there is the expectation that the reviewers will agree that it should be published. Conversely, if there are faults in design, analysis, or interpretation of a study, there is also the expectation that each reviewer will uncover these faults and make a recommendation to reject a manuscript based on a study's shortcomings. Reviewers are expected to know whether certain faults are serious enough to render a manuscript unpublishable and which faults can be corrected with revisions.

Chapter Two on rejected manuscripts and Chapter Three on editors and editorial boards shows a fair amount of consensus regarding publication criteria for rejection (Table 2-1 and Table 2-2) or acceptance (Table 3-2). Table 2-1 provides a list of editors' theoretical reasons for rejection, Table 2-2 their actual reasons, and Table 3-2 summarizes a number of investigators' normative publication criteria. If manuscripts have those qualities described in the normative publication criteria, there is some expectation that the reviewers will agree with each other and accept a manuscript. Likewise, if a manuscript has the characteristics described in Tables 2-1 or 2-2 it is expected that the reviewers would recommend rejection.

In 1977, Williams thought that it was time to study how reviewers did their job. He lamented that little was known about the degree to which reviewers agreed. "There are many reasons why referees disagree, of course, and research in this area should be broadly based" (p. 131) (Williams, 1977). This chapter examines what has been learned through studies of reviewer agreement and the importance of reviewer agreement to the editorial peer review process.

*Question*

To what degree do reviewers agree with each other when evaluating the same manuscript?

*Criteria for inclusion*

~ any study that examined agreement among reviewers for a defined set of manuscripts.

*Comparable studies*

Only one study was located that asked multiple reviewers to evaluate a single manuscript.

Ernst and colleagues conducted a straightforward experiment (Ernst et al., 1993). One manuscript submitted to a medical journal was sent to 45 experts, each holding editorial board appointments for journals that publish articles with subject matter similar to that of the submitted manuscript. Each of these experts was asked to evaluate the manuscript against eight measures of quality. In writing up the study, the investigators gave no details about the manuscript, nor did they say if the manuscript was eventually published and, if so, to what extent it was revised prior to acceptance. Thirty-one (68.9 percent) reviewers completed the evaluations (Table 6-1). Almost every measure received both the worst and the best rating by reviewers. From two-thirds to three-quarters of reviewers rated the manuscript fair to good, about 20 percent rated the manuscript in the accept to excellent category, about 12 percent found the statistics unacceptable, and less than 10 percent recommended rejection.

| Discipline | Number of reviewers | Accept excellent | Fair good | Reject unacceptable | Reference |
|---|---|---|---|---|---|
| medicine—overall | 31 | 17.2% | 75.8% | 6.9% | (Ernst, Saradeth, & Resch, 1993) |
| scientific merit | | 16.1% | 77.4% | 6.4% | |
| clarity of description | | 26.7% | 70.0% | 3.3% | |
| statistical method | | 22.6% | 64.5% | 12.9% | |
| methodology | | 20.0% | 73.3% | 6.7% | |

**Table 6-1: Multiple reviewer ratings of one manuscript**

Ernst and colleagues concluded that "the absence of reliability ... seems unacceptable for anyone aspiring to publish in peer-reviewed journals" (p. 296). This is a very small study that illustrates the range of opinions that can be solicited from just one manuscript. It also illustrates the important role of the editor, who must decide how to proceed after receiving conflicting recommendations. The range of recommendations indicates that submitting a manuscript for more review might not solve an editor's dilemma. The investigators of this study maintained that they had chosen a noncontroversial manuscript and expressed dismay that even the linguistic category received a range of ratings, although none rated the author's linguistics unacceptable. With this 1993 study Ernst and colleagues echoed Williams' 1977 sentiment: the "method of evaluating scientific papers by peer review is unreliable and open to bias and should itself be submitted to evaluation" (p. 296).

In addition to this study in which one manuscript received multiple reviews, a number of studies have examined agreement among reviewers who were asked to evaluate abstracts, papers presented at meetings, or published articles. Abstracts by their very nature are an abbreviated representation of a study. Reviewers of abstracts are asked to make a recommendation to accept or reject a work with little knowledge of the entire endeavor. One would expect studies of reviewer agreement of abstracts to show a relatively high level of reviewer disagreement, and in fact, studies of reviewer agreement in the evaluation of abstracts submitted for consideration for presentations at a meeting do just that (Cicchetti & Conn, 1975), (Cicchetti & Conn, 1976), (McReynolds, 1991), and (Rubin, Redelmeier, Wu, & Steinberg, 1993). The 1976 study by Cicchetti and Conn found that reviewer agreement varied considerably depending upon which statistical test was applied to data in studies that evaluated abstracts. Since these studies do not address reviews of manuscripts submitted to journals, they are not included in the analysis in this section.

Bowen, Perloff, and Jacoby's study comparing reviewer ratings of a group of papers being considered for recognition after presentation at a meeting also found a great variation in ratings (Bowen, Perloff, & Jacoby, 1972). However, these are probably not comparable reviews, since criteria established to evaluate papers for awards usually consider a number of factors in addition to the scientific merits of a study.

There have been studies that assessed rater agreement for published articles, not for overall publishability, but for specific aspects of the merits of the work. One of these studies tested rater agreement on the clinical relevance of articles published in three journals: the *American Journal of Medicine*; *Annals of Internal Medicine*; and the *New England Journal of Medicine* (Dixon, Schonfeld, Altman, & Whitcomb, 1983). Another study assessed agreement among raters for "the consistency of an index of the scientific quality of research overviews" (p. 91) for 36 published review articles (Oxman et al., 1991). A third study assessed inter-rater reliability for "the methodological quality and clinical relevance of drug studies" (p. 101) published in symposium proceedings and peer reviewed bio-medical journals (Cho & Bero, 1994). Cho and Bero's study tested the validity of a scoring system for evaluating reviewers' reports and is discussed in Chapter Five. These studies are mentioned here because they are often included in discussions of studies of reviewer agreement, but because they did not evaluate bona fide manuscripts they are excluded from further discussion.

Zuckerman and Merton discuss reviewer agreement for 172 manuscripts submitted to *The Physical Review* between 1948-1956 (Zuckerman & Merton, 1971). For five manuscripts the reviewers completely disagreed, and for two-thirds of the manuscripts there was only minor disagreement. No other details of this study were given. In addition, Zuckerman and Merton also refer to a reviewer agreement study conducted by Orr and Kassab of 1,572 biomedical manuscripts. Each manuscript in Orr and Kassab's study was reviewed by at least two referees, who agreed with each other 75 percent of the time in recommending acceptance or rejection. (The results of this study were presented at the International Federation for Documentation in Washington, D.C., on October 15, 1965. Proceedings from this meeting have not been located.) Lazarus claimed only about 10 percent to 15 percent of reviewers agreed to accept or reject a manuscript for *Physical Review Letters* during the first round of reviewing (Lazarus, 1982). He provided no other details and argued that reviewer disagreement would be greater if editors did not use anonymous review. Kahn and colleagues examined reviewer agreement for the journal *Psychology of Women Quarterly* on eight manuscript characteristics, providing data only on the highest, lowest, and median percentages of agreement (Kahn, Presbury, Moore, & Driver, 1990). This research focused mainly on different characteristics of accepted and rejected manuscripts (see Chapter Two). However, none of these studies gave sufficient detail for further analysis.

Table 6-2 provides summary information on reviewer agreement studies. In these studies reviewers' reports of manuscripts submitted to 32 journals and one group of journals published by the American Psychological Association were tested for reviewer agreement. Each study used a similar methodology—the reviewers' recommendations were compared after a manuscript had been reviewed according to the particular journal's standard peer review process. For each study, the set of manuscripts used were either received in the editorial office during a certain time period or received starting with a particular date until there were sufficient manuscripts. Each of the reviewer agreement studies examined a group of bona fide reviewers' reports. Reviewers in these studies would have had no way of knowing that their reports would be part of a study.

Reviewers' reports were analyzed using a number of methodologies. Some studies tested for the overall percentage of reviewer agreement; others looked for the concurrence of general agreement to either accept or reject. Most subjected the data to one of several statistical tests. Most studies compared ratings between two reviewers. Some investigators considered reviewers to agree only when there was an exact agreement, others considered reviewers to agree if their recommendations were within one step of each other. For example, a recommendation to accept a manuscript with no revisions might be considered to be the same level of agreement as a recommendation to accept with minor revisions.

The analysis of reviewer agreement studies has two sections. The first summarizes the discussions of statistical tests used in reviewer agreement studies; the second discusses what can be learned from these studies despite the questions about the statistical analysis used.

## Statistics used to analyze studies of reviewer agreement

A variety of statistical tests have been used to calculate the degree of reviewer agreement. There is debate as to which of these tests is the most reliable.
Each of the following statistical tests has been used in at least one of the studies in Table 6-2:

### Finn's *r*:

*Compares the variance within manuscripts to the variance
that would have been obtained if the ratings had been assigned randomly (p. 74) (Whitehurst, 1983).*

*Finn's r can be interpreted as the proportion of the corre-
spondence of the observed ratings that is not due to chance
(p. 25) (Whitehurst, 1984).*

### Kappa:

*The proportion of agreement corrected for chance and scaled
to vary from -1 to +1 so that a negative value indicates poorer
than chance agreement, zero indicates exactly chance agreement, and a positive value indicates better than chance agreement (p. 613) (Fleiss & Cohen, 1973).*

*A kappa coefficient of 0.14 indicates that referees agreed in
their evaluation on 14 percent more of the manuscripts than
would have been expected on the basis of pure chance. Kappa
coefficients between zero and 0.40 point to a relatively low
level of agreement. Kappa coefficients between 0.41 and 0.80
are described as reflecting substantial agreement, and values
greater than 0.81 indicate excellent agreement (p. 235)
(Daniel, 1993). Kappa is appropriate when all disagreements
may be considered equally serious, and weighted kappa is
appropriate when the relative seriousness of the different
possible disagreements can be specified (p. 323) (Fleiss,
Cohen, & Everitt, 1969).*

### Kendall's coefficient:

*A rank ordering concordance (p. 99) (Feurer et al., 1994).*

### Intraclass correlation coefficient (ICC):

*A procedure for estimating the reliability of sets of ratings ...
based upon the analysis of variance and the estimation of
variance components (p. 3) (Bartko, 1966).*

| Journal | # of manuscripts | Agreement (original investigators) overall | accept | reject | Statistical tests (original investigators) | Statistical tests (additional analysis) | References |
|---|---|---|---|---|---|---|---|
| American Journal of Community Psychology | 220 | | | | .43 rigor of method; .23 significance of issues (intercorrelations) | | (Glidewell, 1988) |
| American Journal of Public Health | 639 | 57.0% | | | 9% complete disagreement | | (Yankauer, 1979) |
| American Psychological Association Journals | 153 | | | | only 31 of 585 possible matches were beyond chance | | (Fiske & Fogg, 1990) |
| American Psychologist | 78 | | 11.5% | 51.7% | | .49[a], 79%[b], 54[c]; .54[d] | (Scarr, 1978) |
| | 71 | | 12.0% | 57.0% | .59 (equal interval); .64 (RC model) | .74 and .78[f] | (Hargens & Herting, 1990) |
| American Sociological Review  accepted  rejected  rejected | 394  361  322 | | 12.0% | 58.0% | .37-.45 (R²)  .28 (equal interval); .29 (RC model) | 0.29[d]; .44 and .44[f] | (Bakanic, McPhail, & Simon, 1987)  (Hargens & Herting, 1990a), (Hargens & Herting, 1990b) |
| Angewandte Chemie | 449 | | 5.0% | 10.0% | .14 (kappa); .20 (weighed kappa); .25 (intraclass) | | (Daniel, 1993) |
| Annals of Internal Medicine  accepted manuscripts | 113 | 69%-77% | | | | | (Justice, Berlin, Fletcher, Fletcher, & Goodman, 1994) |
| Australian and New Zealand Journal of Psychiatry | 500 | 50.0% | | | .23 (Cramer's V); 6% complete disagreement | | (Parker, Barnett, Holmes, & Manicavasagar, 1984) |
| British Medical Journal | 707 | 62%-68% | | | | .31[d] | (Lock, 1985) |
| Canadian Journal of Behavioural Sciences | 120 | | | | .42 (intercorrelation) | | (Linden, Craig, & Wen, 1992) |
| Developmental Review | 184 | | | | .62 (Finn's r); .44 (intraclass) | .44[c] .44[d] | (Whitehurst, 1983) |
| Journal of Abnormal Psychology | 1067 | 67.0% | 42.0% | 74.0% | .17-.28 (intraclass) | .19[c], .19[d] | (Cicchetti & Eron, 1979) |
| Journal of the American Academy of Child & Adolescent Psychiatry | 272 | | | | .27 (intraclass); .43 (after new rating scale) | | (Strayhorn, McDermont, & Tanguay, 1993) |
| Journal of Applied Behavior Analysis | 40 | 81%-98% | | | 12% complete agreement | | (Boice, Barlow, Johnson, & Klosko, 1984), (Boice, Pecker, Zaback, & Barlow, 1985) |
| Journal of Clinical Anesthesia  pairs of reviewers  editorial board | 422 | 40.0%  32.0% | | | | | (Cullen & Macaulay, 1992), (Cullen & Macaulay, 1994) |
| Journal of Clinical Investigation | 1000 | 67%-80% | 36.2% | | | | (Scharschmidt, DeAmicis, Bacchetti, & Held, 1994) |

**Table 6-2: Studies of reviewer agreement**

| Journal | # of manuscripts | Agreement (original investigators) | | | Statistical tests (original investigators) | Statistical tests (additional analysis) | References |
|---|---|---|---|---|---|---|---|
| | | overall | accept | reject | | | |
| Journal of Counseling Psychology | 263 | | | | .37 (Finn's r); .28 (intraclass) | | (Munley, Sharkin, & Gelso, 1988) |
| Journal of Education Psychology | 325 | | | | .34 (intraclass) | .34[c], .34[d] | (Marsh & Ball, 1981) |
| | 278 | | | | .30 (intraclass) | | (Marsh & Ball, 1989) |
| Journal of Health and Social Behavior | 120 | 41.0% | | | | | (1989), (Gallagher & Ferrante, 1991) |
| Journal of Personality and Social Psychology | 287 | | | | .07-.37 (intraclass) | .26[c], .26[d], 70%[e] | (Scott, 1974) |
| Journal of Vascular and Interventional Radiology | 23 | | | | .84 (intraclass); .94 (Kendall's) | | (Feurer et al., 1994) |
| Law and Society Review | 251 | | 6.0% | 60.0% | .17 (equal interval); .23 (RC model) | .23[d], .29 and .36[f] | (Hargens & Herting, 1990b) |
| New England Journal of Medicine | 496 | 41.8% | 50.5% | 39.7% | | .26[d] | (Ingelfinger, 1974) |
| Personality and Social Psychology Bulletin | 177 | | | | .54-.62 (intraclass) | .091[a], .21[c], .21[c], 80%[e] | (Hendrick, 1976) |
| | 177 | | | | .21 (corrected) | | (Hendrick, 1977) |
| | 177 | | 13.0% | 18.0% | .23-.27 (equal interval); .28-.30 (RC model) | .37 and .46[f] | (Hargens & Herting, 1990b) |
| Physical Therapy<br>no revision<br>unsolicited | 223<br>284 | | | | .0079 (kappa)<br>.116 (kappa) | | (Bohannon, 1986) |
| Physiological Zoology | 209 | | 11.0% | 26.0% | .28 (equal interval); .31 (RC model) | .31[d] .44 and .47[f] | (Hargens & Herting, 1990b) |
| Research Quarterly for Exercise & Sports Review | 363 | 40.0% | | | .11 (kappa); .37 (intraclass) | | (Morrow, Bray, Fulton, & Thomas, 1992) |
| Rural Sociology | 337 | | 63.0% | 95.0% | | | (Warner, Eberley, Johnson, & Albrecht, 1985) |
| | 279 | | | | .57 (rank order); .36 (correlation with outcome) | | (Eberley & Warner, 1990) |
| Social Problems | 193 | 75.2% | 22.7% | 49.8% | | .29[c] .40[d] | (Smigel & Ross, 1970) |
| Social Work Research | 54 | 14%-32% | | | -.015 to .404 (intraclass); 55%-69% (one-step agreement) | | (Kirk & Franke, 1997) |
| Sociological Quarterly | | | 20.0% | 30.0% | | 70%[e] | (McCartney, 1973) |
| Sociometry<br>accepted<br>rejected | 28<br>75 | | 3.5% | 14.7% | | | (Seeman, 1966) |
| | 140 | | | | .21 | .21[c], .21[d], 75%[e] | (Hendrick, 1976) |
| South African Journal of Psychology | 164 | | | | .34 (single-reviewer reliability) | | (Plug, 1993) |
| *Average* | | 49.3% | 22.0% | 44.9% | | .27[c] | |

a. Kappa (Watkins, 1979)
b. % overall agreement (Cicchetti, 1980)
c. Single-reviewer reliability (Marsh, 1989)

d. Kappa or R (Cicchetti, 1991)
e. % overall agreement (Crandall, 1978)
f. Equal-interval scale values and RC association model for two referees (O'Brien, 1991)

**Table 6-2: Studies of reviewer agreement (continued)**

> *The intraclass correlation coefficient ($R_1$) can vary between -1
> and +1. The higher the $R_1$ scores, the more the observer agree-
> ment (p. 375) (Cicchetti & Conn, 1976). There are numerous
> versions of the ICCs that can give quite different results when
> applied to the same data (p. 420) (Shrout & Fleiss, 1979). Any
> cutoff value [for reliable interjudge agreement] is somewhat
> arbitrary (p. 94) (Oxman et al., 1991). The row and column
> effects (RC) association model of intraclass correlation em-
> pirically estimates distances between referee recommenda-
> tion categories [and] researchers can avoid using arbitrary
> assumptions about these distances (p. 3-4) (Hargens &
> Herting, 1990b).*

### Single-reviewer reliability:

> *The correlation between two independent reviews of the same
> manuscript across a large number of manuscripts submitted
> for publication (p. 152) (Marsh & Ball, 1989).*

> *The reliability of the average of two or more reviewers will be
> higher than the reliability of a single rater (p. 873) (Marsh &
> Ball, 1981). Once the value of a single rater is determined the
> average of two or more reviewers can be obtained with the
> Spearman-Brown equation.*

These definitions are from the reports themselves and are briefly summarized here as an introduction to the terminology and to some of the issues with
reviewer agreement studies. The definitions give a sense of some of the sub-
tleties of statistical issues that underlie the statistical analyses of reviewer
agreement studies. When a statistical test listed in Table 6-2 is not defined
above, the investigator did not provide a definition. The following discussion is
not a mathematical discussion, but a presentation of the issues and the problems
associated with statistical analyses of reviewer agreement data.

In an example of the complication of the mathematical concepts surrounding reviewer agreement studies, Cicchetti provides formulae for the kappa, weighted
kappa, and three variations of the intraclass correlation coefficient ($R_i$): $R_{i(Model\ I)}$,
$R_{i(Model\ II)}$, and $R_{i(Model\ III)}$ (Cicchetti, 1991). The reader is referred to references cited
above for details of definitions, variations in the statistical tests, and precise formulae.

Several investigators have subjected their data to more than one statistical
test (Whitehurst, 1983), (Munley et al., 1988), (Hargens & Herting, 1990a),
(Eberley & Warner, 1990), (Morrow et al., 1992), (Daniel, 1993), (Feurer et al.,
1994), and (Kirk & Franke, 1997). Both Marsh and Ball (Marsh & Ball, 1989)
and Cicchetti (Cicchetti, 1991) reworked the statistics used in a number of studies in Table 6-2; results of these recalculations with the statistical tests used to

recalculate are also found in Table 6-2. Some examples should help to show the difficulties with some of the statistical issues.

Given the number of possible statistical tests appropriate for an examination of reviewer agreement data and the nuances in their application and interpretation, it is not surprising that these studies have generated considerable controversy on the proper statistical tests to use for particular studies. Indeed, several commentaries on reviewer agreement have questioned the interpretation of the results of a previous study or questioned the correctness of a statistical test applied to some of the data. For example, Hendrick studied reviewer agreement for the journal *Personality and Social Psychology Bulletin*, calculated a correlation of from +0.54 to +0.62, and reported he was "quite pleased at the relatively high level of reviewer agreement" (p. 207) (Hendrick, 1976). Later, after revising his previous conclusion, his optimism over his results was replaced with "embarrassment and disappointment" (p. 1). Hendrick had failed to use the intraclass correlation, and the recalculation gave an intraclass coefficient of +0.21, which indicated a low level of agreement among reviewers (Hendrick, 1977).

Crandall argued that when some reviewer agreement studies were examined slightly differently, results are markedly better (Crandall, 1978). For example, in a reexamination of the Hendrick's study of *Personality and Social Psychology Bulletin*, Crandall showed there was complete agreement in 33 percent of the cases. An additional 27 percent of reviewers' recommendations are within one category of each other. In only 4 percent of the cases did reviewers entirely disagree. Crandall concluded that 80 percent of the ratings are in general agreement about the publishability of manuscripts for *Personality and Social Psychology Bulletin*. In this same report, Crandall further analyzed data from reviewer agreement studies of both the *Journal of Personality and Social Psychology* (Scott, 1974) and *Sociological Quarterly* (McCartney, 1973). From this additional analysis, Crandall concluded that reviewer agreement averaged about 70 percent if one simply calculated the percentage of agreement among those reviewers who thought the manuscript was generally publishable (Crandall, 1978). Watkins also examined the Hendrick data, applied an additional statistical test, the kappa statistic, and calculated a very low level of reviewer agreement: a kappa of 0.091 (Watkins, 1979). After calculating the kappa, Watkins argued that it is "apparent that a statistic such as $\kappa$ [kappa] should be used in place of simple percentage of agreement so as not to obscure the role played by chance." (p. 797).

Watkins also reexamined data from the Scarr and Weber study of reviewer agreement for the *American Psychologist*, which had originally found that reviewers' agreed in 57 out of 87 pairs of ratings (Scarr, 1978). While Scarr and Weber concluded "interrater reliability is quite high and gives us new faith in ourselves as casual observers" (p. 935). Watkins calculated the kappa for this study at 0.49, revealing a rate of about 50 percent reviewer agreement after excluding agreement likely to happen by chance. Gilmore (Gilmore, 1979) argued that conclusions of the Scarr and Weber study showed that 47 percent agreement would be expected for "*totally unreliable* judgment conditions" and

suggested that "some creative experimentation with new rules of journal reviewing" (p. 157) might be needed.

Whitehurst believed the most appropriate statistical test for reviewer agreement studies was Finn's *r* (Whitehurst, 1984). He maintained that "comparisons across journals using the intraclass correlation are impossible if there are
significant differences in rejection rates. Finn's *r* solves this and related problems by comparing the obtained variance within manuscripts to that which
would have been obtained if manuscript ratings had been assigned randomly"
(p. 27). Cicchetti critiqued Whitehurst's arguments by demonstrating "that the
$r_I$ [intraclass correlation coefficient] is a much more sensitive statistic than
Finn's" (p. 563) (Cicchetti, 1985). He went on to argue that "it is a well-known
statistical fact that overall agreement levels are simply weighted averages between levels of agreement on specific categories of classification" (p. 563).
Whitehurst then suggested that when "conscientious reviewers are faced with
a preponderance of low-quality manuscripts and a restricted range of manuscript quality, they are likely to agree mostly on reject decisions. They cannot
obtain a respectable intraclass correlation coefficient under those conditions"
(p. 569) (Whitehurst, 1985).

In 1988, Lindsey reviewed a number of reviewer agreement studies and suggested that results indicated "highly selective decision-making with imprecise
reviewers results in outcomes ... that are only slightly better than chance" (p.
75) (Lindsey, 1988). He concluded that the study of reviewer agreement "within
a proper statistical framework suggests substantial imprecision in the manuscript review process" (p. 80). One solution, from Lindsey's perspective is that
editors should use three or more reviewers per manuscript.

A study of reviewer agreement for the *Journal of Health and Social
Behavior* found overall agreement of 79 percent between pairs when comparing agreement between acceptance versus rejection recommendations.
However, when testing for agreement on recommendation of the same specific
category—the reviewers were asked to select from one of six ratings—the level
of agreement was only 41 percent (1989).

Hargens and Herting's studied reviewer agreement in five scholarly journals,
one from each of five disciplines (sociology, zoology, law, psychology, and social psychology) (Hargens & Herting, 1990a). Each journal Hargens and Herting
studied is listed separately in Table 6-2. They found reviewers most likely to
agree on a rejection recommendation. Hargens and Herting "point to analytical
difficulties that confront researchers who wish to compare levels of referee
agreement exhibited by different journals." (p. 1). According to the investigators,
when researchers "calculate measures of agreement, researchers implicitly assume that manuscripts vary on a latent dimension of publishability, but measures
of agreement themselves provide little evidence about the existence of such a dimension. By examining the statistical fit of the RC associate model and the referee recommendation scale values yielded by that model, researchers can obtain
more direct evidence on the adequacy of the assumption. (p. 14).

O'Brien recalculated Hargens and Herting's data, maintaining that these authors had not taken the number of reviewers per manuscript into account (O'Brien, 1991). O'Brien's recalculation was based on the ICC, using the same two measures Hargens and Herting used (the equal-interval scale values and the RC associate model), but for one, two, or three referees. For example, single reviewer rating for *Physiological Zoology* is 0.28, while the reliability based on two reviewers is 0.44, and this increases to 0.54 for three reviewers. O'Brien concluded that "used in conjunction with weights derived from the RC associate model the levels of reliability found in previous studies are seen to be more pessimistic than warranted" (p. 327). As can be seen from Table 6-2, in each case O'Brien's recalculation resulted in a higher level of reviewer agreement than Hargens and Herting found.

Lindsey took a different approach with Hargens and Herting's (Hargens & Herting, 1990) analysis from the perspective of sociology journal reviewers (Lindsey, 1991). Lindsey argued that not all journal editors perform their tasks well, and in order "to improve the quality of published work journals need to reduce the low reliability of the current manuscript review process" (p. 313). Lindsey questioned Hargens and Herting's finding that the reviewer agreement coefficients were between 0.2 and 0.3 for the *American Sociological Review.* Lindsey argued that if his own model were used "almost half of the papers that should be published are not and they are replaced with papers that should not have been published" (p. 323). Of course, Lindsey only addressed referee agreement here and ignores the role of the editor, who can override reviewer recommendations. The findings do not shed light on the manuscripts that are not published.

Both Marsh and Ball and Cicchetti also recalculated data from reviewer agreement studies (Table 6-2), basing their recalculations on the single-reviewer reliability measure (Marsh & Ball, 1989) (Cicchetti, 1991). Marsh and Ball found that reviewer agreement "between different reviewers on each separate dimension, on the unweighted sum of these dimensions, and on various empirically weighted sums of these dimensions was no better than for the overall recommendation by itself" (p. 151).

Taking another approach in the examination of reviewer agreement studies, Cicchetti felt that several statistical tests assume that recommendations to accept, to reject, and to revise each occur with the same frequency (Cicchetti, 1991). However, many journals have high rejection rates, and there is the expectation that a rejection recommendation would occur at a different rate from an acceptance recommendation, thus rendering measures of chance agreement invalid. Cicchetti described the conditions under which certain statistics were appropriate. For example, the $R_{i(Model\ I)}$ is the statistic of choice for assessing reviewer agreement when manuscripts are evaluated by different sets of reviewers, and the $R_{i(Model\ II)}$ is the statistic of choice when three or more reviewers evaluate the same set of manuscripts. Cicchetti examined results of several of the studies in Table 6-2, giving the original investigators' kappa statistic if available or calculating it if not. Cicchetti found that reviewers and editors agree more on rejection than on acceptance for the general and diffuse journals (e.g., general fields of medicine and social psychology), and more on acceptance than rejection for the specific and focused journals (e.g., medical specialties and behavioral neuroscience) (Cicchetti, 1991).

Of all the studies of reviewer agreement, the study by Feurer and colleagues showed the highest level of reviewer agreement. The intraclass correlation was .84 and a Kendall's correlation was .94, indicating excellent reviewer agreement for the *Journal of Vascular and Interventional Radiology* (Feurer et al., 1994). However, their sample of 23 manuscripts was also the smallest sample of all the studies, and the purpose of the Feurer study was to test a new scoring system for evaluating reviewers' reports.

Two additional studies were designed to test a reviewer scoring system (Strayhorn et al., 1993), (Kirk & Franke, 1997). Strayhorn and colleagues tested a new reviewer rating scale: reviewers assigned a value from "zero" to "five" to each of nine questions about the manuscript. Zero points were assigned if the reviewer judged the manuscript as failing to meet the criterion or a question was answered negatively and five points were assigned if the reviewer judged the manuscript as successfully meeting the criterion or a question was answered positively. Criteria were detailed, for example: "The statistical analyses were described specifically enough to be evaluated" (p. 952). Reviewers' reports were evaluated before and after the implementation of the rating scale. Reliability increased, leading the investigators to conclude that "ratings of scientific articles may be improved by increasing the number of rating scale points, eliciting ratings of separate, concrete items rather than a global judgment, using training manuals, and averaging the scores of multiple reviewers" (p. 947).

Kirk and Franke tested the level of reviewer agreement for the journal *Social Work Research* using four different statistical measures for each of nine questions from the reviewer's form. The four measures were the percentage of agreement, one-step agreement, intraclass correlation, and 95 percent confidence intervals (Kirk & Franke, 1997). Exact agreement occurred less than one-third of the time, but one-step agreement occurred about two-thirds of the time. The intraclass measure showed weak agreement, and most items did not reach statistical significance (p. 123). This experiment illustrated how different statistical measures give different results, which then need to be carefully interpreted.

After their reanalysis of several studies of reviewer agreement, Marsha and Ball were discouraged: "There is a disappointingly small amount of empirical research on the validity of such strategies [on tests of reviewer agreement] or even actual policy practices that comprise the peer review process" (p. 168) (Marsh & Ball, 1989).

This discussion of the statistical difficulties of analyzing data from reviewer agreement studies raises two important issues. One, what is the correct statistical test for reviewer agreement studies? And two, what is the meaning or importance of results of reviewer agreement studies? One conclusion seems irrefutable: there is not a lot of agreement among reviewers, regardless of measure used to analyze data. Nor is there a lot of agreement as to which test is the best or most reliable statistic to apply to data on reviewer agreement. After reviewing a number of studies of reviewer agreement, Kirk had this thought: "as with many measures that depend on human judgment, there is some degree of measurement error that expresses itself in disagreement among referees in their assessment of quality. How much disagreement there actually is among reviewers depends on how you calculate disagreement and interpret the scores" (p. 3) (Kirk, 1993).

Together these studies show that analysis and interpretation of reviewer agreement studies is complicated, not straightforward, and open to various interpretations. The most important benefit of reviewer agreement studies might be what they reveal about the editorial peer review process in general and the value of reviewers' reports to editors even when reviewers disagree.

## What can be learned from reviewer agreement studies

The previous section demonstrated a fair amount of disagreement on how to analyze reviewer agreement studies. If these studies are examined from a different perspective, they can offer insight into the editorial peer review process itself, even without perfect statistical analysis of the studies themselves. What are the reasons for reviewer disagreement? What can editors learn from these studies? Should reviewer agreement be a worthy goal from an editor's perspective?

If one uses a simple example of a possible reason for reviewer disagreement, the importance of the role of the editor is clear. For example, if one reviewer finds a major methodological problem with the design of a study (and the editor agrees with the reviewer's analysis), the fact that a number of other reviewers did not catch this fault is of course not an argument to salvage a manuscript. The outcome should be clear: a seriously flawed manuscript should be rejected and more review would be pointless.

If one looks at the averages of the percentages for overall agreement, agreement to accept, and agreement to reject in Table 6-2, one sees that on the average, reviewers are twice as likely to agree on rejection than on acceptance. An average of 44.9 percent of the reviewers agree when they make a rejection recommendation while an average of 22.0 percent agree when they make an acceptance recommendation. In addition, the average likelihood of overall agreement is very close 50 percent.

Ingelfinger also discovered most agreement was obtained between reviews when the paper was poor. Could not an editor make a rejection judgment without sending the manuscript for review, he wondered, since "a poor paper is recognized with reasonable consistency" (p. 690) (Ingelfinger, 1974)? Concurring with Ingelfinger, Gordon maintained that reviewer agreement studies have demonstrated that "outstandingly poor papers ... are recognised with reasonable consistency" (p. 342) and these views seem to be borne out in the studies that have been conducted since Ingelfinger and Gordon made these observations (Gordon, 1977). Agreement between referees correlated with the manuscript's outcome particularly for manuscripts ultimately rejected (Eberley & Warner, 1990). However, according to Eberley and Warner, agreement is also "a good predictor of a manuscript's final outcome" (p. 217).

Investigators have noted that reviewer agreement studies have shown that some reviewers provide better reviews than others, that reviewers have an ability to recognize the most important or the least important manuscripts in a discipline, and that reviewer disagreement can actually help an editor make a decision about a manuscript.

- Cicchetti and Eron's study of the *Journal of Abnormal Psychology* concluded: "the final recommendation correlates the highest with what reviewers consider the importance of the research to the field in general" (p. 597) (Cicchetti & Eron, 1979).

- Munley, Sharkin, and Gelso correlated reviewer agreement with final disposition of the manuscript. Reviewers had the highest correlation with editorial decisions on methodology, importance of the manuscript, interpretation of results, and conclusions (Munley et al., 1988).

- Cullen and Macaulay found more reviewer agreement when reviewers were not members of the editorial board than when they were board members (Cullen & Macaulay, 1992). They offered two explanations, but tested neither: referees from different countries might provide different levels of rigorous review or younger reviewers might "be more rigorous, detailed, and effective in their reviews" (p. 858).

- Justice and colleagues asked readers and reviewers to rate manuscript quality of works already accepted for publication by the *Annals of Internal Medicine* on 10 attributes (Justice et al., 1994). They found that while agreement was high among all groups, agreement was hardly better than chance. Most agreement was for categories of the correctness of the abstract and the clarity of defining the patient population, while the least was for relevance to the reviewers' work. The authors speculated that the "tendency toward high grades may reflect a uniformly high level of quality among these manuscripts" (p. 118).

- In another study that added insight to reviewers' decisions for the *Journal of Clinical Investigation*, Scharschmidt and colleagues noticed that reviewers avoided ranking manuscripts at the extreme ends of the scales; they infrequently recommended acceptance with no revisions or outright rejection. They appeared to want to give authors a chance to revise and in so doing offered constructive comments to authors (Scharschmidt et al., 1994).

- In a related study of the journal *Social Work Research*, the highest level of agreement was reached on the reviewers' assessment of the importance of the information in the manuscript to the discipline and on the author's citing the significant studies. The lowest agreement was attained on the reviewers' assessment of statistical analysis (Kirk & Franke, 1997). Examining the specific areas of reviewer agreement and disagreement might be more enlightening than recognizing the mere fact that there is disagreement.

Gordon pointed out that one of the problems with reviewer agreement studies is the differing expectations among editors (Gordon, 1977). There is little agreement among editors on which points they want a reviewer to evaluate. Unless they receive a clear statement as to evaluation criteria, reviewers' judgment may (and do) vary considerably. Different reviewers spend different amounts of time on a manuscript, which may, in turn, contribute to inconsistent recommendations. Echoing this view Williams contended that the "there are many reasons that reviewers disagree, of course, and research in this area should be broadly based. The decision-making process of the editor is also very complex and should be the focus of empirical investigation" (p. 131) (Williams, 1977). Gottfredson suggested that rather than focus on reviewer agreement a more useful approach might be to "increase the reliability of peer judgments of article quality" (p. 920) (Gottfredson, 1978).

Some investigators think reviewer agreement need not be a goal in the editorial peer review process. There had been speculation that "a substantial source of disagreement is probably inherent in the differing perspective of referees; this cannot reasonably be eliminated simply by improving the rating form" (p. 700) (Scott, 1974).

At the time he was editor of the *Canadian Medical Association Journal* Morgan discussed the dilemma reviewer disagreement presented for editors (Morgan, 1983). He maintained that editors often pick reviewers with diverse backgrounds, different expectations, and differing abilities to review and communicate. Morgan pointed out that a decision made by an editor is more complex than merely siding with the majority opinion of the reviewers. A disagreement between reviewers may in fact reassure the editors that their reviewers are not limited to "a small, elite group that controls the publications of other scientists" (p. 1173).

Taking a philosophical view, Glidewell at the end of 13 years as editor of the *American Journal of Community Psychology* maintained "that one of an editor's best safeguards against routinization and its partners, bias and diminution (one's own and one' reviewers), was low agreement between reviewers" (p. 766) (Glidewell, 1988).

Munley and colleagues also supported the view that reviewers might be selected because they have different perspectives (Munley et al., 1988). One manuscript may be sent to a reviewer with a solid theoretical base and another one with knowledge of methodological techniques. Their view was that "disagreement among reviewers is not necessarily a reflection of error in the classical sense of being a mistake or error in judgment" (p. 201). Kraemer also subscribed to the view that editors intentionally sought reviewers of different expertise (Kraemer, 1991).

According to the editor of the *Journal of Health and Social Behavior*, the purpose of editorial peer review is to "get a set of informed evaluations in front of the editor. Thus assisted, the editor can make more broadly based, wiser decisions" (p. iv), (1989). Even though editors seek a variety of opinions, many solicit more review when faced with reviewer disagreement. Depending on the size of a journal, between 30 percent and 40 percent of medical journal editors opted for more review when reviewers disagreed; the rest resolved the disagreement by themselves, sought input from an associate editor, or discussed the next steps at an editorial meeting (Weller, 1990). In another study of editors of 221 leading medical journals Wilkes and Kravitz found similar results: 43 percent of responding editors sent a manuscript with opposing recommendations from reviewers out for more review (Wilkes & Kravitz, 1995).

Hargens and Herting argue that reviewer agreement studies alone do not give a complete picture of the scholarly communication process (Hargens & Herting, 1990a). They point out that in some disciplines one journal publishes a major portion of the scholarly literature—*Astrophysical Journal* in astronomy and *Physical Review* in physics, for example. These core journals then function by "serving as high-prestige general outlets and large numbers of more specialized ... journals making up the remainder of the prestige hierarchy" (p. 102). If a manuscript is rejected because of reviewer disagreement, in many disciplines there are other publication options for the authors, but not in disciplines with only one major journal. Steig also discussed the roles of journals in certain disciplines (Stieg, 1983). For example, history has only one major journal, the *American Historical Review*. After a rejection by the *American Historical Review* there is simply "no single journal to try" (p. 115). In many disciplines a number of journals serve as the core and any one journal publishes only a small percentage of the literature of the field. The success of authors when they resubmit rejected manuscripts in medicine illustrates the options these authors have.

It is interesting to note that of the 32 journals listed in Table 6-2, 10 (31.5 percent) originate from psychology, seven (21.8 percent) from sociology, and 10 (31.5 percent) from medicine. These three disciplines comprise 84.8 percent of all journal titles from studies of reviewer agreement. Several disciplines had only one reviewer agreement study each: chemistry, law, sports and exercise, and zoology. It should be noted that each of these studies found reviewer agreement levels to be similar to the other studies and relatively low. However, Cicchetti thought his analysis of reviewer agreement studies showed a tendency for reviewers to agree on rejection more in general and diffuse fields than in specific and focused fields (Cicchetti, 1991). As a result of their study of reviewer agreement, Linden and colleagues found only low to moderate agreement among reviewers and recommended that the behavioral sciences "as a discipline ... pursue with even more vigour the question of what constitutes an adequate experimental design and what is important research" (p. 439) (Linden et al., 1992).

Studies originating from general and diffuse disciplines (psychology, sociology, general medicine) investigate many ramifications of human behavior and human dynamics. As pointed out by Chase normative publication criteria might be less certain in fields of behavioral sciences with less developed paradigms than the natural sciences, making the likelihood of reviewer agreement more uncertain in the general and diffuse disciplines (Chase, 1970). Reviewer agreement studies and the range of reviewers' opinions documented by them seem to indicate that it is more difficult to judge normative publication criteria in practice than it is in theory.

Reviewer disagreement has proven to be a tool by which editors can evaluate manuscripts. There is more to be gained from reviewer agreement studies than simply the degree to which reviewers agree or disagree. Given the inclination of editors to select reviewers of different perspectives, one wonders if reviewer agreement should continue to be an issue. Some editors have used reviewer agreement studies as a way to evaluate their processes and at least one study (Strayhorn et al., 1993) indicated that detailed instructions to reviewers might produce a better quality of review than very general instructions and might produce more reviewer agreement.

## Guidelines for reviewer agreement

Do editors use results of studies of reviewer agreement to a journal's advantage? A number of investigators of reviewer agreement studies viewed the studies themselves as an opportunity to evaluate procedures and make some improvements to the process, such as making evaluation forms more explicit.

Bohannon, after finding reviewer agreement was almost what could have been predicted by chance for the journal *Physical Therapy*, recommended that editors use subject experts, rate reviewers' level of expertise, ask reviewers to identify biases, and consider the authors' expertise in deciding the disposition of the manuscript (Bohannon, 1986).

After a reviewer agreement study, editors of the *Research Quarterly for Exercise and Sports Review* decided that one strategy to improve reviewer agreement was to provide reviewers with feedback by giving each reviewer copies of other reviewer reports (Morrow et al., 1992). Others have suggested this as a way to improve the review process in general (see Chapter Five). Editors also decided to evaluate reviewers' reports themselves (after the names had been removed) and included information on these evaluations in the reviewer file. Reviewers' names were deleted if the reviews were not satisfactory. Morrow and colleagues also recommended that more descriptive objectives could be provided for reviewers or reviewers could be trained either at professional meetings or as graduate students.

In their study to test a scoring system for evaluating reviews, Feuer and colleagues found that the grading system could be completed by an editor in about one minute (Feurer et al., 1994). The system not only provided information on reviewer agreement, but as suggested by Morrow and colleagues (Morrow et al., 1992), provided a method to track the quality of individual reviewers.

Evidence seems to support the idea that guidelines might be helpful for reviewers. Bowen argued a number of years ago for a "standardized, structured, and formalized manuscript evaluation system" (p. 224) (Bowen et al., 1972). Publication of standards, he added, would help authors submit a better manuscript. Although editors have not yet developed standardized reviewer guidelines, since 1972 there has been a move toward standards in manuscript submissions through such work as the International Committee of Medical Journal Editors and a move in the medical community for structured abstracts. Bowen promoted the adoption of a standardized evaluation system by which a relatively unskilled person could be trained to evaluate manuscripts. This idea appears to have received little support, and if implemented it could ultimately defeat the purpose of editorial peer review by trivializing it to a mechanical process.

*Limitations of studies on reviewer agreement*

• There is limited documentation on the need for or value of reviewer agreement.

• What seems clear from the commentaries accompanying the statistical analyses of the studies of reviewer agreement is that there is no indisputable proper or correct statistical test for assessing data from reviewer agreement studies. Investigators have applied a number of statistical tests to data on reviewer agreement (Table 6-2). Experts have engaged in considerable debate on the subject of proper statistical tests for reviewer agreement studies but the issues remain unresolved. It is thus difficult to draw meaningful conclusions from reviewer agreement studies or to try to suggest alternate studies that might identify ways to improve the editorial peer review process.

• Only reviewers' recommendations were used in the analyses. Reviewers' comments were not evaluated in detail; nor were the reviewers' recommendations juxtaposed with the editors' final decision. Reviewers could easily make similar comments on a given manuscript, but one reviewer might suggest the comments warranted rejection, while another reviewer might recommend revision. For example, Table 2-2 listed several reasons for rejecting a manuscript, some of which were correctable problems, others which were not. Thus, individual reviewers make their own judgment calls as to the likelihood that a subsequent revision would correct any manuscript deficiencies. Reviewer agreement studies compare recommendations of reviewers and examine them for consistency. Armstrong suggest that reviewers not be asked to make a recommendation to accept or reject, but only to make comments for improvement (Armstrong, 1996).

• Reviewers' recommendations could be based on different qualities of a manuscript. That is, reviewer disagreements might stem not so much from true disagreement, but from each reviewer analyzing different aspects of the manuscript. Fiske and Fogg point out that under these circumstances each reviewer's recommendation could be both "appropriate and accurate"

(p. 591) for the part of the manuscript each reviewer focused on (Fiske & Fogg, 1990).

- There are many interrelated factors in the editorial peer review process. Reviewer disagreement should not be evaluated in isolation. Rather, one must consider such factors as why particular reviewers were selected, what type of guidelines they received, what the differences are between different journals, and what can be learned from the disagreements.

*Recommendations*

- Additional reviewer agreement studies will undoubtedly continue to find that there is a high level of reviewer disagreement. However, very few studies have approached reviewer agreement with the purpose of identifying the actual reasons behind reviewer disagreement. In-depth studies that address these issues might prove to be fruitful avenues for future investigation.

- Reviewer agreement studies should be designed to look for ways to improve the peer review process and to provide a basis for developing reviewer guidelines. Those editors that were testing a new rating scale showed more reviewer agreement than studies that did not take this approach.

- Although reviewers will in all likelihood continue to disagree, studies of the editorial processes vis-à-vis the value of the reviewers' reports to editors could result in improving the process.

- Editors' sharing reviewers' reports with all reviewers of a particular manuscript would undoubtedly be a valuable educational tool for reviewers. The chance to read other reports for the same manuscript they evaluated would give reviewers pointers on ways to improve their own reviewing skills.

## Conclusions about reviewer agreement studies

Not all editors see reviewer disagreement as a negative factor, but many see it as a positive method of evaluating a manuscript from a number of different perspectives. If reviewers are selected for their opposing viewpoints, there seems little reason to conduct more studies of reviewer agreement. If the purpose of a reviewer agreement study is to serve as the conduit for altering editorial peer review processes, a study should be designed with that in mind (and some have been). For example, an analysis of the precise points of agreement and disagreement could be more important to the study of editorial peer review than a statistical analysis of the degree of reviewer disagreement.

Generally, reviewer agreement studies found more agreement among reviewers when there was a recommendation to reject. Some studies concluded that clustering recommendations into only accept, revise, or reject categories improves reviewer agreement. Other studies suggested that standardizing the rating scale would improve reviewer agreement, while still others found that more categories for reviewers to choose from improved agreement. Some authors saw an advantage to reviewer disagreement. Many authors disagreed on how to analyze the data gathered. Reviewer agreement studies in Table 6-2 with the subsequent discussions and recalculations of the data show the difficulty in reaching any conclusions that might assist editors in their process of evaluating editorial peer review.

Bornstein suggested that studies of reviewer agreement raises sufficient questions about the review process that it is time to assess the "predictive and discriminant validity of peer review. Altering the peer review process ... may be difficult, ... costly, ... and somewhat risky ... The costs and risk associated with changing— even experimenting with—the review process are far less than the costs and risks of continuing to support uncritically a process that, in its current form, has many significant flaws" (p. 139) (Bornstein, 1991). Not all share this negative view.

The discussion of reviewer agreement studies has produced little commentary on the research methodology used in reviewer agreement studies. However, it is very straightforward. The studies compare ratings of reviewers for the same set of manuscripts. The discussions of many of these studies center on statistical tests used in data analysis. Statisticians look at reviewer agreement studies as a way to resolve the fine points of some important statistical questions, but this sheds little light on the editorial peer review process itself.

The most important considerations are not *that* reviewers disagree, but the reasons for the disagreement. If reviewers disagree because one reviewer believes a study was done improperly and another believes the same study used sound methodology, then the editor obviously needs to resolve the dilemma. However, if the disagreement stems from different ideological views, for example, of a theoretician vs. a practitioner, a nutritionist vs. a pharmacist, or a physical therapist vs. a physician, there may be valid reasons for the disagreements with no right or wrong "camp."

Some discipline differences were apparent in reviewer agreement studies. Many of the studies were conducted in psychology and sociology and to some degree medicine, where the subject matter is human behavior and human health. These areas are less precise and absolute than other sciences and, therefore, it might be expected that there are more discussions of reviewer agreement. Cicchetti suggested this as an area for more research.

The fact that reviewers are most likely to agree on rejection is somewhat reassuring. After all, it is the truly unsound or poor research that should not be published. If reviewer agreement studies have provided an opportunity for editors to rethink their editorial peer review process they have served a very useful purpose. The two quotations at the beginning of this chapter from two different editors as well as some of the discussion in this chapter have indicated that reviewer disagreement need not be viewed as a negative factor; it may be exactly what an editor is seeking. It certainly confirms the need for the editor. The editor weighs reviewers' opinions against his or her own and then makes an informed decision.

# References

(1989, September). Peer review always helps but never cures. *Journal of Health and Social Behavior, 30*(3), iv-v.

Armstrong, J. S. (1996, October 25). We need to rethink the editorial role of peer reviewers. *Chronicle of Higher Education, 43*(9), B3-B4.

Bakanic, V., McPhail, C., & Simon, R. J. (1987, October). The manuscript review and decision-making process. *American Sociological Review, 52*(5), 631.

Bartko, J. J. (1966). The intraclass correlation coefficient as a measure of reliability. *Psychological Reports, 19*, 3-11.

Bohannon, R. W. (1986, September). Agreement among reviewers. *Physical Therapy, 66*(9), 1431-1432.

Boice, R., Barlow, D. H., Johnson, K., & Klosko, J. (1984). Behaviorists as peer reviewers: do they misbehave? *Behavior Therapist, 7*(6), 105-107.

Boice, R., Pecker, G., Zaback, E., & Barlow, D. H. (1985). A challenge to Peters and Ceci's conclusion with an examination of editorial files for reviewer appropriateness. *Behavioral and Brain Sciences, 8*(4), 744-745.

Bornstein, R. F. (1991, March). The predictive validity of peer review: a neglected issue. *Behavioral and Brain Sciences, 14*(1), 138-139.

Bowen, D. D., Perloff, R., & Jacoby, J. (1972, May). Improving manuscript evaluation procedures. *American Psychologist, 27*(3), 221-225.

Chase, J. M. (1970, August). Normative criteria for scientific publication. *American Sociologist, 5*(3), 263-265.

Cho, M. K. & Bero, L. A. (1994, July 13). Instruments for assessing the quality of drug studies published in the medical literature. *JAMA, 272*(2), 101-104.

Cicchetti, D. V. (1980, March). Reliability of reviewers for the *American Psychologist*: A biostatistical assessment of the data. *American Psychologist, 35*(3), 300-303.

Cicchetti, D. V. (1985, May). A critique of Whitehurst's "Interrater agreement for journal manuscript reviews": De omnibus, disputandem est. *American Psychologist, 40*(5), 563-568.

Cicchetti, D. V. (1991). The reliability of peer review for manuscript and grant submissions: a cross-disciplinary investigation. *Behavioral and Brain Sciences, 14*, 19-86.

Cicchetti, D. V. & Conn, H. O. (1975, June). Reviewer agreement and systemic bias in evaluation medical abstracts. *Biometrics, 31*(2), 592.

Cicchetti, D. V. & Conn, H. O. (1976, September). A statistical analysis of reviewer agreement and bias in evaluating medical abstracts. *Yale Journal of Biology and Medicine, 49*(4), 373-383.

Cicchetti, D. V., & Eron, L. D. (1979). *The reliability of manuscript reviewers for the Journal of Abnormal Psychology.* Paper presented at the American Statistical Association, Washington, DC.

Crandall, R. (1978, June). Interrater agreement on manuscripts is not so bad! *American Psychologist, 33*(6), 623-624.

Cullen, D. J. & Macaulay, A. (1992, December). Consistency between peer reviewers for a clinical specialty journal. *Academic Medicine, 67*(12), 856-859.

Cullen, D. J. & Macaulay, A. (1994). Consistency of peer reviewers who evaluate scientific articles. In R. A. Weeks & D. L. Kinser (Eds.), *Editing the refereed scientific journal* (pp. 13-16). New York: IEEE Press.

Daniel, H-D. (1993). An evaluation of the peer review process at *Angewandte Chemie*. *Angewandte Chemie, 32*(2), 234-238.

Dixon, G. F., Schonfeld, S. A., Altman, M., & Whitcomb, M. E. (1983, March). The peer review and editorial process: a limited evaluation. *American Journal of Medicine, 74*(3), 494-495.

Eberley, S. & Warner, W. K. (1990, Fall). Fields or subfields of knowledge: rejection rates and reviewer agreement in peer review. *American Sociologist, 21*(3), 217-231.

Ernst, E., Saradeth, T., & Resch, K. L. (1993, May 27). Drawbacks of peer review. *Nature, 363*, 296.

Feurer, I. D., Becker, G. J., Picus, D., Ramirez, E., Darcy, M. D., & Hicks, M. E. (1994, July 13). Evaluating peer reviews; pilot testing of a grading instrument. *JAMA, 272*(2), 98-100.

Fiske, D. W. & Fogg, L. (1990, May). But the reviewers are making different criticisms of my paper! *American Psychologist, 45*(5), 591-598.

Fleiss, J. I. & Cohen, J. (1973). The equivalence of weighted Kappa and the intraclass correlation coefficient as measures of reliability. *Educational and Psychological Measurements, 33*, 613-619.

Fleiss, J. L., Cohen, J., & Everitt, B. S. (1969). Large sample standard errors of kappa and weighted kappa. *Psychological Bulletin, 72*(5), 323-327.

Gallagher, E. B., & Ferrante, J. (1991). *Agreement among peer reviewers for a middle-sized biomedical journal.* Paper presented at the First International Congress on Peer Review in Biomedical Publication, Chicago, Il.

Gilmore, J. B. (1979). Illusory reliability in journal reviewing. *Canadian Psychology, 20*(3), 157-158.

Glidewell, J. C. (1988). Reflections on thirteen years of editing AJCP. *American Journal of Community Psychology, 16*(6), 759-770.

Gordon, M. D. (1977, February 10). Evaluating the evaluators. *New Scientist, 73*, 342-343.

Gottfredson, S. D. (1978, October). Evaluating psychological research reports; dimensions, reliability, and correlates of quality judgments. *American Psychologist, 33*(10), 920-934.

Hargens, L. L. & Herting, J. R. (1990a). Neglected considerations in the analysis of agreement among reviewers. *Scientometrics, 10*(1-2), 91-106.

Hargens, L. L. & Herting, J. R. (1990, March-b). A new approach to referees' assessment of manuscripts. *Social Science Research, 19*(1), 1-6.

Hendrick, C. (1976). Editorial comment. *Personality and Social Psychology Bulletin, 2,* 207-208.

Hendrick, C. (1977, Winter). Editorial comment. *Personality and Social Psychology Bulletin, 3*(1), 1-2.

Ingelfinger, F. J. (1974, May). Peer review in biomedical publication. *American Journal of Medicine, 56*(5), 686-692.

Johnson, S. H. (1996, Fall). Dealing with conflicting reviewers' comments. *Nurse Author and Editor, 6*(4), 1-3.

Justice, A. C., Berlin, J. A., Fletcher, S. W., Fletcher, R. H., & Goodman, S. N. (1994, July 13). Do readers and peer reviewers agree on manuscript quality? *JAMA, 272*(2), 117-119.

Kahn, A. S., Presbury, J. H., Moore, H. B., & Driver, J. D. (1990). Characteristics of accepted versus rejected manuscripts. *Psychology of Women Quarterly, 14,* 7-14.

Kirk, S. A. (1993, June). The puzzles of peer perusal. *Social Work Research and Abstracts, 29*(2), 3-4.

Kirk, S. A. & Franke, T. M. (1997, June). Agreeing to disagree: a study of reliability of manuscript reviews. *Social Work Research, 21*(2), 121-126.

Kraemer, H. C. (1991). Do we really want more "reliable" reviewers? *Behavioral and Brain Sciences, 14*(1), 152-154.

Lazarus, D. (1982). Interreferee agreement and acceptance rate in physics. *Behavioral and Brain Sciences, 5*(2), 219.

Linden, W., Craig, K. D., & Wen, F. K. (1992, October). Contributions of reviewer judgements to editorial decision-making for the *Canadian Journal of Behavioural Sciences:* 1985-86. *Canadian Journal of Behavioural Science, 24*(4), 433-441.

Lindsey, D. (1988, July). Assessing precision in the manuscript review process: a little better than a dice role. *Scientometrics, 14*(1), 75-82.

Lindsey, D. (1991). Precision in the manuscript review process: Hargens and Herting revisited. *Scientometrics, 22*(2), 313-325.

Lock, S. (1985). *A difficult balance. Editorial peer reviewed in medicine.* Philadelphia: ISI Press.

Marsh, H. W. & Ball, S. (1981, December). Interjudgmental reliability of reviews for the Journal of Educational Psychology. *Journal of Educational Psychology, 73*(6), 872-880.

Marsh, H. W. & Ball, S. (1989, Winter). The peer review process used to evaluate manuscripts submitted to academic journals: interjudgmental reliability. *Journal of Experimental Education, 57*(2), 151-169.

McCartney, J. L. (1973). Manuscript reviewing. *Sociological Quarterly, 14*(3), 290, 440-446.

McReynolds, P. (1991, April). Reliability of ratings of research papers. *American Psychologist, 26*(4), 400-401.

Morgan, P. P. (1983, December 1). When reviewers disagree. *Canadian Medical Association Journal, 129*(4), 1172-1173.

Morgan, P. P. & Yankauer, A. (1987). The editor and conflicting referees: how to referee among referees. *CBE Views, 10*(5), 79.

Morrow, J. R., Jr., Bray, M. S., Fulton, J. E., & Thomas, J. R. (1992). Interrater reliability of 1987-91 *Research Quarterly for Exercise and Sports Review. Research Quarterly for Exercise and Sports Review, 63*(2), 200-204.

Munley, P. H., Sharkin, B., & Gelso, C. J. (1988, April). Reviewer ratings and agreement on manuscripts for the *Journal of Counseling Psychology. Journal of Counseling Psychology, 35*(2), 198-202.

O'Brien, R. M. (1991, September). The reliability of composites of referee assessments of manuscripts. *Social Science Research, 20*(3), 319-328.

Oxman, A. D., Guyatt, G. H., Goldsmith, C. H., Hutchison, B. G., Milner, R. A., & Streiner, D. L. (1991). Agreement among reviewers of review articles. *Journal of Clinical Epidemiology, 44*(1), 91-98.

Parker, G., Barnett, B., Holmes, S., & Manicavasagar, V. (1984, March). Publishing in the parish. *Australian and New Zealand Journal of Psychiatry, 18*(1), 78-85.

Plug, C. (1993). The reliability of manuscript evaluation for the South African Journal of Psychology. *South African Journal of Psychology, 23*(1), 43-48.

Rubin, H. R., Redelmeier, D. A., Wu, A. W., & Steinberg, E. P. (1993, May). How reliable is peer review of scientific abstracts? *Journal of General Internal Medicine, 8*(5), 255-258.

Scarr, S. (1978, October). The reliability of reviews for the American Psychologist. *American Psychologist, 33*(10), 935.

Scharschmidt, B. F., DeAmicis, A., Bacchetti, P., & Held, M. J. (1994, May). Chance, concurrence, and clustering, analysis of reviewers' recommendations on 1,000 to the *Journal of Clinical Investigation. Journal of Clinical Investigation, 93*, 1877-1880.

Scott, W. A. (1974, September). Interreferee agreement on some characteristics of manuscripts submitted to the Journal of Personality and Social Psychology. *American Psychologist, 29*(9), 698-702.

Seeman, M. (1966, November). Report of the editor of *Sociometry. American Sociologist, 1*(5), 284-285.

Shrout, P. E. & Fleiss, J. L. (1979, March). Intraclass correlations: uses in assessing rater reliability. *Psychological Bulletin, 86*(2), 420-428.

Smigel, E. O. & Ross, H. L. (1970, February). Factors in the editorial decision. *American Sociologist, 5*(1), 19-21.

Stieg, M. F. (1983, February). Refereeing and the editorial process: the AHR and Webb. *Scholarly Publishing, 14*(2), 99-122.

Strayhorn, J., Jr., McDermont, J. F., & Tanguay, P. (1993, June). An intervention to improve the reliability of manuscript reviews for the *Journal of the American*

*Academy of Child and Adolescent Psychiatry. American Journal of Psychiatry, 150*(6), 947-952.

Warner, W. K., Eberley, S., Johnson, B. L., & Albrecht, S. L. (1985, Winter). Discriminants of editorial decision outcomes. *Rural Sociology, 50*(4), 614-625.

Watkins, M. W. (1979, September). Chance and interrater agreement on manuscripts. *American Psychologist, 34*(9), 796-798.

Weller, A. C. (1990, March 9). Editorial peer review in U.S. medical journals. *JAMA, 263*(10), 1344-1347.

Whitehurst, G. J. (1983). Interrater agreement for reviews for Developmental Reviews. *Developmental Reviews, 3*(1), 73-78.

Whitehurst, G. J. (1984, January). Interrater agreement for journal manuscript reviews. *American Psychologist, 39*(1), 22-28.

Whitehurst, G. J. (1985, May). On lies, damned lies, and statistics: measuring interrater agreement. *American Psychologist, 40*(5), 468-469.

Wilkes, M. S. & Kravitz, R. L. (1995, August). Policies, practices, and attitudes of North American medical journal editors. *Journal of General Internal Medicine, 10*(8), 443-450.

Williams, J. (1977, September). Quality in the review process. *IEEE Transactions on Professional Communication, PC-20*(2), 131-132.

Yankauer, A. (1979, March). Editor's report: peer review. *American Journal of Public Health, 69*(3), 222-223.

Zuckerman, H. & Merton, R. K. (1971, January). Patterns of evaluation in science: institutionalisation, structure and functions of the referee system. *Minerva, 9*(1), 66-100.

# Chapter Seven

# Reviewers and Their Biases

*Anonymity is increasing difficult to defend.*
(Maddox, 1989, p. 657)

Ideally a reviewer approaches a manuscript with every intention judging impartially and evaluating the manuscript solely on its merits. The only relevant factors for the reviewer are the quality and importance the research; its design, methodology, analysis, discussion, and conclusions; and the logic of the thought process. Table 3-2 identifies a set of normative criteria for scientific publications; these are the very criteria reviewers should use. The criteria mentioned most frequently in Table 3-2 are logical rigor, contribution to knowledge, research design, methodology, objectivity, topic selection, writing style, and organization. Information such as an author's prestige, institutional affiliation, country, gender, ethnicity, source of funding, or any information unrelated to the research project should not influence reviewers' comments or recommendation; nor should reviewers' personal research agendas or particular views on a given topic. The practices of anonymous and blind review have been championed to help reduce any reviewer bias.

In 1967, a professor of sociology wrote a letter to the editor of the *American Sociologist* asserting that "as an author, I can state unhesitatingly that I want to be known under my proper name when submitting a contribution—I do not want to be author "X." I do not think that any author who is worth his salt will feel otherwise." (p. 98) (Cahnman, 1967). Of course, this sounds dated, definitely not gender-neutral (a term unheard of in 1967), strikingly opinionated, and quite self-assured. But the letter gets to the heart of the problem with reviewer bias—the author knew that his signature, "professor of sociology, Rutgers University," came as the result of years of hard work and probably wanted reviewers to know that. This example illustrates two potential reviewer biases: bias in favor of a known author or in favor of a prominent institution. It is exactly this line of reasoning that impels another group of researchers and scholars, the young, the unknown, the untenured, or the first-time author to support blind review.

Even if the manuscripts are blinded to the reviewers, editors know who the authors are. This factor, according to Fye, might influence the review process:

> *All authors are not created equal in the eyes of the editor or the reader. Those with a record of publishing high quality papers in prestigious journals are more likely to be successful in subsequent attempts at authorship. In addition to the reputation of the author, the prestige of the institution or research group in which he or she works may affect the review process* (p. 321) (Fye, 1990).

Murphy defined bias as "a process at any stage of inference tending to produce results that depart systematically from the true values" (p. 239). (Murphy, 1976). He went on to identify six places in the scientific process where bias may enter: bias of design, observation, estimation, hypothesis testing, interpretation, and reporting. In other words, bias may slip in at any step of the research process. Building on Murphy's definition from a reviewer's perspective, Owen listed 25 potential reader or reviewer biases in a commentary in the *Journal of the American Medical Association* (*JAMA*) (Owen, 1982). These have been grouped into the broad categories of personal biases, methodology biases, conclusion biases, and prestige biases.

- Personal biases: rivalry, personal habits, moral, clinical practice, resource allocation (funds should be spent on other projects), financial advantage, friendship, omission (did not read the manuscript carefully), tradition, territory, benevolence;

- Methodology biases: favored study design, empirical data, too much reliance on methods of previous studies, pro-technology;

- Conclusion biases: "do something," supports "my" practice, substituted the question (considered results in light of a different research question than that asked by the researcher); and

- Prestige biases: journal, author's institution, flashy article title, geography, academic degrees of authors, known professor.

Two additional types of biases, publication bias (a bias against studies that find no statistically significant differences among the comparison groups) and replication bias (a bias against redoing an already conducted study), are discussed in Chapter Eight on statistical review of manuscripts. In fact, a study that examined opinions of reviewers of six psychology journals ("not a random sample" of journals, but a sample that was "broadly based") (p. 23) found that most reviewers felt little journal space should be devoted to replication studies (Neuliep & Crandall, 1993). However, 92 percent of these reviewers had never reviewed a manuscript that was a report of a replication study.

Depending on the exact types of bias one identifies, Owen's list could be longer or different. There are probably limitless ways to bring some degree of bias into the evaluation of a manuscript and, furthermore, it is probably not possible for a reviewer to evaluate a manuscript without a certain degree of bias. What is important is not so much a bias *per se*, but the potential for a groundless negative report or outcome because of a bias. Is the publication of any valid research delayed, published in a "less prestigious" journal, or simply not published as a result of reviewers' biases? How can editors compensate for the fact that each and every reviewer does bring some degree of bias into the review process?

This chapter analyzes studies that have investigated reviewer bias. Studies look at potential biases from a number of perspectives, often they sought evidence of review bias under blind or anonymous conditions. To establish baseline data, the first section investigates the degree to which editors use anonymity or blind review. This is followed by discussions of:

- studies that tested the ability of reviewers to identify authors when authors' names have been removed from manuscripts (blind review)

- studies that looked for any evidence that reviewers' recommendations are influenced by their ideological views

- studies that compared reviewers' recommendations in blind and nonblinded conditions

- studies that examined journals with a policy of signed reviewers' reports

  There are four variations of reviewers' and authors' knowledge of each other:

- neither author nor reviewer know each other (blind review, also known as double-blind review)

- both author and reviewer know each other (open review)

- the reviewer knows the author, but the author does not know the reviewer (anonymous)

- the author knows the reviewer, but the reviewer does not know the author (signed reviews)

The editor decides which option to use. If blind review is used, the editor might provide guidelines for preparing a manuscript for blind review in the instructions to authors or might remove authors' identification in the editorial office. The editor, of course, cannot control reviewers or authors ability to either obtain or guess each other's names.

## Editorial policies on anonymous and blind review

An editorial in *Nature* expressed some commonly held opinions about the reasons for anonymity: referees should not have to endure encounters with angry authors, anonymous reviewers do not make negative comments simply because they can remain anonymous, and the reviewer serves as an anonymous reader whose opinion should not be dismissed (1974-a).

Debakey presented pluses and minuses of blind review. Arguments in favor of anonymity include editorial integrity and the reduced risk of authors' retaliation to reviewers following a negative review (DeBakey, 1990). The minuses included the potential increases of intellectual theft and bias of the reviewers.

The Ad Hoc Committee on Double-Blind Refereeing appointed by the Institute of Mathematical Statistics in 1992 studied the advantages and disadvantages of blind reviewing (Cox, Gleser, Perlman, Reid, & Roeder, 1993). As outlined by the ad hoc committee, these are the advantages of double-blind review:

• It permits the merits of a manuscript to be evaluated without regard to author characteristics.

• It eliminates the perception of decisions being made on author characteristics.

• It is easy to implement.

• It confirms that the name of the author is not relevant.

They also found disadvantages:

• It makes extra assistance often given new researchers less available.

• It is more difficult for new researchers to publicize their prepublication work through the refereeing process.

• It eliminates a relevant piece of information: the name of the author.

• It introduces distortions by referees' trying to guess the author.

• It increases the editor's burden.

After weighing these advantages and disadvantages and examining the literature on the subject, the ad hoc committee suggested that the Institute of Mathematical Statistics appoint a second ad hoc committee to design an experiment and conduct a pilot test (Benedetti, Green, Lee, & Crowley, 1993). The ad hoc committee suggested that randomly selected manuscripts undergo review by four reviewers, two blinded to the authors and two not blinded to the authors. Each reviewer would use the same rating scales and the magnitude of interrater variability would be determined. The ad hoc committee recommended that the pilot test examine only one journal, then determine the feasibility of expanding the study after completion and analysis of the data. No results of this study have been located.

Table 1-2 lists those journals whose editors have published information about their editorial peer review process. Of the 139 journals in Table 1-2, about half discussed the use of anonymity or blind review; 23 percent of these stated that they used a double-blind review process. When the percentage of these editors are added to the 2.8 percent of editors who said they blind the authors' names to the reviewer, a total of 25.8 percent used blind review. The editors who said they used blind review might also have used anonymous review; however, they did not provide that information in their editorials. An additional 28 percent stated in the editorials that they use anonymous review. The practice of not revealing reviewers' names to authors is the accepted practice. So common, in fact, that most commentaries on editorial peer review appear to assume editors use anonymous review and discussions of anonymity surface only when editors deviate from that practice. A study now over 10 years old revealed that in the instructions to authors of medical journals, depending on the category of journal, only 12 percent to 15 percent state that the journal uses anonymous review, while none mention that they use blind review (Weller, 1987). Information provided by editors in editorials or instructions to authors, while informative to the journal readership, does not provide data on how common anonymous or blind review is or what variations exist among disciplines.

Several reports indicate that reviewers themselves may accept a blind review policy. In 1972, the editor of the *American Economic Review* undertook a study to test the decisions on manuscripts subjected to either blind or nonblind (anonymous) review (Borts, 1974). Of 311 manuscripts, about half underwent blind review and the others received nonblind review. Of those that underwent blind review 47.7 percent were accepted, and of those that underwent nonblind review 38.1 percent were accepted. Borts found that referees were "favorably disposed" to blind review and felt it was fair (p. 478). Some reviewers commented to Borts that they spent more time with the manuscript when the author's identity was removed from the manuscript.

The editors of *William and Mary Quarterly* asked reviewers how they felt about blind review (McGiffert, 1988). Only 11 percent of the respondents wanted to know the names of the authors while 23 percent of reviewers had no objection to the disclosure of their identity to authors.

The editorial board of the *American Journal of Public Health* instituted a policy of blind review in 1976. The editor was initially skeptical of the policy, but followed through with a survey of reviewers, who overwhelmingly favored blind review. During the next 13 years, only two of over 1,000 reviewers refused to review a manuscript because the authors had not been identified (Yankauer, 1991).

In areas of the world with limited-interest research coupled with a very small number of investigators, the reviewer is almost certain to be able to guess the name of the author correctly (Hodder, 1979). For example, editors who receive manuscripts on geology written by scientists in New Zealand have only a handful of potential reviewers to choose from. There is the possibility that two researchers will review each other's manuscripts, because there is no one else qualified to review these specialized reports. The small pool of reviewers led Hodder to speculate that in these circumstances the overall tone of the reviews may be "a little less brutal" (p 163) than it might otherwise be.

*Question*

How common is the practice of anonymous or blind review? Are there differences in practices among disciplines?

*Criteria for inclusion*

~ any study that queried a group of editors about their practices of anonymous or blind review.

*Comparable studies*

Fifteen studies surveyed a defined group of editors about their policies on anonymous or blind review (Table 7-1).

| Discipline | Anonymity* | Blind review** | Open review*** | Conclusion about anonymous or blind review | References |
|---|---|---|---|---|---|
| earth sciences | 55.7% | 4.4% | | | (Glen & Konigsson, 1976) |
| economics | | 25.6% | | Except in two categories (manuscript "too speculative" and "too esoteric"), reasons for blind and nonblind rejected manuscript the same. | (Coe & Weinstock, 1967) |
| | assumed? | 38.0% | | Manuscript evaluation may be influenced by knowledge of author's identity and institution. | (Coe & Weinstock, 1968) |
| engineering | assumed? | no, for most | | Editors said blind review would make no difference in outcome. | (Christiansen, 1974) |
| library science | 18.2% | 9.1% | | Journals should adopt double-blind reviewing. | (O'Connor & Van Orden, 1978) |
| | 41.7% | 31.2% | | | (Budd, 1988) |
| | 50.0% | 39.7% | | | (Via, 1996) |
| medicine (top journals) | 100.0% | 0.0% | | Anonymous review is standard practice; leading medical journals use blind review less than specialized journals. | (Weller, 1990) |
| (randomly selected journals) | 96.5% | 32.9% | | | |
| nursing | | 58.1% | | | (McElmurry, Newcomb, Barnfather, & Lynch, 1981) |
| | | 52.0% | | | (Swanson & McCloskey, 1982,) |
| | | 86.8% | | | (Fondiller, 1994) |
| pharmacy | assumed? | 18.6% | | The burden of proof of the value of blind review rests with advocates. No journals blinded the editor to the authors. | (Cleary & Alexander, 1988) |
| psychology British American | assumed? | 66.7% 31.6% | | | (Hartley, 1988) |
| psychology | | | 77% | An open review system is clearly warranted. | (Bornstein, 1993) |
| mulit-discipline: 12 groups | assumed? | 11.5% | | | (Miller & Serzan, 1984) |
| *Average* | 60.4% | 33.7% | | | |

*Anonymity: author does not know reviewer; **Blind review: reviewer does not know author; ***Open review: both author and reviewer know each other.

**Table 7-1: Blind review and anonymity—surveys of editors by discipline**

Many of these studies are discussed elsewhere in this monograph; such information as journal selection criteria and percentage of respondents to these surveys is provided in Table 3-1. Two studies, the Cleary study and the Bornstein study, focused only on the degree of anonymous or blind review for a group of journals (Cleary & Alexander, 1988) (Bornstein, 1993). A number of investigators tallied the percentages of anonymous or blind review for a group of journals, but did not comment on their findings in the discussions or conclusions. In these cases, the conclusion column of Table 7-1 is left blank; only conclusions directly related to anonymous or blind review have been included in this column.

In a 1995 survey, Wilkes and Kravitz received responses from senior editors of 221 "leading medical journals" in the United States and Canada who answered questions about their opinions on anonymous and blind review. Only 8 percent of the editors thought authors should learn the names of the reviewers, while 46 percent thought reviewers should be blinded to authors' names and institutions (Wilkes & Kravitz, 1995). The Wilkes study is not included in Table 7-1, since it was an opinion survey and did not ask editors about their actual practices. Another study of 16 of the top medical journals found that 100 percent used anonymous review while none used blind review (Weller, 1990), demonstrating a possible ambiguity between theory and practice in light of the Wilkes and Kravitz study. However, the two studies were conducted a few years apart and undoubtedly included different titles or, even if there was overlap of journal titles, the editorships of the journals could have changed.

Nine of the 15 surveys in Table 7-1 asked editors about blind review, but not anonymous review. From the discussions in several of these studies, it appears likely that the investigators had assumed that anonymous review was standard editorial practice. This is particularly true of five of the studies (Coe & Weinstock, 1968), (Christiansen, 1974) (Miller & Serzan, 1984) (Cleary & Alexander, 1988), and (Hartley, 1988). In the other four of the nine studies it was unclear if the investigators assumed anonymous review. However, for those studies that asked editors specifically about anonymity, with the exception of the highest ranked medical journals, which all used anonymous review, every group included journals that did not use anonymous review.

A few trends are noteworthy. On the average about one-third of the editors in Table 7-1 used blind review, and about twice as many used anonymous review. For each study that asked editors about both anonymous and blind review, anonymous review was always used more than blind review. For comparison purposes, it is interesting to note that roughly 25 percent of the editors who have published information about their review process (Table 1-2) stated that they used blind review, fairly close to the average percentage (33.7 percent) of all journals in the 15 studies in Table 7-1. These studies show a wide range of editorial practices from discipline to discipline for both anonymous and blind review: for blind review they range from zero (top medical journals) to 86.8 percent (nursing) and for anonymous review from 18.2 percent (library science) to 100 percent (top medical journals). For those few disciplines with more than one study (with the exception of one study in nursing), the more recent the study, the higher the percentage of editors who used blind review. Of the eight disciplines represented in these studies, nursing journals appear most likely to employ a system of blind review, from 52 percent in one study to 87 percent in another. Findings for medical journals using blind review range from 0.0 percent to 32.9 percent, library science from 9.1 percent to 39.7 percent, and economics from 25.6 percent to 38.2 percent. Library science showed an increase in the percentage of editors who used anonymous review—from 18.2 percent to 50.0 percent over an 18-year period. The multidisciplinary study conducted by Miller and Serzan found education, communications, the social sciences, psychology, psychiatry, history, political science, religion, and philosophy more likely than the sciences to use blind review (Miller & Serzan, 1984).

## Name recognition

One of the standard arguments against the use of blind review is that the reviewers are very likely to guess the authors' names anyway, so there is little purpose in editors' spending the time needed to blind manuscripts. This argument has been made rather recently by DeBakey who thought the practice of blind review was "impractical because experienced reviewers can recognize clues to authorship in the text and in references cited" (p. 346) (DeBakey, 1990).

From the editors' perspective it is not always possible to remove identification of authors from the text of the manuscript itself (Goudsmit, 1967). In fact, in recognizing the benefit peer review offers to known authors when their names remain on a manuscript, the editor of the *New England Journal of Medicine* tried a system of double-blind review in the late 1960s (1970). The editor eventually discontinued the practice of blind review as it "inevitably broke down under the persistent weight of authors whose identity was regularly disclosed by their subject matter, bibliographic citations and well-labeled illustrations as well as of those referees who considered their objective integrity impugned thereby" (p. 394). Some years later Relman, at the time he was editor of the *New England Journal of Medicine*, maintained that since there were many manuscripts "from which it is impossible to expunge the traces of authorship simply by omitting the authors' names.... A system that blinded reviewers only some of the time wouldn't be equitable, and to ensure anonymity of every article would be more trouble than it is worth" (p. 899) (Relman, 1982). Of course these observations were made before computers eased the task of reworking manuscripts, charts, photographs, tables, and the like to remove all traces of authors' names.

Several authors have suggested that reviewers can guess the authors' names correctly. Bradley asked a group of authors in psychology and statistics if they felt that the standard blind refereeing procedure was "highly effective in preventing a referee from deducing the author's identity" (p. 33) (Bradley, 1981). Over 75 percent thought it was not. Adair and colleagues in a "rather rough experiment" (p. 15) thought about 80 percent of the reviewers for *Physical Review Letters* could guess authors' names given the specific details covered in most manuscripts (Adair, Carlon, & Sherman, 1981). Scarr, editor of *Developmental Psychology* and associate editor of *American Psychologist*, estimated that the double-blind review process worked for "more than half—perhaps two-thirds" of manuscripts (Scarr, 1982). Ceci and Peters asked a random sample of members of the American Psychological Association (APA) "what proportion of reviewers for a journal that practices blind review in your field can deduce the authors' identities when the title page has been removed and the usual precautions taken?" (p. 1492) (Ceci & Peters, 1984). Respondents estimated that reviewers could identify the authors about 72 percent of the time. Has this assumption been tested and, if so, how close are these estimates to the reviewers' actual ability to guess authors' names? From the studies discussed here, anywhere from 50 percent to 80 percent of those asked guessed that reviewers could identify authors' names.

*Question*

Are reviewers able to identify authors or institutions after the names have been removed from manuscripts?

*Criteria for inclusion*

~ any study that tested reviewers' ability to identify the authors or institutions.

*Comparable studies*

Nine studies tested reviewers' ability to identify authors or their institutions in a manuscript from which the names of authors and institutions had been removed (Table 7-2).

Rosenblatt and Kirk collected data on 33 manuscripts sent to 115 reviewers for the *Journal of Social Service Research* (Rosenblatt & Kirk, 1980). Thirty-three percent of the time reviewers were able to guess the authors' name correctly. When they did identify the authors, the correct name came from within the manuscript itself 64 percent of the time.

Ceci and Peters asked editors of 15 psychology journals to participate in a study in which reviewers of blinded manuscripts were asked to identify authors (Ceci & Peters, 1984). Only six editors agreed to participate and did so by blinding the next 20 to 30 manuscripts they received and then asking reviewers to name authors. Overall, only 35.6 percent of the 146 reviewers were able to identify authors correctly or to name at least one author in multi-authored manuscripts. In Ceci and Peters' study, there were several cases of "mechanical detection" caused by oversights in the editorial office that made it possible to identify the authors from information in the manuscript. If these had been corrected prior to review, reviewers' ability to identify authors' might have dropped to about 25 percent of the time. Ceci and Peters concluded that the actual ability of the reviewers to detect authorship was probably not much more than "weak hunches," (p. 1493) quite limited, and considerably less than the percentage that authors and reviewers thought they would be able to identify.

| Journal title or subject | # of mss. | # of reviews | Identified authors | Did not try to identify author(s) | Guessed wrong | Source of identification | | | References |
|---|---|---|---|---|---|---|---|---|---|
| | | | | | | self-citations | knew research | other | |
| *Journal of Social Services Research* | 33 | 115 | 33.3% | 56.0% | 4.0% | | | 64% from contents of manuscript | (Rosenblatt & Kirk, 1980) |
| Editors of 6 psychology journals | | 146 | 35.6% | | 8.0% | | | 0-19% mechanical detection | (Ceci & Peters, 1984) |
| *Journal of Neuropathology & Experimental Neurology* | 33 | 85 | 34.0% | 55.0% | 11.0% | | | 45 manuscripts excluded because of self-citations | (Moossy & Moossy, 1985) |
| *Australian & New Zealand Journal of Psychiatry* | 32 | 32 | 25.0% | | | | | 16% identified institution | (Parker, 1986) |
| *Journal of General Internal Medicine* | 127 | 127 | 27.0% | | | 31.0% | | 23% editorial error; 19% other | (McNutt, Evans, Fletcher, & Fletcher, 1990) |
| *American Economic Review* | 151 | | 13.2% | | | | | self-citations or other knowledge of research | (Borts, 1974) |
| | | 1,164 | 45.6% | | 10.0% | | | | (Blank, 1991) |
| *American Journal of Public Health* | 228 | 312 | 83.0% | | 16.0% | 61.8% | 38.2% | 85% identified institution | (Yankauer, 1991) |
| *Journal of Developmental and Behavioral Pediatrics* | 57 | 108 | 46.0% | 48.0% | 6.0% | 44.0% | 39.0% | 17.0% | (Fisher, Friedman, & Strauss, 1994) |
| *Averages* | | | 38.1% | 53.0% | 9.2% | 45.6% | 38.6% | | |

**Table 7-2: Blind reviewing—identification of authors**

Moossy and Moossy conducted a study of manuscripts submitted to the *Journal of Neuropathology and Experimental Neurology* but eliminated manuscripts from which they were sure the reviewers would be able to identify the authors, particularly manuscripts in which the authors "referred repeatedly to their published papers" (p. 225). Using this criterion, 45 of the 78 (57.7 percent) manuscripts were excluded from the study. Of those manuscripts that qualified for the study, reviewers correctly identified 34 percent of the authors, 33 percent of the departments, and 34 percent of the institutions. Eleven percent of the authors were incorrectly identified, and 55 percent of the reviewers made no attempt to identify authors (Moossy & Moossy, 1985).

Parker found that author name recognition occurred more frequently than institutional name recognition (Parker, 1986). While 25 percent of the reviewers identified the author correctly, in only 16 percent of the cases were they able to identify the correct institution. McNutt and colleagues were successfully able to blind authors to reviewers 73 percent of the time (McNutt, Evans, Fletcher, & Fletcher, 1990). The blinding process took the editors about 15 minutes. In the Blank study of the *American Economic Review*, 45.6 percent of authors were identified correctly by reviewers (Blank, 1991). Blank suggested that those authors who were identified were those who were "better known or who belong to networks that distribute their working papers more widely" (p. 1052).

Yankauer found that for the *American Journal of Public Health* reviewers were equally adept at identifying authors and institutions—approximately 85 percent of the time reviewers were able to identify both authors and institutions correctly (Yankauer, 1991). Manuscripts generating from public health may be written differently from other disciplines, revealing enough information to identify authors; indeed 61.8 percent of the authors were identified by self-citations, and the remaining 38.2 percent were identified by the reviewers' knowledge of the authors' work.

Fisher, Stanford, and Strauss sent reviewers a survey after each had completed a review (Fisher, Friedman, & Strauss, 1994). One-half of the reviewers had received blinded manuscripts, and the other half received manuscripts with the authors' names. For those manuscripts that had been blinded to the authors, reviewers were asked to identify the authors. The reviewers correctly guessed authors' names 46 percent of the time, mostly from self-citations within the article or knowledge of the authors' work. This study also examined quality of reviews for blind and nonblind manuscripts; this aspect of the Fisher study is discussed in the next section.

Most studies tried to determine which clues made detection possible. On the average, referees identified 38.1 percent of the authors and of these 45.6 percent (or 17.4 percent of the total) came from self-citations in the manuscript. If self-citations were used more judiciously, or in some cases eliminated, data then suggest that 17.4 percent of the authors could still be identified through other means. Instructions to authors could direct authors not to refer to themselves in self-citations; indeed some instructions to authors do contain such guidelines. It would be impossible, of course, to eliminate author identification totally because the reviewer has expertise in the area of research. For only a relatively small percentage (about 14 percent) of the manuscripts were reviewers able to identify the authors from knowledge of the research: 38.1 percent of authors were identified and 38.6 percent of those were identified because the reviewer had knowledge of the research. As mentioned above, a study of instructions to authors contained in medical journals showed about 12 percent to 15 percent of the instructions do require that authors prepare a manuscript with blind review in mind (Weller, 1987). With the exception of one study in public health, reviewers appear less likely to be able to identify authors of blinded manuscripts than predictions indicated they could. It is also interesting to note (Table 7-2) that in the three studies that asked reviewers to guess the authors of a blinded manuscript, an average of 53 percent of the reviewers did not attempt to name the authors.

Looking at the other side of author-referee identification, a group of researchers asked authors if they were able to identify the reviewers of the manuscripts that these authors had sent to *Psychological Medicine* (Wessely, Brugha, Cowen, Smith,

& Paykel, 1996). As one would expect, authors performed less well at guessing reviewers' names than reviewers at guessing authors' names. Only 5.9 percent of authors correctly named the reviewers; 14.9 percent incorrectly identified referees' names; 79.7 percent of the authors had no idea who the referees were.

## Reviewer bias and name recognition

A large survey of about 4,000 scholars in the United States conducted in the mid-1980s by the American Council of Learned Societies found that "three out of four respondents considered the peer review system for journals in their disciplines biased, especially in favor of established scholars. Nearly half say reform is needed" (p. 1) (Morton & Price, 1986).

Crane studied publication patterns in the *American Sociological Review* before and after editors established a blind review policy (Crane, 1967). From 1946 to 1955, before blind review was begun, 26 percent of *American Sociological Review* authors worked in major universities. From 1956 to 1965, after blind review was begun, 33 percent of authors were from major universities. Crane concluded that blind review "does not produce the expected results" (p. 198). Crane had expected that, after establishing a policy of blind review, the percentage of authors from major universities would not increase. A study that followed institutional affiliation of authors in three economic journals (*American Economic Review*, the *Journal of Political Economy*, and the *Quarterly Journal of Economics*) over four decades (from the 1950s through the 1980s) found that the share of pages from major universities declined through the 1970s and then stabilized (Siegfried, 1994). Siegfried speculated that double-blind reviewing might be responsible for journals becoming "less parochial in their article selection procedure" (p. 383) than at the time of the Crane study. One additional study of articles published in the *Journal of Applied Psychology* found that of 162 articles only 39 percent originated from the top 20 institutions (McIntosh & Ross, 1987). McIntosh and Ross concluded that authors from highly ranked institutions were not necessarily publishing more than their peers at other institutions. They did not suggest that blind review was responsible for this trend.

Garfunkel and colleagues (Garfunkel, Ulshen, & Lawson, 1994) wanted to know if manuscripts from prestigious institutions were more likely to be accepted for publication than those from less prestigious institutions. Their retrospective study of manuscripts submitted to the *Journal of Pediatrics* found that major manuscripts from prestigious institutions were no more likely to be accepted than those from less prestigious institutions. However, the investigators did find that brief reports were more likely to be rejected when they originated from less prestigious institutions. Although the investigators did not state if the *Journal of Pediatrics* used a nonblind or blind review process, the implication of the article, of course, was that the nonblind review process was being evaluated.

Marsden maintained that the only way to assure that a review is based solely on the merits of the research and not on such factors as "reputation, sex, race and institutional affiliation" (p. 698) is to use blind review (Marsden, 1990). But it appears that for a certain percentage of manuscripts, it is impossible to remove all traces of the authors' identity. The next logical question then is to ask to what degree, if any, is the reviewer influenced by a knowledge of authors' names or institutions? How does this knowledge influence the overall quality of the review or the final recommendation of the reviewer?

*Question*

To what degree have studies demonstrated measurable reviewer bias in the reviewers' reports or recommendations when authors' names or institutions are known to reviewers?

*Criteria for inclusion*

~ any study that measured bias in the review of a group of manuscripts or articles that could be directly traced to reviewers' knowledge of authors' names or institutions.

*Comparable studies*

Ten studies looked for reviewers' biases that could be attributed to their knowledge of the authors' names or institutions; seven of these studies are summarized in Table 7-3 and three are discussed separately. The three discussed separately are a study by Peters and Ceci on resubmitted manuscripts (Peters & Ceci, 1982), and two studies, one by Perlman and one by Laband and Piette, on

| Journal title | # of manuscripts | # of reviews | Reviewers' score | | | | References |
|---|---|---|---|---|---|---|---|
| | | | blind | nonblind* | scale** | statistical significance | |
| *Australian & New Zealand Journal of Psychiatry* | 32 | | 2.78 | 2.66 | 4-point | none | (Parker, 1986) |
| *Journal of General Internal Medicine* | 123 | 246 | 3.5 | 3.1 | 5-point | Wilcoxon matched-pairs tests; p<.02 for all measures | (McNutt et al., 1990) (Evans, McNutt, Fletcher, & Fletcher, 1993) |
| | 131 | 226 | 51% | 36% | 4 or 5 on a 5-point scale | p<.03 | |
| *American Economic Review* | 311 | | 47.7% | 38.1% | | | (Borts, 1974) |
| *American Economic Review* | 832 blind; 666 nonblind | | 10.6% accepted | 14.1% accepted | | | (Blank, 1991) |
| *Journal of Development & Behavioral Pediatrics* | 57 | 112 blind; 108 nonblind | 20% accepted | 20% accepted | 5-point | Wilcoxon sign rank test; no difference | (Fisher et al., 1994) |
| *British Medical Journal* | 487 | | | | | no significant differences | (Goldbeck-Wood, 1997) |

\* Nonblind: reviewer knows name of author; \*\* Scale: higher number for better quality of reviews

**Table 7-3: Quality of blind versus nonblind reviews**

citation patterns following publication in journals that used either anonymous or blind review (Perlman, 1982) (Laband & Piette, 1994a).

In each of the three studies that are discussed separately, it was not possible to trace reviewer bias as such to knowledge of the authors or their institutions. However, they were designed to examine potential reviewer bias based on reviewers' knowledge of the authors. In the first of these three studies, Peters and Ceci resubmitted manuscripts that had been published by well-known psychology journals, changing only the names of authors and institutions (Peters & Ceci, 1982). The resubmitted manuscripts were the same in each case, with the exception that fictitious authors and institutions were exchanged for real authors and institutions. Each altered manuscript was resubmitted to the same journal that had originally published it. Nothing else was altered. The editors detected the resubmission in of three of the 12 manuscripts. Of the remaining nine manuscripts, eight were rejected.

Peters and Ceci's study was published in *Behavioral and Brain Sciences*. This journal is peer reviewed and publishes commentaries following each article. The Peters and Ceci article is followed by 56 commentaries that address many ethical, practical, and emotional issues raised by the study. The Peters and Ceci study has not been replicated but continues to be frequently cited, often as an example of problems with the editorial peer review process. Indeed, it may have received more commentary than any other study on editorial peer review. A search of *Web of Science* revealed that by mid-1999 it had been cited 196 times.

Some of the many negative comments raised in the commentaries following this article include:

- Peters and Ceci's manuscript had been rejected by *Science* (Armstrong, p. 197).

- Its generalizableness was questioned (Beaver, p. 199).

- The study was designed to ensure the results it found (Beyer, p. 203).

- Peters and Ceci did not have a full experimental design (Crandall, p. 207).

- Peters and Ceci did not obtain permission to copy the articles (DeBakey, p. 208).

- The authors violated six of 10 ethical principles for research with human subjects (Fleiss, p. 210).

- The study will have little impact on journal publication practices (Hogan, p. 216).

- The study used no control group, no independent variable (Rosenthal, p. 235).

Peters and Ceci acknowledged that 14 commentaries mentioned problems with the design of their study, particularly the lack of a control group. However, they maintained that "to test all the special factors necessitated a grand design that would have been impossible to carry out without the cooperation of the journal editors, which, unfortunately, was not forthcoming" (p. 246).

Many others saw the study as strong evidence of the need for reform of editorial peer review:

• Peters and Ceci showed that two or three reviewers are not enough (Belshaw, p. 200).

• Evidence from the study indicates a "need for improvement in the review process of academic journals" (Glenn, p. 212).

• Peter and Ceci's findings "reveal a grim state of affairs" (Howe, p. 218).

• Peters and Ceci used solid methodological techniques and obtained permission from all but one of the original authors (Millman, p. 225).

• The study "calls for some new and bold policy experiments in science" (Mitroff, p. 228).

• The study offers evidence that reviewers should be blinded to authors and paid (Perloff & Perloff, p. 232).

Two studies tested reviewer bias by comparing the number of citations to articles published in journals that used either blind or nonblind review (Perlman, 1982) (Laband & Piette, 1994b), (Laband & Piette, 1994c). The Laband and Piette study was published in two journals (neither cited the other).

Perlman tracked the number of citations to articles published in two psychology journals, the *Journal of Abnormal Psychology* (nonblind review) and the *Journal of Personality and Social Psychology* (blind review) in 1980. Authors from high-status institutions were cited an average of 3.7 times in two years and those from low-status institutions were cited an average of 1.4 times (the differences were statistically significant). Perlman found that, regardless of the type of reviewing practices used by these journals, articles written by authors from high-status institutions were cited more frequently than articles written by authors from low-status institutions.

Laband and Piette determined the number of citations for 1,051 articles published in 28 economics journals of which 13 used double-blind review and 15 used single-blind (anonymous) review. Articles published in the journals that used double-blind review were cited an average of 6.7 times per article in a five-year period, while those published in 15 journals that used anonymous were cited 7.3 times during the same five years. Laband and Peitte named the journals, but neither explained their selection process, the circulation of these journals, nor other factors that might have influenced citations to these articles. Laband and Piette felt that their study showed that "journals using nonblinded peer review publish a larger fraction of papers that should not have been published than do journals using blinded peer review. When reviewers know the identity of the author(s) of an article, they are able to (and evidently do) substitute particularistic criteria for universalistic criteria in their evaluation" (p. 147) (Laband & Piette, 1994c). Laband and Piette offered no evidence that the less-cited articles should not have been published, that either blind or anonymous review was responsible for the number of citations, or that the differences in number of citations between the two groups was a statistically significant difference. None of the investigators of these three studies could have known whether articles had undergone the review process according to the guidelines published by the editors. While Perlman thought that author affiliation influenced number of citations, Laband and Piette considered that the anonymity of the review process influenced the number of citations. In addition, Laband and Piette found that longer articles were cited more than shorter ones, a phenomenon that has been identified in other studies (Laband & Piette, 1994-b) (Campanario, 1996).

Three of the seven studies included in Table 7-3 used a similar study design. In each of these three studies, the same manuscript was reviewed by two reviewers: one reviewer received a blinded manuscript and the other received a nonblinded manuscript (Parker, 1986), (McNutt et al., 1990), (Evans et al., 1993), and (Fisher et al., 1994). (The McNutt study and the Evans study each report on different aspects of the same study.) Parker found that blind reviewers returned a slightly more favorable rating than nonblinded reviewers, but that the differences were not statistically significant. McNutt and colleagues compared two sets of reviewers' reports for the same manuscripts: one set of manuscripts had the authors' names and institutions removed; the other set retained both. These investigators found that, using the Wilcoxon matched-pairs test, the quality of the reviews were higher when reviewers received blinded manuscripts. Fisher and colleagues designed a similar study but found that there was no difference in the two sets of reviewers' reports using the Wilcoxon Sign Rank Test. One finding of the Fisher study was puzzling to the investigators: when the number of publications were obtained from authors' curriculum vitae, "senior authors with more previous articles received significantly better scores from the blinded reviewers, but not from the nonblinded reviewers" (p 145). Comparing the scores given by reviewers, Fisher and colleagues saw "no significant overall differences between blinded and nonblinded scores" (p. 144) and found that the blinded reviewers gave better scores to authors with a greater number of previous publications. The McNutt and Evans studies showed statistically significant differences between blind and nonblind review with those performing blind review receiving higher ratings than those performing nonblind review (McNutt et al., 1990) (Evans et al., 1993). None of the other studies showed statistically significant differences.

Blank studied the results of double-blind vs. anonymous review for the *American Economic Review* (Blank, 1991). She found that in raw numbers, double-blind manuscripts had a lower acceptance rate. Like the Fisher study that had the opposite findings, Blank uncovered some confounding results. "These results indicate that blind papers were accepted at a lower rate than nonblind papers over the sample period.... [I]t is also true that blind papers have worse referee ratings. Given that all the other aspects of these papers are identical in both samples, this indicates that these two reviewing practices do not produce identical results." (p. 1053).

In a study of the *British Medical Journal* (*BMJ*), Godlee reported that an independent review of referees' reports from 487 manuscripts randomly allocated to either a blind or a nonblind review found no statistically significant differences between the two types of review in overall quality, recommendations, or reviewing time (Goldbeck-Wood, 1997).

Studies listed in Table 7-3 uncovered less-striking differences for acceptances and rejections based on blind versus nonblind review than the results found by Peters and Ceci. There is inconclusive evidence from these studies to state whether reviewers perform better or worse when the manuscript is blinded. Studies in Table 7-3 offer a good methodological approach to investigating differences in blind versus nonblind review. Studies designed with bona fide manuscripts in real situations with assistance from editors would not raise the same ethical and methodological concerns as those raised in the Peters and Ceci study. By the nature of their design, studies of this type need to use data from editorial offices to avoid the issues of fabricated manuscripts and artificial settings, factors that have limited the generalizability of the Peters and Ceci study.

## Bias of ideological framework

If reviewers agree with a particular ideology, philosophy, or scientific technique presented in a manuscript, are they more likely to recommend the manuscript for acceptance than if they do not agree with the author's viewpoint? Six studies explored this question; all used fabricated abstracts or manuscripts.

The first study looked for bias by asking psychologists to evaluate one of two fabricated abstracts in astrology, one showed positive findings and the other negative (Goodstein & Brazis, 1970). Psychologists who received the abstracts with negative findings rated the study "as better designed, more valid, and as having more adequate conclusions" (p. 835) than those who received the abstracts with the positive findings. As has already been pointed out, the brevity of abstracts makes analyzing reviewers' recommendations from them somewhat problematic.

Abramowitz wrote two brief fabricated manuscripts in the field of political science (Abramowitz, Gomes, & Abramowitz, 1975). The manuscripts differed only in that one supported a proactivist viewpoint while the other supported an antiactivist viewpoint. Liberal and less-liberal subpopulations were identified through APA divisional membership and by journals in which they choose to publish. The liberal-designated group held membership in APA Division 9, the Society for the Psychological Study of Social Issues, or had published in the *Journal of Social Issues* during the five previous years. The less-liberal-designated group held membership in APA Division 8, Social and Personality, or had published in one of four journals during the same five-year period: *Journal of Personality and Social Psychology*, the *Journal of*

*Consulting and Clinical Psychology*, the *Journal of Personality*, and *Sociometry*. A manuscript was mailed to 400 psychologists in each group. Results showed that "the probability that a paper would receive a very firm publication endorsement was a good deal greater when it was sent out to an ideologically sympathetic referee (irrespective of whether his politics was more or less left) than to an unsympathetic one" (p. 196).

Gordon sent an anonymously authored psychology manuscript to 75 referees in the United States (Gordon, 1977). The manuscript was "adjusted to give results which were either congruent with, or contradictory to, the referees' presumed theoretical standpoints" (p. 232). Few details were given about the nature of the fabricated studies used in this experiment and no numerical results were provided. Gordon concluded that manuscripts were "consistently rejected when the results were opposed" (p. 232) to reviewers' theoretical framework. A second summary of this study was also published in *Earth & Life Sciences Editing* (Gordon, 1978a).

Mahoney conducted a similar study, asking 75 reviewers to evaluate a manuscript that had identical experimental procedures in cognitive psychology. One version of the manuscript had positive results, one negative results, and one mixed results (Mahoney, 1977). Mahoney saw little reviewer agreement and thought reviewers were "strongly biased against manuscripts which reported results contrary to their theoretical perspective" (p. 161).

Epstein sent two versions of a fabricated manuscript, one version with positive findings and the other version with negative findings, to 53 social work journals (Epstein, 1990). There was more support for acceptance of the positive manuscript than the negative one: 35.3 percent versus 25.0 percent. (This study is discussed further in Chapter Eight in the section on publication bias.) Mahoney expressed concern with several problems he saw in the Epstein study: the quality of the manuscript itself, the imbalance in the sampling procedure, the absence of independent raters, inadequate and inappropriate statistics, and a bias in emphasizing qualitative rather than quantitative results (Mahoney, 1990).

A study by Ernst and colleagues identified 33 investigators who had expressed an opinion on transcutaneous electrical nerve stimulation (TENS) (Ernst, Resch, & Uher, 1992). The 33 investigators were sent a fabricated manuscript on TENS reporting positive results. Of the 16 reviewers who did return the manuscript, eight were from the "pro" camp and eight were from the "con" camp. Those in favor of the procedure judged the manuscript more favorably then those who were against the procedure (p <0.02).

Studies that showed reviewers' tendency to favor manuscripts that agree with their viewpoints have findings similar to the studies that looked for reviewer agreement in Chapter Six. When reviewers with different viewpoints are selected to review particular manuscripts, they make recommendations based on their own beliefs or viewpoints.

## Gender and ethnicity biases

When Owen itemized in *JAMA* 25 potential biases, he failed to mention potential biases based on either the ethnicity or gender of the author (Owen, 1982). Since Owen cautioned readers 17 years ago to put aside their own opinions when reading reports, we have seen profound changes in the way women and members of ethnic groups in the United States have advanced professionally and altered their own expectations and efforts towards education, careers, and professions. This section reviews studies that investigated gender or ethnicity of authors as potential sources of reviewer bias.

In a study that examined reviewers' recommendations for the *Journal of Applied Behavior Analysis*, Boice and colleagues found no evidence of "reliable bias toward authors of a particular gender or from high status institutional affiliations" (p. 107) (Boice, Barlow, Johnson, & Klosko, 1984). The primary purpose of this study was to investigate reviewer agreement, and the authors did not provide the data from the portion of the study that discussed these findings.

The following analysis of gender and ethnic issues in the editorial peer review process looks for evidence of any changes that have occurred over time. A primary purpose of editorial peer review is to weed out flawed studies and to retain those of scientific and scholarly merit. There are some classic examples of highly publicized studies from the late 1800s that purported to prove that brain sizes were different in different ethnic groups (and, therefore, the studies concluded, intelligence was different in different ethnic groups). These studies were taken as correct and valid, and cited for years. Stephen Gould has written a fascinating treatise that discredited the whole series of these studies and critiques study design guaranteed to give results the investigators were looking for (Gould, 1996). While these studies were probably not peer reviewed by today's standards, they stand as an example of flawed studies that were not weeded out prior to publication.

The only example identified for this monograph of a claim of ethnic bias not uncovered by the peer review process was made in an article written by Leslie who critiqued an article published in *Social Science & Medicine* by Rushton (Leslie, 1990) (Rushton & Bogaert, 1989). The Rushton study, which was peer reviewed prior to publication, attributed the epidemiology of AIDS to ethnic variations, and according to Leslie, the article contained stereotypical reasoning. Leslie stated that Rushton's conclusions needed to be interpreted to fit both data and the explanation for the data (p. 908). Leslie affirmed that he was in favor of peer review, but he thought that it was often imperfect, as in his example. He suggested that Rushton's manuscript should have been reviewed by anthropologists or biologists who specialize in research on human evolution and who then might have uncovered these shortcomings.

In order to protect against biases toward those less-known researchers, women, or those from ethnic groups, in 1974, the Publications of the Modern Language Association (PLMA) adopted a policy of "author anonymous review "(p. 4), which meant that reviewers did not know names of authors. In a commentary in 1980,

Herbert quoted Mary Lefkowitz as stating that there had been a 100 percent increase in the number of accepted papers by women since the adoption of this policy (Herbert, 1980) by the PLMA. In one of the commentaries following the Peters and Ceci article, Horrobin also mentioned the experience of the PLMA, claiming there "was a dramatic rise in the acceptance of papers by female authors" (p. 217) (Horrobin, 1982). In a different example of anecdotal information, Edwards and Ferber quoted the results of an unpublished study of economics journals by Coughlin and O'Brien presented at the annual ASSA [sic] meeting in 1985 (Edwards & Ferber, 1986). According to Coughlin and O'Brien when the *American Economic Review* adopted a policy of double-blind review it published "significantly more pages by authors from non-elite institutions and women" (p. 5) than the *Journal of Political Economy*, which did not use double-blind review. Neither of the primary sources of the PLMA or the economic studies was located.

The APA serves as an example of steps taken by one association to work toward equal access to the publication process for all its members. In October 1970, the APA appointed a Task Force on the Status of Women in Psychology. The charge of the task force was to make recommendations to ensure that "women be accepted as fully enfranchised members of the profession" (p. 1) (American Psychological Association, 1972a). The task force conducted a survey of APA women members and made a series of recommendations based on the findings. The report did not include the specific questions on publication experiences that were asked in the survey. The final recommendations covered a range of proposed actions aimed at increasing participation by women in APA professional activities. The third recommendation of the task force was that the APA should institute blind review for a trial period of one year. As a result of this recommendation, eight of the APA's journals initiated blind review in 1972. The *APA Monitor* called this move controversial but pointed out that several other associations had a similar policy on blind review: American Sociological Association, American Political Science Association, and American Personnel and Guidance Association (American Psychological Association, 1972b).

In a letter to the editor published in the *APA Monitor*, Levinger wrote that in his experience the removal of authors' names only worked about half of the time (Levinger, 1973). He suggested an empirical study be conducted to prove the benefits of blind review before journals changed policies. Levinger's estimation that removing the authors name was only successful in blinding a manuscript about 50 percent of the time was similar to the percentage found in studies summarized in Table 7-2. Table 7-2 shows that an average of 38.1 percent reviewers could identify authors after the manuscript had been blinded.

By 1980, this task force was called the APA's Committee on Women in Psychology (American Psychological Association, 1980). The committee undertook a survey of journal editors in 1980 to determine what, if any, barriers existed that might hinder women or members of ethnic groups from participating in the review process. Of the 76 returned surveys, 64 percent of the editors said they took special steps to include women and members of ethnic groups in the review process, usually including them on the editorial board. An open call to solicit volunteers to review manuscripts was used by 23.7 percent of the editors. Only 22 percent of the journal editors had some provision for actively including women and members of ethnic groups as reviewers; 11 percent did not answer that question. The committee concluded that "qualified women continue to be underrepresented in this process, although some progress has been made in the attempts to increase their participation" (p.1110).

In most academic fields career advancement requires a substantial scholarly publication record. Any prejudice shown toward women or other groups in the publication process could have financial and career implications. As stated by Huth: "authorship is a meal ticket" (p. 266) (Huth, 1983).

In 1986, Yankauer, the editor of the *American Journal of Public Health*, wrote about the first 75 years of the *Journal*. He reflected on the changes these years have had on the number of women as authors. Until the 1930s, only 3 percent of all authors were women who, for the most part, were nurses or laboratory workers. During the next 40 years, the percentage of women as first authors steadily increased: 20 percent by 1970 and 30 percent by 1980. Women authors continue to increase their contributions to "many more of the disciplines covered by the public health umbrella" in addition to nursing and medical technicians. He added that "there is reason to hope that the shift will continue until equity is attained" (p. 810) (Yankauer, 1986). It is this very change in thinking that makes it important to consider the date of a particular study before attributing seemingly unequal publication patterns within gender or ethnic groups to bias in the editorial peer review process.

*Question*

Is the submission versus acceptance rate for manuscripts different depending on the gender or ethnicity of the author?

*Criteria for inclusion*

~ any study that compared the treatment or outcome of a group of manuscripts base on the gender or ethnicity of the authors.

*Comparable studies*

Six studies (Table 7-4) examined the review process of a group of manuscripts with the gender of the author as the variable; each study used fabricated manuscripts. Other than the one example discussed above by Rushton and Bogaert, no studies tried to identify reviewer bias originating from the authors' ethnicity (Rushton & Bogaert, 1989).

In order to determine if women showed prejudice against women, women college students ("girls" in the article) were asked to rate several articles from six disciplines (Goldberg, 1968). The 40 participants were divided into two groups. Each was asked to rate the same six articles—three articles received obvious male names as authors and three articles received obvious female

| Discipline; number of manuscripts | # and gender of reviewers | Female judge | | Both judge | Male judge | | Both judge | Statistical significance | Rating criteria | References |
|---|---|---|---|---|---|---|---|---|---|---|
| | | female author | male author | female author | female author | male author | male author | | | |
| one manuscript from each of six disciplines | 40 women | 2.81 | 2.53 | | | | | yes | 9 criteria on persuasiveness, value, and profundity | (Goldberg, 1968) |
| one manuscript from each of six disciplines | 79 men, 55 women | | | 3.57 | | | 3.55 | no | 5 criteria on writing, competence, persuasiveness, author's ability, and value | (Levenson, Burford, Bonno, & Davis, 1975) |
| one psychology essay | 58 men | | | | 3.01 | 2.59 | | $p<0.025$ | status criteria | (Ward, 1981) |
| | | | | | 2.21 | 1.84 | | $p<0.05$ | competence criteria | |
| | | | | | | | | no | 5 criteria | |
| one manuscript from each of three disciplines | 180 men, 180 women | 3.00 | 2.30 | | 3.00 | 1.90 | | not overall | 9 criteria | (Paludi & Bauer, 1983) |
| | | | | | | | | $p<.01$ | 3 criteria | |
| one manuscript from each of three disciplines | 150 men, 150 women | 3.10 | 2.00 | | 3.00 | 2.40 | | $p<0.05$ | 9 criteria | (Paludi & Strayer, 1985) |
| one manuscript from behavioral sciences | 35 men, | 2.81 | 4.20 | | | | | $p<0.015$ | 4 criteria: accept to reject | (Lloyd, 1990) |
| | 28 women | | | | 3.84 | 3.80 | | no | | |
| *Average* | | 2.93 | 2.76 | 3.57 | 3.01 | 2.51 | 3.55 | | | |

* Rating scale: 1 high, 5 low

**Table 7-4: Gender differences in evaluation of fabricated manuscripts**

authors' names. There were two sets of these six articles, one-half of the college students evaluated one set and the other half evaluated the second set. The sets differed only in that in the two sets the names of authors were reversed. The study found that male authors received more favorable ratings in all six disciplines. Articles authored by males received statistically significant better ratings for the "masculine" fields of city planning and law. Articles authored by males also received higher ratings, although the differences were not statistically significant, in the predominately "female" fields of dietetics and education, as well as in the "neutral" fields of linguistics and art history.

The Goldberg study was replicated seven years later, with the addition of evaluations by men as well as women (Levenson et al., 1975). Levenson and colleagues asked 134 college freshmen to evaluate six articles. As in the Goldberg study, they divided the students into two groups using fabricated articles in the same disciplines as those used by Goldberg. Each group evaluated one of the two sets of articles with each set again switching names of authors from obviously male to obviously female names. Levenson and colleagues found that both men and women rated female authors slightly higher than male authors, but the differences were not statistically significant. In addition, they found no statistically significant differences in the ratings of the articles for the variables of sex of the raters or type of occupation for either a predominately "male" or "female" occupation.

Using the same methodology Ward also found no statistically significant differences with respect to ratings of the articles for style, content, persuasiveness, profundity, and professionalism (Ward, 1981). However, there was "a marked tendency for males to denigrate the female author" (p. 163). The two ratings of "status" and "competence" (Table 7-4) were the only data supplied by Ward. Paludi and Bauer conducted a similar study to Ward's two years later and found, like Goldberg, that an article attributed to a person with an obvious male name was given a higher rating than the same article attributed to a person without an obvious male name (Paludi & Bauer, 1983). And 17 years after the Goldberg study, Paludi and Strayer reached the same conclusions as Goldberg: an article "written by a male was valued more positively than if the author were not male" (p. 353) (Paludi & Strayer, 1985).

These five studies used the same study design, with slightly different approaches. Goldberg only used female subjects to review the manuscripts. Levenson aggregated data by combining data from both the male and female ratings of manuscripts. Ward gave only data on the cases in which statistically significant differences were found. The Goldberg study, the Levenson study, and the Paludi and Strayer study each divided manuscripts into either "male" professions or "female" professions. The Ward study and the Paludi and Bauer study did not designate manuscripts by male or female professions and studied effects of only one manuscript (with different authors' names).

A study in the behavioral sciences by Lloyd took a slightly different approach, but similar to the studies of college students, used a fabricated manuscript and examined reviewers' recommendations based on the gender of the author (Lloyd, 1990). Lloyd obtained reviewers' names from editors of five behavioral journals. She fabricated a manuscript that described research conducted in a preschool setting. The same manuscript was sent to two sets of reviewers; in one set the manuscripts had an obviously female author and in the other set the manuscript had an obviously male author. Lloyd found that female reviewers recommended acceptance for 62 percent of female-authored manuscripts compared to only 10 percent for male-authored manuscripts. This large difference was, not surprisingly, a statistically significant difference. Men showed similar same-gender preferences but to a much lesser degree than the women. Men recommended acceptance of 30 percent for the male-authored manuscripts and 21 percent for the female-authored manuscripts. Lloyd's understated conclusions ring true: "Information unrelated to the quality of the manuscript appears to have influenced reviewers' decisions" (p. 539). One could speculate that the study by Lloyd showed a backlash by women; that women were inclined to recommend female-authored manuscripts for acceptance to help undo perceived past injustices. But Lloyd did not make that speculation. She did, however, hope that her findings would prompt the editors of behavioral sciences journals to reconsider their long-standing policies against blind review.

Data in Table 7-4 have been converted to a five-point scale: "1" is the highest or most positive rating, and "5" is the lowest or least positive rating. Five studies engaged college students to evaluate fabricated papers. Three studies have summary data for females judging a fabricated article authored by either a male or a female and males judging a fabricated article authored by either a male or a female (Goldberg, Paludi and Strayer, and Paludi and Bauer). In each of these studies, data indicate that both college males and females rate male-authored manuscripts higher than female-authored manuscripts. This trend did not change in the 18 years from the earliest study to the most recent. Ward studied evaluations by male reviewers and found they slightly favored male authors. Levenson reach a different conclusion when he did not find a bias against female authors. The behavior at a professional rather than a college level could be quite different. Since these studies used students to evaluate manuscripts, they are not a study of the editorial peer review process *per se*. Whether these results could be replicated for professionals would be very interesting to know, and this argues for more study. Indeed the Lloyd study has done just that and had disquieting findings. Lloyd did not find much of a difference when males judged either male or females, but she found a marked favoritism when females positively judged female authors and not male authors. The studies show a tendency of the reviewers to rank the same manuscript differently depending on the gender of the author.

All studies in Table 7-4 used fabricated manuscripts. There is a strong possibility that fabricated manuscripts were written with less care than an author would give to the preparation of a bona fide manuscript. A less well-written or constructed manuscript might be a likely candidate for receiving mixed reviews. With a less well-prepared manuscript, reviewers might place more weight on secondary characteristics of a manuscript (like the gender of author) than they might for a more carefully constructed manuscript. Since an artificial situation was created in each study, it was not possible to follow the fabricated manuscripts through to a final publication decision. In other words, it is not known if a positive or negative review in any of these examples would actually have resulted in the acceptance or rejection of the manuscript.

Another group of studies more directly related to the editorial peer review process than the previous studies examined acceptance and rejection of manuscripts based solely on the gender of the author (Table 7-5).

Six studies investigated the influence of blind versus nonblind review on recommendations of the reviewers, focusing on the influences of the author's gender (Table 7-5). Each study compared the gender of the reviewers and the gender of authors with reviewers' recommendations to either accept or reject a manuscript in both blind and nonblind reviews.

| Field; # of journals | Gender of authors | Acceptance with blind review | Difference in male or female rate of acceptance with blind review | Favors male | Acceptance: nonblind review | Difference in male or female rate of acceptance for nonblind review | Favors male | Difference in acceptance between blind and nonblind review | References |
|---|---|---|---|---|---|---|---|---|---|
| Economics; 12 | female<br>male | 22.9%<br>19.0% | 3.9% | | 12.8%<br>15.2% | 2.4% | x | 10.1%<br>3.8% | (Ferber & Teiman, 1980) |
| Organization; 1 | female<br>male | 26.0%<br>32.3% | 6.3% | x | | | | | (Bernard, 1980) |
| Economics; 12 | female and male | 26.4% | | | 13.6% | | | 12.8% | (Edwards & Ferber, 1986) |
| Psychology; 1 | female<br>male | 15.0%<br>35.0% | 20.0% | x | | | | | (Glidewell, 1988) |
| Economics; 1 | female<br>male | 10.0%<br>11.0% | 1.1% | x | 11.2%<br>15.0% | 3.8% | x | 1.2%<br>4.0% | (Blank, 1991) |
| Medicine; 1 | female<br>male | | | | 41.0%<br>41.0% | 0.0% | | | (Gilbert, Williams, & Lundberg, 1994) |
| *Average* | | 22.0% | 7.8% | | 21.4% | 2.1% | | 6.4% | |

**Table 7-5: Gender differences in blind and nonblind manuscript review**

The American Economics Association supported a study designed to determine if women had the same success in collaborating as their male counterparts (Ferber & Teiman, 1980). Ferber and Teiman studied authorship patterns from 1974 to 1978 in 14 economics journals selected to represent a "good cross section of different journals" (p. 190). They found that there were fewer articles coauthored by men and women than would be expected by randomly pairing men and women authors. Ferber and Teiman also compared rejection rates of manuscripts authored by only male authors, by male and female authors, and only female authors under both double-blind and open reviewing systems. In each comparison, women both with and without male coauthors tended to have a higher acceptance rate when manuscripts had undergone a blind review. Edwards and Ferber used some of the same data as the Ferber and Teiman study, supplied additional data on coauthored manuscripts, and found the same pattern as Ferber and Teiman (Edwards & Ferber, 1986). Laband used the same set of articles studied by Ferber and Tieman and assigned them a measure of quality based on number of citations, type of article, length, theory, and coauthorship. Laband found "no particular qualitative difference between material published by members of each sex" and concluded that "there is no reason to believe that journal editors in the economics profession discriminate against female authors, in terms of the qualitative standards for an affirmative publication decision" (p. 152). (Laband, 1987). Laband refers to unpublished remarks by Ferber where she argued that citation patterns favor male authors.

Of the 592 manuscripts with identifiable gender names processed by the editor of *Human Organization* during the four years of his tenure, 26 percent of the female authors and 32.3 percent of the male authors were accepted (Bernard, 1980). Although more male-authored articles were accepted, the difference was not statistically significant, leaving Bernard to conclude that "aggregated data indicate no gender bias for getting into print in *Human Organization*" (p. 369).

Glidewell, the editor of the *American Journal of Community Psychology*, compared acceptance and rejection rates of male versus female authors from 1981 to 1986 (Glidewell, 1988). During this time the rejection rate for female first authors was 85 percent while the rejection rate for male first authors was 65 percent (p. 765). Glidewell seemed genuinely puzzled by this finding, especially given his policy of blind review, and promised further investigation. However, his tenure as editor was ending at the time he wrote his analysis and no follow-up data were located.

In a study of the *American Economic Review* Blank found that women authors had an overall 10.6 percent acceptance rate that was slightly lower but not a statistically significant difference than the 12.7 percent acceptance rate for men. As can be seen in Table 7-5, the acceptance rate for women was only marginally higher with nonblind review: 11.2 percent (nonblind) compared to 10 percent (blind) (p. 1052). This study did not control for age, experience, or institutional affiliation, and the authors conceded that no statement could be made about any gender bias in the review process for the *American Economic Review* (Blank, 1991).

The editors of *JAMA* were interested in finding out if there were different peer review and manuscript processing characteristics based on the gender of the author, reviewer, or editor (Gilbert et al., 1994). Gilbert and colleagues found that while gender differences existed in editor and reviewer characteristics (for example, women editors worked fewer hours but handled more manuscripts than male editors), there was "no apparent effect on the final outcome of the peer review process or acceptance for publication" (p. 139) of manuscripts authored by women compared to those authored by men.

These studies show strikingly less difference between the recommendations of male and female reviewers than found in studies of fabricated manuscripts. Differences in these two sets of studies support the argument that fabricated manuscripts do not make the best material for a study of the editorial peer review process. Studies also do not support the supposition that there are changes over time one way or the other. The data also do not provide solid evidence of a systematic gender bias, and no study looked for evidence of ethnic bias. Studies that measured manuscript outcome without an analysis of the reviewers' reports cannot measure the influence of the editor on manuscript outcome.

## Signed reviewers' reports

The subject of reviewers signing their reports has received scant attention in the literature and generated very little data. Even if the editor employs an anonymous review process, reviewers may sign their reports without an invitation from the editor to do so. In turn, the editor decides whether to leave signatures on reports when they are sent to the authors.

Fraenkel-Conrat wrote a letter to the editor in *Nature* supporting an open review system in which authors are given reviewers' names. As editor of *Comprehensive Virology*, he found reviewers were more likely to submit constructive criticism over their signatures than when they did not sign the reports (Fraenkel-Conrat, 1974). He viewed anonymous review as bringing out "the worst in people and it causes undesirable aspects of the reviewing system" (p. 8).

Referring to the fact that book reviewers regularly sign their names to the reviews, Jones suggested that reviewers should also sign their reports when evaluating journal manuscripts (Jones, 1974). Editors of the *BMJ* countered Jones' comments with the thought that "few referees would be prepare to wound with the unvarnished truth, and the practice would almost certainly lead to personal conflicts between them and the authors" (p. 185) (1974-b). Mirman believed that when reviewers sign their reports they have a strong personal incentive to do a good job (Mirman, 1975). Ingelfinger, commenting on the uncharitable words used by some reviewers, remarked that he had "never seen an abrasive or insulting word used by a reviewer who identified himself" (Ingelfinger, 1975). Relman claimed that approximately 15 percent of the reviewers for the *New England Journal of Medicine* sign their reviews, and he left the option of signing reports to the discretion of each reviewer (Relman, 1981). The editor of *Journal of Aerosol Science* always disclosed the names of the referees to the authors. During a nine-year period, he experienced no difficulties when he passed on both favorable and unfavorable reviewers' comments to the author (Davies, 1978).

In order to open the review system and foster interaction among scientists, the editor of the *Journal of Laboratory and Clinical Medicine* encouraged reviewers to sign their reports (Knox, 1981). Knox kept a tally of those reviewers who chose to sign the reviews and those who did not during nine months in 1977 and nine months in 1980. Reviewers were slightly more likely to sign their reports when manuscripts were ultimately accepted—about 10 percent more for each time period studied. The percentage of those signing reviews did not increase during the study period, leading the editor to conclude that his argument in favor of signing reviews had not convinced reviewers to alter their practices. However, a rather high percentage of reviewers did sign their reports: in 1977, 68 percent of reviewers signed reports for those manuscripts eventually accepted and 59 percent signed for those manuscripts eventually rejected; in 1980, percentages of those signing reports were 60 percent and 50 percent, respectively. It is interesting to note that for both accepted and rejected manuscripts more reviewers signed their reports in 1977 than in 1980. Contrary to speculation, signed reviews were not "bland and meaningless" (p. 3) as predicted. Reviewers participating in this study had split opinions about signing reports: 48 percent of reviewers favored signing, while 52 percent favored anonymity for reviewers. The editor decided to continue with the policy of offering referees the option of signing their reports. The editor of the *Journal of General Internal Medicine* also encouraged reviewers to sign reports (Kern, 1988).

In surveying a random sample of journal editors in multiple disciplines, Miller and Serzan determined that 16.8 percent of editors left the reviewers' names on signed reports when sending them to authors (Miller & Serzan, 1984). These investigators found that journals in medicine, health, psychology, and life sciences were more likely than journals in humanities to send signed reviewers' reports to authors.

Brady pointed out a potential problem with signed reviewers' reports: reviewers who sign their names could be "unduly flattering: a younger referee would not want to offend a senior investigator who might be in a position to influence his career" (p. 823) (Brady, 1985). The editors of *Plastic and Reconstructive Surgery* worried that a signed report would produce a "bland review, like the polite discussion" following a presentation at a meeting (p. 398) (Goldwyn, 1989).

A study conducted by McNutt and colleagues investigated the quality of anonymous versus signed review. Reviewers were given the option. Forty-three percent chose to sign and there was no difference in quality between signed and unsigned reports (McNutt et al., 1990). Other details of this study are discussed above in the section on reviewer bias and name recognition.

However, as an example of the continued ambivalence toward disclosing the names of reviewers, a survey of reviewers for *Cardiovascular Research* showed that 83 percent of the reviewers and 70 percent of the authors favored maintaining reviewers' anonymity (Fabiato, 1994). Referring to the Fabiato survey, Hearse reported that 39 percent of respondents thought that revealing the identity of the reviewer would improve peer review, and 39 percent thought it would make peer review worse (Hearse, 1994). These opposing opinions were puzzling, but the editors of *Cardiovascular Research* concluded, given the results, they would maintain a policy of anonymous review.

These examples on signed reports illustrate a mix of editorial and reviewers opinions. Editors who collected data on the percentage of reviewers who signed their reports found that anywhere from 10 percent to 68 percent of reviewers' were willing to sign their names on reviewers' reports. Editors who retained reviewers' names on returned reports have not appeared to encounter any problems.

## Guidelines for addressing reviewer bias

A number of authors have suggested changes to the editorial peer review process to lessen the impact of reviewer bias. Hunt thought referees should be given the option of being named, particularly if the final article incorporated a number of reviewers' recommendations. He also thought reviewers who consistently do a good job should be acknowledged (Hunt, 1971). Guenin suggested that only senior scientists should review manuscripts since this group has no vested interest in the outcome and can remain objective (Guenin, 1996).

Gordon urged the adoption of an "optional published refereeing" system in which an author could publish a criticized or rejected manuscript on the condition that anonymous comments of referees be published as well. He recommended that this suggestion be tested in a number of physics journals (Gordon, 1978b). Agreeing with most of Gordon's recommendations, Kumar thought that under the optional published refereeing system authors should have a chance to refute the reviewers' comments (Kumar, 1979). Gordon then implied that variations to his proposal were possible, but that the important idea was that "a contested manuscript ... be published along with the critical comments of the referee in such a form as to encourage a subsequent objective evaluation of the important points in question" (p. 609) (Gordon, 1980). No more information about this recommendation has been located.

In a variation to the "optional published refereeing" system recommended by Gordon, the journal *Behavioral and Brain Sciences* uses a system in which signed commentaries follow each article. However, in *Behavioral and Brain Sciences* each manuscript undergoes traditional editorial peer review and is accepted for publication before comments to accompany the published article are solicited and the authors do not learn the names of the reviewers.

Arguments for and against anonymous review have been spelled out by Fabiato, who wanted to get both sides on the table for further discussion (Fabiato, 1994). Fabiato's arguments favoring revealing the reviewers' identity include:

- Reviewers maintain balance between their judgment role and the role of helping authors.

- Credentials of reviewers add to the credibility of their comments.

- Reviewers become more accountable.

- Abuses of the editorial peer review system are eliminated, such as an unscrupulous reviewer delaying publication.

- Controversial areas of research are more easily resolved.

- Politeness is maintained and peer review is less disagreeable.

- New technologies may render open review a necessity.

- Respectable scientific communities have little room for secrecy.

Arguments against revealing the reviewers' identity include:

- Junior reviewers fear reprisals.

- An "old boy" network favors established scientists.

- Resentment and animosity are created.

- A higher acceptance rate would result.

- More work and problems for the editor would be created.

- A system that now works has no reason to change.

Although Fabiato favored opening the review system, he saw that "neither the reviewers nor the authors are ready for such a change" (p. 1134) for the time being. Futhermore, as long as he remained editor of *Cardiovascular Research*, he was not going to change the policy. He went on to recommend changes that would improve the peer review system:

• Reveal names of reviewers to each other.

• Use guest editors.

• Publish lists of reviewers and guest editors.

• Maintain confidentiality of reviewers' reports.

• Arbitrate conflicts between authors and reviewers.

• Use one set of policies for all authors and reviewers.

Bornstein asked editors, associate editors, and reviewers of psychology journals their opinions about opening the review process by revealing reviewers' identity to authors (Bornstein, 1993). More than one-half of all respondents thought open reviewing would result in authors retaliating against reviewers, in less negative reviews, in less critical reviews, in fewer researchers willing to review, and in decreased reviewer objectivity.

This section has presented the standard and logical arguments for and against anonymous and blind review. The Fabiato article presents a particularly complete set of arguments. It is clear that without further study one cannot reach any definitive conclusions about the merits of one method over the other. Data collected thus far have not provided a lot of help. Even the International Committee of Medical Journal Editors has remained noncommittal on issues of blind and anonymous review. The peer review section includes only the statement that "the reviewing procedures, and the use made of the reviewers' opinion may vary, and therefore each journal should publicly disclose its policies" (p. 571) (International Committee of Medical Journal Editors, 1997).

## Limitations to studies of reviewer bias

• Studies and discussion appear to assume that anonymous review is the standard procedure for journal editors. Several studies have made that assumption and collected data without verifying current editorial practices. Future studies should review existing practices and then evaluate the merits of procedures or policies.

• Several studies that investigated gender bias in manuscript review used fabricated manuscripts that were judged by college students. These students might not have taken their task as seriously as they would have had they been professionals. Some of these studies found statistically significant differences between ratings of male and female judges for the same manuscript, depending on the gender of the author. When similar studies were done using bona fide manuscripts, results were less dramatic.

- The few studies that tested for biases in the review process under anonymous or blind review came from behavioral sciences, economics, medicine, psychiatry, and sociology. Each discipline was subjected to only one or two studies and, with the exception of the Ceci and Peters' study, each investigated only one journal. They were such small studies that generalizations are problematic.

- Studies that debate the merits or prejudices of reviewers' reports under either anonymous or blind review do not account for the role of the editor, who presumably weighs the merits or correctness of a manuscript against reviewers' comments. Editors could, and probably do, balance negative reviews, if they have some concerns about comments on the reviewers' reports.

- Data from these studies provide little guidance for editors when they set policies aimed at reducing review bias.

## *Recommendations*

- There appears to be little point in pursing studies of editorial peer review with fabricated manuscripts. Any such study could be critiqued on the overall quality of a fabricated manuscript alone. In fact, in a reference to the quality of a fabricated manuscript in the Epstein study (Epstein, 1990), Mahoney pointed to the "poor choice of an experimental manuscript" (p. 52) as one of several problems with the study (Mahoney, 1990). This may be true for similar studies as well. In addition, fabricated manuscripts will by their nature always bring up ethical issues: particularly the issues of the presentation of false data and the waste of editors' and reviewers' time. In addition there is the possibility that studies that use fabricated manuscripts are designed to reach conclusions the authors are seeking. There are sufficient sources of real manuscripts and these sources should be tapped.

- There are very few studies that have compared reviewers' recommendations when reviewers blinded or not blinded to the authors. This very interesting line of inquiry suggests that additional studies of this nature, with a design similar to the Evans and McNutt study or the design proposed by the Institute of Mathematical Statistics, but on a larger scale, might resolve the debate on blind versus not blind review. Control studies are needed and these two methodologies provide solid approaches for further investigation. The studies that showed evidence that reviewers who were blinded to the authors produce better reviews is argument enough to pursue this question with a large, comprehensive study.

- The observation that young researchers might provide the best reviews, with some evidence to support the observation, gives a powerful argument to the recommendation that reviewers remain anonymous. Unless data in the future show otherwise, together they make a case for the recommendation that a double-blind review system is the fairest.

## Conclusions from studies of bias of reviewers

In writing on the practice of anonymous authoring in the seventeenth and eighteenth centuries, Kronick draws a parallel to the practice of anonymous reviewing (Kronick, 1988). "While many authors chose the prerogative of remaining anonymous in the earlier period, the practice rarely occurs today, and when it does, it is not as easily condoned" (p. 234).

Some have made the argument that manuscript reviewers are similar to monograph reviewers: monograph reviewers sign their names, so why not the same for manuscript reviewers? However, there is a difference between a reviewer of a monograph and a reviewer of a manuscript. Experts in a field usually are selected to evaluate a monograph, so their careers are not on the line as might be the case for a young, new researcher who is asked to critique a manuscript of a well-known researcher or scholar. Scientific monographs often do not present new data as such, but are a compilation or analysis of data or information already published. Therefore, the reviewer is not critiquing new science as much as commenting on the analysis. Monograph reviews are also relatively infrequent compared to the number of manuscripts in need of review.

Peer review is inherently a human process, subject to the imperfections of human behavior. Reviewer bias for or against a particular characteristic (place, theory, method, result—you name it) is so fundamental to human nature that erasing such bias is simply not possible. Reviewer bias surely exists, but may also be a different type of a bias from that described by Murphy as a bias of "moving from the truth." Reviewer bias may be a bias of personal experience and beliefs. It might be expected that studies that investigated reviewer bias in the evaluation of manuscripts that express opinions and beliefs, not scientific principles, would result in recommendations based on beliefs of the reviewers. As has been demonstrated in some examples in this chapter, there have been questions about the study design itself in several of the studies of reviewer bias. The Peters and Ceci study is an excellent case in point. Like their study, most studies on editorial peer review have not examined the whole process, only a portion of it. Therefore drawing conclusions embracing the whole process may be unwarranted.

There have been changes in practices of anonymous and blind review over the years with a trend toward more anonymous and more blind review. The suggestion by a physicist that editors remove the authors' name and affiliation from manuscripts was probably rather radical in 1966 (Coffman, 1966), but is fairly common practice in some fields today.

Anonymous review has been supported on the grounds that it protects the young investigator who might find fault with a senior author, and it also protects professional friendships. Discussions on anonymous and blind review tend to generate two types of arguments. On one hand, there are the discussions about the fairness of reviews when reviewers have information about the authors. On another hand, there are the discussions about the impossibility of producing a manuscript free of author-identification markings. These discussions tend to produce circuitous opinionating and offering little resolution. The data are not overly helpful but do show a weak support for a blind-review system.

Removing the authors' identity from all manuscripts appears to be impossible. Some editors view this fact alone as reason not to pursue a blind review system. However, reviewers appear to be less likely to identify authors accurately than they thought they could. Reviewers guessed they could identify between 65 percent and 80 percent of authors if the manuscripts were blinded, whereas studies have found the percentage closer to 40 percent. More important, the identification of an author by a reviewer is not *ipso facto* proof that there is any reviewer bias that might unjustly affect the outcome of a manuscript. In fact, those few studies that examined differences in the quality of reviews between blind and nonblind reviewers found mixed results. A certain percentage of reviewers (about one-half each time the question was asked) seem not to be interested in guessing who the authors might be.

Cultural factors appear to be at work when one examines the differences in the way men and women rate each other's work. This fascinating line of inquiry requires more study. Similar to other studies that used fabricated manuscripts, recent studies of actual peer review seem to confirm that the impact of any gender biases may not be as strong as it was a number of years ago. These studies, even if flawed, have been included in this discussion because they illustrate some of the complexities involved in the evaluation of someone's work by another person.

The studies that examined outcome of the editorial peer review process present an incomplete picture. There are many variables at play when a reviewer undertakes the review of a manuscript. For example, harsh criticisms by reviewers, even if done anonymously, do not escape judgment by the editor. Some editors do maintain evaluations of reviewers' reports. Manheim noted the role of the editor is infrequently mentioned as a check on anonymous review (Manheim, 1973). Also, those studies that have looked for bland judgments when reviewers are identified have also not found it.

Data from the studies of reviewer bias must be considered in light of studies that have shown that researchers and scholars from major institutions publish more than researchers and scholars from less prominent institutions. While some researchers claimed blind review helps researchers from less prominent institutions, many complex factors are at work. These studies did not investigate any relationship between a more productive publishing record and its connection with either anonymous or blind reviewing. Nor did they examine the impact of resubmissions of rejected manuscripts, which data show is a very prevalent practice.

Studies from this chapter have demonstrated the difficulties of measuring any type of reviewer bias. Clearly, this is an area ripe for more research. Some methodologies have been developed that could be used for additional, comparative studies, similar to the Evans and McNutt study. But any new studies on this topic should be large, use random samples of manuscripts, and have a well-defined control group.

More information is needed to help editors decide on a course of action fairest to all. There is a move toward more closed review rather than open review. The Internet, with its easy potential for an open review system, has the real potential to change scientific communication. There is an urgent need for answers to these questions about reviewer bias and the value of editorial peer review as the Internet becomes a viable option for a different form of publication of important scholarly and scientific information: publication with no review.

# References

(1970, February 12). "There shall be weeping and gnashing of teeth." *New England Journal of Medicine, 282*(7), 393-394.

(1974, April 27-a). Both sides of the fence. *British Medical Journal, 2*(5912), 185-186.

(1974, June 14-b). In defence of the anonymous referee. *Nature, 249*, 601.

Abramowitz, S. I., Gomes, B., & Abramowitz, C. V. (1975). Publish or politic: referee bias in manuscript review. *Journal of Applied Social Psychology, 5*(3), 187-200.

Adair, R. K., Carlon, H. R., & Sherman, C. (1981, June). Anonymous refereeing. *Physics Today, 34*(6), 13-15, 80-81.

American Psychological Association. (1972, September-a). *Report of the task force on the status of women in psychology*: American Psychological Association.

American Psychological Association. (1972, June-b). Eight APA journals initiate controversial blind reviewing. *APA Monitor, 3*(5), 1, 5.

American Psychological Association. (1980, December). A survey of the selection of reviewers of manuscripts for psychology journals. APA Committee on women in psychology. *American Psychologist, 35*(12), 1106-1110.

Benedetti, J., Green, S., Lee, M.-L., & Crowley, J. (1993, August). Report of the Ad Hoc Committee on Design of an experiment on double-blind refereeing. *Statistical Science, 8*(3), 318-330.

Bernard, H. R. (1980, Winter). Report from the editor. *Human Organization, 39*(4), 366-369.

Blank, R. M. (1991, December). The effects of double-blind versus single-blind reviewing: experimental evidence from *The American Economic Review. American Economic Review, 81*(5), 1041-1067.

Boice, R., Barlow, D. H., Johnson, K., & Klosko, J. (1984). Behaviorists as peer reviewers: do they misbehave? *Behavior Therapist, 7*(6), 105-107.

Bornstein, R. F. (1993). Costs and benefits of reviewer anonymity. *Journal of Social Behavior and Personality, 8*(3), 355-370.

Borts, G. H. (1974, May). Report of the managing editor *American Economic Review*. *American Economic Review, 64*(2), 476-481.

Bradley, J. V. (1981, January). Pernicious publication practices. *Bulletin of the Psychonomic Society, 18*(1), 31-34.

Brady, J. P. (1985, August). Journal referees: gatekeepers of science. *Biological Psychiatry, 20*(8), 823-824.

Budd, J. (1988, September 1). Publication in library and information science: the state of the literature. *Library Journal, 113*(14), 125-131.

Cahnman, W. J. (1967, February). For the abolition of the anonymity rule. *American Sociologist, 2*(1), 97-98.

Campanario, J. M. (1996, March). The competition for journal space among referees, editors, and other authors and its influence on journals' impact factors. *Journal of the American Society for Information Science, 47*(3), 184-192.

Ceci, S. J. & Peters, D. P. (1984, December). How blind is blind review? *American Psychologist, 39*(12), 1491-1494.

Christiansen, D. (1974, August). Who gets published? Part II: transactions. *IEEE Spectrum, 11*(8), 31.

Cleary, J. D. & Alexander, B. (1988, July/August). Blind versus nonblind review: survey of selected medical journals. *Drug Intelligence and Clinical Pharmacy, 22*(7/8), 601-602.

Coe, R. K. & Weinstock, I. (1967, Winter). Editorial policies of major economic journals. *Quarterly Review of Economics and Business, 7*(4), 37-43.

Coe, R. K. & Weinstock, I. (1968, January). Publication policies in major business periodicals. *Southern Journal of Business*, 1-10.

Coffman, M. L. (1966, November). Objective editorial decisions. *Physics Today, 19*(11), 12.

Cox, D., Gleser, L. J., Perlman, M., Reid, N., & Roeder, K. (1993, August). Report of the Ad Hoc Committee on Double-Blind Refereeing. *Statistical Science, 8*(3), 310-317.

Crane, D. (1967, November). The gatekeepers of science: Some factors affecting the selection of articles for scientific journals. *American Sociologist, 2*(4), 195-201.

Davies, C. N. (1978, November). Refereeing physics papers. *Physics Bulletin, 29*(11), 499.

DeBakey, L. (1990, March). Journal peer reviewing. Anonymity or disclosure? *Archives of Ophthalmology, 108*(3), 345-349.

Edwards, L. N. & Ferber, M. A. (1986). Journal reviewing practices and the progress of women in the economics profession: is there a relationship? *Newsletter of the Committee on the Status of Women in the Economics Profession*, 1-7.

Epstein, W. M. (1990, Winter). Confirmational response bias among social work journals. *Science, Technology, & Human Values, 15*(1), 9-38.

Ernst, E., Resch, K. L., & Uher, E. M. (1992, June 1). Reviewer bias. *Annals of Internal Medicine, 116*(11), 958.

Evans, A. T., McNutt, R. A., Fletcher, S. W., & Fletcher, R. H. (1993, August). The characteristics of peer reviewers who produce good-quality reviews. *Journal of General Internal Medicine, 8*(8), 422-428.

Fabiato, A. (1994). Anonymity of reviewers. *Cardiovascular Research, 28,* 1134-1139.

Ferber, M. A. & Teiman, M. (1980, August-October). Are women economists at a disadvantage in publishing journal articles? *Eastern Economic Journal, VI*(3-4), 189-193.

Fisher, M., Friedman, S. B., & Strauss, B. (1994, July 13). The effects of blinding on acceptance of research papers by peer review. *JAMA, 272*(2), 143-146.

Fondiller, S. H. (1994, March). Is nursing at risk? *Nursing & Health Care, 15*(3), 142-148.

Fraenkel-Conrat, H. (1974, March 1). Is anonymity necessary? *Nature, 248,* 8.

Fye, W. B. (1990, August 15). Medical authorship, traditions, trends, and tribulations. *Annals of Internal Medicine, 113*(4), 317-325.

Garfunkel, J. M., Ulshen, M. H., & Lawson, E. E. (1994, July 13). Effect of institutional prestige on reviewers' recommendations and editorial decisions. *JAMA, 272*(2), 137-138.

Gilbert, J. R., Williams, E. S., & Lundberg, G. D. (1994, July 13). Is there a gender bias in JAMA's peer review process? *JAMA, 272*(2), 139-142.

Glen, J. W., & Konigsson, K. L. (1976). Refereeing in earth-science journals. *Earth Science Editing, 3,* 11-13.

Glidewell, J. C. (1988). Reflections on thirteen years of editing AJCP. *American Journal of Community Psychology, 16*(6), 759-770.

Goldbeck-Wood, S. (1997, September 27). Blinding reviewers to authors' identity does not improve quality. *British Medical Journal, 315.*

Goldberg, P. (1968, April). Are women prejudiced against women? *Trans-Action, 5*(5), 28-30.

Goldwyn, R. M. (1989, February). Peer review for publication. *Plastic and Reconstructive Surgery, 83*(2), 398-399.

Goodstein, L. D. & Brazis, K. L. (1970, December). Psychology of scientist. XXX. Credibility of psychologists: an empirical study. *Psychological Reports, 27*(3), 835-838.

Gordon, M. D. (1977). *Refereeing reconsidered: an examination of unwitting bias in scientific evaluation.* Paper presented at the First International Conference of Scientific Editors, Jerusalem.

Gordon, M. D. (1978-a). Maintaining quality: refereeing. *Earth & Life Science Editing, 6,* 12-13.

Gordon, R. A. (1978, October-b). Optional published refereeing. *Physics Today, 31*(10), 81.

Gordon, R. A. (1980). The advantages of a simple system of optional published refereeing. *Speculations in Science and Technology, 3*(5), 607-609.

Goudsmit, S. A. (1967, January). Reviewer and author anonymity. *Physics Today, 20*(1), 12.

Gould, S. J. (1996). *The mismeasure of man* (Revised and expanded ed.). New York: W. W. Norton.

Guenin, L. M. (1996, March 29). Confidentiality. *Science, 271,* 1790.

Hartley, J. (1988, November). Editorial practices in psychology journals. *Psychologist, 1*(11), 428-430.

Hearse, D. J. (1994). Anonymity of reviewers—editorial comment. *Cardiovascular Research, 28,* 1133.

Herbert, W. (1980, April). Blind reviewing, hotly debated, taking hold in humanities journals. *Humanities Report, 2,* 4-6.

Hodder, P. (1979, February). Refereeing for limited-interest research. *Scholarly Publishing, 10*(2), 161-169.

Horrobin, D. (1982, June). Peer review: a philosophically faulty concept which is proving disastrous for science. *Behavioral and Brain Sciences, 5*(2), 217-218.

Hunt, E. (1971, March). Psychological publications. *American Psychologist, 26*(3), 311.

Huth, E. J. (1983, August). Responsibility of coauthorship. *Annals of Internal Medicine, 99*(2), 266-267.

Ingelfinger, F. J. (1975, December 25). Charity and peer review in publication. *New England Journal of Medicine, 293*(26), 1371-1372.

International Committee of Medical Journal Editors. (1997, February 15). Additional statements from the International Committee on Medical Journal Editors. *Canadian Medical Association Journal, 156*(4), 571-574.

Jones, R. (1974, March 21). Rights, wrongs and referees. *New Scientist, 61*(89), 758-9.

Kern, D. E. (1988, January/February). JGIM manuscript review policies. *Journal of General Internal Medicine, 3*(1), 98.

Knox, F. G. (1981, January). No unanimity about anonymity. *Journal of Laboratory and Clinical Medicine, 97*(1), 1-3.

Kronick, D. A. (1988, July). Anonymity and identity: editorial policy in the early scientific journal. *Library Quarterly, 58*(3), 221-237.

Kumar, K. (1979, April). Optional published refereeing. *Physics Today, 32*(4), 13, 15.

Laband, D. N. (1987, April-June). A qualitative test of journal discrimination against women. *Eastern Economic Journal, 13*(2), 149-153.

Laband, D. N. & Piette, M. J. (1994, February-b). Favoritism versus search for good papers: empirical evidence regarding the behavior of journal editors. *Journal of Political Economy, 102*(1), 194-302.

Laband, D. N. & Piette, M. J. (1994, April-a). Does the "blindness" of peer review influence manuscript selection efficiency? *Southern Economic Journal, 60*(4), 896-906.

Laband, D. N. & Piette, M. J. (1994, July 13-c). A citation analysis of the impact of blind peer review. *JAMA, 272*(2), 147-149.

Leslie, C. (1990). Scientific racism: reflections on peer review, science and ideology. *Social Science and Medicine, 31*(8), 891-909.

Levenson, H., Burford, B., Bonno, B., & Davis, L. (1975, January). Are women still prejudiced against women? A replication and extension of Goldberg's study. *Journal of Psychology, 89*, 67-71.

Levinger, G. (1973). "Blind" reviewing. *APA Monitor, 4*(1), 2, 8.

Lloyd, M. E. (1990, Winter). Gender factors in reviewer recommendations for manuscript publication. *Journal of Applied Behavior Analysis, 23*(4), 539-543.

Maddox, J. (1989, June 29). Can journals influence science? *Nature, 339*(6227), 657.

Mahoney, M. J. (1977). Publication prejudices: an experimental study of confirmatory bias in the peer review system. *Cognitive Therapy and Research, 1*(2), 161-175.

Mahoney, M. J. (1990, Winter). Bias, controversy, and abuse in the study of the scientific publication system. *Science, Technology, & Human Values, 15*(1), 50-55.

Manheim, F. T. (1973, May). Referees and the publication crisis. *EOS Transactions of the American Geophysical Union, 54*(5), 532-537.

Marsden, J. E. (1990, April 19). Blind Reviews. *Nature, 344*(6268), 698.

McElmurry, B. J., Newcomb, B. J., Barnfather, J., & Lynch, M. S. (1981). The manuscript review process in nursing publications. *Current Issues in Nursing*, 129-143.

McGiffert, M. (1988, October). Is justice blind? An inquiry into peer review. *Scholarly Publishing, 20*(1), 43-48.

McIntosh, E. G. & Ross, S. (1987, June). Peer review in psychology: institutional ranking as a factor. *Psychological Reports, 60*(2), 1049-1050.

McNutt, R. A., Evans, A. T., Fletcher, R. H., & Fletcher, S. W. (1990, March 9). The effects of blinding on the quality of review. *JAMA, 263*(10), 1371-1376.

Miller, A. C. & Serzan, S. L. (1984, November/December). Criteria for identifying a refereed journal. *Journal of Higher Education, 55*(6), 673-699.

Mirman, R. (1975, September). For open refereeing. *American Journal of Physics, 43*(9), 837.

Moossy, J., & Moossy, Y. R. (1985, May). Anonymous authors, anonymous referees: an editorial exploration. *Journal of Neuropathology and Experimental Neurology, 44*(3), 225-228.

Morton, H. C., & Price, A. J. (1986, Summer). The ACLS survey of scholars. Views on publications, computers libraries. *Scholarly Communication, 5*(1-16).

Murphy, E. A. (1976). Bias. *The logic of medicine* (pp. 239-262). Baltimore: Johns Hopkins University Press.

Neuliep, J. W., & Crandall, R. (1993). Reviewer bias against replication research. *Journal of Social Behavior and Personality, 8*(6), 21-29.

O'Connor, D., & Van Orden, P. (1978, September). Getting into print. *College and Research Libraries, 39*(5), 389-396.

Owen, R. (1982, May 14). Reader bias. *JAMA, 247*(18), 2533-2534.

Paludi, M. A. & Bauer, W. D. (1983). Goldberg revisited: what's in an author's name? *Sex Roles, 9*(3), 387-390.

Paludi, M. A. & Strayer, L. A. (1985). What's in an author's name? Differential evaluations of performance as function of author's name. *Sex Roles, 12*(3/4), 353-361.

Parker, G. (1986, June). On blinding the journal assessor. *Australian and New Zealand Journal of Psychiatry, 20*(2), 241-242.

Perlman, D. (1982). Reviewer "bias": do Peters and Ceci protest too much? *Behavioral and Brain Sciences, 5*(2), 231-232.

Peters, D. P. & Ceci, S. J. (1982, June). Peer review practices of psychological journals: the fate of published articles, submitted again. *Behavioral and Brain Sciences, 5*(2), 187-255.

Relman, A. S. (1981). Journals. In K. S. Warren (Ed.), *Coping with the biomedical literature* : Praeger Special Studies.

Relman, A. S. (1982). Editorial review. *New England Journal of Medicine, 307*(14), 899.

Rosenblatt, A. & Kirk, S. A. (1980, Summer). Recognition of authors in blind review of manuscripts. *Journal of Social Services Research, 3*(4), 383-394.

Rushton, J. P., & Bogaert, A. F. (1989). Population differences in susceptibility to AIDS: an evolutionary analysis. *Social Science and Medicine, 28*(12), 1211-1220.

Scarr, S. (1982). Anosmic peer review: a rose by another name is evidently not a rose. *Behavioral and Brain Sciences, 5*, 237-238.

Siegfried, J. J. (1994, Winter). Trends in institutional affiliation of authors who publish in three leading general interest economics journals. *Quarterly Review of Economics and Business, 34*(4), 375-386.

Swanson, E. A. & McCloskey, J. (1982, October). The manuscript review process of nursing journals. *Image, 14*(3), 72-76.

Via, B. J. (1996, July). Publishing in the journal literature of library and information science: a survey of manuscript review process and acceptance. *College and Research Libraries, 57*(4), 365-376.

Ward, C. (1981). Prejudice against women: who, when, why? *Sex Roles, 7*(2), 163-171.

Weller, A. C. (1987, October). Editorial policy and the assessment of quality among medical journals. *Bulletin of the Medical Library Association, 75*(4), 310-316.

Weller, A. C. (1990, March 9). Editorial peer review in U.S. medical journals. *JAMA, 263*(10), 1344-1347.

Wessely, S., Brugha, T., Cowen, P., Smith, L., & Paykel, E. (1996, November 9). Do authors know who refereed their paper? A questionnaire survey. *British Medical Journal, 313*(7066), 1185.

Wilkes, M. S. & Kravitz, R. L. (1995, August). Policies, practices, and attitudes of North American medical journal editors. *Journal of General Internal Medicine, 10*(8), 443-450.

Yankauer, A. (1986, July). Then and now, the *American Journal of Public Health*, 1911-85. *American Journal of Public Health, 76*(7), 809-815.

Yankauer, A. (1991, July). How blind is blind review? *American Journal of Public Health, 81*(7), 843-845.

# Chapter Eight

# Peer Review and Statistical Review

*Some of the most enduring findings in medical research originate from studies that are methodologically imperfect.*

(Davies, 1987, p. 371)

In a unique study for the time, Goldberger and colleagues investigated the effect of changing the diet of institutionalized orphans on the progress of a disease called pellagra. Pellagra disappeared in all but one of the 172 children studied when the children's diet was widened to include oatmeal, meat, milk, eggs, and beans. The disease reappeared within nine months in 40 percent of the children when they were again given the traditional diet of grits (Goldberger, Waring, & Tanner, 1923). The study contained no statistical analysis of the data. Today this study, as conducted, would probably not pass the scrutiny of any institutional review board whose job it is to evaluate the ethical aspects of human research. Both the study of institutionalized children as subjects and the return to the detrimental diet when the study was completed are two examples of areas that would be considered problematic today. Even without statistical analysis, the results were dramatic and unarguable: pellagra disappeared with the enhanced diet. The pellagra study was probably not peer reviewed before publication. Despite its shortcomings, it is a classic example of good study design. One variable (diet) was altered and outcome was observed (presence or absence of pellagra). The control group comprised those children at other institutions who continued to receive the traditional diet of grits. The study was important in that for the first time there was evidence that the absence of something could lead to a disease.

The use of statistics to analyze data to test for the significance of a study's findings is a relatively recent addition to the journal literature. The *British Medical Journal* (*BMJ*) first mentioned the use of statistics in 1936 when it published an article on chance in clinical medicine. Two years later, a paper on a similar topic appeared in the *Canadian Medical Association Journal*. By the

1940s published studies that contained some type of statistical analysis were a regular part of articles in the *BMJ* (Smith, 1990).

Today, of course, it is expected that statistical analysis be part of any well-designed, well-conducted, and properly analyzed study. The media regularly report on the statistical significance of particular studies, especially medical ones. The public expects a report of a medical study to include such statements as "... a statistically significant number of the participants improved after receiving this procedure, ..." which typically is a drug therapy or a surgical intervention. Not infrequently, some reports of medical findings are followed by long debates about the real significance, importance, or validity of the study. Topics such as the long-term effects of caffeine on human health or the role that diet plays in the control of cholesterol and heart disease are two examples of topics that have frequently been discussed in the press.

Studies that test the statistical validity of manuscripts or published articles ask a number of questions: was the study designed correctly and, if so, was the statistical analysis appropriate for the data? If the study was designed correctly, and if the authors used proper statistical tests, were the conclusions correct, given any limitations of the study design? An analysis of a study could verify that an adequate control group was used or that an adequate randomization of subjects had taken place, but concluded that the correct statistical tests were not applied. For example, in a study with a proper control group, the authors might have used a chi-square test (which is usually used for comparing percentages) when the *t*-test (usually used for analysis of a continuous timeline) might have been more appropriate.

An examination of a study designed to test the value of all-day versus half-day kindergarten illustrates some difficulties with statistical analyses (Sergesketter & Gilman, 1988). Researchers tested children's ability to learn to read based on whether children attended full-day or half-day kindergarten. The researchers concluded that full-day kindergarten proved to be beneficial in helping children learn to read. In a reexamination of the data, Fusaro and Royce argued that the original data were incorrectly analyzed and the authors did not prove that full-day kindergarten students faired better at learning to read than half-day students (Fusaro & Royce, 1995). Fusaro and Royce maintained that Sergesketter and Gilman had computed the "*t* tests with unpooled variances and found significant differences in favor of full-day kindergarten." This approach failed to consider that "degrees of freedom reflect a downward adjustment when unpooled variances are used in the computation of the *t* tests" (p. 858). When this statistical fact is taken into account, there was no difference in the ability of kindergartners to learn to read based on the length of their school day. Few nonstatisticians would understand the nuances of degrees of freedom and its relation to unpooled variances. Fusaro and Royce suggested that readers of research studies should take care before believing conclusions of articles that have not undergone "scrupulous" peer review. Sergesletter and Gilman's work was published as an ERIC document and, therefore, not peer reviewed.

In a similar example, Feinstein critiqued three studies that received a great deal of media attention at the time each was published (Feinstein, 1988). One study found an increased risk of breast cancer after exposure to resperine, another found an increased risk of pancreatic cancer in coffee drinkers, and the third identified an increased risk of breast cancer with alcohol consumption. Feinstein uncovered methodological faults with each study. Contrary to the example of all day kindergarteners' ability to learn to read, all three of these studies had been subjected to the editorial peer review process prior to publication. Subsequent studies found the first two relationships to be without merit, while debate about any connection between breast cancer and alcohol consumption continues today (Smith-Warner, Spiegelman, Yaun, Van den Brandt, & Folsom, 1998).

Discussions of the statistical merits of a particular study are very difficult for lay people and professionals alike to decipher. A reader of a published medical or scientific article has the right to expect that information presented, particularly the conclusions and subsequent recommendations, is correct. Those who are familiar with the scholarly and scientific publication process also expect that articles have been subjected to the editorial peer review process prior to publication and that this process has filtered out the inaccurate, incomplete, or improperly designed or analyzed studies. Each reader has the right to assume that a study published in a peer-reviewed journal was properly designed and analyzed and that the conclusions with carefully defined limitations and generalizability are correct.

What level of statistical review do manuscripts undergo during the editorial peer review process? Are flawed studies filtered out (rejected) through proper application of the review process? This chapter examines several aspects of statistical review of manuscripts. The first section identifies baseline data of journals' editorial practices. Studies of statistical review of manuscripts prior to their publication are analyzed, followed by an investigation into the statistical validity of studies after they have successfully undergone the peer review process and been published. The next section discusses the complexity of statistical tests in the published literature and the degree to which a study has statistically significant results before acceptance for publication, a phenomenon referred to as publication bias. Finally, the role of editorial peer review in publication bias is examined.

## Editorial use of a statistical reviewer

Reviewers are asked to review the contents of a manuscript and make a recommendation to accept, revise, or reject based on its accuracy. Editors might assume that reviewers critically examine all statistical analyses in a manuscript or they might specifically ask reviewers to conduct a thorough statistical review.

Referring to the fact that few medical journal editors used a statistician in manuscript review, Altman called for a comprehensive statistical refereeing system for medical manuscripts (Altman, 1982). Altman made this recommendation citing common statistical errors in design, analysis, interpretation, presentation of results, and omission of information.

*Question*

What level of statistical review do editors require of reviewers during the review process?

*Criteria for inclusion*

~ any study that examined a group of editors regarding their editorial peer review requirements for review of manuscripts that contain statistical analyses.

*Comparable studies*

Only three surveys were identified that asked editors about the statistical review of manuscripts and each came from medicine (Table 8-1).

| Journals surveyed | Response rate | Statistician as consultant or on editorial board | Editorial policy to use statistical reviewer | Editor published statistical review policy | References |
|---|---|---|---|---|---|
| 98 | 85.0% | 35.0% | 16.0% | 12.0% | (George, 1985) |
| 16 | 100.0% | | 37.5% | | (Weller, 1990) |
| 124 | 69.4% | | 30.5% | | (Weller, 1990) |
| 15 | 80.0% | 83.3% | | | (Schulman, Sulmasy, & Roney, 1994) |

**Table 8-1: Surveys of statistical review in medical journals**

George surveyed 98 editors of major medical journals to determine the degree to which articles contained statistics and, if so, to what degree statistical review was undertaken. Journal titles for this sudy were selected using a number of criteria: a journal's peer review status, a high impact factor, and its publication of original research. Journals were selected from a number of medical fields: general medicine, cancer, cardiology, hematology, pediatrics, and psychiatry. George admitted that the list was "ultimately subjective" (p. 109) (George, 1985). Only 16 percent of the responding editors had a policy that guaranteed statistical review prior to publication, and 61 percent of the journal editors said they decided if a statistical reviewer was needed for any one manuscript. George's study was published in *Medical and Pediatric Oncology.* An editorial accompanying this study declared that the editor was following George's advice and would begin using a statistical reviewer for all manuscripts reporting on clinical trials or containing statistical analysis (Mauer, 1985).

Weller queried two groups of medical journal editors about a variety of editorial peer review issues (Weller, 1990). Group one contained journals that met a more selective set of criteria than journals in group two. In the Weller study, 37.5 percent of group one editors and 30.5 percent of group two usually or always sought statistical review for a manuscript with statistical analysis. Often (43.8 percent for group one and 67.1 percent for group two) the editors relied on the reviewers to question the statistical analysis before a statistician was called on to assess the manuscript. The two groups differed in the degree to which an editor assumed a reviewer would serve as a statistical reviewer: 12.5 percent for group one and 41.3 percent for group two. Schulman and colleagues asked editors of 15 leading medical journals if they used a statistical reviewer. Ten of the 12 (83.3 percent) respondents reported having a statistician among their editors (Schulman et al., 1994). Both the Shulman and Weller studies focused on a number of editorial policies and asked relatively few questions about practices of statistical review itself. Weller sought information about different peer review practices in different categories of medical journals, and Shulman asked about the use of ethicists and health economic specialists as reviewers as well as about the use of statistical reviewers.

While these studies show that some editors use a form of statistical review, there are little data on the topic. All of these studies were in medicine, and each queried a rather select group of journal editors. These three studies alone present a very incomplete picture of editors' reliance on statistical review for manuscripts containing statistical analysis. Each researcher asked slightly different questions and queried a different set of journal editors. Questions concerning statistical review of manuscripts were often not asked in surveys of editors.

Statistical reviewers can come from the pool of reviewers, can be present on editorial boards, or can be brought in as special consultants by editors as needed. Data are insufficient to say much more than some medical editors use statistical reviewers and a small select group of journals appear more likely to have statisticians on the editorial board than a larger, less selected group of medical journals. Even among rather highly selective medical journals not all editors regularly used statistical reviewers for manuscripts that contain statistical analyses.

## Statistical review of manuscripts

The previous section summarized the small number of studies that asked editors about their statistical review practices and found there are little data on this topic. A few medical journals (12 percent) were found to have a formal policy in place, but the surveys of editors provide little insight into the regularity with which statistical review takes place. The next section examines what is known about how manuscripts are evaluated for their statistical content.

*Question*

To what types of statistical review are manuscripts usually subjected?

*Criteria for inclusion*

~ any study that evaluated the degree of statistical review a set of manuscripts has undergone.

*Comparable studies*

Given the fact that only editors and editorial staff have access to submitted manuscripts, studies that analyze manuscripts must come either directly from a

journal's editorial offices or editors would have to make manuscripts or reviewers' reports available to researchers. It is, therefore, not surprising that only six
studies met the criterion of examining statistical review in a set of submitted
manuscripts (Table 8-2).

| Journals | Number of manuscripts | Acceptable after standard review | Acceptable after statistical review | Revisions needed after statistical review | Rejected after statistical review | Acceptable after statistical revisions | References |
|---|---|---|---|---|---|---|---|
| medical journals | 514 | 100.0% | 26.0% | 67.0% | 7.0% | 74.0% | (Schor & Karten, 1966) |
| JAMA | 614 | 24.0% | | 69.2% | 7.0% | 75.0% | (Schor, 1967) |
| BMJ | 200 | 100.0% | | | 37.0% | | (Gardner, Altman, Jones, & Machin, 1983) |
| BMJ | 103 | | 16.5% | | | | (Gardner, Machin, & Campbell, 1986) |
| BMJ | 45 | | 8.8% | 80.0% | 11.1% | | (Gardner, Machin, & Campbell, 1986) |
| BMJ | 45 | | 11.0% | | | 84.0% | (Gardner & Bond, 1990) |
| Lancet | 191 | 100.0% | 54.0% | 32.0% | 14.0% | | (Gore, Jones, & Thompson, 1992) |
| *Average* | | 81.0% | 23.3% | 62.1% | 15.2% | 77.7% | |

**Table 8-2: Statistical evaluation of manuscripts**

In addition to these six, there is an additional study in which the investigators prepared a fictitious "but believable" (p. 504) manuscript with deliberate
statistical errors and mailed it to reviewers used by the *Annals of Emergency
Medicine* (Baxt, Waeckerle, Tintunalli, Knopp, & Callaham, 1996). Of the 262
reviewers who received this manuscript, 203 (78 percent) were returned and
119 (58.6 percent) of the reviewers recommended the manuscripts be rejected.
Of those recommending rejection, 36 percent did so on the grounds of statistical errors in the manuscript. However, the reviewers, even those recommending
rejection, did not "identify the majority of preconceived errors placed in the
manuscript" (p. 504). Since over half of the reviewers recommended rejection,
and only about one-third of those on the grounds of the statistical analysis, the
manuscript with its fictitious data may have had other serious problems in addition to the statistical errors. These problems could have led to a rejection recommendation regardless of the statistical analysis in the manuscript. For this
reason the study has not been included in Table 8-2.

Schor and Karten evaluated the statistical methods of 514 manuscripts that
were initially judged by reviewers to be clinically acceptable. They determined
that only 26 percent were statistically acceptable and 7 percent were not salvageable (Schor & Karten, 1966). Of the remaining manuscripts, 74 percent

were corrected and subsequently published. The authors recommended that "a statistician be part of the research team or be consulted before a study is attempted" (p. 150). As a result of the findings of this study, the editors of *Journal of the American Medical Association* (*JAMA*) began to use statistical consultants to evaluate the statistical accuracy of manuscripts. Of the first 614 manuscripts subjected to statistical review after *JAMA* began regular statistical review, 7 percent were rejected outright with no further review, 75 percent were acceptable after revision, and 2.1 percent were rejected because statistical problems within the manuscripts were not corrected (Schor, 1967).

The *BMJ* published a series of studies investigating their own statistical review process. Over a seven-year period, Gardner and colleagues undertook three studies of statistical accuracy of manuscripts submitted to the *BMJ* (Gardner et al., 1983), (Gardner et al., 1986), and (Gardner & Bond, 1990). The first Gardner study from 1983 found that 37 percent of 200 manuscripts that had initially received a positive review were rejected after statistical review. At that time the *BMJ* received approximately 5,000 manuscripts per year, many of which contained no statistical analysis. The manuscripts that were targeted for additional statistical review comprised about 2 percent of the total number of manuscripts received by *BMJ* for the time period studied.

As a result of the first Gardner analysis, *BMJ* editors decided to assist reviewers with the statistical portion of the review process. Reviewers were provided with a 12-item statistical checklist covering characteristics of statistical importance: study design, conduct, analysis and presentation, and overall recommendations. By 1986, *BMJ* was using two checklists as part of the standard review process for the assessment of manuscripts that contained some statistical analyses. A 12-item checklist was designed for use during statistical review of general studies, and a 26-item checklist was designed for use during statistical review of reports of clinical trials.

The second Gardner study reported on the initial experience with the two checklists (Gardner et al., 1986). The general checklist was tested on 103 manuscripts. Only 17 (16.5 percent) of these manuscripts had acceptable statistical analysis. The checklist for clinical trials was tested on 45 studies of which 31 (68.9 percent) had conclusions that were considered unjustified. Five (11.1 percent) were viewed as unsalvageable and unacceptable for publication, and three of these had not been properly randomized at the start of the investigation. The authors advocated the use of a statistical checklist by statistical reviewers, editors, and particularly by researchers at the time a study is designed.

In 1990, the third Gardner study found that statistical review increased the number of statistically acceptable manuscripts to 84 percent once statistical problems had been corrected by the authors (Gardner & Bond, 1990). The statistical problems of the remaining 16 percent of the manuscripts could not be corrected. Gardner's and colleagues' 1990 conclusion was similar to the conclusion of their second study in 1986. They found that "statistical assessment is beneficial but that further efforts by authors and assessors could make it even more effective" (p. 1355).

Gore and colleagues reviewed the outcome of 191 manuscripts that had already received favorable review for the *Lancet* (Gore et al., 1992). Following statistical review, only 54 percent of them were either acceptable or accepted after one revision.

These studies used a number of different analytical approaches. Schor in 1966, Gardner in 1983, and Gore in 1992 scrutinized a set of manuscripts after the manuscripts had received initial favorable review. In the 1983 Gardner study, 37 percent of the manuscripts were rejected after statistical review, but given the large number of manuscripts received by the *BMJ*, this percentage increased *BMJ's* rejection rate by only 0.74 percent (2 percent of all manuscripts that required further statistical review times 37 percent is 0.74 percent). Neither the Schor studies in 1966 and 1967 nor the Gore study provided figures on the total number of manuscripts received by the journals during the period of the investigation. Schor in 1967 and the remaining Gardner studies in 1986 and 1990 examined statistical review after it had been instituted at *JAMA* and *BMJ* respectively. These studies all concluded that statistical review improved statistical analyses in the manuscripts.

These few studies of statistical review of manuscripts make an initial compelling argument in support of formal statistical review for all manuscripts containing data analysis. These three studies were conducted over a period of 25 years, and each showed that about three-fourths of the manuscripts were acceptable after revisions following statistical review. It is during the review process that statistical inaccuracies or outright mistakes that were not identified by authors *should* be uncovered. One obvious conclusion from these few studies is that the peer review process worked effectively, and for three-fourths of the manuscripts statistical review performed as expected. The remaining 25 percent of the manuscripts still had unacceptable statistical analyses and these would presumably be rejected or, if not rejected, conclusions would need to be restated to explain limitations of the findings.

## Statistical review of published studies

After a manuscript is reviewed, revised, and deemed acceptable by the editor, it is published. This section reviews those studies that have examined the statistical accuracy of published articles.

As already stated, reports of statistical inaccuracies in the published literature surface fairly regularly. Examples of inaccuracies of statistical analysis in medical articles are particularly disturbing when they become public debates, legitimately confusing practitioners and health care consumers alike who are trying to make sound medical decisions. However, individual examples offer little insight into the extent of a problem. Are instances that receive media attention aberrations or are they indicative of a larger problem? How successful is statistical review of manuscripts at preventing the publication of unsound research or overstated conclusions about the importance or meaning of the findings?

*Question*

What kind of statistical errors have been identified through studies of published articles?

*Criteria for inclusion*

~ any study that evaluated the accuracy or appropriateness of statistical analysis in a set of published articles.

*Comparable studies*

Thirty-four studies were identified that examined the validity of statistics used in published scientific studies. These studies were conducted over a period of nearly 50 years and are summarized in chronological order by publication date in Table 8-3. Thirty-three (97.1 percent) studies came from some arena of the medical sciences; one studied the social work literature.

The 33 studies of the medical literature examined published articles from 39 named journals, one monograph, and one group of published articles in the Cochrane database. All but one of 31 studies of journals provided the names of the journals from which the articles were taken. All named medical journals were indexed in *Index Medicus*. Of the 30 studies that named journal titles, 25 (83.3 percent) were published in one of the 39 named journals. Seventeen of the studies (56.7 percent) evaluated articles published in a single journal and all but three of these (82.3 percent) were published in the journal whose articles were analyzed. The studies covered journals published in the United States, Great Britain, Canada, Australia, and New Zealand. Five journals were subjected to four or more studies: *BMJ*, the *Canadian Medical Association Journal*, *JAMA*, the *Lancet*, and the *New England Journal of Medicine*. Each of these journals is among the most well-known medical journals.

Armitage described five categories of statistical errors (Figure 8-1) (Armitage, 1971). When appropriate, data from studies in Table 8-3 have been grouped according to these five categories: inadequate description of basic data, disregard for statistical independence, errors related to randomization, errors with the student *t*-test, and errors with chi-square tests. While there are other ways to group types of statistical tests, Armitage's categories give a sense of the different levels of complexity of statistical tests.

Investigators of the studies summarized in Table 8-3 took a variety of different approaches and examined a number of different statistical tests. Overall, an average of 65.8 percent of the published articles evaluated in these studies contained at least one statistical problem. Statistical problems of studies in Table 8-3 range from an average of 26.0 percent to 95 percent of the articles per study.

Ross was the first investigator to disclose the presence of statistically inadequate studies in the published literature (Ross, 1951). Ross evaluated the first 100 articles published from January to June 1950 in five different medical journals (*JAMA, American Journal of Medicine, Annals of Internal Medicine, American*

| Discipline | # of journals | # of articles | well-controlled | category I error | category II error | category III error | category IV error | category V error | serious problems or reject | some problems present | References |
|---|---|---|---|---|---|---|---|---|---|---|---|
| | | | Statistical problems in articles with statistics | | | | | | | | |
| medicine | 5 | 100 | 27.0% | | | | | | | 73.0% | (Ross, 1951) |
| medicine | 2 | 103 | 25.1% | | | | | | | 41.5% | (Badgley, 1961) |
| drug trials | 1 | 203 | 34.5% | | | 24.1% | | | | 95.0% | (Mahon & Daniel, 1964) |
| medicine | 10 | 149 | | | | | | | 5.0% | 73.0% | (Schor & Karten, 1966) |
| drug trials | 1 | 264 | 44.3% | | | 20.8% | | | | 84.1% | (Reiffenstein, Schiltroth, & Todd, 1968) |
| drug trials | 1 | 103 | 52.5% | | | 17.5% | | | | 80.5% | (Reiffenstein, Schiltroth, & Todd, 1968) |
| therapeutic trials | 4 | 141 | | | | | | | 32.6% | 48.9% | (Lionel & Herxheimer, 1970) |
| medicine | 5 | 345 | | | | | 44.0% | 35.0% | | | (Feinstein, 1974) |
| medicine | 1 | 62 | | 16.1% | 9.7% | 12.9% | 17.7% | 19.3% | | 51.6% | (Gore, Jones, & Rytter, 1977) |
| medicine/RCT* | 20 | 71 | | | | | | | | 80.3% | (Freiman, Chalmers, Smith, & Kuebler, 1978) |
| medicine/RCT* | 2 | 172 | | | | 66.7% | | | | 66.7% | (Ambroz et al., 1978) |
| psychiatry | 1 | 139 | | 12.9% | | 12.9% | 9.3% | 8.6% | | 45.3% | (White, 1979) |
| cancer/RCT* | 1 | 164 | | | | 69.4% | | | | 76.0% | (Mosteller, Gilbert, & McPeek, 1980) |
| medicine | 1 | 59 | | | | | 46.0% | | | | (Glantz, 1980) |
| medicine | 1 | 142 | | | | | 27.0% | | | | (Glantz, 1980) |
| medicine | 4 | 67 | | | | 81.0% | | | | 44.0% | (DerSimonian, Charette, McPeek, & Mosteller, 1982) |
| medicine | 1 | 184 | | | | | 67.0% | | | | (Hall, 1982) |
| medicine | 1 | 64 | 2.0% | | | 13.0% | | | | 95.0% | (MacArthur & Jackson, 1984) |
| medicine | 1 | 47 | | 13.0% | 2.0% | | 4.0% | 6.0% | | 60.0% | (Felson, Cupples, & Meenan, 1984) |
| medicine | 1 | 74 | | 9.0% | 5.0% | | 24.0% | 5.0% | | 66.0% | (Felson, Cupples, & Meenan, 1984) |
| surgery | 6 | 84 | 41.0% | | | 11.0% | | | | 41.0% | (Emerson, McPeek, & Mosteller, 1984) |
| medicine | 2 | 243 | 15.6% | 9.0% | | 42.8% | | | | 85.0% | (Avram, Shanks, Dykes, Ronai, & Stiers, 1985) |
| medicine | 1 | 48 | | 35.0% | | | 17.5% | | | 42.5% | (Wainapel & Kayne, 1985) |
| veterinary | 1 | 100 | | 19.0% | | | | | | 31.0% | (Shott, 1985) |

**Table 8-3: Statistical shortcomings of published articles**

| Discipline | # of journals | # of articles | well-controlled | Statistical problems in articles with statistics | | | | | | serious problems or reject | some problems present | References |
|---|---|---|---|---|---|---|---|---|---|---|---|---|
| | | | | category I error | category II error | category III error | category IV error | category V error | | | | |
| veterinary | 1 | 535 | | 18.0% | | | | | | | 26.0% | (Shott, 1985) |
| social work | 1 | 59 | | | | | 8.8% | 24.6% | 32.0% | | 66.0% | (Huxley, 1986) |
| comparative trials | 3 | 45 | | | | | | | | | 89.0% | (Pocock, Hughes, & Lee, 1987) |
| psychiatry | 2 | 29 | | | | | | | | | 79.0% | (Davies, 1987) |
| medicine | 1 | 28 | | | | | | | 14.0% | | 79.0% | (Murray, 1988) |
| surgery | 1 | 103 | | | | | | | | | 75.0% | (Morris, 1988) |
| medicine | 1 | 167 | | 12.4% | | 12.4% | | | | | 88.5% | (Cruess, 1989) |
| medicine/RCT* | 4 | 80 | | | | 30.0% | | | | | 41.0% | (Altman & Dore, 1990) |
| medicine | 1 | 25 | | | | | | | | | 44.0% | (Garfunkel, Ulshen, Hamrick, & Lawson, 1990) |
| medicine/RCT* | 4 | 206 | 45.0% | | | 68.0% | | | | | 78.0% | (Schulz, Chalmers, Grimes, & Altman, 1994) |
| medicine/RCT* | 3 | 102 | | | | | | | | | 68.0% | (Moher, Dulberg, & Wells, 1994) |
| medicine | 1 | 59 | | 39.0% | | | | | | 15.0% | 80.0% | (Kanter & Taylor, 1994) |
| medicine/RCT* | | 500 | | | | | | | | | 76.0% | (Schulz, Chalmers, Hayes, & Altman, 1995) |
| veterinary | 1 | 133 | 94.7% | | | 16.5% | | | | 5.0% | 66.0% | (McCance, 1995) |
| *Average* | | | 37.9% | 20.4% | 5.6% | 33.3% | 26.5% | 16.4% | | 17.3% | 65.8% | |

* RCT: randomized control trial

**Table 8-3: Statistical shortcomings of published articles (continued)**

| Categories of statistical errors* | |
|---|---|
| Category I | Inadequate description of basic data |
| Category II | Disregard for statistical independence |
| Category III | Errors related to randomization |
| Category IV | Errors with student t-test |
| Category V | Errors with chi-square tests |

*(Armitage, 1971)

| Types of statistical errors** | |
|---|---|
| Type I | The null hypothesis is rejected when it is true. The null hypothesis assumes that the population means are equal. |
| Type II | The null hypothesis is accepted when it is false and a false negative conclusion is reached, often because of small number of subjects |

**(Davies, 1987)

**Figure 8-1: Types of statistical errors**

*Journal of Medical Sciences*, and *Archives of Neurology and Psychiatry*). He looked for the presence of a proper control group in each study (for example, a group of patients received a treatment or procedure compared to a similar group that did not receive the treatment or procedure). A control group is the corner-stone of a clinical study and was the logical focus of the first study of the statis-tical validity of published articles. Ross included in this study any article that reported on a group of cases that used some "procedure or some form of therapy that was recommended or condemned" (p. 73) as a result of the analysis. He found that 45 percent of these articles had no control group when one was required, 18 percent had an inadequate control group; 10 percent did not need a control group, and only 27 percent had a well-controlled group of subjects.

In his conclusion, Ross emphasized the need to have a proper control group in the study design; however, he did not recommend that the review process evaluate a manuscript for correct statistical methodology. He recommended that a "skeptical attitude be maintained toward all therapy or procedures proposed as effective unless adequate untreated parallel cases are compared" (p. 75). This statement remains valid today. Badgley used Ross's methodology to examine a set of articles published in two Canadian journals: the *Canadian Medical Association Journal* and the *Canadian Journal of Public Health* (Badgley, 1961). Badgley's findings were similar to Ross's findings. Only 25.1 percent of the published articles in the study were well controlled, while 41.5 percent had one or more problems with sampling technique, control group, or statistical analysis. Schor and Karten published in *JAMA* an analysis similar to Ross's (Schor & Karten, 1966). These investigators studied published reports from 10 of the most frequently read medical journal and judged that a full 73 percent of the articles had conclusions that were not justified by the data presented in the written description of the study. An accompanying editorial to the Schor and Karten study in *JAMA* decried the quality of statistics taught in medical school and stated that the editors of *JAMA* used a statistical consultant for reviewing manuscripts with statistics.

Mahon and Daniel assessed reports of drug trials in the *Canadian Medical Association Journal*. They found that a scant 5 percent of the studies fulfilled the requirements that they considered were needed for a valid report (Mahon & Daniel, 1964). Reiffenstein and collaborators conducted a follow-up of the Mahon and Daniel study of published drug trials (Reiffenstein et al., 1968). The investigators found a significant improvement ($p < 0.01$) in the statistical reporting of drug trial's appearing in the *Canadian Medical Association Journal* from the time of the first study in 1964 to their 1967 study. The improvement was seen in areas of study design and control group. However, the investigators still found that only about half of the studies were well con-trolled. Overall, Reiffenstein identified some degree of statistical problems in 80 percent to 85 percent of drug trials.

Editors of four British nonspecialist journals prepared a checklist of 44 ques-tions to help reviewers with the systematic assessment of reports of clinical trials.

Reviewers were asked to use the checklist and evaluate the statistics in published studies. Lionel and Herxheimer found that nearly half of the published reports had some statistical problems, and a full third of them were unacceptable because they lacked one or more of the features required in a valid report (Lionel & Herxheimer, 1970).

Feinstein surveyed statistical procedures used in published articles from five journals (*BMJ*, the *Canadian Medical Association Journal*, *JAMA*, the *Lancet*, and the *New England Journal of Medicine*) during a six-month period in 1973. He determined that the *t*-test had been used incorrectly in 44 percent of the reports and the chi-square test had been used incorrectly in 35 percent of the reports (Feinstein, 1974).

The five categories of errors described by Armitage were used by Gore and colleagues in a study that analyzed statistical tests from articles published in the *BMJ*. They found 51.6 percent of original articles in 13 consecutive issues of *BMJ* had statistical errors (Gore et al., 1977). A study from the *British Journal of Psychiatry* looked for a number of statistical errors. Problems were identified with methods of randomization, descriptions, *t*-tests, and chi-square tests. Errors were present in 45.3 percent of the published articles that White examined (White, 1979).

Freiman and colleagues investigated the likelihood that studies contained either Type I errors (the null hypothesis is rejected when it is true) or Type II errors (the null hypothesis is accepted when it is false) (see Figure 8-1) (Freiman et al., 1978). A rejection of the null hypothesis means that the study found statistically significant differences between two or more characteristics of the study population. When the null hypothesis is not rejected, there were no statistically significant differences among the comparison groups. The Freiman investigation studied 71 control trials that showed no therapeutic improvement to patients as a result of a particular therapy. The investigators wanted to determine if the published studies had used a large enough sample to detect any potential therapeutic improvements. The investigators concluded that 57 (80.3 percent) of the negative outcomes might have had different results if an adequate sample size had been used. Their study raised the concern that "many of the therapies discarded as ineffective after inconclusive 'negative' trials may still have a clinically meaningful effect" (p. 694). Kupfersmid argued that the publication of a study containing a Type I error was more serious than the publication of a study with a Type II error (Kupfersmid, 1988). The appearance of a Type I error "often stops researchers from studying the phenomena and/or reporting nonsignificant results" (p. 637).

Glantz looked for one type of error—inappropriate use of the *t*-test—in one volume each of two circulation journals: *Circulation Research* and *Circulation*. Glantz found 46 percent and 27 percent of the published articles, respectively, from each journal inappropriately used the *t*-test (Glantz, 1980). He concluded that "errors are so widespread that the present system of peer review has not been able to control them" (p. 1). Hall reviewed the literature discussed by

Feinstein (Feinstein, 1974), declared that the 67 percent of the published articles that used the *t*-test in the *British Journal of Surgery* from 1979 and 1980 made "unjustifiable assumptions about normality," and suggested Feinstein's study had only uncovered "the tip of the iceberg" (p. 56) (Hall, 1982).

A study of reports of clinical trials in the *New England Journal of Medicine*, *BMJ*, and *JAMA* examined 11 components of design and analysis and found that 56 percent of the articles were clearly reported (DerSimonian et al., 1982). However, only 19 percent of the studies reported on the method the researchers used to randomize subjects. DerSimonian pointed out that readers were confused "when the author merely tucks in such expressions as 'p<0.05' without identifying the statistical test" (p. 1335). Using DerSimonian's 11 items to analyze 84 articles in six surgical journals, Emerson and colleagues reported that 11 percent of the studies lacked proper randomization (Emerson et al., 1984).

An examination of the *Journal of Infectious Diseases* found that almost all articles that used statistics had at least one statistical error (MacArthur & Jackson, 1984). A full 95 percent had a "statement of a probability value without a complete summary of the statistical results" (p. 349). An additional study of two anesthesiology journals, *Anesthesia and Analgesia* and *Anesthesiology*, determined 85 percent of the articles from both journals had least one major error in the statistical analysis (Avram et al., 1985).

In an examination of rehabilitation literature, Wainapel and Kayne critically reviewed 40 studies that used analytical statistics (Wainapel & Kayne, 1985). Only 23 (57.5 percent) were found acceptable in both description and methodology. The three categories of deficiencies identified were "(1) inadequate description of methods, (2) misuse of the *t*-tests, and (3) the absence of appropriately complex statistical analysis" (p. 322).

Felson and colleagues compared statistical methods used in articles published in *Arthritis and Rheumatism* in 1967 and 1968 to those published in 1982 (Felson et al., 1984). Their broad conclusions were that 60 percent of these published articles and 66 percent of the articles published in 1982 that used statistical tests had analytical errors. In addition, they also found that 9 percent of articles in 1967 and 1968 contained multiple statistical tests and, in 1982, 41 percent of the articles contained multiple statistical tests. The authors pointed out that software packages easily perform complex data analysis which "may underly the emergence of multiple testing errors" (p. 1018). They thought that "sophistication with statistical techniques has not kept pace with increasingly complex data" (p. 1020).

Davies identified 10 methodological errors in 29 analytical articles in 1985 from the *Australian and New Zealand Journal of Psychiatry* and the *American Journal of Psychiatry* (Davies, 1987). While Davies found that 79 percent of published articles had at least one error, he also cautioned that care should be taken before reaching a broad conclusion from his study and emphasized that "statistical errors do not necessarily invalidate research" (p. 371). Certain errors are much more damaging than other errors, for example, errors in design are more problematic than errors in analysis.

Pocock and colleagues identified 45 reports of comparative trials published in *BMJ*, the *Lancet*, and the *New England Journal of Medicine* (Pocock et al., 1987). Only 13 percent of the trials used confidence intervals, and only 11 percent mentioned the intended number of patients. The investigators pointed out that the tendency to favor statistically significant results when reporting on a clinical trial "appears to be biased toward an exaggeration of treatment differences" and suggested that trials needed to have "a clearer predefined policy for data analysis and reporting" (p. 426) than they usually do before a study is undertaken. In a study of statistical reporting in the *Journal of Bone and Joint Surgery*, Morris revealed that conclusions were often unjustified because of inadequate sample sizes and pointed out that statistical techniques should have been used more frequently in the published literature (Morris, 1988).

Cruess found an overall 88.5 percent error rate for articles with statistical analysis published in the *American Journal of Tropical Medicine* (Cruess, 1989). He seemed troubled that this percentage was remarkably similar to studies of other journals. He suggested a year of statistics should be required in the curriculum for tropical medicine. An accompanying editorial to the Cruess study emphasized that the errors described by Cruess usually did not have the effect of altering the conclusions of the studies (Tigertt, 1989). While admitting that statistical standards were needed, Tigertt's editorial did not discuss the possibility of changing the journal's policy on statistical review as a result of Cruess' findings.

Murray audited the statistics present in 28 articles published in the *British Journal of Surgery* and, acting as statistical reviewer for these articles, decided that 14 percent should have been rejected, 25 percent needed substantial revisions, 39 percent should have had minor revisions, and only 21 percent required no modification (Murray, 1988). An analysis of 59 articles published in *Transfusion* found 80 percent of the articles had some type of statistical deficiency (Kanter & Taylor, 1994). As did other investigators, these authors conceded that critiques of published articles were subjective and that not every statistical error was a serious error, although Kanter and colleagues considered that 15 percent of the articles had conclusions unsupported by the data.

Two studies examined the statistical validity of the veterinary medicine literature. Shott compared statistical errors in two veterinary medicine journals from the years 1982 to 1984. Shott reported that of the 100 articles with statistical analysis published in the *Journal of the American Veterinary Association* and of the 535 articles in the *American Journal of Veterinary Medicine* during that period, 19 percent and 18 percent, respectively, had insufficient information to allow evaluation. Twelve percent and 8 percent, respectively, contained statistical errors, and close to one-third of the articles in each journal had some statistical problems (Shott, 1985). In another study of published articles in the veterinary medicine literature, McCance found statistical problems similar to reports in the medical sciences. Thirty percent of the contributions had weaknesses in the study design, 45 percent had deficiencies in analysis, 33 percent had insufficient information about data collection or the statistical analysis, and 26 percent had conclusions not supported by the statistical analysis (McCance, 1995).

In the one nonmedical study of this set, Huxley examined statistical errors in the *British Journal of Social Work* and found results similar to the studies in medicine: 66 percent of the articles had statistical errors and 32 percent had serious errors (Huxley, 1986).

Seven studies examined statistical tests used in reports of randomized control trials (RCT) (Freiman et al., 1978), (Ambroz et al., 1978), (Mosteller et al., 1980), (Altman & Dore, 1990), (Schulz et al., 1994), (Moher et al., 1994), and (Schulz et al., 1995). Overall, all of these investigations reached the same conclusions as other studies that evaluated statistical analysis in published articles: from 41 percent to 80 percent of all RCT contained some statistical problems with description, design, analysis, or conclusions. Schulz and colleagues' conclusions repeat many earlier similar conclusions about the statistical analysis of published studies with the thought that their study "provides empirical evidence that inadequate methodological approaches in controlled trials ... are associated with bias. Readers of trial reports should be wary of these pitfalls, and investigators must improve their design, execution, and reporting of trials" (p. 408).

Data from these studies point to an array of statistical problems. Some authors pointed out that flaws identified by investigators might be flaws of description and reporting, not necessarily errors in analyses. Description and reporting problems are potentially correctable; however, articles with inappropriate reporting could also turn out to have methodological problems as well. Only six of the 34 investigators (17.1 percent) tried to determine if an article should have been rejected because of serious statistical errors. Of those that identified the percentage of serious statistical errors, the investigators thought that an average of 17.3 percent of the articles should have been rejected. Many of the studies summarized in Table 8-3 examined only a few statistical tests. Those data in Table 8-3 have, therefore, uncovered minimum percentages of statistical problems in the published literature. The exact percentage of articles with correctable problems cannot be determined from these studies. However, few of the investigators were willing to suggest that the published article should have been rejected based on their statistical review of the studies.

Figure 8-2 is a scatter diagram of the data from the studies listed in Table 8-3. In Figure 8-2, the year of each study is plotted against the average percentage of articles in each study in which some statistical problems were uncovered. This diagram does not reveal a trend toward an improvement with the use of statistical analyses in the published literature over time. This chart shows, simply, that evaluations of the statistics in the published literature continue to uncover a high percentage of studies that lack proper statistical analysis or proper descriptions of the statistical analysis. The degree of scrutiny might be more rigorous today than it was when the early reports were published. These early reports only examined some very basic statistical tests.

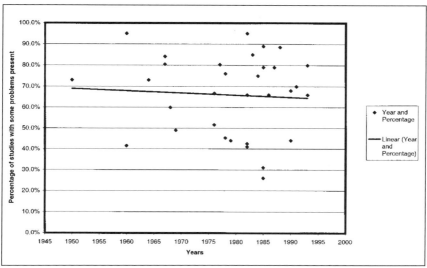

**Figure 8-2: Scatter diagram of statistical problems in articles over time**

## Complexity of statistical tests in published studies

The previous sections reviewed studies that evaluated the completeness and correctness of statistical tests both in submitted manuscripts and in the published literature. How complex are statistical tests in manuscripts?

*Question*

To what degree could a reviewer without training in statistics accurately review manuscripts containing some statistical tests?

*Criteria for inclusion*

~ any study that examined the statistical complexity of published studies.

*Comparable studies*

Ten studies were located that examined the complexity of statistical tests in the published medical literature (Table 8-4). Several of these studies compared data from more than one year, and each year is a separate entry in Table 8-4.

Hayden tracks changes in the complexity of statistics in the journal *Pediatrics* at 10-year intervals from 1952 to 1982 (Hayden, 1983). He found that statistical procedures had become more common and more varied during these 30 years. From 1952 to 1982 the percentage of articles in *Pediatrics* that used either no statistical tests or only one of four simple statistics (measures of dispersion, *t*-test, chi-square, and Pearson's correlation) decreased from 97 percent to 65 percent. During this same time period, those published studies with interpretative statistical procedures increased from 13 percent to 48 percent.

| Field of study; journal | Number of articles | Number of journals | Percentage of articles with statistical tests | | | No statistics | % easy to understand | Year of Study | References |
|---|---|---|---|---|---|---|---|---|---|
| | | | descriptive* | dispersion** | interpretive*** | | | | |
| *Pediatrics* | 67 | 1 | | 21% | 13% | 66% | 97% | 1952 | (Hayden, 1983) |
| *Pediatrics* | 98 | 1 | | 20% | 20% | 59% | 95% | 1962 | (Hayden, 1983) |
| otolaryngology | 306 | 4 | 35% | | 6% | 58% | | 1969 | (Rosenfeld & Rockette, 1991) |
| *Archives of Ophthalmology* | 168 | 1 | 53% | 27% | 46% | | | 1970 | (Juzych, Shin, Seyedsadr, Siegner, & Juzych, 1992) |
| *Pediatrics* | 115 | 1 | | 27% | 28% | 45% | 88% | 1972 | (Hayden, 1983) |
| medicine | 2238 | 9 | | 9% | 25% | 73% | most | 1973 | (Daubs, 1980) |
| medicine | 1165 | 5 | | 5% | 30% | 65% | 73% | 1973 | (Feinstein, 1974) |
| otolaryngology | 415 | 4 | 42% | | 11% | 47% | | 1979 | (Rosenfeld & Rockette, 1991) |
| *Archives of Ophthalmology* | 214 | 1 | 56% | 39% | | 42% | | 1980 | (Juzych et al., 1992) |
| *New England Journal of Medicine* | 760 | 1 | 58% (or none) | | | | 73% | 1980 | (Emerson & Colditz, 1983), (Emerson & Colditz, 1992) |
| *Pediatrics* | 151 | 1 | | 23% | 48% | 30% | 65% | 1982 | (Hayden, 1983) |
| medicine | 3299 | 9 | 44% | 21% | | 42% | 90% | 1983 | (Hokanson, Stiernberg, McCracken, & Quinn, 1987) |
| rehabilitation | 128 | 1 | 37% | | | 62% | | 1982 | (Wainapel & Kayne, 1985) |
| *New England Journal of Medicine* | 115 | 1 | 12% (or none) | | 27-36% | | | 1989 | (Emerson & Colditz, 1992) |
| otolaryngology | 541 | 4 | 33% | | 27% | 39% | 90% | 1989 | (Rosenfeld & Rockette, 1991) |
| rehabilitation | 1039 | 2 | 66% | | | 34% | | 1990 | (Schwartz, Sturr, & Goldberg, 1996) |
| ophthalmology | 592 | 3 | 65% | 50% | | 34% | 89% | 1990 | (Juzych et al., 1992) |
| *Average* | | | 48% | 24% | 23% | 49% | 84% | | |

\* percentages, means, mode      \*\* standard error, standard deviation, range      \*\*\* t test, chi-square, Pearsons, etc.

**Table 8-4: Complexity of statistical test in published articles in medicine**

Rosenfeld and Rockette carried out a study similar to Hayden's study when they evaluated articles from four otolaryngology journals (*Annals of Otolaryngology, Archives of Otolaryngology—Head & Neck Surgery, Laryngoscope,* and *Otolaryngology Head and Neck Surgery*) comparing the statistical complexity in articles published in 1969, 1979, and 1989 (Rosenfeld & Rockette, 1991). While an average of 67 percent of all articles from these three time periods contained no statistics at all or only descriptive statistics, the investigators considered that knowledge of five statistical techniques was sufficient to understand the statistics of 90 percent of all articles: *t*-tests, contingency tables, analysis of variance, life tables, and nonparametric statistics. The investigators cautioned however that their study suggested that articles would continue to increase in statistical complexity.

Using a similar study design, Juzych and colleagues looked at statistical analysis in articles in ophthalmology journals at decade intervals from 1970 to 1990 (Juzych et al., 1992). The number of articles published in *Archives of Ophthalmology* without statistics decreased from 46 percent in 1970, to 42 percent in 1980, to 34 percent in 1990. Researchers also found differences in the percentages of articles that contained statistics among the journals for 1990: 67 percent for *Ophthalmology*, and 55 percent for the *American Journal of Ophthalmology*. The difference among the three journals is statistically significant. For 1990, a total of 66 percent of all articles in these journals contained some statistical analysis. The authors calculated that 89 percent of all articles were "statistically accessible" (p. 1227) if the reader had knowledge of 10 statistical techniques. These 10 included: measures of central tendency, dispersion statistics, *t*-test, contingency tables, nonparametric tests, analysis of variance, linear regression, Pearson's correlation coefficient, survival analysis, and multiple comparisons.

Feinstein determined that a basic knowledge of standard deviation, standard errors, *t*-test, and chi-square was enough to understand 73 percent of statistics used in five major medical journals in 1973 (Feinstein, 1974). Emerson and Colditz (Emerson & Colditz, 1983) in a study of 760 articles from the *New England Journal of Medicine*, found that the reader needed a knowledge of three basic statistics (description, *t*-test, and contingency tables) to understand the statistics in 73 percent of the articles. Ten years later Emerson and Colditz adding to the 1983 data determined that only 12 percent of the articles in one volume of the *New England Journal of Medicine* had no statistical analysis or only descriptive statistics (Emerson & Colditz, 1992). Emerson and Colditz's 1992 study did not cite their 1983 one, but the 1992 study found that in every category reporting of statistical tests had increased.

A review of two years of otolaryngology literature led Hokanson and colleagues to conclude that 90 percent of 3,299 articles could be understood knowing fewer than 10 basic statistical procedures (Hokanson et al., 1987). Daubs' conclusion from a study of nine medical journals was similar "most of the procedures used could be explained in an introductory coverage of statistics, yet clinicians rarely show an interest in this subject" (p. 801) (Daubs, 1980).

Wainapel and Kayne determined that 37 percent of the 128 articles published in 1982 in the *Archives of Physical Medicine and Rehabilitation* used some type of statistical methodology (Wainapel & Kayne, 1985). Schwartz, Sturr, and Goldberg updated the Wainapel study and documented the use of statistics in two rehabilitation journals from 1990 to 1993: the *American Journal of Physical Medicine and Rehabilitation* and the *Archives of Physical Medicine and Rehabilitation* (Schwartz et al., 1996). The sample of articles contained 66 percent research articles. These investigators confirmed that more statistical tests and more complex statistical tests were used by rehabilitation journals in the early 1990s than in 1982.

As Figure 8-3 illustrates, there is a trend toward the increased use of statistics in the medical literature. One additional study of the complexity of published statistical tests was conducted in psychology (Reis & Stiller, 1992). Reis and Stiller examined changes in research patterns in the *Journal of Personality and Social Psychology* using the 1968, 1978, and 1988 volumes. Similar to the studies of medicine, the investigators found a "growing complexity both in the kinds of theoretical questions that social-personality researchers ask and in the methodologies and statistics they use to answer them" (p. 465).

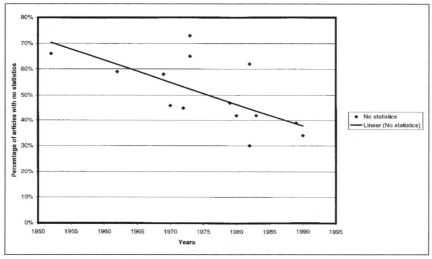

**Figure 8-3: Percentage of medical articles with no statistics**

In Figure 8-3, one can see that studies since 1980 indicate that from 30 percent to 40 percent of all articles contain no statistical analysis, while in the 1950s and 1960s this percentage was closer to 60 percent. An average of 84 percent of all statistics in published articles was easy to understand. Which statistics are easy to understand of course could be different for different investigators, so clearly this average is only an estimate. An average of 25 percent of these studies contain either dispersion statistics or interpretive statistics, while an average of 50 percent include only descriptive statistics. These data seem to strengthen the argument that reviewers of medical manuscripts should have an understanding of statistics. Investigators of these studies did not try to determine if manuscripts had undergone statistical review prior to publication.

## Publication bias and replication studies

"Publication bias" is a term used to describe the tendency to publish only studies with statistically significant results. Publication bias is present when authors decide not to submit studies for publication that do not have statistically significant outcomes, when reviewers recommend these manuscripts for rejection, or when editors reject these manuscripts once submitted. Replication studies (studies that repeat the design of a previously completed study) face similar difficulties: authors are reluctant to carry out a replication study, assuming that neither reviewers nor editors are interested in seeing these studies in print. Both publication bias and replication studies are important topics for editorial peer review. There is debate about the value of and need for both types of studies in the literature. This section examines the role of editorial peer review in the publication of studies without statistically significant findings and the publication of replication studies.

Dickersin reviewed the literature on publication bias and pointed out that there are no guidelines as to when a study should or should not be published (Dickersin, 1990). Dickersin observed that the tendency of researchers to wait for a noticeable impact before deciding to publish any results has been around a long time. Dickersin referred to the laments of the seventeenth century chemist, Robert Boyle, who complained that scientists did not write up the results of one study, but waited until they "had a 'system' worked out that they deemed worthy of formal presentation" (p. 1386).

The editor of the *Journal of Experimental Psychology* admitted in a 1962 editorial that he had "a strong reluctance to accept and publish results related to the principal concern of the research when those results were significant at the .05 level" (p. 554) (Melton, 1962). Melton preferred significance at the 0.01 level. Furthermore, he made a similar rejection decision for studies that did not disprove the null hypothesis.

Since publication bias is a tendency *not* to publish, in order to study the phenomenon one must be able to identify what has not been published. Surveys and registers do not include all unpublished studies and it is probably impossible to locate all unpublished studies. But there are several approaches that do shed light on the effects of publication bias. The first approach is to examine positive outcomes of studies published in the literature. This approach looks for the percentage of published studies in which the null hypothesis is not rejected. A second approach is to identify investigations approved by institutional review boards and determine if more of the approved studies with statistically significant results have been published than studies without statistically significant results. A third approach is to fabricate a manuscript similar in all respects except that one version of the manuscript has statistical significant differences, while the other version has nonsignificant results. Any of these approaches has limitations according to Moscati and colleagues (Moscati, Jehle, Ellis, Fiorello, & Landi, 1994).

An editorial in the *New England Journal of Medicine* acknowledged the perception that journals do not publish negative studies. Yet in the same issue, the *Journal* published a report that concluded that vitamins taken by pregnant women did not affect the incidence of neural-tube defects in their offspring (Angell, 1989). A study that was published in *JAMA* determined that newspapers were more likely to publish reports of studies with positive results than reports of studies with no effects or adverse effects (Koren & Klein, 1991).

*Question*

What evidence is there that the editorial peer review process is likely to reject manuscripts with no statistically significant differences in outcome (studies that do not reject the null hypothesis)?

*Criteria for inclusion*

~ any study that looks for a connection between the editorial peer review process and publication bias.

*Comparable studies*

Three approaches have been used to study publication bias: (1) studies that look for published articles with statistically significant outcomes, (2) studies that identify the outcome of approved research projects, and (3) studies that examined outcomes of fabricated manuscripts.

## Studies with statistically significant outcomes

Six reports examined publication bias within a group of published articles (Table 8-5). The first report of this phenomenon came from a psychology article that discussed the statistically significant results of published reports. Sterling studied 362 research reports from four psychology journals *(Experimental Psychology, Comparative and Physiological Psychology, Clinical Psychology,* and *Social Psychology)* (Sterling, 1959). Of all published reports studied, 81.2 percent used some tests of statistical significance and only 2.2 percent of these failed to reject the null hypothesis. There were no studies that replicated a previously published study.

In 1972, Bozarth and Roberts using Sterling's methodology, found that 94 percent of 1,046 research articles reported rejection of the null hypothesis in three psychology journals *(Journal of Consulting and Clinical Psychology, Journal of Counseling Psychology,* and *Personnel Guidance Journal)* (Bozarth & Roberts, 1972).

In a private communication to Dickersin and Min, Sterling reported that when updating his study 40 years later using the same four journals, he had virtually the same results: about 95 percent of the articles had statistically significant findings (Dickersin & Min, 1993). Dickersin and Min conducted a study that was similar to Sterling's study and used the same four psychology journals in addition to three medical journals *(American Journal of Epidemiology, American Journal of Public Health,* and *New England Journal of Medicine).*

| Field of study | Number of articles | Number of journals | Studies examined statistically significant results | Studies examined non-significant trend | Studies examined failed to reject the null hypothesis | Replication studies | Year | References |
|---|---|---|---|---|---|---|---|---|
| psychology | 362 | 4 | 81% | | 2% | 0% | 1955 | (Sterling, 1959) |
| psychology | 1046 | 3 | 94% | | | >1% | 1970 | (Bozarth & Roberts, 1972) |
| psychology | 597 | 4 | 95% | | 4% | | 1986-87 | (Dickersin & Min, 1993) |
| medicine | 456 | 3 | 86% | | 14% | | 1986-87 | (Dickersin & Min, 1993) |
| medicine–emergency | 177 | 2 | 80% | 5% | 15% | | 1994 | (Moscati et al., 1994) |
| medicine–general | 211 | 2 | 80% | 4% | 16% | | 1994 | (Moscati et al., 1994) |
| medicine–general | 383 | 3 | 73% | | | | 1975-90 | (Moher et al., 1994) |
| tobacco–peer reviewed | 44 | | 57% | | 11% | | 1965-93 | (Bero, Glantz, & Rennie, 1994) |
| tobacco–not reviewed | 19 | | 47% | | 26% | | 1965-93 | (Bero et al., 1994) |
| *Averages* | | | 77% | 5% | 13% | | | |

**Table 8-5: Evidence of publication bias and replication studies in published articles**

Again their findings were similar to Sterling's. The medical journal articles failed to reject the null hypothesis more frequently than the psychology journals, from 12 percent to 19 percent of the time. Dickersin found that "despite the fact that the overwhelming majority of trials were published, there was still strong evidence of publication bias" (p. 139) in favor of those studies with statistically significant findings. As pointed out by Dickersin, the data appear to contradict the popularly held notion that editors do not publish studies with no statistically significant findings. It is usually the investigators that make the decision not to pursue publication (Dickersin, Min, & Meinert, 1992).

Moscati and colleagues looked for positive outcome bias in two emergency medicine journals (*Annals of Emergency Medicine* and *American Journal of Emergency Medicine*) compared to two general medical journals (*JAMA* and *New England Journal of Medicine*) (Moscati et al., 1994). Both groups of journals yielded the same results: about 80 percent of the original contributions had statistically significant findings.

Commenting on the study by Moscati and colleagues, the editor of *Academic Emergency Medicine*, pointed out that publication bias:

> *cannot be interpreted apart from the many other factors affecting a study's suitability for publication. Whether publication bias must be condemned or whether it can be tolerated depends on the definition used, the availability of accessible repositories for study results, the ability to assess the impact of unavailable data, and the function of journal publication* (p. 208) (Olson, 1994).

A review of 383 articles published in *JAMA*, *Lancet*, and the *New England Journal of Medicine* over a 15-year period found that 27 percent of all RCTs had negative results (Moher et al., 1994). Bero and colleagues conducted a study of published articles that measured the health effects of tobacco exposure (Bero et al., 1994). Contrary to the tobacco industry's claim, Bero and colleagues uncovered "no publication bias against statistically nonsignificant results on ETS [environmental tobacco smoke] in the peer-reviewed literature" (p. 133).

Summaries from Table 8-5 show that an average of 13 percent of published studies did not reject the null hypothesis and three-fourths were statistically significant. There are no data on the percentage of manuscripts that are rejected simply because they do not reject the null hypothesis. Nor do data show what percentages of research studies in general are likely to reject the null hypothesis.

## Publication of approved studies

A second approach to the study of publication bias is to document publication outcomes of studies approved by organizations, funding bodies, or institutional review boards and then determine if those eventually published studies had statistically significant findings. Unpublished studies can also be located by querying authors about any studies they have completed, but were rejected after submission or were never submitted for publication. Six studies looked for evidence of publication bias in the publication outcomes of a group of research projects (Table 8-6).

| Field of study | Number of studies (% published) | Published studies | | | Unpublished studies | | | Year | References |
|---|---|---|---|---|---|---|---|---|---|
| | | Statistically significant results | Non-significant trend | Failed to reject the null hypothesis | Statistically significant results | Non-significant trend | Failed to reject the null hypothesis | | |
| psychology | 134 (74%) | 86% | 14% | | 60% | 40% | | 1986 | (Coursol & Wagner, 1986) |
| medicine | 1312 (80%) | 55% | 16% | 29% | 15% | 22% | 62% | 1963-81 | (Dickersin, Chan, Chalmers, Sacks, & Smith, 1987) |
| medicine | 285 (48%) | 67% | 9% | 22% | 41% | 15% | 43% | 1984-87 | (Easterbrook, Berlin, Gopalan, & Matthews, 1991) |
| public health | 172 (66%) | 62% | | 38% | | | | 1980 | (Dickersin et al., 1992) |
| medicine | 342 (81%) | 61% | | 39% | | | | 1980 | (Dickersin et al., 1992) |
| medicine | 280 | 62% | | 38% | | | | 1980-87 | (Dickersin & Min, 1993) |
| medicine | 216 | 69% | 8% | 22% | | | | 1979-88 | (Stern & Simes, 1997) |
| medicine–clinical trials | 119 | 61% | 11% | 33% | | | | 1979-88 | (Stern & Simes, 1997) |

**Table 8-6: Evidence of publication bias in research project outcomes**

In a study of psychologists, Coursol and Wagner queried 1,000 American Psychological Association members about their participation in outcome studies of counseling and psychotherapy (Coursol & Wagner, 1986). Respondents who had performed at least one outcome study were much more likely to submit a report for publication if the study had a positive outcome. After submission, editorial acceptance was more likely for those studies with a positive outcome.

Dickersin and colleagues investigated the influence of statistically significant outcomes of RCTs on eventual publication of research reports (Dickersin et al., 1987). The investigators queried 156 authors and obtained information on 271 unpublished and 1,041 published studies. Of studies with no statistically significant differences, nonsignificant trends among therapies, or trends that favored standard therapies 45 percent were published. On the other hand, 85 percent of the studies that showed no statistically significant differences or nonsignificant trends remained unpublished. Their findings "suggest that the results of published RCTs are more likely to favor the new therapy than are the results of unpublished RCTs" (p. 351).

Easterbrook and colleagues surveyed 487 research projects approved by the Central Oxford Research Ethics Committee from 1984 to 1987 and discovered that "studies with statistically significant results were more likely to be published than those finding no difference between the study groups" (p. 867) (Easterbrook et al., 1991). The studies with statistically significant differences were also more likely to be published in a greater number of publications and presented at scientific meetings, in addition to being published in journals with a high impact factor. In a similar study, Stern and Simes tracked the publication of studies submitted to the ethics committee at the University Hospital in Sydney, Australia, over a 10-year period (Stern & Simes, 1997). Studies with statistically significant results were much more likely to be published than those without statistically significant results. Also, positive studies were much more likely to be published in a shorter time frame (a median of 4.8 versus 8.0 years).

Dickersin (1990) reviewed data from four studies [(Simes, 1986), (Dickersin et al., 1987) (Sommer, 1987), (Chalmers et al., 1990a)]. In each study publication was more likely when statistically significant results were found. Dickersin called for the registration of all clinical studies, pointing out that registers now exist in several areas: perinatal trials, cancer, and AIDS. In a second analysis of clinical studies, Dickersin reported on the publication outcome of approved clinical trials from Johns Hopkins School of Medicine's institutional review board, the Johns Hopkins School of Hygiene and Public Health's institutional review board, and the National Institutes of Health, excluding those funded by the National Cancer Institute (Dickersin & Min, 1993). In this investigation, 62 percent of all studies had statistically significant differences.

In an additional analysis of publication bias, Dickerson and colleagues merged data from several of these studies, including data from the Easterbrook study (Dickersin et al., 1992). Since several studies summarized in Table 8-6 were discussed in more than one article, these data have not been averaged in the table. While the averages for each study range from 55 percent to 69 percent, they still fall short of the 77 percent of studies published with statistically significant results (Table 8-5).

## Fabricated manuscripts

The third approach investigators used to study publication bias was the examination of reviewer behavior when evaluating a fabricated manuscript. Fabricated manuscripts present an opportunity to control for one variable. In a study designed to look for the existence of a bias in favor of studies reporting statistically significant results, Atkinson and colleagues asked editing consultants to evaluate three versions of one study. The studies differed only with respect to the level of statistically significant findings (Atkinson, Furlong, & Wampold, 1982). The version that reported no statistical significant findings was recommended for rejection three times as often as the version reporting statistically significant differences. Following this report, Fagley and McKinney questioned the statistics used in the Atkinson study (Fagley & McKinney, 1983). After conducting a statistical power analysis, Fagley and McKinney determined that the power of the study was low. "Low power in a study reporting nonsignificant findings is a valid reason for recommending not to publish. Therefore, differential acceptance recommendations for bogus manuscripts differing only in the statistical significance of the results were justified" (p. 298). Continuing the discussion of the Atkinson study, Wampold, Furlong, and Atkinson countered that the bogus study did have sufficient "power to detect a large experimental effect and that attempts to design studies sensitive to small experimental effects are typically impractical" (p. 459) (Wampold, Furlong, & Atkinson, 1983). This discussion is similar to the one in the beginning of the chapter in which the statistical validity of a study on the merits of all day versus half-day kindergarten is discussed. In addition, it is another example of problems with the study and analysis of fabricated manuscripts.

In an additional example of the problems with fictitious manuscripts, Kemper, in an editorial in 1991 in the *Journal of Clinical Epidemiology*, discussed a study of a rejected manuscript similar to the Atkinson study (Kemper, 1991). In this study, versions of a fictitious manuscript that differed only in the statistical significance of the outcome were submitted to 140 journals. The editorial focused on the deception of the study and the ethical aspects of this research approach and claimed that a report of the study had been rejected by at least one journal. The study Kemper referred to was written by Epstein and was published in 1989 in a journal cited as "*Int Rev Board.*" This original article was not located.

A number of studies using fabricated data were designed to test for potential bias for or against a certain theoretical or ideological framework. These studies all found that reviewers were likely to recommend for publication studies that supported their particular viewpoint. These studies did not test for publication bias as such and are discussed in Chapter Seven on reviewer biases.

After reviewing the literature on publication bias, Rennie and Flanagin suggested editors drop the use of words "positive" and "negative" when describing study outcomes and concluded that "no one, from the researcher testing a new notion to the physician prescribing new drugs, would do so unless moved by the bias of optimism. And so it is with reviewers, editors, reporters, and readers." (p. 412) (Rennie & Flanagin, 1992). In fact, they maintained there is little evidence that reviewers or editors do engage in the practice of publication bias.

## Replication studies

Brown and colleagues critiqued the description of clinical trials and the degree to which they could be replicated as reported (Brown, Kelen, Moser, Moeschberger, & Rund, 1985). They concluded that controlled trials are not being reported with enough detail to be replicated. The authors suggested that journal editors should adopt publication standards to assure that a replication study could be conducted.

Bornstein suggested that the social sciences should increase the number of replication studies, and he saw both researchers and editors sharing responsibility for accomplishing this end (Bornstein, 1990). Bornstein maintained that social science in particular is perceived as "less rigorous, less robust, less replicable and less cumulative than research in other branches of science" (p. 80).

*Question*

How commonly are replication studies published?

*Criteria for inclusion*

~ any study that determined likelihood of publication of replication studies.

*Comparable studies*

Neuliep and Crandall surveyed editors of social and behavioral science journals and found a "strong bias against publishing replications" (p. 85) (Neuliep & Crandall, 1990). These investigators also queried reviewers of social science journals about their view of replication studies and determined that reviewers were biased against replication studies as well (Neuliep & Crandall, 1993). (See Chapters Three and Seven, respectively).

Two studies determined the percentage of published studies that were replication studies (Table 8-5). Sterling's study of 362 research reports from four psychology journals discussed in the previous section found that less than 1 percent, only eight articles, were replication studies (Sterling, 1959). Similarly, and Bozarth and Roberts repeated Sterling's study and found less than 1 percent of all published studies in three psychology journals were replication studies (Bozarth & Roberts, 1972).

## Guidelines and checklists

Statistical problems in the published medical literature are a well-documented phenomenon. Since the first study of this type in 1951, every study that has investigated statistical analysis of medical articles has identified a number of statistical errors or shortcomings in a group of published articles containing statistical analyses. A number of authors have outlined steps or developed guidelines for authors, editors, and reviewers to use when writing or reviewing reports with statistical analyses. Some journal editors have altered their statistical review process after seeing a statistical analysis of published articles and then established guidelines for authors and reviewers as a result of these critiques. Several authors have offered opinions and recommendations for correcting some of the many problems that have been identified by those who have studied statistical difficulties in published articles. This section summarizes these recommendations as well as measures journal editors have taken to try to improve the statistical reporting in their journal, particularly in the five medical journals that have been the subject of four or more studies (Table 8-3).

In a letter to the editor, Feige addressed the problem of publication bias in the field of political economy and suggested a change of editorial policy: do not count statistical significance of study results, but consider "relevance of the proposed research and adequacy of design of the hypothesis-testing procedures" (p. 1293) (Feige, 1975). The editors of the *Journal of Political Economy* countered that implementing Feige's suggestion would be extremely expensive, but they thought that there was merit in the journal publishing alternative statistical tests of a hypothesis. In fact, in a note appended to Feige's comment, the editors thought that authors should be willing to make all of their data available to other scholars. The editors also stated that they would add a section titled "Confirmations and Contradictions" for authors who tried to replicate data in *Journal of Political Economy* articles (p. 1296). A perusal of the *Journal of Political Economy* revealed that the editor did indeed add a section on "Confirmations and Contradictions" that included about 20 items over the five years following this announcement.

O'Fallon and colleagues summarized a panel discussion of a 1978 meeting of the Biometric Society where the topic was a question: should there be statistical guidelines for medical research papers (O'Fallon et al., 1978)? The panel developed a list of suggestions, including some of particular interest to editors and the review process:

- Editors should give publication preference to controlled clinical trials.

- Statisticians should be involved from the beginning of a research project.

- Editorial boards should develop standards for statistical content of manuscripts.

- Raw data should be made available to the reviewers by researchers.

- Biostatisticians should be required as reviewers.

- Statistics courses should be required for medical school students.

Chalmers, Frank, and Reitman suggested several steps editors could take to minimize any publication bias relevant to peer review (Chalmers, Frank, & Reitman, 1990b):

- Insist on high-quality research and literature reviews.

- Ask reviewers to state any conflict of interest.

- Publish high quality research, independent of outcome.

- Replace review articles with meta-analysis.

Those who have carried out studies of the statistical accuracy in published articles have made many recommendations. Some of these suggestions could be implemented by educators, some by researchers, and some by editors. Other than the suggestion to use a statistical reviewer, these suggestions are not directed at reviewers. The numerous suggestions illustrate the difficulty of identifying a workable solution to the problem of accurate statistical reporting in the peer reviewed literature. These suggestions include:

*In education*

- Increase the teaching of statistics in medical school and in postgraduate training programs (Feinstein, 1974), (Wainapel & Kayne, 1985), (Davies, 1987), and (Altman & Bland, 1991).

*In research*

- Add a statistical consultant to the research team (Gore et al., 1977) (Avram et al., 1985).

- Give more attention to planning clinical trials (Freiman et al., 1978).

*For institutions*

- Require institutional review boards to pay more attention to study design (Glantz, 1980).

- Maintain a registry of research projects (Dickersin et al., 1992) (Stern & Simes, 1997).

- Advise ethics committees on statistical issues (McCance, 1995).

*For editors*

- Work to refute the currently held belief that one study can establish the importance of a research finding; do not publish only studies with statistically significant findings (Walster & Cleary, 1970).

- Accept only the experimental design for review (Walster & Cleary, 1970).

- Use more careful statistical reviewing (White, 1979) (Cruess, 1989).

- Set standards for reporting controlled clinical trials (Mosteller et al., 1980).

- Improve the reporting of clinical trials by giving authors information on the important statistical and methodological points to cover in their manuscript (DerSimonian et al., 1982), (MacArthur & Jackson, 1984), and (Rennie & Flanagin, 1992).

- Publish statistical guidelines, publish raw data in articles, and use a statistical reviewer (Altman, 1982), (Shott, 1985), and (McCance, 1995).

- Publication of a manuscript should be based on study design and relevance, not on outcome (Moscati et al., 1994).

*For authors*

- Report the power of the statistical tests used in a study, report findings in terms of confidence intervals, and report on an index of effect of size (p. 299) (Fagley & McKinney, 1983).

- Write brief descriptions of all statistics used in a study (Wainapel & Kayne, 1985).

- Undertake projects with partners and collaborate in research projects (Morris, 1988).

Tutorials have been published to help authors, reviewers, and editors understand the correct use of statistics. Like the recommendations above, these tutorials cover a wide range of recommendations and suggestions. Examples include the following:

- Explain the basic principles of statistics in medical research (Schoolman, Becktel, Best, & Johnson, 1968).

- Understand the use and misuse of statistics (Weech, 1974).

- Identify statistical errors (1977).

- Assist the reader in interpreting clinical trials (1978).

- Understand the null hypothesis and appreciate statistical significance versus medical significance (Sheehan, 1980).

- Improve the quality of statistics in medical journals (Altman, 1981).

- Explain statistics to contributors (Altman, Gore, Gardner, & Pocock, 1983).

- Aid the reviewer with statistical review (Ederer, 1985).

- Explain use and misuse of statistics (Robinson, 1985).

- Assist the average reader of a medical article in assessing the reliability of published reports (Bulman, 1988).

- Explain statistical guidelines to authors (Evans, 1989) (Murray, 1991).

- Improve physicians' understanding of statistics (Altman & Bland, 1991).

- Explain basic statistics to authors (Finney & Clarke, 1992).

## Efforts of individual journals

Of those studies summarized in Table 8-3, five journals were subjected to more statistical analyses than other journals: *BMJ, Canadian Medical Association Journal, JAMA, Lancet,* and *New England Journal of Medicine.* Fourteen of the 34 studies (41.2 percent) summarized in Table 8-3 investigated the statistical methodologies of articles in at least one of these journals. The attention that the editors of these five journals have given to the subject of statistical review of manuscripts is of interest. Three of these five journals have published guidelines for statistical review of manuscripts for their reviewers: *BMJ, Canadian Medical Association Journal*, and *Lancet*. Editors of these three journals have stated through editorials or descriptions of their process in the journals that they have a statistical review process in place and have published their criteria. While such published criteria are public statements of statistical review policies, the fact that an editor has not published a statement is by no means an indication that statistical review is not a part of the editorial review process. In fact, since the editorials of many journals are not indexed, there probably are any number of such statements by editors of other medical journals. In addition, editors may use a statistical reviewer as a matter of policy, without informing authors or reviewers of this practice. On the other hand, editors occasionally do make announcements about the use of a statistical reviewer. For example, in 1968, the editor of *Diseases of the Chest* reported that "major communications" were reviewed by staff biostatisticians (p. 3) (Soffer, 1968). Soffer added that biostatisticians frequently requested more information from the authors about the investigators' scientific protocols or statistical tests. Exactly how common it is to use staff statisticians in medical journals has not been fully investigated. A summary of the published accounts of these five journals provides some insight into the issues of statistical review.

### BMJ

Lionel published the first report of statistical assessment of published reports (Table 8-3) in the *BMJ* (Lionel & Herxheimer, 1970). A number of years later, in 1977, the *BMJ* published an editorial about prepublication statistical review of manuscripts. In this editorial, accompanying the Gore study (Table 8-3) (Gore et al., 1977), the editors held that not all statistical errors were of equal gravity, pointing out that many of the errors uncovered by Gore were errors of omission. The *BMJ* urged caution and thought that Gore's suggestion of adding a statistician to the research team was an impractical suggestion, as statisticians, particularly medical statisticians, are often available only in large research centers and not small centers (1977). An editorial the next year suggested that care needed to be taken with the interpretation of results of clinical trials (1978). The editorial cautioned that "most *BMJ* readers probably believe that when a controlled trial shows 'no significant differences ($p<0.05$)' between a drug and a placebo the results are conclusive. In fact, they may not be: for ... the report is incomplete unless the confidence limits are also given" (p. 1318).

In 1981, Altman argued for comprehensive guidelines for statistical reporting in the *BMJ*. He outlined guidelines on the more important statistical aspects of writing a report with sufficient statistical details: the design, data collection, analysis, presentation of results, and interpretation of results (Altman, 1981). In 1982, when the editors of *BMJ* first discussed with a group of referees the possibility of using a statistical reviewer, Smith quoted Altman as observing that "it was symbolic of the status given to statistics that the meeting had discussed references and punctuation before statistics." Others at the meeting countered that "statistics is no more of an exact science than clinical medicine." Those attending this meeting did agree that "the poor statistics in medical papers was a disgrace" (p. 1260). However, the consensus at this meeting was that statistical refereeing for *BMJ* needed improvement. The editors determined to study in a scientific manner what they could do to improve refereeing of the statistical portion of a manuscript (Smith, 1982, October 30).

By 1983, Altman developed more detailed guidelines intended to help authors present statistically acceptable reports of studies (Altman et al., 1983). A checklist for *BMJ* for use by statistical reviewers was developed by Gardner and colleagues (including Altman) and was tested on a set of submitted manuscripts (Gardner et al., 1983). The checklist was refined and retested three years later (Gardner et al., 1986). Results of an additional test of this checklist were presented at the first International Conference on Peer Review in Biomedical Literature and subsequently published in *JAMA* (the American Medical Association was the conference's sponsor) (Gardner & Bond, 1990). The results of these three studies are summarized in Table 8-2. In 1986 when he was editor of *BMJ*, Lock published a monograph: *A Difficult Balance: Editorial Peer Review in Medicine*. In it he included *BMJ*'s statistical guidelines for editors and referees as well as the statistical review checklist (Lock, 1985). And, by 1990, Smith revealed that Haynes had urged clinical journals to publish only reports of RCTs or structured review articles (Haynes, 1989) (Smith, 1990). Smith argued that Haynes has too narrow a view of the general medical journal. Smith contended that the general medical journal serves a series of purposes: "of informing, educating, entertaining, and amusing" (p. 758), and the publication of only RCTs would be too restrictive for a general medical journal. Altman emphasized the need for randomization to decrease biases in clinical reports (Altman, 1991). Altman, when he discussed the overall quality of medical research maintained that "The issue here is not one of statistics as such.

Rather it is a more general failure to appreciate the basic principles underlying scientific research ... We need less research, better research, and research done for the right reasons. Abandoning using the number of publications as a measure of ability would be a start" (pp. 283-284) (Altman, 1994).

In 1987, in the *BMJ*, Newcombe addressed the issue of publication bias, suggesting that editors and funding bodies should require protocols for peer review that detail study design at the planning stage (Newcombe, 1987). Newcombe stressed the importance of a proper sample size for all clinical trials. In a letter to the editor to *BMJ*, Mullee and colleagues suggested that statisticians should have recognition for their work by being listed as coauthors (Mullee, Lampe, Pickering, & Julious, 1995). They maintained that "mere acknowledgement of a statistician does not guarantee that appropriate statistical analysis has been done or its interpretation published" (p. 869).

*BMJ* again addressed the issue of publication bias with a study that examined delayed publication and publication bias (see Table 8-6) (Stern & Simes, 1997).

## Canadian Medical Association Journal

The *Canadian Medical Association Journal* published three studies in the 1960s that examined statistical methodologies of published articles in the *Journal*. Each of the studies is summarized in Table 8-3 (Badgley, 1961), (Mahon & Daniel, 1964), and (Reiffenstein et al., 1968). The *Canadian Medical Association Journal*, like *BMJ*, developed a set of questions for reviewers to use when reviewing studies with statistical analysis (Squires, 1989) and with clinical trials (Squires, 1990). Squires urged authors to engage a statistician at the beginning of a research project, to follow the statistician's advice, to ask a statistician for help with the analysis and interpretation, and to have a statistician read a manuscript before submission (Squires, 1990). If these are not followed, Squires suggested, the statistical review might not proceed well for the authors.

## Journal of the American Medical Association (JAMA)

In what appeared to be an attempt to counterbalance criticism about engaging in publication bias, about once a month between 1962 and 1968 *JAMA* published a column entitled "Negative Results" (Dickersin, 1990). *JAMA* editors in the 1990s were not able to learn details about the rationale for adding this feature to the journal. This is very similar to the action taken by the *Journal of Political Economy* in the 1970s with the publication of the "Confirmation and Corrections" column discussed earlier in this chapter. In 1991, a *JAMA* study confirmed media bias against negative studies (Koren & Klein, 1991).

*JAMA* was the first journal to publish a study that revealed the presence of statistically flawed studies in the medical literature (Ross, 1951). Fifteen years later, Schor and Karten replicated Ross' findings (Schor & Karten, 1966). In an accompanying editorial to this report, the editors of *JAMA* stated that the *Journal* "has for some time now availed itself of the services of biostatistical consultants for reviewing the statistical aspects of manuscripts" (p. 167) (1966).

In a *JAMA* editorial, 10 years later, Shuster and colleagues suggested that statistical review be added to the editorial peer review process for any article containing even elemental statistics (Shuster et al., 1976). They suggested that editors accept investigators' assumptions about statistical models, that statistical reviewers not critique the medical aspects of a study, and that reviewers keep in mind that authors often have minimal training in statistics. Vaisrub, a statistician for *JAMA*, discussed her role as a statistical reviewer and added a list of statistical problems that tend to be correctable and a corresponding list of incorrectable statistical problems (Vaisrub, 1985).

In 1990, *JAMA* published the proceedings from the First International Congress on Peer Review in Biomedical Publications. Five of these articles focused on statistics in biomedical articles and are discussed in this chapter (Chalmers et al., 1990a), (Chalmers et al., 1990b), (Dickersin, 1990), (Gardner & Bond, 1990), and (Garfunkel et al., 1990). Similarly, proceedings from the Second International Conference were published in 1994 in *JAMA*, and four of these articles dealt with statistical issues in the medical literature (Bero et al., 1994), (Moher et al., 1994), (Schulman et al., 1994), and (Schulz et al., 1994). The subjects of publication bias (Dickersin et al., 1992) and inadequate methodologies of controlled clinical trials (Schulz et al., 1995) have also been covered in additional articles in *JAMA*.

## Lancet

*Lancet* published an editorial on the subject of statistical review in 1991 and announced that after conventional review, if appropriate, manuscripts would also receive statistical review. *Lancet* also published two of the studies discussed in this analysis: the study by Gore and colleagues that examined statistical problems in *Lancet* articles (Table 8-3) (Gore et al., 1992) and the study by Easterbrook and colleagues that investigated issues of publication bias (Table 8-4) (Easterbrook et al., 1991).

Altman and Dore analyzed questions of proper randomization in articles published in several journals, including *Lancet*, and made a number of suggestions for improving reports of RCTs (Altman & Dore, 1990).

## New England Journal of Medicine

The *New England Journal of Medicine* has regularly published information on statistics in medical articles. In 1978, the explanation of the importance of type II error and sample size (Figure 8-1) was reported in the *New England Journal of Medicine* (Freiman et al., 1978).

In an editorial in 1978, Rennie commented: "our goal is the publication of data that are correctly observed and properly analyzed. Notwithstanding that dream, we hope our readers will continue to receive what we publish with their usual healthy skepticism" (p. 829) (Rennie, 1978). In a 1984 letter to the editor following the 1983 Emerson study, Boyer stressed the need to teach statistics to medical professionals (Boyer, 1984).

The *New England Journal of Medicine* published four studies included in Table 8-3 (Freiman, 1978), (DerSimonian et al., 1982), (Emerson & Colditz, 1983), and (Pocock et al., 1987). Emerson and colleagues published an updated study of the *New England Journal of Medicine* in a monograph on medical statistics (Emerson & Colditz, 1992).

In the same issue of the *New England Journal of Medicine* that published the DerSimonian study, Relman announced that this article was the first in a new series of articles in the *Journal* on biostatistics (Relman, 1982). The series was aimed at helping the *Journal's* readers understand statistical analysis. This series included such articles as "Bias in treatment assignment in controlled clinical trials" (Chalmers, Celano, Sacks, & Smith, 1983), "Use of statistical analysis in the *New England Journal of Medicine*" (Emerson & Colditz, 1983), and "Statistical analysis in the *New England Journal of Medicine*" (Boyer, 1984). Each of these articles is discussed in this chapter.

## Additional published statistical review guidelines

In addition to the five journals listed above, a number of other journals have published guidelines, checklists, or statistical tutorials to help with statistical review:

- Cancer clinical trials: *Journal of Clinical Oncology* (Zelen, 1983)

- Drug trials: *Drug Therapy* (Weintraub, 1982)

- Internal medicine: *Archives of Internal Medicine*, (Goldberg & Dalen, 1997)

- Medical literature in general; *Statistics in Medicine* (Altman, 1982) and *Annals of Internal Medicine* (Bailar & Mosteller, 1988)

- Pediatrics: *American Journal of Diseases of Children* (Brown, 1985)

- Pharmacology: *Clinical Pharmacology and Therapeutics,* (Feinstein, 1974; Feinstein, 1975; and Feinstein, 1976)

The third edition of the International Committee of Medical Journal Editors' "Uniform Requirements for Manuscripts Submitted to Biomedical Journals" included guidelines for the authors on the preparation of the statistical portion of the manuscript (International Committee of Medical Journal Editors, 1997). These guidelines are directed at authors, not editors or reviewers, and do not suggest that a statistician be part of a research team. Figure 8-4 is a copy of the two paragraphs on the statistical guidelines from the most recent statement of the International Committee. These guidelines are often published with a list of "participating" journals. It is not known to what degree these journals, in practice, have changed any editorial policy or whether they use these guidelines exclusively or in addition to their "instructions to authors." But acceptance of the "Uniform Requirements" does seem to indicate a move by editors toward more statistical accountability in the publication of studies with statistical analyses.

Describe statistical methods with enough detail to enable a knowledgeable reader with access to the original data to verify the reported results. When possible, quantify findings and present them with appropriate indicators of measurement error or uncertainty (such as confidence intervals). Avoid relying solely on statistical hypothesis testing, such as the use of $p$ values, which fails to convey important quantitative information. Discuss the eligibility of experimental subjects. Give details about randomization. Describe the methods for and success of any blinding of observations. Report complications of treatment. Give numbers of observations. Report losses to observation (e.g., dropouts from a clinical trial). When possible, references for the study design and statistical methods should be to standard works (with page numbers stated) rather than to papers in which the designs or methods were originally reported. Specify any general-use computer programs used.

Put a general description of methods in the Methods section. When data are summarized in the Results section, specify the statistical methods used to analyze them. Restrict tables and illustrations to those needed to explain the argument of the paper and to assess its support. Use graphs as an alternative to tables with many entries; do not duplicate data in graphs and tables. Avoid nontechnical uses of technical terms in statistics, such as "random" (which implies a randomizing device), "normal," "significant," "correlations," and "sample." Define statistical terms, abbreviations, and most symbols.

*The Uniform Requirements for Manuscripts Submitted to Biomedical Journals is not copyrighted and may be reproduced freely.

---

* (International Committee of Medical Journal Editors, 1997)

**Figure 8-4: Statistics Section**
**Uniform requirements for manuscripts submitted to biomedical journals**

While admitting that the International Committee's statement was helpful, in 1994 the *Annals of Internal Medicine* published a list of recommendations for *Reporting of Clinical Trials* (Working Group on Recommendations for Reporting of Clinical Trials in the Biomedical Literature, 1994). The report included a checklist of information that should be included in reports of clinical trials. The checklist covered information on conducting a clinical trial as well as points to include in each section of the report of the trial. The Working Group suggested that editors were in a position to promote reporting that is better than the current norm, and that guides for evaluating clinical trials should be available to editors and reviewers. Results of the Working Group's investigation were published two years later with a revised checklist (Asilomar Working Group on Recommendations for Reporting of Clinical Trials in the Biomedical Literature, 1996). The group suggested that the checklist published with the report be used as a guideline to improve clinical trial reports.

## *Limitations of studies of statistical review*

• The studies of statistical validity of published articles have a few limitations. As a group they have found that published studies containing statistical analysis are frequently inadequate. Most of these studies originate from medicine and an important concern is the clinical validity of a medical study. The link between statistical significance and clinical importance is critical, and frequently reports do not distinguish between a faulty design and a faulty description of the design. This distinction is crucial to understanding the difference between a serious problem (clinically important) and a potentially less-serious problem (not clinically important). Available information makes generalizations or dire predictions about statistical problems probably unwarranted. The degree that statistical problems lead to improper conclusions is not clear.

- The authors of a number of studies that found statistical faults in the published literature commented that not all statistical faults are serious and many could be corrected with a better written description of the study design or statistical analysis. There are two types of errors: errors of reporting and errors of analysis. Investigators of studies summarized in Table 8-3 might not know which error is present without an examination of the raw data from each and every study. A study that took this approach might prove to be valuable in understanding the importance of statistical shortcomings within the published literature.

- Those published articles subjected to statistical evaluation were from some of the most respected journals in medicine. There is no indication that any other journals do a different job, either better or worse.

*Recommendations*

- Studies of the statistical analysis present in published articles have provided valuable information about the need for statistical review as part of the editorial peer review process. There should continue to be studies that monitor the statistical quality of the published article.

- Manuscripts with statistical analysis should be reviewed by a statistical reviewer.

- Studies that use fabricated manuscripts have been shown to be problematic. Studies of bona fide manuscripts eliminate issues about the quality of a fabricated manuscript and the ethical problems of asking editors and reviewers to contribute their time and expertise to a fabricated manuscript. Studies designed to evaluate the review of manuscripts containing statistics should evaluate bona fide manuscripts or published articles.

- A comprehensive study of the degree of statistical review required by journal editors should be conducted.

## Conclusions about statistical review

This chapter has examined the statistical analysis of manuscripts prior to and after publication. Studies published since 1951 have found that, per study, an average of from 26 percent and 95 percent of published studies contain some degree of statistical shortcomings. These studies also found that most published studies used relatively simple statistics and statistical review improves the use of statistics in the published literature. These studies have scrutinized some of the most respected medical journals. There are different levels of inappropriate use of statistics and not all errors are serious. Even taking into account the serious errors, an average per study of anywhere from 5 percent to 32 percent of articles still had problems of a serious enough nature that those who examined the reports thought they should have been rejected. The studies also showed that most published studies do not have enough detail for replication. It has also been shown that the statistics used in recent studies are more complex than they were a few years ago, and the tendency toward statistical inaccuracies or shortcomings has remained level. These two trends are a sign that the efforts of editors and researchers who for a number of years have championed the use of standards may have had some impact.

These studies show that there has been a steady attempt by editors and statisticians to tackle the problem of using and reporting appropriate statistics in the analysis of studies containing data. These studies together offer evidence of the complicated issues statistics present to authors, reviewers, and editors.

Formal statistical review increases the statistical correctness of the subsequently published articles. Statistical software packages make the execution of statistical tests easier than previously, but do little to help investigators understand the underlying theory or reasons for the selection of a particular statistical test to analyze data.

This chapter has identified a considerable number of statistical inadequacies of studies. Many investigators have made a number of recommendations for improving what looks like dismal statistical analysis within the published literature, particularly in the medical arena. Many of these authors have suggested methods of improving the outcome of statistical reporting at almost every step of the research and publication process, from initial considerations during the study design stage to the final published article. So far, recommendations, tutorials, and admonitions do not seem to have solved the problem of inadequate statistics in the literature. But through these studies an understanding of the issues and ways to improve statistical analysis have developed. A number of journal editors, by publishing findings of studies of their own journals, showed an openness to identifying problems associated with statistics in manuscripts and the published literature.

The party responsible for correcting the statistical issues has been suggested at every level: from institutions, to statisticians, to educators, to authors, to editors, and, of course, to reviewers. Many of the suggested guidelines have a common sense ring to them, but they have proven difficult to implement. The suggestions made for the past 40 years tend to be similar. Many of those writing on the subject recommend statistical review of every manuscript that uses statistical methodologies. Given the results of these studies, it is difficult not to defend this position. The addition of statistical review to each manuscript that contains statistics undoubtedly adds considerable work to the production of a journal. Editors might be reluctant to take on the additional amount of work required for statistical review without being certain that this step is necessary to produce analytically solid research reports.

It was not always easy to tell from the studies summarized in this chapter if the identified statistical errors were errors of reporting or errors of using inappropriate or wrong statistics. If details of design are lost in shortening a manuscript, for example, the lack of information in the published article does not *ipso facto* mean that the research had been sloppy. While there is a tendency to publish few studies on nonsignificant results and replication studies, there is little evidence that publication bias is a direct result of negative reviewers' reports or negative editorial views. There is evidence that reviewers are not good at detecting statistical errors in manuscripts and, indeed, they may often not have enough information to evaluate correctly the statistical aspects of a manuscript. It seems fairly obvious that if an editor wants a good statistical review, a statistical reviewer must be called upon to perform the task. The data have made an irrefutable argument for statistical review of each and every manuscript containing statistical analysis.

## References

(1966, March 28). A pillar of medicine. *JAMA, 195*(13), 1145.

(1977, January 8). Statistical errors. *British Medical Journal, 1*, 66.

(1978, November 11). Interpreting clinical trials. *British Medical Journal, 2*, 1318.

(1991, January 12). Statistical review for journals. *Lancet, 337*, 84.

Altman, D. G. (1981, January 3). Statistics and ethics in medical research. VIII. Improving the quality of statistics in medical journals. *British Medical Journal, 282*, 44-47.

Altman, D. G. (1982). Statistics in medical journals. *Statistics in Medicine, 1*, 59-71.

Altman, D. G. (1991, June 22). Randomisation: essential for reducing bias. *British Medical Journal, 302*(6791), 1481-1482.

Altman, D. G. (1994, January 29). The scandal of poor medical research. *British Medical Journal, 308*(6923), 283-284.

Altman, D. G. & Bland, J. M. (1991). Improving doctors' understanding of statistics. *Journal of the Royal Statistical Society. A., 154*(Part 2), 223-267.

Altman, D. G. & Dore, C. J. (1990, January 20). Radomisation and baseline comparison in clinical trials. *Lancet, 335*, 149-153.

Altman, D. G., Gore, S. M., Gardner, M. J., & Pocock, S. J. (1983, May 7). Statistical guidelines for contributors to medical journals. *British Journal of Psychiatry, 286*(6376), 1489-1493.

Ambroz, A., Chalmers, T. C., Smith, H., Schroeder, B., Freiman, J. A., & Shareck, E. P. (1978, April). Deficiencies of randomized control trials. *Clinical Research, 26*(3), 280A.

Angell, M. (1989, August 17). Negative studies. *New England Journal of Medicine, 321*(7), 464-466.

Armitage, P. (1971). *Statistical methods in medical research*. New York: John Wiley & Sons Inc.

Asilomar Working Group on Recommendations for Reporting of Clinical Trials in the Biomedical Literature. (1996, April 15). Checklist of information for inclusion in reports of clinical trials. *Annals of Internal Medicine, 124*(8), 741-743.

Atkinson, D. R., Furlong, M. J., & Wampold, B. E. (1982, March). Statistical significance, reviewer evaluations, and the scientific process: Is there a (statistically) significant relationship? *Journal of Counseling Psychology, 29*(2), 189-194.

Avram, M. J., Shanks, C. A., Dykes, M. H. M., Ronai, A. K., & Stiers, W. M. (1985, June). Statistical methods in anesthesia articles: an evaluation of two American journals during two six-month periods. *Anesthesia and Analgesia, 64*(6), 607-611.

Badgley, R. F. (1961, June 29). An assessment of research methods reported in 103 scientific articles from two Canadian medical journals. *Canadian Medical Association Journal, 85*, 246-250.

Bailar, J. C. & Mosteller, F. (1988, February). Guidelines for statistical reporting in articles for medical journals. Amplifications and explanations. *Annals of Internal Medicine, 108*(2), 266-273.

Baxt, W. G., Waeckerle, J. F., Tintunalli, J. E., Knopp, R. K., & Callaham, M. L. (1996, May). Evaluation of the peer reviewer: performance of reviewers on a factitious submission. *Academic Emergency Medicine, 3*(5), 504.

Bero, L. A., Glantz, S. A., & Rennie, D. (1994, July 13). Publication bias and public health policy on environmental tobacco smoke. *JAMA, 272*(2), 133-136.

Bornstein, R. F. (1990). Publication politics, experimenter bias and the replication process in social science research. *Journal of Social Behavior and Personality, 5*(4), 71-81.

Boyer, W. F. (1984, March 8). Statistical analysis in the *New England Journal of Medicine. New England Journal of Medicine, 310*(10), 659.

Bozarth, J. D. & Roberts, R. R., Jr. (1972, August). Signifying significant significance. *American Psychologist, 27*(8), 774-775.

Brown, C. G., Kelen, G. D., Moser, M., Moeschberger, M. L., & Rund, D. A. (1985, October). Methodology reporting in three acute care journals: replication and reliability. *Annals of Emergency Medicine, 14*(10), 986-991.

Brown, G. W. (1985, March). Statistics and the medical journal. *American Journal of Diseases of Children, 139*(3), 226-228.

Bulman, J. S. (1988, September 10). A critical approach to the reading of analytical reports. *British Dental Journal, 165*(5), 180-182.

Chalmers, I., Adams, M., Dickerson, K., Hetherington, J., Tarnow-Mordi, W., Meinert, C., Tonascia, S., & Chalmers, T. C. (1990, March 9a). A cohort study of summary reports of controlled trials. *JAMA, 263*(10), 1401-1405.

Chalmers, T. C., Celano, P., Sacks, H. S., & Smith, H., Jr. (1983, December 1). Bias in treatment assignment in controlled clinical trials. *New England Journal of Medicine, 309*(22), 1358-1361.

Chalmers, T. C., Frank, C. S., & Reitman, D. (1990, March 9b). Minimizing the three stages of publication bias. *JAMA, 263*(10), 1392-1395.

Coursol, A. & Wagner, E. E. (1986). Effect of postive findings on submission and acceptance rates: a note on meta-analysis bias. *Professional Psychology: Research and Practice, 17*(2), 136-137.

Cruess, D. F. (1989, December). Review of the use of statistics in *The American Journal of Tropical Medicine and Hygiene* for January-December 1988. *American Journal of Tropical Medicine and Hygiene, 41*(6), 619-626.

Daubs, J. (1980). A survey of biostatistics in clinical journals. *American Journal of Optometry & Physiological Optics, 57*(11), 801-807.

Davies, J. (1987, September). A critical survey of scientific methods in two psychiatry journals. *Australian and New Zealand Journal of Psychiatry, 21*(3), 367-373.

DerSimonian, R., Charette, L. J., McPeek, B., & Mosteller, F. (1982, June 3). Reporting methods in clinical trials. *New England Journal of Medicine, 306*(22), 1332-1337.

Dickersin, K. (1990, March 9). The existence of publication bias and risk factors for its occurrence. *JAMA, 263*(10), 1385-1389.

Dickersin, K., Chan, S., Chalmers, T. C., Sacks, H. S., & Smith, H. J. (1987, December). Publication bias and clinical trials. *Controlled Clinical Trials, 8*, 343-353.

Dickersin, K., & Min, Y-I. (1993). Publication bias: the problem that won't go away. *Annals of the New York Academy of Medicine, 703*, 135-148.

Dickersin, K., Min, Y-I., & Meinert, C. (1992, January 15). Factors influencing publication of research results. Follow-up of applications submitted to two institutional review boards. *JAMA, 267*(3), 374-378.

Easterbrook, P. J., Berlin, J. A., Gopalan, R., & Matthews, D. R. (1991, April 13). Publication bias in clinical research. *Lancet, 337*(8746), 867-872.

Ederer, F. (1985, November). Refereeing clinical research papers for statistical content. *American Journal of Ophthalmology, 100*(5), 735-737.

Emerson, J. D. & Colditz, G. A. (1983, September 22). Use of statistical analysis in the *New England Journal of Medicine. New England Journal of Medicine, 309*(12), 709-713.

Emerson, J. D. & Colditz, G. A. (1992). Use of statistical analysis in the *New England Journal of Medicine.* In J. C. Bailar & F. Mosteller (Eds.), *Medical use of statistics* (2nd ed., pp. 45-57). Boston, MA: NEJM Books.

Emerson, J. D., McPeek, B., & Mosteller, F. (1984, May). Reporting clinical trials in general surgical journals. *Surgery, 95*(5), 572-579.

Evans, M. (1989, December). Presentation of manuscripts for publication in the *British Journal of Surgery. British Journal of Surgery, 76*(12), 1131-1134.

Fagley, N. S. & McKinney, I. J. (1983, April). Reviewer bias for statistically significant results: a reexamination. *Journal of Counseling Psychology, 30*(2), 298-300.

Feige, E. L. (1975, December). The consequences of journal editorial policies and a suggestion for a revision. *Journal of Political Economy, 83*(5), 1291-1296.

Feinstein, A. R. (1974, January). Clinical biostatistics. XXV. A survey of the statistical procedures in general medical journals. *Clinical Pharmacology and Therapeutics, 15*(1), 97-107.

Feinstein, A. R. (1975, October). Clinical biostatistics. XXXIV. The other side of 'statistical significance': alpha, beta, delta, and the calculation of sample size. *Clinical Pharmacology and Therapeutics, 18*(4), 491-505.

Feinstein, A. R. (1976, December). Clinical biostatistics. XXXVII. Demeaned errors, confidence games, nonplussed misuses, inefficient coefficients, and other statistical disruptions of scientific communication. *Clinical Pharmacology and Therapeutics, 20*(6), 617-631.

Feinstein, A. R. (1988, December 12). Scientific standards in epidemiologic studies of the menace of daily life. *Science, 242*(4883), 1257-1262.

Felson, D. T., Cupples, L. A., & Meenan, R. F. (1984, September). Misuse of statistical methods in *Arthritis and Rheumatism* 1982 versus 1967-68. *Arthritis and Rheumatism, 27*(9), 1018-1022.

Finney, D. J. & Clarke, B. C. (1992). Editorial code for presentation of statistical analyses. *Proceedings of the Royal Society of London B, 249*, 1-2.

Freiman, J. A., Chalmers, T. C., Smith, H. J., & Kuebler, R. R. (1978, September 28). The importance of beta, the type II error and sample size in the design and interpretation of the randomized control trial. *New England Journal of Medicine, 299*(13), 690-694.

Fusaro, J. A. & Royce, C. A. (1995, December). A reanalysis of research data. *Perceptual and Motor Skills, 81*(3, pt. 1), 858.

Gardner, M. J., Altman, D. G., Jones, D. R., & Machin, D. (1983, May 7). Is the statistical assessment of papers submitted to the "British Medical Journal" effective? *British Medical Journal, 286*(6376), 1485-1488.

Gardner, M. J. & Bond, J. (1990, March 9). An exploratory study of statistical assessment of papers published in the *British Medical Journal. JAMA, 26*(10), 1355-1357.

Gardner, M. J., Machin, D., & Campbell, M. J. (1986, March 22). Use of check lists in assessing the statistical content of medical studies. *British Medical Journal, 292*(6523), 810-812.

Garfunkel, J. M., Ulshen, M. H., Hamrick, H. J., & Lawson, E. E. (1990, March 9). Problems identified by secondary review of accepted manuscripts. *JAMA, 263*(10), 1369-1371.

George, S. L. (1985). Statistics in Medical Journals: A survey of current policies and proposals for editors. *Medical and Pediatric Oncology, 13*, 109-112.

Glantz, S. A. (1980, January). Biostatistics: How to detect, correct and prevent errors in medical literature. *Circulation, 61*(1), 1-7.

Goldberg, R. J., & Dalen, J. E. (1997, February 24). Enhancing peer review of scientific manuscripts. *Archives of Internal Medicine, 157*(3), 380-382.

Goldberger, J., Waring, C. H., & Tanner, W. F. (1923). Pellagra prevention by diet among institutional inmates. *Public Health Reports, 38*(41), 2361-2368.

Gore, S. M., Jones, G., & Thompson, S. G. (1992, July 11). The *Lancet*'s statistical review process: areas for improvement by authors. *Lancet, 340*, 100-102.

Gore, S. M., Jones, I. G., & Rytter, E. C. (1977, January 8). Misuse of statistical methods: critical assessment of articles in BMJ from January to March 1976. *British Medical Journal, 1*, 85-87.

Hall, J. C. (1982, January). Use of the *t* test in the *British Journal of Surgery*. *British Journal of Surgery, 69*(1), 55-56.

Hayden, G. F. (1983, July 1). Biostatistical trends in *Pediatrics*: implications for the future. *Pediatrics, 72*(1), 84-87.

Haynes, R. B. (1989). Organising and accessing the literature. *Bulletin of the New York Academcy of Medicine, 65*, 673-686.

Hokanson, J. A., Stiernberg, C. M., McCracken, M. S., & Quinn, F. B., Jr. (1987, January). The reporting of statistical techniques in otolaryngology journals. *Archives of Otolaryngology—Head and Neck Surgery, 113*(1), 45-50.

Huxley, P. (1986, December). Statistical errors in papers in the *British Journal of Social Work*. *British Journal of Social Work, 16*(6), 645-648.

International Committee of Medical Journal Editors. (1997, January 15). Uniform requirements for manuscripts submitted to biomedical journals. *Canadian Medical Association Journal, 156*(2), 270-277.

Juzych, M. S., Shin, D. H., Seyedsadr, M., Siegner, S. W., & Juzych, L. A. (1992, September). Statistical techniques in ophthalmic journals. *Archives of Ophthalmology, 110*, 1225-1229.

Kanter, M. H. & Taylor, J. R. (1994, August). Accuracy of statistical methods in *Transfusion*: a review of articles from July/August 1992 through June 1993. *Transfusion, 34*(8), 697-701.

Kemper, K. J. (1991). Pride and prejudice in peer review. *Journal of Clinical Epidemiology, 44*(4/5), 343-345.

Koren, G. & Klein, N. (1991, October 2). Bias against negative studies in newspaper reports of medical research. *JAMA, 266*(13), 1824-1826.

Kupfersmid, J. (1988, August). Improving what is published, a model in search of an editor. *American Psychologist, 43*(8), 635-642.

Lionel, N. D. W. & Herxheimer, A. (1970). Assessing reports of therapeutic trials. *British Medical Journal, 3*(5723), 637-640.

Lock, S. (1985). *A difficult balance. Editorial peer reviewed in medicine.* Philadelphia: ISI Press.

MacArthur, R. D. & Jackson, G. G. (1984, March). An evaluation of the use of statistical methodology in the *Journal of Infectious Diseases*. *Journal of Infectious Diseases, 149*(3), 349-354.

Mahon, W. A., & Daniel, E. E. (1964, February 29). A method for the assessment of reports of drug trials. *Canadian Medical Association Journal, 90*(8), 565-569.

Mauer, A. M. (1985). Editorial review policies for manuscripts. *Medical and Pediatric Oncology, 13*, 113.

McCance, I. (1995, September). Assessment of statistical procedures used in papers in the Australian Veterinary Journal. *Australian Veterinary Journal, 72*(9), 322-328.

Melton, A. W. (1962, December). Editorial. *Journal of Experimental Psychology, 64*(6), 553-557.

Moher, D., Dulberg, C. S., & Wells, G. A. (1994, July 13). Statistical power, sample size, and their reporting in randomized controlled trials. *JAMA, 272*(2), 122-124.

Morris, R. W. (1988, March). A statistical study of papers in the *Journal of Bone and Joint Surgery [Br]* 1984. *Journal of Bone and Joint Surgery, 70-B*(2), 242-246.

Moscati, R., Jehle, D., Ellis, D., Fiorello, A., & Landi, M. (1994). Positive-outcome bias: comparison of emergency medicine and general medicine literatures. *Academic Emergency Medicine, 1*, 267-271.

Mosteller, F., Gilbert, J. P., & McPeek, B. (1980, May). Reporting standards and research strategies for controlled trials. Agenda for the editor. *Controlled Clinical Trials, 1*(1), 37-58.

Mullee, M. A., Lampe, F. C., Pickering, R. M., & Julious, S. A. (1995, April 1). Statisticians should be coauthors. *British Medical Journal, 310*, 869.

Murray, G. D. (1988, July). The task of a statistical referee. *British Journal of Surgery, 75*(7), 664-667.

Murray, G. D. (1991, July). Statistical guidelines for the *British Journal of Surgery*. *British Journal of Surgery, 78*(7), 782-784.

Neuliep, J. W. & Crandall, R. (1990). Editorial bias against replication research. *Journal of Social Behavior and Personality, 5*(4), 85-90.

Neuliep, J. W. & Crandall, R. (1993). Reviewer bias against replication research. *Journal of Social Behavior and Personality, 8*(6), 21-29.

Newcombe, R. G. (1987, September 12). Towards a reduction in publication bias. *British Medical Journal, 295*(6599), 656-659.

O'Fallon, J. R., Dubey, S. D., Salsburg, D. S., Edmonson, J. H., Soffer, A., & Colton, T. (1978, December). Should there be statistical guidelines for medical research papers? *Biometrics, 34*(4), 687-695.

Olson, C. M. (1994, May/June). Publication bias. *Academic Emergency Medicine, 1*(3), 207-208.

Pocock, S. J., Hughes, M. D., & Lee, R. J. (1987, August 13). Statistical problems in the reporting of clinical trials. A survey of three medical journals. *New England Journal of Medicine, 317*(7), 426-432.

Reiffenstein, R. J., Schiltroth, A. J., & Todd, D. M. (1968, December 14). Current standards in reported drug trials. *Canadian Medical Association Journal, 99*, 1134-1135.

Reis, H. T. & Stiller, J. (1992, August). Publication trends in *JPSP*: a three-decade review. *Personality and Social Psychology Bulletin, 18*(4), 465-472.

Relman, A. S. (1982, June 3). A new series on biostatistics. *New England Journal of Medicine, 306*(22), 1360-1361.

Rennie, D. (1978, October 12). Vive la Difference (p<0.05). *New England Journal of Medicine, 299*(1), 828-829.

Rennie, D. & Flanagin, A. (1992, January 15). Publication bias. The triumph of hope over experience. *JAMA, 267*(3), 411-412.

Robinson, R. G. (1985, September 25). Journal matters. *New Zealand Medical Journal, 98*(787), 797.

Rosenfeld, R. M. & Rockette, H. E. (1991, October). Biostatistics in otolaryngology journals. *Archives of Otolaryngology—Head and Neck Surgery, 117*, 1172-1176.

Ross, O. B. J. (1951, January 13). Use of controls in medical research. *JAMA, 145*(2), 72-77.

Schoolman, H. M., Becktel, J. M., Best, W. R., & Johnson, A. F. (1968, March). Statistics in medical research: principles versus practice. *Journal of Laboratory and Clinical Medicine, 71*(3), 357-367.

Schor, S. (1967, February). Statistical reviewing program for medical manuscripts. *American Statistician, 21*(1), 28-31.

Schor, S. & Karten, I. (1966, March 23). Statistical evaluation of medical journal manuscripts. *JAMA, 195*(13), 1123-1128.

Schulman, K., Sulmasy, D. P., & Roney, D. (1994, July 13). Ethics, economics, and the publication policies of major medical journals. *JAMA, 272*(2), 154-156.

Schulz, K. F., Chalmers, I., Grimes, D. A., & Altman, D. G. (1994, July 13). Assessing the quality of randomization from reports of controlled trials published in obstetric and gynecology journals. *JAMA, 272*(2), 125-128.

Schulz, K. F., Chalmers, I., Hayes, R. J., & Altman, D. G. (1995, February 1). Empirical evidence of bias. Dimensions of methodological quality associated with estimates of treatment effects in controlled trials. *JAMA, 273*(5), 408-412.

Schwartz, S. J., Sturr, M., & Goldberg, G. (1996, May). Statistical methods in rehabilitation literature: a survey of recent literature. *Archives of Physical Medicine and Rehabilitation, 77*, 497-500.

Sergesketter, K. & Gilman, D. (1988). *The effect of length of time in kindergarten on reading achievement* (ERIC Document Reproduction Service ED 324-664).

Sheehan, T. J. (1980, April). The medical literature: let the reader beware. *Archives of Internal Medicine, 140*(4), 472-474.

Shott, S. (1985, July 15). Statistics in veterinary research. *Journal of the American Veterinary Association, 187*(2), 138-141.

Shuster, J. J., Binion, J., Moxley, J., Walrath, N., Grassmuck, D., Mahnks, D., & Schmidt, J. (1976, February 2). Statistical review process. Recommended procedures for biomedical research articles. *JAMA, 235*(5), 534-535.

Simes, R. J. (1986, October). Publication bias: the case for an international registry of clinical trials. *Journal of Clinical Oncology, 4*(10), 1529-1541.

Smith, J. (1990, October 3). Journalology—or what editors do. *British Medical Journal, 301*(6754), 756-758.

Smith, R. (1982, October 30). Steaming up windows and refereeing medical papers. *British Medical Journal, 285,* 1259-1261.

Smith-Warner, S. A., Spiegelman, D., Yaun, S. S., Van den Brandt, P. A., & Folsom, A. R. (1998, February 18). Alcohol and breast cancer in women: a pooled analysis of cohort studies. *JAMA, 279*(7), 535-540.

Soffer, A. (1968, November). Alienated readers and frustrated editors. *Diseases of Chest, 54*(5), 3.

Sommer, B. (1987). The file drawer effect and publication rates in menstrual cycle research. *Psychology of Women Quarterly, 11,* 233-242.

Squires, B. P. (1989, November 1). Descriptive studies: what editors want from authors and peer reviewers. *Canadian Medical Association Journal, 141*(9), 879-880.

Squires, B. P. (1990, February 1). Statistics in biomedical manuscripts: what editors want from authors and peer reviewers. *Canadian Medical Association Journal, 142*(3), 213-214.

Sterling, T. D. (1959). Publication decisions and their possible effects on inferences drawn from tests of significance—or vice versa. *Journal of the American Statistical Association, 54,* 30-34.

Stern, J. M. & Simes, R. J. (1997, September 13). Publication bias: evidence of delayed publication in a cohort study of clinical research projects. *British Medical Journal, 315,* 640-645.

Tigertt, W. D. (1989, December). Editor's page. *American Journal of Tropical Medicine and Hygiene, 41*(6), 617-618.

Vaisrub, N. (1985, June 7). Manuscript review from a statistician's perspective. *JAMA, 253*(21), 3145.

Wainapel, S. F. & Kayne, H. L. (1985, May). Statistical methods in rehabilitation literature. *Archives of Physical Medicine and Rehabilitation, 66,* 322-324.

Walster, G. W. & Cleary, A. T. (1970, April). A proposal for a new editorial policy in the social sciences. *American Statistician, 24*(2), 16-19.

Wampold, B. E., Furlong, M. J., & Atkinson, D. R. (1983). Statistical significance, power and effect size: a response to the reexamination of reviewer bias. *Journal of Counseling Psychology, 30*(3), 459-463.

Weech, A. A. (1974, December). Statistics: use and misuse. *Australian Paediatric Journal, 10*(6), 328-333.

Weintraub, M. (1982, July). How to critically assess clinical drug trials. *Drug Therapy, 12,* 131-148.

Weller, A. C. (1990, March 9). Editorial peer review in U.S. medical journals. *JAMA,* *263*(10), 1344-1347.

White, S. J. (1979, October). Statistical errors in papers in the British Journal of Psychiatry. *British Journal of Psychiatry, 135,* 336-342.

Working Group on Recommendations for Reporting of Clinical Trials in the Biomedical Literature. (1994, December 1). Call for comments on a proposal to improve reporting of clinical trials in the biomedical literature. *Annals of Internal Medicine, 121*(11), 894-895.

Zelen, M. (1983, February). Guidelines for publishing papers on cancer clinical trials: responsibilities of editors and authors. *Journal of Clinical Oncology, 1*(2), 164-169.

# Chapter Nine

# Peer Review in an
# Electronic Environment

*With the electronics revolution continuing unabated, further*
*impacts on scientific communication are inevitable.*
(Abelson, 1980)

This chapter reviews the evolution and growth of electronic journals and describes the various emerging models of editorial peer review in an electronic environment. There is some debate about whether the traditional model of editorial peer review should be altered. Medicine, physics, and psychology are taking different approaches to editorial peer review in an electronic environment. Studies to date have focused on attitudes toward electronic publications and citation patterns of electronic journals. Future trends and levels of acceptance of the new models are discussed.

Electronic journals (ejournals), which evolved from electronic newsletters and electronic conferencing networks, first appeared about 20 years ago. Sondak and Schwartz are credited with the concept of a scholarly electronic journal (Lancaster, 1995-a). They envisioned a "paperless journal" consisting of "computer output microform" that provided an opportunity for instantaneous data analysis and transmission with electronic publications (Sondak & Schwartz, 1973). Roistacher in 1978 coined the term "virtual journal" and proposed a computer network that would "combine the referee system of conventional journals with the rapidity of dissemination and unlimited page capacity found in technical information services" (p. 18) (Roistacher, 1978). By 1991, ejournals were prevalent enough for the Association of Research Libraries (ARL) to publish a *Directory of Electronic Journals, Newsletters and Academic Discussion Lists* (http://www.arl.org/scomm/edir/pr97.html). The term ejournal encompasses a range of publication types as indicated by the title of the directory itself. In 1991, the *ARL Directory* listed a total of 636 electronic publications, of which 81.2 percent were electronic conferences and 1.1 percent were peer-reviewed journals. The seventh edition in 1997 listed a total of 9,182 publications, of which 41.5 percent were electronic conferences and 11.4 percent (1,049) were peer-reviewed journals. The trend toward a smaller percentage of electronic conferences and a larger percentage of peer-reviewed ejournals indicates a shift toward the publication of more scholarly material online. In the fields of science, technology, and medicine, Hitchcock and colleagues identified 115 peer-reviewed ejournals in 1995 (Hitchcock, Carr, & Hall, 1996). Only 35 of these did not have a print counterpart.

An example illustrates the difficulty of locating information about electronic peer-reviewed journals on the Internet. A search of the term "electronic peer review" in the search engine AltaVista yielded 215 postings in January 2000. Most postings had some relationship to electronic publishing. Some postings were not relevant, like "English through Web Page Creation" (http://www.xlrn. ucsb.edu/~hshetzer/fall97/web.html) and some relevant-sounding postings had inactive URLs, like the "Electronic Peer Review Project, UIUC, UCSB" (http:// www.xlrn.ucsb.edu/~hshetzer/fall97/uiucucsb.html). On the other hand, some postings were very relevant, like the one that listed 15 peer-reviewed ejournals (http://www.cudenver.edu/~mryder/peer/peer_review.html); however, this posting gave no criteria as to how these particular 15 peer-reviewed ejournals were selected. Of the 15, three URLs were not available, two URLs pointed to the same journal, one URL had been changed, and the 10 remaining had URLs that were available on the first try. These 10 journals all had a statement that peer review was used to evaluate manuscripts prior to electronic publication (Table 9-1).

How has the traditional process of peer review been altered within this complex, rapidly changing and, to some extent, unstable electronic environment? Is there any difference between the traditional, nonelectronic, print-based peer-review process and peer review after the advent of the World Wide Web?

## Models of editorial peer review in an electronic environment

Table 9-1 serves to illustrate that in each case there was no alteration to the standard editorial peer-review process in any of these all-electronic publications. However, some publishers and professional associations are experimenting with a number of different models and approaches to peer review as scholarly publishing shifts from print to electronic. Models currently in use and proposed are reviewed here. Included are examples of traditional peer review, no prepublication peer review, and a combination of pre- and postpublication peer review.

## A model in medicine

The editors of *JAMA* predicted that "these new modes of communicating scientific facts will certainly break some barriers for print publications, allowing for faster, more collaborative, and perhaps even more altruistic communication among scientists" (p. 2374) (Flanagin, Glass, & Lundberg, 1992). Kassirer seconded this view while stating that in the electronic environment the process of

| Online journal title | URL | Peer review description |
|---|---|---|
| First Monday | http://www.firstmonday.dk/idea.html#process | "This initial peer-reviewing process is private." |
| JAIR (Journal of Artificial Research) | http://www.cs.washington.edu/research/ jair/submission-info.html | "Articles sent to JAIR will be reviewed and a decision returned to the authors in approximately 7-9 weeks." |
| Sociological Research Online | http://www.socresonline.org.uk/socresonline/ 1/1/editors.html#top | "We insist on refereeing as a crucial element of quality control in the electronic publishing process." |
| TOSEM (Transactions on Software Engineering and Methodology) | http://www.acm.org/pubs/tosem/Referees.html | "Your report should be sent to the Editor-in-Chief by regular mail or, preferably, by email.... An anonymous copy of your review will be emailed to the authors." |
| PRD (Physical Review D) | http://publish.aps.org/PRD/noted.html | "... the acceptability or otherwise of a paper can normally be expected after no more than two rounds of reviewing ... extended anonymous review cannot be used as a vehicle to develop an otherwise unacceptable paper into an acceptable one." |
| EJTES (Electronic Journal of Terrestrial Ecosystem Software) | http://www.arsusda.gov/ejtes/sc14.html | "Before publication each article will be review [sic] by two or more people familiar with the subject matter." |
| Australian Mammology | http://ikarus.jcu.edu.au/mammal/aminfo.html# Editorial Policy | "Manuscripts submitted as research articles will be sent to two referees for critical comment." |
| Research on Contemplative Life: An Electronic Quarterly (RCL) | http://140.190.128.190/merton/peer.html | "At least three affirmative reviews by qualified reviewers" |
| RhetNet | http://www.missouri.edu/~rhetnet/call.html | "... selecting appropriate work by a more-or-less conventional peer review process" |
| Psycoloquy | http://www.princeton.edu/~harnad/psyc.html | "All contributions are refereed." |

**Table 9-1: Descriptions of peer review practices of ejournals (http://www.cudenver.edu/~mryder/peer/peer_review.html)**

reviewing and editing manuscripts is unchanged, but electronic communication does shorten the time needed to publish (Kassirer, 1992).

As pointed out in Chapter One, editors of some medical journals have insisted that nothing that has received prior publication will be published in their journals. This policy was first articulated by Franz J. Ingelfinger, editor of the *New England Journal of Medicine* from 1967 to 1977. The "Ingelfinger rule" as it has come to be called was revisited and reaffirmed in 1995 by the editor, Jerome P. Kassirer. Kassirer reaffirmed that the *New England Journal of Medicine* will "not consider a manuscript for publication if its substance has already been reported elsewhere." He added that "posting a manuscript, including its figures and tables, on a host computer to which anyone on the Internet can gain access will constitute prior publication" (p. 1709) (Kassirer & Angell, 1995).

The International Committee of Medical Journal Editors recently made a statement on electronic publications, supporting the Ingelfinger rule. "Most journals do not wish to receive papers on work that has already been reported in large part in a published article or is described in a paper that has been submitted or accepted for publication elsewhere, in print or in electronic media" (p. 271) (International Committee of Medical Journal Editors, 1997-a). The International

Committee has also warned publishers to review the health sites to which they link their own pages. A link "from one health or medical Internet site to another may be perceived as a recommendation of the quality of the second site" (p. 1808) (International Committee of Medical Journal Editors, 1997-b).

Huth, past editor of the *Annals of Internal Medicine*, introduced the first medical peer-reviewed ejournal with the *Online Journal of Current Clinical Trials* (*OJCCT*) (Huth, 1992). Huth guaranteed that all accepted manuscripts would undergo the traditional peer review process. *OJCCT* was the first ejournal without a print counterpart to be indexed in *Index Medicus*. The first all electronic nursing journal, the *Online Journal of Knowledge Synthesis for Nursing*, also guaranteed that "manuscripts will be peer reviewed so there is assurance of the same quality one finds in paper journals" (p. 8) (Barnsteiner, 1993).

In a currently successful variation to the *OJCCT* model, in 1997, the Optical Society of America launched an ejournal with no print counterpart, *Optics Express* (http://epubs.osa.org/opticexpress). This ejournal is unique in that there is no subscription fee. The cost of mounting the journal comes from author fees: an initial \$50 for peer review of the manuscript and a minimum of \$300 more once the manuscript is accepted (1998).

In an additional example, the ESPERE project (Electronic Submission and Peer Review project) began in 1996 and has completed the research phase of the project. The ESPERE project is lead jointly by the University of Ulster and a number of association partners. The project focuses on the electronic peer review of papers submitted to associations in the United Kingdom, initially in the biomedical area. For the research phase, a questionnaire was sent to 200 biomedical authors, one focus group was held, and an author's group was established to provide trial material and feedback to the project. Authors are "genuinely enthusiastic" about the idea with 63 percent being interested in submitting material electronically and 70 percent of publishers prepared to accept papers for review by this method. In January 2000, ESPERE listed nine partners: Biochemical Society, British Society for Immunology, Company of Biologists, Oxford University Press, Society for Endocrinology, Society for General Microbiology, The Royal Society, John Wiley & Sons Ltd., and the University of Nottingham (http://www.espere.org/).

## A model in high-energy physics-theory

In 1988, the American Physical Society (APS) formed a Task Force on Electronic Information Systems. The Task Force was charged (among other things) to develop a strategy that would "utilize these new information technologies in order to distribute to the physics community most effectively, information now published in APS journals ... and integrate the plan into the present APS editorial and journal production system" (p. 1119) (American Physical Society, 1991). In 1988, the electronic advantages were viewed as email, electronic manuscript submission, and electronic referee reports' submission. Those writing the report did envision a time when full-text databases with graphics would be readily available. They also saw the potential for electronics to network large amounts of raw data.

In 1991, three years after this task force was formed, Ginsparg at the Los Alamos National Laboratory (LANL) began an electronic preprint archives (eprint) of high-energy physics theory research reports. Physicists were primed to embrace this new format for information exchange from their tradition of sharing preprints with each other (Butler, 1996). The eprints of high-energy physics theory are not peer reviewed prior to electronic publication. Readers can add comments or suggestions to the eprints. According to Ginsparg, authors are "meticulous about updating their articles with changes suggested by colleagues" (p. 78) (1998). By 1994, Ginsparg discussed with physicists a plan to review submissions to the database and suggested that reviewers would not be anonymous. The outcome of the review process would depend on a scoring system that would take such elements as quality of research and presentation into account. The APS encouraged the experimentation with this model of peer review for the eprints (Taubes, 1994). By 1996, there was a plan to use the archives as the formal submission route for further publication considerations in fully peer-reviewed journals (Taubes, 1996).

By 1996, the Los Alamos eprints server had material on 17 disciplines within physics and handled over 13,000 submissions annually (Taubes, 1996). By August 1998, the eprint archives were receiving about 2,000 submissions per month and had material in 33 categories of physics, 31 categories of mathematics, six categories of nonlinear sciences, and one category of computation and language. Most of these disciplines are theoretical and lend themselves to a discussion format. On the eprint archives homepage, Ginsparg indicates that there is a small degree of quality control with the statement: "We reserve the right to reject any inappropriate submissions" (http://xxx.lanl.gov/help/general). The APS has shown support of the LANL's eprints by giving access to it from APS's homepage. APS has a similar eprint archives, which is also not peer reviewed. This file serves as the point from which articles are sent out for review and possible publication in one of APS's print journals (Taubes, 1996).

These examples from physics and medicine illustrate very different models of editorial peer review. The APS permits submission to its journals after the authors have posted the article in the preprint file: "Many authors post papers here that are submitted to non-APS journals for formal publication" (http://publish.aps.org/eprint/docs/faq.html#journals). Authors who submit preprints to the Los Alamos eprint archives are also free to submit their manuscripts to peer reviewed journals for formal publication. APS' eprint homepage cautions: "This eprint system is NOT a publication of the American Physical Society, and therefore no editorial control is extended to the content. That means you use the material here at your own risk ... all the information provided here is exactly what the authors posted. However incoming materials are now screened to ensure they have some relationship to physics" (http://publish.aps.org/eprint/docs/).

Rogers and Hurt have suggested a variation to the physics model in which a paper could be published on the Internet for about six months without peer review (Rogers & Hurt, 1990). During this time period scholars would be given the opportunity to comment on the merits of the publication. After six months, authors would revise the paper and a review board would make the equivalent of an acceptance or rejection decision. LaPorte and colleagues proposed (possibly intending to start a debate on the topic) that readers rate electronic articles and those articles that rated highest would be put in a permanent file (LaPorte et al., 1995). LaPorte and coauthors wrote this in the *British Medical Journal* and therefore the piece stands as opposing the stated policies of the mainstream medical profession.

## A model in psychology

The all-electronic journal, *Psycoloquy,* began publication in 1990. *Psycoloquy* covers such topics in psychology as cognitive sciences, neuroscience, and behavioral biology. Harnad, editor of *Psycoloquy* and a proponent of "open peer review," has attempted "to provide a model for electronic scholarly periodicals" by publishing "refereed peer commentary on those articles, as well as authors' responses to those commentaries" (p.109) (Harnad, 1996). In Harnad's "open peer review" model the manuscripts are reviewed prior to publication. The commentaries are also peer reviewed, providing a form of continuous peer review.

*Psycoloquy* is sponsored on an experimental basis by the American Psychological Association (APA). To date it is not included on the APA's homepage under their list of published journals. A link from APA's homepage includes an interview with *Psycoloquy*'s editor, Harnad, in which he stated, "As part of APA's special science initiative, the Association is funding the experimental transformation of the electronic psychology journal, *Psycoloquy*, into a hypertext format" (http://www.apa.org/psa/sepoct95/interv.html). Harnad admitted that "the best authors are still afraid to submit to *Psycoloquy*" (Taubes, 1996).

## Emerging models

In a model similar to *Psycoloquy*, in 1996, the editors of the *Medical Journal of Australia (MJA)* announced the creation of a Web page for *MJA*. The Internet site would contain "selective research articles that have gone through [the] traditional peer review process and have been accepted by the *MJA*. The manuscripts would be published electronically together with comments provided by the peer reviewers" (p. 9) (Bingham & Coleman, 1996). The articles would be available immediately after acceptance and readers could add any comments. Both the authors and reviewers would be given the opportunity to revise or suggest revisions, respectively, prior to publication. This electronic version of the *MJA (eMJA)* is listed under the ESPERE project discussed above. Articles submitted for publication to *eMJA* are circulated to reviewers on the Internet (using password-protected access) and the review process is conducted as an online discussion between the journal editors, reviewers, authors and a small panel of consultants. When an article is accepted for publication, both the article and the record of its review process are published on the Internet where it undergoes open review. After four weeks of open review, the article is finalized and published in print. In the fall of 1999, six articles had been accepted and five articles were undergoing review. *eMJA* is now in a second phase that will study the electronic journal by comparing a control group of 50 articles undergoing standard review with 50 articles undergoing open electronic peer review. Main outcome measures from this study will include: participation rates of authors, reviewers, and others; performance scores for reviewers; and evaluation questionnaires completed by authors, reviewers, and editors.

A similar model was proposed after the announcement of a new ejournal, *Earth Interactions* (Simpson & Seitter, 1995). Segal and colleagues suggested a manuscript would receive an anonymous, formal review, which would then be published in *Earth Interactions* along with the manuscript. Comments to these anonymous reviews would be elicited from anyone in the field. Then both author and reviewers would have a chance to address the "public" comments (Segal, Turner, & Yarger, 1995). Similarly, Bloom suggested that authors in *Science* could add electronic addenda to their papers as they receive feedback. This would both reduce the number of new submissions and reduce the time that it takes for a new manuscript to work its way through the review process (Bloom, 1996).

Whalley and colleagues stated the ejournal *Glacial Geology and Geomorphology* would use conventional peer review (Whalley, Munroe, Landy, Trew, & MacNeil, 1996). They added that the editors were looking for a "private" Internet channel that would permit double-blind review and copyediting all online prior to permitting subscribers to have access to the article.

These models in a number of disciplines illustrate different approaches to peer review in the electronic scholarly communication environment. With the exception of the Los Alamos eprint files, some form of traditional peer review is present in each model described here. In a number of proposed and working models, the traditional model of peer review has been retained and a postpublication review has been added. The "public" is given the opportunity to comment on the merits, limitations, or inaccuracies of the manuscript. The "public" is defined differently by different models. Some models call for private communication, others for public communication to the authors or reviewers after electronic publication. Once the "post publication review" has been completed, the manuscript would either remain in an electronic format only or would be published in a more permanent, paper format.

## Studies of peer review in an electronic environment

*Question*

Have any studies documented a change in editorial peer review practices in an electronic environment?

*Specific criteria*

~any study that examines a group of electronic journals for procedures for editorial peer review.

*Comparable studies*

The approximately 20 years since the advent of ejournals provide a very limited time period for a formal investigation into any transformation of the editorial peer review process. Few studies have been identified that either directly or indirectly examine editorial peer review in an electronic environment.

Six studies have investigated the attitudes of scholarly communities towards peer review in an electronic environment. A survey of academics in Australia, the United States, and the United Kingdom examined attitudes towards potential contributors to scholarly communications in an electronic environment. Schauder found that among scholars peer review was still highly regarded and that these scholars were not very concerned about its perceived weaknesses (p. 88). Scholars viewed electronic publishing as a means of providing a greater diversity in publication choices for them (Schauder, 1994). Lancaster surveyed administrators of large academic institutions, mostly library directors or academic research administrators. Lancaster found that this group viewed the electronic environment as facilitating the expeditious processing of peer review and thought that "open peer review was desirable." He did find that respondents were not enthusiastic about the ability of postreview discussions to stimulate further research or grant ideas (Lancaster, 1995-b).

Cronin and Overfelt studied the impact that ejournals might have on tenure decisions. The investigators found that although promotion and tenure documents did not address the media of communication, the implication was that electronic publications were not perceived as being peer reviewed (Cronin & Overfelt, 1995). Butler surveyed 511 authors and editorial boards of ten electronic journals in the field of sociology. Butler concluded that authors felt publications in electronic journals were viewed as less important than those in print publications (Butler, 1995). Gomes and Meadows surveyed staff in British universities and asked them about their impressions of print and electronic publications. Only 6.3 percent of the respondents thought the peer review process was more acceptable in an electronic environment, 32 percent thought print more acceptable, and close to one-half of the respondents did not know (Gomes & Meadows, 1998). They identified the major problem for authors: "the perceived lack of prestige of electronic journals" (p. 180).

Wood examined some very practical issues relevant to the implementation of electronic peer review. He surveyed the publishers of seven learned societies to determine their readiness to move to an electronic environment and also surveyed 200 authors and reviewers. The publishers were ambivalent. They were enthusiastic about electronic peer review, but worried about the practical aspects of receiving files electronically: reading the files, "decoding" them, printing them. However, 63 percent of the authors would like to submit manuscripts electronically and 69 percent of the authors and referees were willing to receive manuscripts electronically for reviewing as long as they could print them after receiving them electronically (Wood, 1998).

Harter and Kim compiled a list of 131 peer-reviewed ejournals and identified access problems and related issues. They found that 55 percent of the ejournals could not be accessed on the first try and that most problems originated with the ejournals themselves. One-fifth of the journals had incomplete archives and one-quarter had "probably ceased publication" (p. 454) (Harter & Kim, 1996). Harter has also analyzed citations to ejournals (Harter, 1998). He wanted to determine the degree to which scholars and researchers were aware of or influenced by electronic publications. Using Hitchcock's (1995) list and other sources, Harter identified 39 peer-reviewed journals and studied citations to these journals. Of the 39 journals, 28 had no print counterpart. The most cited ejournal, the *Bulletin of the Mathematical Society* (which has a print counterpart) was cited 1,500 times, *OJCCT* was cited 111 times, and *Psycoloquy* was cited 35 times. Thirteen of the ejournals had been cited between one and five times, and 15 had never been cited. Harter carefully pointed out the limitations of his study: it is too early to do a meaningful study of this nature, ejournals are new, most citation studies are conducted on older journals, and a random sample of journals was not used. This study provides benchmark data for future studies. Harter concluded: "... almost none of the scholarly, peer-reviewed electronic journals in the sample have had a significant impact on formal scholarly communication in their respective fields" (p. 515).

## Conclusions about peer review in an electronic environment

No studies have been conducted yet that have comprehensively investigated models of peer review in an electronic environment. The little data available indicate that peer review of ejournals is similar to the traditional process of editorial peer review. Different approaches to editorial peer review in different disciplines may be due to the very nature of the disciplines. Some fields rely on wide discussion and input, while other fields rely on empirical data.

Scientists who attended a conference in Denmark sponsored by the Organization for Economic Cooperation and Development (OECD) were almost unanimous in thinking that the electronic environment would change not the tradition of peer review for scientific publications. There was wide agreement about the benefits of the Internet for the exchange of scientific information, specifically the speeding up of peer review and the developing use of the Internet for distribution of "preprints" that allow "open peer commentary" (1996). This sentiment has been mirrored by the studies that have examined the attitudes of professionals to the electronic publication.

Harnad's open peer review model of *Psycoloquy* parallels the traditional "letters-to-the-editor" format, a standard addition to scholarly communication after publication. The advantage of an online "letter" or commentary is the decrease in turnaround time. Authors can also respond quickly and a "conversation" may ensue. In print, the discussion usually ends after one round of letters to the editor.

Kuhn (1962) has argued that as paradigms shift the usual pattern is to layer a new practice or theory on the traditional, existing one, trying to get both old and new to work together, until eventually the old model or theory is no longer valid and a new one emerges. Scholarly publication is undergoing such a shift and many of the current practices are trying to bend and twist the traditional model to fit the new emerging electronic environment. Anonymity of reviewers, for example, will need to be reexamined in the electronic environment. But a solid, workable new model that replaces editorial peer review has not yet emerged. The traditional model of peer review is being retained while in some cases a post-publication review has been layered on top of the traditional peer review.

Editors and publishers may find it is increasingly difficult to maintain a traditional peer review model in an electronic environment. Scholars may want to reevaluate their view of the value of electronic publications. New models of editorial peer review have been suggested and some are being experimented with that either alter or eliminate the traditional model of peer review. It is most important that any new model maintain the integrity of science and scholarly communication. These issues need to be discussed and studied by scholars, publishers, academics, learned societies, and information specialists.

An article based on this chapter appeared in the December 2000 issue of *JASIS*.

## References

(1996, June 22). Re-engineering peer review. *The Economist, 239*, 78-79.

(1998, January 24). Publishing, perishing, and peer review. *The Economist, 346*(8052), 77-78.

Abelson, P. H. (1980, July 4). Scientific communication. *Science, 209*, 60-62.

American Physical Society. (1991, April). Report of the APS task force on electronic information systems. *Bulletin of the American Physical Society, 36*(4, Series II), 1119-1151.

Barnsteiner, J. H. (1993, Spring). The *Online Journal of Knowledge Synthesis for Nursing. Reflections, 19*(1), 8.

Bingham, C., & Coleman, R. (1996, January 1). Enter the web: an experiment in electronic research peer review. *Medical Journal of Australia, 164*(1), 8-9.

Bloom, F. E. (1996, January 26). Refining the on-line scholar's tools. *Science, 271*, 429.

Butler, D. (1996, February 29). Peer review "still essential," says researchers. *Nature, 379*, 758.

Butler, H. J. (1995). Where does scholarly electronic publishing get you? *Journal of Scholarly Publishing, 26*(4), 234-246.

Cronin, B. & Overfelt, K. (1995, October). E-journals and tenure. *Journal of the American Society for Information Science, 46*(9), 700-703.

Flanagin, A., Glass, R. M., & Lundberg, G. D. (1992, May 6). Electronic journals and duplicate publication; Is a byte a word? *JAMA, 267*(17), 2374.

Gomes, S. & Meadows, J. (1998, April). Perceptions of electronic journals in British universities. *Journal of Scholarly Publishing, 29*(3), 174-181.

Harnad, S. (1996). Implementing peer review on the net: scientific quality control in scholarly electronic journals. In R. P. Peek & G. B. Newby (Eds.), *Scholarly publishing: the electronic frontier* (pp. 103-118). Cambridge MA: MIT Press.

Harter, S. P. (1998, May 1). Scholarly communication and eletronic journals. *Journal of the American Society for Information Science, 49*(6), 507-516.

Harter, S. P. & Kim, H. J. (1996, September). Accessing electronic journals and other e-publications: an empirical study. *College and Research Libraries, 57*, 440-456.

Hitchcock, S., Carr, L., & Hall, W. (1996, January 15). *A survey of STM online journals 1990-95: the calm before the storm* (http://journals.ecs.soton.ac.uk/survey/survye.html).

Huth, E. J. (1992, April 30). *Online Journal of Current Clinical Trials. New England Journal of Medicine, 326*(18), 1227.

International Committee of Medical Journal Editors. (1988, February). Uniform requirements for manuscripts submitted to biomedical journals. *Annals of Internal Medicine, 108*(2), 258-265.

International Committee of Medical Journal Editors. (1997, Jan. 1-a). Uniform requirements for manuscripts submitted to biomedical journals. *Canadian Medical Association Journal, 156*(2), 270-277.

International Committee of Medical Journal Editors. (1997, June 11-b). Policies for posting biomedical journal information on the Internet. *JAMA, 277*(22), 1808.

Kassirer, J. P. (1992, January 16). Journals in bits and bytes. Electronic medical journals. *New England Journal of Medicine, 326*(3), 195-197.

Kassirer, J. P. & Angell, M. (1995, June 22). The Internet and the *Journal. New England Journal of Medicine, 332*(25), 1709-1710.

Kuhn, T. S. (1962, June 1). Historical structure of scientific discovery. *Science, 136*, 760-764.

Lancaster, F. W. (1995, Spring-a). Attitudes in academia toward feasibility and desirability of networked scholarly publishing. *Library Trends, 43*(4), 741-752.

Lancaster, F. W. (1995, Spring-b). The evolution of electronic publishing. *Library Trends, 43*(4), 518-527.

LaPorte, R. E., Marler, E., Akazawa, S., Sauer, F., Gamboa, C., Shenton, C., Glosser, C., Villasenor, A., & Maclure, M. (1995, May 27). The death of the biomedical journal. *British Medical Journal, 310*(6991), 1387-1390.

Rogers, S. J. & Hurt, C. S. (1990, January). How scholarly publication should work in the 21st century. *College and Research Libraries, 51*(1), 5-6, 7.

Roistacher, R. C. (1978). The virtual journal. *Computer Networks, 2,* 18-24.

Schauder, D. (1994). Electronic publishing of professional articles: attitudes of academics and implications for the scholarly communication industry. *Journal of the American Society for Information Science, 45*(2), 73-100.

Segal, M., Turner, R., & Yarger, D. (1995, November). On scientific electronic journals and conferences. *Bulletin of the American Meteorological Society, 76*(11), 2245-2246.

Simpson, J. & Seitter, K. (1995, May). *Earth Interactions*: a new electronic journal. *Bulletin of the American Meteorological Society, 75*(5), 653.

Sondak, N. E. & Schwartz, R. J. (1973, January). The paperless journal. *Chemical Engineering Progress, 69*(1), 82-83.

Taubes, G. (1994, November 11). Peer review in cyberspace. *Science, 266,* 967.

Taubes, G. (1996, February 9). Electronic preprints point the way to "author empowerment." *Science, 271,* 767-768.

Taubes, G. (1996, July 19). APS starts electronic preprint service. *Science, 273,* 302.

Whalley, B., Munroe, G., Landy, S., Trew, S., & MacNeil, J. (1996, July/August). Publishing a scholarly journal on the World Wide Web. *Aslib Proceedings, 48*(7/8), 171-176.

Wood, D. J. (1998, March). Peer review and the web: the implications of electronic peer review for biomedical authors, referees and learned society publishers. *Journal of Documentation, 54*(2), 173-197.

# Chapter Ten

# Conclusions about
# Studies of Editorial Peer Review

*Even at its best, the peer review process has inherent limitations.*
(Relman, 1990, p. 522)

This monograph has systematically reviewed all identified studies on the editorial peer review process published prior to 1998. This final chapter outlines the strengths and weaknesses of editorial peer review that are intuitive and particularly those that have been identified through investigations. The chapter considers designs of studies of editorial peer review and discusses a number of the more important studies in terms of their weaknesses and strengths. There are suggestions for directions for future study and a discussion about improving peer review using guidelines and recommendations that are based on data from studies. There is an examination of some new working and proposed models of editorial peer review, especially in an electronic environment. The chapter concludes with some thoughts on the value of the editorial peer review process to the integrity of scientific communication and the need to preserve editorial peer review as scientific and scholarly communication becomes more and more electronic.

The studies reviewed have uncovered both the strengths and weaknesses of the editorial peer review process. However, certain strengths are irrefutable and independent of any data derived from any studies. Almost everyone engaged in scientific and scholarly communication today has contributed to or been affected by the editorial peer review process. Through this process scientists and scholars have regularly evaluated the work of their peers. Rarely is there a work that cannot be improved. The primary goal of editorial peer review is to assure that all information contained in a published document has been carefully evaluated and any problems corrected prior to publication.

Simply stated, the underlying strength of editorial peer review is the concerted effort by large numbers of researchers and scholars who work to assure that valid and valuable works are published, and conversely, to assure that invalid or nonvaluable works are not published. Underpinning all editorial peer review is the unquestionable goodwill provided by reviewers. Secondary strengths include its educational value, its support of open communication and prepublication sharing of knowledge, and its foundation of the trust of researchers who know their studies remain confidential until publication.

One of the interesting factors of editorial peer review is that it is not a separate discipline in itself, but a process that encompasses almost every discipline with a journal publication outlet. As has been demonstrated, the literature of peer review is also widely dispersed over numerous disciplines.

There is no doubt that the review process presents some indisputable advantages to the reviewer. Through critiquing the work of their peers, reviewers learn how to conduct a better research project, write more clearly, organize and summarize a research project, state limitations and conclusions of a study more clearly and, of course, how to write a critique.

Authors, knowing their manuscripts will be reviewed, undoubtedly devote more time on manuscript preparation then they might otherwise. Authors are not objective judges of their own work. Reviewers' suggestions for revisions almost always improve manuscripts' presentations and produce a better piece of literature.

A more subtle strength of the culture of peer review is the openness with which editors are willing to examine its functions, evaluate the process itself, and explore ways to improve it. Editors now have a sizeable literature to consult when they make policy decisions or implement procedural details.

It has been shown that "bias" on the part of reviewers is part of any review process and that it is both a strength and weakness. Reviewers rely on the knowledge and experience that they bring to the table each and every time they review a manuscript; they could never be totally "unbiased." To be completely unbiased, reviewers would have no knowledge of or experience with a subject and would then, by definition, not be a "peer." "Bias," of course, can be detrimental and cloud a reviewer's judgment about certain theories, procedures, or approaches. However, any detrimental impact of unwarranted negative reviews has been difficult to document.

Peer review's outstanding weakness is that errors of judgment, either unintentional or intentional, are sometimes made. Asking someone to volunteer personal time evaluating the work of another, possibly a competitor, by its very nature invites a host of potential problems, anywhere from holding a manuscript and not reviewing it to a careless review to fraudulent behavior. Fraudulent behavior on the part of a researcher has not been discussed, primarily because of the limited ability of reviewers or editors to identify fraudulent activities or fabricated data. Fraud is an ever-present problem and deserves a separate and thorough study. *Betrayers of the Truth* by William Broad and Nicholas Wade (Broad & Wade, 1982) and *Stealing into Print: Fraud, Plagiarism, and Misconduct in Scientific Publishing* by Marcel LaFollette (LaFollette, 1992) are interesting analyses of scientific fraud.

Another weakness of editorial peer review is the lack of guidelines and standards. Editors have great flexibility in their implementation of the process in their journals. Peer review has been demonstrated to be different for different disciplines, different journals, and different editorships. There is not one solid, accepted definition of what constitutes "peer review." While a number of definitions of editorial peer review were summarized in Chapter One, except for the broadest definition (evaluation by one's peers), no one definition has been accepted as a standard.

## Design of studies of editorial peer review

Studies of the editorial peer review process *must* be subjected to the same rigorous scientific standards as any other research. If these studies are to offer meaningful guidance to editors or to further the understanding of scientific communication, then the studies themselves must be conducted under the umbrella of good science. This means the studies must begin with a specific question and a methodology carefully designed to answer it. The studies must give sufficient details for replication, provide summary data of findings, and base conclusions and any subsequent recommendation on data analysis.

Bailar and Patterson called for leadership in the area of research into the editorial peer review process:

> *Studies of journal peer review have languished largely, we believe, because there has been little high-level interest, no identifiable source of funds for such work, and no comprehensive public analysis of needs. As a result, the work that we found was often poorly conceived, methodologically weak, based on small samples, undertaken by persons without a major long term commitment to studies of journal peer review or related matters, and irrelevant to policy* (p. 657) (Bailar & Patterson, 1985).

Although the number of publications devoted to editorial peer review has increased since Bailar and Patterson wrote this critique (Figure 1-2), these criticisms remain valid. Many of the studies of editorial peer review can be conducted with minimum expenses incurred by the researcher. Several types of studies make up the majority of studies of editorial peer review:

- surveys of opinions or processes of a group of editors, reviewers, or authors

- studies of processes of one journal (e.g., rejection rates, reviewer selection, quality of reviewers' reports, reviewer agreement, statistical review)

- studies of processes and outcomes of prestigious journals

- studies of processes and outcomes of a group of journals in the same discipline

- studies of disciplinary differences in the editorial peer review process

- studies of reviewer behavior under different conditions (e.g., blind versus nonblind review)

## Weaknesses of studies of editorial peer review

Many studies of editorial peer review show an incongruity: on the one hand, studies of editorial peer review evaluate a process designed to assure that only the best is published and, on the other, the studies themselves are often very flawed. A number of common problems or weaknesses in studies of editorial peer review are noteworthy. Some of the studies themselves were subjected to long debates about methodology, data analysis, or generalizability after their publication in a peer-reviewed journal. The relatively limited number of studies on any one topic, many with a very narrow focus, often make generalizations difficult or problematic. The lack of strict scientific methodology in many studies discussed in this monograph has been pointed out in the appropriate chapters. The vast majority fall short in the discussion of sample size, randomization, control groups, and statistical limits. Within the study of editorial peer review there is a troubling amount of duplicate publication; these have also been identified in the relevant chapters.

In many of the studies, investigators made assumptions about the editorial peer review process that were not tested before conducting a study. For example, investigators have made the following assumptions:

- Editors treat all manuscripts in the same way; for example, often no distinction is made between solicited or unsolicited manuscripts, or between a group of manuscripts (e.g., conferences or symposia) and manuscripts not part of the group.

- The best journals in a discipline are obvious or easy to determine.

- Reviewer agreement is a worthy goal.

- Reviewer bias is detrimental to peer review.

- Reviewers know how to review a manuscript.

- Reviewers verify the statistical analysis in a manuscript.

- Editors agree with and follow reviewers' recommendations.

- There is a correlation between certain variables. For example, studies that looked for a correlation between citation patterns and the use of either blind or nonblind review did not account for additional factors that might influence the number of citations to an article (e.g., differences in subject coverage of journals or differences in length of published articles).

- Results of studies of fabricated manuscripts can be generalized to include bona fide manuscripts.

From commentaries about editorial peer review, it seems clear that even without revalidation findings and conclusions of some of the early studies continue to be assumed valid today:

- A study that identified differences in rejection rates by disciplines (Chapter Two) (Zuckerman & Merton, 1971).

    *While Zuckerman and Merton's study revealed a high rejection rate for journals in the "hard" sciences of chemistry and physics, these investigators gathered data from very few of the most prestigious journals in each discipline. Therefore, generalizations about the rejection rate of a discipline in general might not have been warranted, since rejection rates were based on a skewed, not a representative set of journals in each discipline. A study that compared rejection rates of such samples of journals would be valuable.*

- A study that found a negative impact of the rejection of a manuscript on the careers of investigators (Chapter Two) (Garvey, Lin, & Tomita, 1972).

    *Garvey and colleagues' large study of 12,000 scientists and engineers was conducted long before it was rather common to reject researchers' manuscripts. Later studies have shown that a large percentage of rejected manuscripts are eventually published. Any relationship between rejection and a negative career impact needs to be verified in today's publication environment.*

- A study that found that most editors come from major universities (Chapter Three) (Crane, 1967).

    *Assumptions about important departments within disciplines from 1967 and the degree to which these departments continue to generate the bulk of editorships have to be validated in today's academic climate.*

- A study that found differences in the distinction and achievement of editorial board members in psychology and the social sciences (Chapter Three) (Lindsey, 1976).

    *Lindsey's study assumed the same publication standards for different disciplines. Interdisciplinary studies should always take into account potentially different publication patterns in different disciplines.*

- A study that found a high level of interrater reliability (Chapter Six) (Scarr, 1978).

  > *Data from the Scarr and Weber study were re-evaluated by four researchers (Table 6-2). Reviewer agreement studies have been regularly subjected to re-evaluations, some of those subsequent recalculations agreed with the authors of the original studies and others found different results. The lack of agreement on how to evaluate a reviewer agreement study is an issue. But more important, the lack of a rationale as to why reviewer agreement should be a goal is missing from these studies. The assumption of all reviewer agreement studies is that reviewer agreement should be achieved.*

- A study that found a high rejection rate for previously published, slightly altered, resubmitted manuscripts (Chapter Seven) (Peters & Ceci, 1982).

  > *Peters and Ceci's study is one of the most frequently cited studies in editorial peer review and has remained controversial since its publication. The controversy stems from ethical aspects of a study in which published manuscripts were altered (fabricated) and resubmitted to the publishing journals. The validity of both the study design and the generalizability of the conclusion have been questioned.*

- A study that identified gender biases (Chapter Seven) (Goldberg, 1968).

  > *In the Goldberg study, college students were asked to evaluate fabricated manuscripts. It is not clear that one can conclude that differences in manuscript evaluation in this example were due to real gender biases or due to problems with the general quality of the fabricated manuscripts.*

## Strengths of studies of editorial peer review

Studies that documented weaknesses of editorial peer review proved easier to identify than studies that document its strengths, but this fact should not obscure the strengths of the studies of peer review. The studies of editorial peer review are themselves evolving and providing a growing cadre of study methodologies and baseline data on which to build additional studies. There are studies that have already helped to explain the process, reevaluate some of the assumptions often made, and look for new ways to solve problems.

Many of the studies of editorial peer review are conducted by editors themselves who, by virtue of the fact that they are publishing information about their journals, show a commitment to evaluate the process, to communicate its shortcomings to readers, and to try to improve the peer review system. By discussing processes and revealing inadequacies in their own journals, these editors have engaged in a public self-evaluation. Fully one-quarter (25.9 percent) of the 1,439 citations identified for this study were written as editorials. Table 1-2 includes 139 journals whose editors explained some part of their process in at least one editorial. The remaining editorials included general comments on editorial peer review, studies of editorial peer review, or congresses on this topic. Journal space is always limited, and it is important to note that editors who devote space in their journals to peer review issues usually do so at the expense of pages that could be devoted to studies in the journals' disciplines.

Each chapter in this monograph ends with a number of recommendations based on data from studies discussed in the chapter. While those recommendations are not repeated here, cumulative data from the studies provide a persuasive argument for additional studies that test for benefits of editorial peer review guidelines. Studies have shown that:

- There is a direct relationship between the theoretical and actual reasons for rejecting a manuscript (Chapter Two).

- There is a direct relationship between publication criteria and reasons for rejecting a manuscript (Chapter Three).

- Authors are generally satisfied with the review process and more satisfied after an acceptance than after a rejection (Chapter Four).

- Review improves the quality of a published article (Chapter Five).

- Findings were mixed for whether younger or more experienced reviewers produced a better review (Chapter Five).

- Once they have been selected, reviewers are likely to review for a number of different journals (Chapter Five).

- Reviewers who do not know the authors show a tendency to produce a better review then those reviewers who know the authors (Chapter Seven).

- Reviewers who receive statistical guidelines provide a better statistical review than those who do not (Chapter Eight).

There are other interesting aspects of studies of editorial peer review that emerged:

- Surveys generally have a relatively high response rate: for example, an average of 78 percent of editors responded to surveys in 27 separate studies of editors (Table 3-3), and an average of 62 percent of reviewers responded to surveys in 17 separate studies of reviewers (Table 5-1). One could speculate that editors have more interest in the process and thus responded in greater percentages to surveys than do reviewers.

- A group of studies examined the reviewers' ability to identify the author (Table 7-2). An average of 53 percent of these reviewers did not attempt to identify the authors, and of those who did, 9.2 percent guessed wrong. For the majority of reviewers, the name of the author appears not to be an important factor.

- From the studies of differences among disciplines, one learns that if a broad definition of editorial peer review is used, the process is similar across disciplines. The more specific the definition, the more variations there are among disciplines. For example, anonymous review is more common in medicine, double-blind review more common in the social sciences (Chapter Seven). Practices are changing and there seems to be a move toward anonymous review.

- Perhaps the strongest studies of editorial peer review have come from those that examined statistical analysis in published articles (Chapter Eight). These studies demonstrated a persistence on the part of investigators to understand and solve the problem of statistical shortcomings in published studies.

A couple of examples of exceptionally well-designed studies of editorial peer review include:

- A randomized study found manuscripts with authors' names removed produced a better review than nonblind review (Chapter Seven) (McNutt, Evans, Fletcher, & Fletcher, 1990).

    *Manuscripts selected for review were sent to two reviewers: one reviewer received the manuscript that retained the authors' names and the other received same manuscript with the authors' names and institutional affiliation removed. Reviews were evaluated by editors, who knew neither authors' nor reviewers' names. The straightforward methodology presents an example of a good study designed to evaluate the difference between blind and nonblind review for the same manuscript.*

- A study identified statistical errors of published studies (Chapter Eight) (Ross, 1951).

    *In Ross' study, the presence of a proper control group and subsequent statistical analyses were the only components of published studies that were evaluated. This study set the stage for many similar studies (Table 8-3), each of which has tried to identify statistical shortcomings of published studies. Generally more sophisticated statistical tests are used today than in 1951, but the methodology remains solid. The overall percentage of statistical problems has remained rather constant in the*

> *published medical literature. This study has remained a model*
> *for a number of additional studies.*

## Areas for future research

Some very basic questions about editorial peer review remain unanswered: Is there an exact, measurable benefit of editorial peer review? Do researchers from major institutions and departments publish more because of a bias in their favor or because they produce a better piece of research or scholarly communication? What criteria are used to define a prestigious journal and what is the relationship, if any, between journal prestige and rejection rate? Even if one could intuitively answer the following questions positively, studies of editorial peer review have not yet provided answers to these questions:

- Do editors who adhere to strict editorial policies produce better published articles than editors who do not have strict editorial policies?

- Do authors who receive detailed guidelines write a better manuscript?

- Do authors who receive statistical guidelines do a better job with statistical analysis and reporting?

- Do reviewers who receive detailed guidelines provide a better review?

While studies of rejection rates do not prove that the best is published and the worst eliminated, these studies raise questions about the importance of the rejection rate for any journal. This needs further investigation. The 15 studies that tracked rejected manuscripts found an average of 51.4 percent (Table 2-4) of them were eventually published. These studies did not determine, however, that the best of the initially rejected manuscripts were published or that the remaining 48.6 percent that were never published had been rightly rejected.

## Recommendations for improving studies of editorial peer review

Some specific suggestions for improving the design of studies of editorial peer review are listed below. While many of these suggestions are obvious, they are listed here because so many studies have not followed principles of good research design, particularly as applied to studies of editorial peer review.

- If a study only includes peer-reviewed journals, define a peer-reviewed journal.

- If a study investigates only peer-reviewed articles, determine which articles in a journal are actually peer reviewed.

- If only one journal is studied, explain why the journal was selected.

- If the top, best, or leading journals are studied, define criteria for inclusion, state how investigators determined which journals meet criteria, and do not draw conclusions beyond the top, best, or leading journals.

- If data about a group of journals in one discipline are desired, explain how this group represents the discipline.

- If a study uses a random sample of journals, editors, reviewers, or authors, provide information on the randomization process.

- If a study compares editorial peer review behavior among disciplines, define each discipline and use similar journal selection criteria for each discipline.

- If a study compares publication patterns of different disciplines, account for disciplinary standards or norms.

- If a study surveys a group of authors, editors, or reviewers, describe criteria for inclusion, sampling techniques, results of the pilot study, response rate, methods used to increase the response rate, and percentage of respondents for each question, etc.

- If a study tests for statistically significant differences, design the study to fit the parameters of the statistical test that will be used to analyze the data.

- If a study tests for comparative reviewer behavior, use a control group.

- If the desired outcome of a study is to develop a set of recommendations, design a study to test the value of the proposed recommendations.

Table 3-4 summarizes guidelines to improve peer review that were proposed by a number of investigators. Many of these recommendations, while sounding very logical, are not based on results of any studies that had attempted to address a problem (e.g., the recommendation to have time limits on editorial appointments or the recommendation that editors should disclose the names of the reviewers at the end of the process). It was often not clear exactly which problem some recommendations were trying to solve (e.g., the recommendation that reviewers should be appointed by the editor and one more person or the recommendation that editors should publish more brief reports). Some of the recommendations are contradictory (e.g., the recommendation that editors should have every manuscript reviewed versus the recommendation that editors should reject inappropriate manuscripts without review). Any guidelines or recommendations developed also need to address issues raised by the electronic environment.

## Current model and alternate models of editorial peer review

Garvey and Griffith studied scientific communication in the 1960s and described a model of scientific communication that is still in place today. Their study determined that about two-and-a-half years elapse from initial work on a research project to its final publication (Garvey & Griffith, 1971). The peer review component in this model added about six months to the publication process. This model continues to be assumed to be valid today; however, the electronic environment may see a transformation of the process.

The Peters and Ceci article was followed by 56 commentaries (Peters & Ceci, 1982). Suggestions in these commentaries for altering peer review ranged from abandoning it entirely to any number of changes: adopting a system of databases, initially publishing only abstracts, publishing letters to the editor only, publishing research reports as substitutes for articles, experimenting with new models, and adopting an optional published refereeing. For the latter system, championed by Gordon, the publication of almost anything would be guaranteed with the requirement that referees' comments be published along with the article (Gordon, 1978). These suggestions present their own problems: some are too general to be meaningful, some are already being used and have unknown impact on the editorial peer review process, some would be very expensive, and none would guarantee the publication of the best manuscripts.

In addition to some of the editorial peer review models discussed in Chapter Nine, there are other proposed models for peer review in an electronic environment.

- Publish summaries of rejected manuscripts along with an accompanying list of reasons for rejection. The manuscript would be made available to anyone who wants it (Kellernberger, 1981).

- Continue to review a manuscript in an open format after it has undergone traditional review, as in the example of *Behavioral and Brain Sciences* (Harnad, 1979). In this model printed commentaries follow the published article. A similar model exists for the electronic journal *Psycholoquy* (discussed in Chapter Nine).

- Robin and Burke suggested that the input of experts should be largely technical. Editors should reserve space for articles of great interest but that receive poor review, they should expedite manuscripts of importance to public health, they should publish unreviewed material with a disclaimer, and they should track the quality of published papers (Robin & Burke, 1987).

- Bornstein has promoted what he calls an "adversary model" of editorial peer review (Bornstein, 1990) (Bornstein, 1991). In this model "the role of the reviewer is shifted to that of 'prosecuting attorney' ... [in which] ... authors can no longer expect an objective assessment of their work, but merely a rigorous and thorough critique" (p. 457) (Bornstein, 1991). After review, the author would have the opportunity to counter reviewers' comments, similar to the response of a defense attorney. Bornstein maintains this model would improve the quality of manuscript review because the authors' are expected to make a rebuttal to the reviewers' criticisms. The associate editor would act as judge and make a final decision, after which, if a rejection was recommended, the author could appeal to the editor. Rychlak and Rychlak suggested a modified version of Borstein's model that maintains the legal analogy, but changes it to one in which the review process resembles a civil lawsuit. In this model, the author of a submitted manuscript "carries the burden of proof to establish the strength of the claim (that the manuscript is worthy of publication)" (p. 469) (Rychlak & Rychlak, 1991).

- Neuhauser suggested what he called a "necessary" model for the health sciences in which a print journal would have a "parallel on-line health services research journal with high acceptance rates, short papers, rapid postings, and the opportunity for reader comments made public" (p. 302). Only a few of the online reports would eventually be published in a print journal and then only after full peer review (Neuhauser, 1997).

Each of these models, while slightly different from the current model, still assumes a certain degree of editorial peer review prior to publication. In discussing models of editorial peer review in an electronic environment, Crawford and colleagues pointed out that peer review can function as it always has or it can be transformed to a very different model (Crawford, Hurd, & Weller, 1996). In an electronic environment transmission of manuscripts, data, and information can happen quicker and more efficiently than in a paper-based model. If electronic transmission merely increases efficiency, the traditional peer review model itself would be maintained. Similarly, a form of traditional peer review could be maintained in a nonjournal electronic model if documents and data are not made public until after formal peer review. In this model, following suggestions and commentaries by peers and revisions by authors, e-articles could be made available on a server. After an article is posted on a server, listserve members could add more commentary and authors could respond. This model is very similar to the current letters to the editor sections now found in many journals except that a server would maintain an archive of all commentaries and any subsequent revisions to the article.

The Crawford and colleagues' unvetted electronic model (discussed as a potential option, but not recommended) strays from the traditional model. In the unvetted model, review takes place on the equivalent of electronic listserves on which any material is posted, and a wide range of viewers are able to add comments about posted documents, data, or commentaries. This model presents an open communication, but one with no control over the quality of the manuscript or subsequent communication.

Some of the above suggestions are not that dissimilar from what is done under the current system. Others, while interesting ideas for discussion, would be hard to implement and some would be hard to justify, particularly a model that championed the publication of unvetted articles.

There are examples of working or proposed models that indicate which directions peer review is most likely to take, if there are changes. Examples discussed here include the following: (1) *Lancet's* fast-track, in which the peer review process is completed quickly; (2) the *Cochrane Database of Systematic*

*Reviews,* in which a level of peer review is added to articles on the same topic after publication; and (3) *PubMed Central* from the National Institutes of Health (NIH), in which studies are published quickly and a distinction is clearly made between peer reviewed and nonpeer reviewed material.

### (1) Lancet's fast-track

In 1997, *Lancet* introduced a "fast-track" publication alternative for any authors who present a convincing case to the editors that their work is worthy of a short publication timeline. The editors promise a four-week turnaround for important studies. After authors request the fast-track status, editors decide if the request has merit. The purpose of this process is to prevent "delays in the publication of important data with major public-health messages" and to stop any leak of research findings prior to publication "perhaps in distorted form, via the mass media" (p. 970) (McNamee & Horton, 1997). *Lancet* editors reported that during the first year, 110 authors had requested the fast track, and 18 requests were immediately denied (McNamee, 1998). The remaining 92 manuscripts were scrutinized, and of these only 14 were selected for peer review. Of the fourteen, seven were accepted for the fast-track, two were rejected during review, and five underwent normal review. Of those seven that were accepted for fast-tracked and published, it took a mean of 27.7 days from receipt to publication.

### (2) The Cochrane Database of Systematic Reviews

There are several examples in currently published ejournals and databases of a peer review model that includes a formal post publication review. One such endeavor is the *Cochrane Database of Systematic Reviews*. According to its mission statement, "The Cochrane Collaboration is an international organisation that aims to help people make well-informed decisions about healthcare by preparing, maintaining and promoting the accessibility of systematic reviews of the effects of healthcare interventions" (http://hiru.mcmasterca/cochrane/default.html). Systematic reviews are prepared for publication in the database by a group of collaborating authors who comprise "an international network of individuals and institutions committed to preparing, maintaining, and disseminating systematic reviews of the effects of health care" (p. 1935) (Bero & Rennie, 1995). One important component of these reviews is that "explicitly defined methods" (p. 1935) are used to reduce the effects of bias. Reviews are prepared by these groups, added to the database, and regularly updated.

### (3) PubMed Central

In May 1999, Harold Varmus, then director of the National Institutes of Health (NIH), proposed an electronic publishing project called E-Biomed, shortly thereafter renamed PubMed Central. PubMed Central is envisioned as an electronic database that "would facilitate a community-based effort to establish an electronic publishing site" for new results and ideas. PubMed Central would:

> *accelerate much-needed public discussion of electronic publi-*
> *cation in the United States and abroad and ... provide the finan-*
> *cial, technical, and administrative assistance to initiate such a*
> *program. PubMed Central will archive, organize and distribute*
> *peer-reviewed reports from journals, as well as reports that*
> *have been screened but not formally peer-reviewed. In addition,*
> *it will coordinate efforts to establish servers for similar inter-*
> *national projects.... The non-peer-reviewed reports will also*
> *enter PubMed Central through independent organizations, which*
> *will be responsible for screening this material. Many of the non-*
> *peer-reviewed reports will be 'preprints,' first deposited in*
> *PubMed Central and then subjected to formal peer review by*
> *journal editorial boards. In other cases, reports may never be*
> *submitted to a journal for traditional peer review, yet will be*
> *deposited in PubMed Central because, in the judgment of the*
> *screening organization, they provide valuable data to the*
> *research community. The non-peer-reviewed material ... will*
> *be clearly distinguishable from the peer-reviewed content of*
> *PubMed Central.... In order to facilitate participation in this*
> *initiative, some of the expenses associated with publication may*
> *shift from readers to authors (http://www.nih.gov/welcome/*
> *director/pubmedcentral/pubmedcentral.htm).*

Arnold Relman's initial reaction to E-Biomed (he was editor of the *New England Journal of Medicine* at that time) was to declare this model "a potential threat to the evaluation and orderly dissemination of new clinical studies" (Relman, 1999). Relman went on to state that, "A system that allowed immediate electronic publication of new clinical studies without the usual careful process of peer review and revision would be risky at best and might well fill the clinical data bases with misleading and inadequately evaluated information" (p. 1828-9). As of January 2000, PubMed Central was still in the planning stage. And the delay may well be due to the concerns similar to Relman's. However, the editors of *Academic Medicine* have taken a different approach and support authors' preference for quick publication with minimum review: "Authors are often frustrated now by the editing required by journals, and they look forward to an electronic future when they can post their articles as written, without the need for editing or reformatting" (p. 9) (Caelleigh, 2000). This approach appears to dismiss categorically the need for any quality control. As has been shown, one is rarely an objective judge of one's own work.

These new models offer a glimpse into how peer review may be transformed in an electronic environment with its easy access to speedy communication.

While the Internet makes it possible to post huge amounts of raw data with relative ease, a debate about the merits of making raw data available to researchers and the public alike has been around for years. In 1986, the National Research Council of the National Academy of Sciences, in a report titled, *Sharing Research Data*, recommended that "sharing research data should be a regular practice" (p. 879) (Neuhauser, 1986). In announcing this recommendation, Neuhauser, editor of *Medical Care,* suggested editors should encourage authors to make data available and he assumed that submitters would make data available to reviewers, if requested. Posting or archiving raw data has been proposed as a means of discouraging fraud (Schuerman, 1989). However, Relman suggested that this practice would be counterproductive, a waste of time, and still would not discourage fraud (Relman, 1990). Few readers would take the time to evaluate raw data or recalculate formulas. Obviously publication on the Internet could not prevent the posting of fraudulent data and the ease of posting information might actually encourage it. The publication of nonreviewed data or information is very troublesome, particularly in medicine, where charlatans are an ever-present threat and the Web is an easy conduit for posting any health-related information.

## Peer review is essential

As the example of *Lancet*'s fast-track model illustrates, an author is rarely objective about his or her own work. In the first year of *Lancet's* project, of the 110 manuscripts considered by authors to be of immediate public health importance, only seven (6.7 percent) were so considered by editors and reviewers. It is for this simple reason that editorial peer review is essential, particularly in an electronic environment. Even if editorial peer review is eventually transformed to a shape somewhat different than the model used today, any new model must protect the integrity of science and scholarly communication.

Electronic publication and editorial peer review are clearly going through a period of transition. In *The Structure of Scientific Revolutions*, Thomas Kuhn discusses scientists' reaction to a crisis (Kuhn, 1970). Kuhn suggested that "crises are a necessary precondition for the emergence of novel theories" (p. 77). The current changes in scholarly and scientific communication precipitated by the electronic environment could certainly be considered a crisis. So, we may be on the cusp of a crisis and ready for a novel theory to emerge. According to Kuhn, the usual result of a scientific crisis is the rejection of a previously accepted theory and the replacement of that theory with a new one. In this chapter and in Chapter Nine there are several examples that illustrate that as peer-reviewed material is posted on the Web, a second, more broadly based review takes place, for example, the *Cochrane Database of Systematic Reviews* and *Psycholoquy.* However, these are not novel theories as such. There are those who suggest that the traditional role of editorial peer review in the publication process be eliminated. If eliminated, there would be no system of quality control and this important point should not be lost on those who want to replace peer review and support an open, nonvetted system of communication.

Relman concluded a discussion of editorial peer review with these thoughts: "Despite its limitations, we need it. It is all we have, and it is hard to imagine how we could get along without it" (p. 522) (Relman, 1990). In the end, editorial peer review should not be changed without some proof that a new communication process would result in publishing better science and scholarship.

Some type of review by someone other than the author is essential. Like a democratic government, scientific publication must maintain a built-in system of checks and balances. Both accidental and deliberate mistakes do happen, but that is not reason to scrap editorial peer review or to underestimate the tremendous importance of editorial peer review to the communication of scholarly and scientific information. Researchers, of course, present their design, results, and conclusions in the best possible light. Reviewers see limitations, skips of logic, alternate meanings of data, or limitations of conclusions not seen by authors. Most important, these opinions of reviewers are just that, and it is the editor who then adjudicates between the author's manuscript and the reviewers' opinions and makes a decision, thereby establishing a system of checks and balances. Another round of checks and balances follows publication through letters to the editor and additional studies build on published works. Like a democracy, editorial peer review is messy and does not always work as it should, but it is essential to the integrity of scientific and scholarly communication.

## References

Bailar, J. C. & Patterson, K. (1985, March 7). Journal peer review. The need for a research agenda. *New England Journal of Medicine, 312*(10), 654-657.

Bero, L. A. & Rennie, D. (1995, December 27). The Cochrane Collaboration, preparing, maintaining, and disseminating systematic reviews of the effect of health care. *JAMA, 274*(24).

Bornstein, R. F. (1990, May). Manuscript review in psychology: an alternative model. *American Psychologist, 45*(5), 672-673.

Bornstein, R. F. (1991, Autumn). Manuscript review in psychology: psychometrics, demand characteristics, and an alternative model. *Journal of Mind and Behavior, 12*(4), 429-467.

Broad, W. J. & Wade, N. (1982). *Betrayers of the truth*. New York: Simon and Schuster.

Caelleigh, A. S. (2000, January). PubMed Central and the new publishing landscape: shifts and tradeoffs. *Academic Medicine, 75*(1), 4-10.

Crane, D. (1967, November). The gatekeepers of science: Some factors affecting the selection of articles for scientific journals. *American Sociologist, 2*(4), 195-201.

Crawford, S., Hurd, J. M., & Weller, A. C. (1996). *From print to electronic: the transformation of scientific communication*. Medford, N.J.: Information Today, Inc.

Garvey, W. D., & Griffith, B. C. (1971, April). Scientific communication: its role in the conduct of research and creation of knowledge. *American Psychologist, 26*(4), 349-362.

Garvey, W. D., Lin, N., & Tomita, K. (1972, October). Research studies in patterns of scientific communication: III. Information-exchange processes associated with the production of journal articles. *Information Storage and Retrieval, 8*(5), 207-211.

Goldberg, P. (1968, April). Are women prejudiced against women? *Trans-Action, 5*(5), 28-30.

Gordon, R. A. (1978, October). Optional published refereeing. *Physics Today, 31*(10), 81.

Harnad, S. (1979, September). Creative disagreement, open peer commentary adds a vital dimension to review procedures. *The Sciences, 19*(7), 18-20.

Kellernberger, E. (1981). Alternatives to peer review. *Trends in Biochemical Sciences, 6*, 11.

Kuhn, T. S. (1970). *The Structure of Scientific Revolutions* (2nd ed.) (Vol. 2). Chicago: The University of Chicago Press.

LaFollette, M. C. (1992). *Stealing into print: fraud, plagiarism, and misconduct in scientific publishing.* Berkeley: University of California Press.

Lindsey, D. (1976, November). Distinction, achievement, and editorial board membership. *American Psychologist, 31*(11), 799-804.

McNamee, D. (1998, February 21). Fast-track publication at the *Lancet. Lancet, 351*(9102), 542.

McNamee, D., & Horton, R. (1997, April 5). Fast-track to publication in the *Lancet. Lancet, 349*(9057), 970.

McNutt, R. A., Evans, A. T., Fletcher, R. H., & Fletcher, S. W. (1990, March 9). The effects of blinding on the quality of review. *JAMA, 263*(10), 1371-1376.

Neuhauser, D. (1986, October). Sharing research data. *Medical Care, 24*(10), 879-890.

Neuhauser, D. (1997, April). Peer review and the research commons. *Medical Care, 35*(4), 301-302.

Peters, D. P. & Ceci, S. J. (1982, June). Peer review practices of psychological journals: the fate of published articles, submitted again. *Behavioral and Brain Sciences, 5*(2), 187-255.

Relman, A. S. (1990, November). Peer review in scientific journals—what good is it? *West Journal of Medicine, 153*, 520-522.

Relman, A. S. (1999, June 10). The NIH "E-Biomed" proposal—a potential threat to the evaluation and orderly dissemination of new clinical studies. *New England Journal of Medicine, 340*(23), 1828-1829.

Robin, E. D. & Burke, C. M. (1987, February). Peer review in medical journals. *Chest, 91*(2), 252-255.

Ross, O. B. J. (1951, January 13). Use of controls in medical research. *JAMA, 145*(2), 72-77.

Rychlak, R. J. & Rychlak, J. F. (1991, Autumn). Problems of burdens and bias: a response to Bornstein. *Journal of Mind and Behavior, 12*(4), 469-477.

Scarr, S. (1978, October). The reliability of reviews for the American Psychologist. *American Psychologist, 33*(10), 935.

Schuerman, J. R. (1989, March). Editorial. *Social Service Review, 63*(1), 1-4.

Zuckerman, H. & Merton, R. K. (1971, January). Patterns of evaluation in science: institutionalisation, structure and functions of the referee system. *Minerva, 9*(1), 66-100.

# About the Author

Ann C. Weller is Associate Professor and Deputy Director at the Library of the Health Sciences, the University of Illinois at Chicago. She previously was head of the Reference Department at the Library of the American Medical Association. Weller conducts research on editorial peer review and has presented results of research at the first two International Congresses on Peer Review in Biomedical Publications. She has investigated and written on users' access to information, and changes in faculty information-seeking behavior in an electronic environment. Results of her research have been published in the *Journal of the American Medical Association*, the *Bulletin of the Medical Library Association*, *College and Research Libraries*, and the *IFLA Journal*. She has published in a *JASIS* Perspectives on *The Transformation of Scientific Communication: Behavioral and Organizational Determinants*. With Susan Y. Crawford and Julie M. Hurd, she has coauthored a monograph on scientific communication: *From Print to Electronic: The Transformation of Scientific Communication*. Weller has spoken at American Society for Information Science and Technology (ASIST) meetings on editorial peer review in an electronic environment, scientific data integrity, and scientific communication and the human genome project. Her committee work with the Medical Library Association (MLA) has focused on research and scholarship. Weller was a member of the Research Task Force that developed MLA's Research Policy Statement: *Using Scientific Evidence to Improve Information Practice*. She has served on the editorial board of the *Bulletin of the Medical Library Association*, served as chair of the Grants and Scholarship Committee, and served on MLA's Credentialing Committee. Weller received a B.A. in chemistry; her M.A. in library science is from the University of Chicago.

# Index

## A

*Abnormal Psychology, Journal of,*
61, 194, 221
abstracts, 44, 48, 49, 198
academic affiliations
  editorial appointments, 85–92
  editorial board appointments, 84
  effect on citations, 221
  impact on publications, 44
  publication criteria, 95
  and review results, 158–159
  study of reviewer bias, 225
*Academic Emergency Medicine,* 269
*Academic Medicine,* 320
*Academy of Management Journal,*
170
acceptances, 92–96, 132, 191–192,
194, 235. *See also* rejections
accountability, 136–141, 235
achievement, measures of, 88–89
acknowledgments, 126
administrative roles, and coauthorship, 125–127
adversary models, 317
*Aerosol Science, Journal of,* 233
ages, 84, 313
AltaVista, 296
AMA. *See* American Medical
Association
*American Anthropology,* 61
American Association of Counseling
and Development, 58
American Association of Higher
Education (AAHE), 130–131
*American Association of Nurse
Anesthetists, Journal of the,*
170

American Chemical Society (ACS),
137–*138*
American Council of Learned
Societies, 119–120
*American Economic Review*
  author recognition, 216–217
  biases, 226, 232
  blind review, 211, 222–223
  editorial appointments, 85
*American Heart Journal,* 49
*American Historical Review,* 67, 196
*American Journal of Medicine,* 4, 49,
183
*American Medical Association,
Journal of the (JAMA)*
  authorship guidelines, 137–140
  categories of biases, 208
  editorial board appointments, 84
  electronic environments, 296–298
  files on reviewers, 153–154
  peer review, 4
  and the press, 45
  publication bias, 270
  rejection letters, 47–48
  rejection rates, 61
  reports on editorial peer review, 12
  statistical review, 253, 255, 258,
260, 279–280
American Medical Association
(AMA), 7, 12
American National Standards
Institute (ANSI), 14
American Physical Society, 100–101
*American Physical Society, Bulletin
of the,* 64
*American Political Science Review,
The,* 25
American Professors of Higher
Education (APHE), 130–131

American Psychological Association
    (APA)
  anonymous blind review, 15
  authorship guidelines, 137–*138*
  burden of reviews, 151
  coauthorship patterns, 122
  editorial appointments, 83
  investigation of bias, 98–99
  journal selection, 58
  resubmission policies, 63
  study of gender bias, 226
  survey of authors, 134
*American Psychologist,* 7, 189, 215
American Society of Agronomy, 48,
    136
*American Sociological Review*
  blind review policies, 218
  citation patterns, 128–129
  editorial appointments, 85
  rejections, 43–44, 60
  reviewer's comments, 169
American Sociological Society, 44
*American Sociologist,* 46, 207
American Statistical Association, 134
*American Veterinary Association,*
    *Journal of the,* 261
analysis of variance, 265
*Analytical Chemistry,* 53
*Anesthesia and Analgesia,* 260
*Anesthesiology,* 4, 260
anonymous reviews
  arguments, 235–236
  benefits of, 313, 314
  and blind review, *212*
  definition, 2
  editorial comments, 25
  policies, *18–24,* 209–214
  use of, 211
*Anthropology, American,* 61
APA. *See* American Psychological
    Association
*APA Monitor,* 226
appeals processes, 63, 65, 67,
    100–101

*Applied Behavior Analysis, Journal*
    *of,* 225
*Applied Psychology, Journal of,* 47,
    61, 170, 218
appropriateness, 161
arbitrariness, 97
arbitration, 82
*ARL Directory,* 295
*Arthritis and Rheumatism,* 260
*Association for Computing*
    *Machines, The Journal of*
    *the,* 152
associations
  annual conferences, 7–8
  appointment of editors, 83
*Astrophysical Journal,* 99, 196
authors
  advantages of review, 308
  assumption of contribution,
      125–129
  citation patterns, 128–129
  coauthorship, 120–129, *121–122*
  department heads as, 127–128
  editors and, 133
  experience of rejection, 43, 48,
      62–67
  first-place, 126
  future submissions, 67
  "gift authorships," 127–128
  informing of, 46–47
  journal selection by, 129–132,
      *131*
  networks, 99–100
  persistence, 70–71
  protection of, 97
  recognition of, 209, 211,
      214–223, *216*
  recommendation of reviewers,
      152
  reputation, 95
  responsibilities of, 139
  on responsibility of editors, 81
  retaliation by, 210
  reviewer biases, 218–223

self-citations, 217
statistical guidelines, 274–277, 276
survey of, 59
value of peer review process, 133–136, *135*
authorship
    coauthorship, 120–129, *121–122*
    conclusions about, 141–143
    definition of, 136–137
    "gift authorships," 127–128
    legitimacy of, 136
    limitations of studies on, 141
    principles and definition, *138*
    principles of, 137–139
    problems of, 119–149

**B**

*Behavioral and Brain Sciences,* 220, 235, 317
behavioral science journals, 54
*Betrayers of the Truth,* 308
biases
    author-editor networks, 99–100
    definition of, 97
    editorial, 96–100, 111
    ethnicity, 225–232
    gender, 225–232, *228,* 312
    ideological framework, 223–224
    length of manuscripts, 99
    perception by authors, 134
    and randomization, 278
    reviewer, 161, 170, 207–246, 234–238, 238–239, 308
    reviewers selection, 197
    studies of, 236–237
    types of, 208
biochemistry journals, 68, 132
*Biological Abstracts,* 11
biology journals, 155

biomedical journals, 122
*Biometrics,* 162
blind reviews
    and anonymity, *212*
    author recognition, 209, *216*
    and authorship problems, 142
    benefits of, 313
    coauthorship patterns, 124–125
    definition, 2
    editorial comments, 25
    and favoritism, 44
    gender differences, *231*
    history of, 207
    journal policies, *18–24*
    physics journals, 100–101
    policies on, 209–214
    quality of, *219*
    time spent, 157
    trends in, 213–214
    use of, 211
*BMJ. See British Medical Journal*
board meeting attendance, 82
*Bone and Joint Surgery, Journal of,* 261
*Boston Medical and Surgical Journal. See New England Journal of Medicine*
*British Medical Journal (BMJ)*
    authorship guidelines, 141
    co-author contributions, 125
    electronic articles, 300
    peer review, 3
    rejection letters, 48
    reviewer guidelines, 161
    reviewer workload, 155
    signed reviews, 233
    statistical review, 247, 253–255, 261, 277–279
    study of blinding, 223
business administration journals, 54
business journals, 49
*Business Periodical Index,* 58

# C

*Canadian Medical Association Journal*
appeals procedure, 64
rejection rates, 61–62
reviewer consensus, 195
reviewer guidelines, 161, 165
statistical review, 247–248, 258, 279
cancer clinical trials, 281
*Cardiology, American Journal of,* 5, 49
*Cardiovascular Research,* 234, 236
career paths, 43
case histories, 51
central tendencies, 265
chance, 191–192, 194
checklists, statistical analysis, 273–277
*Chemical Abstracts,* 11
chemistry journals, 58, 84, 95, 122–123, 123
*Chest,* 63
chi square tests, 248, 255, 259
*Circulation,* 81–82, 259
*Circulation Research,* 5, 259
citations
author affiliations, 222
author-editor networks, 99
author recognition and, 214
benefits of peer review, 136
co-authored articles, 128–129
editorial board members, 88–89
electronic journals, 303
initially-rejected manuscripts, 48
patterns for editors, 91
productivity and, 88
self-citations, 217
clarity, and acceptance, 92
*Clinical Anesthesia, Journal of,* 136
clinical applicability, 51
*Clinical Care Nurse,* 161

*Clinical Epidemiology, Journal of,* 272
*Clinical Investigation, Journal of,* 4, 67, 158, 194
*Clinical Oncology, Journal of,* 122, 281
*Clinical Pharmacology & Therapeutics,* 91, 157, 281
clinical trials, 275, 276, 281, 282
coauthorship, 120–129
*Cochrane Database of Systematic Reviews,* 318–319, 321
codes of practice, 107–108
collaboration, and quality, 276
*College & Research Libraries,* 51, 53
committee members, and coauthorship, 126
communication-of-rejection process, 46–49
*Communication Quarterly,* 27
communications, model in the sciences, 316–322
*Community Psychology, American Journal of,* 195, 232
competition, 26, 169
complaints, 81, 98. *See also* appeals processes
conciliators, 169
conclusions, unwarranted, 51, 53
conferences
new findings, 45
proceedings, 7–8
publication of abstracts, 44–45
publication of manuscripts, 44
sponsored meetings, 49
confidence intervals, 276
confidentiality, 81, 161. *See also* anonymous reviews; blind reviews; secrecy
conflicts of interest, 81, 99, 154, 161, 275
*Consulting and Clinical Psychology, Journal of,* 223–224
contingency tables, 265

contributor listings, 140–141
control groups, 220–221, 258
controversial topics, 27, 93, 96, 97.
    *See also* innovative ideas
conversions, biases, 208
corrections and retractions, 81
costs, 27, 151, *156*
Council of Biology Editors, 12, 164
Counseling and Development,
    American Association of, 58
credibility, coauthorship, 124–125
critic reviewer, 169
*Current Contents: Social & Behavioral
    Sciences,* 48, 67, 130


**D**


data collection, 125–127
databases
    additional keywords, 70
    full text, 299
    review of, 8–10
    of reviewers, 153–154
    summary of search results, *9*
decorative editorial boards, 84
Delphi method, 162
dental journals, 58
department heads, 126, 127
*Dermatology, Archives of,* 5
descriptions
    correctable problems, 262
    inadequate, 255, 260
    statistics use, 276
design, and coauthorship, 125–127
*Developmental Psychology,* 215
*Diabetes Care,* 64
*Difficult Balance: Editorial Peer
    Review in Medicine, A,* 278
*Directory Electronic Journals,
    Newsletters and Academic
    Discussion Lists,* 295

*Directory of Publishing
    Opportunities in Journals
    and Periodicals,* 58
disciplines
    author recognition, *216*
    author value of peer review
        process, *135*
    blind review and anonymity, *212*
    coauthorship patterns, 124
    definition of, 59
    editorial appointments, *86–87*
    guidelines for reviewers, *163–164*
    peer review process, *102–103*
    publication biases, *270*
    publication criteria, *94*
    publication standards, 111
    rejection rates, 54–60, *56–57*, 311
    replication studies, *269*
    reviewer consensus, 196–197, 200
    reviewer workload, *156*
    statistical problems, *256–257*
    value of reviews, *168*
*Disease in Childhood, Archives of,*
    166–167
*Diseases of Children, American
    Journal of,* 3–4, 281
dispersion statistics, 265
distinction, measures of, 88
documentation
    missing, 50
    publication criteria, 95
*Documentation, Journal of,* 68
double-blind review, 314
drug companies, 7
*Drug Therapy,* 281
drug trials, 281
duplicate publications, 51


**E**


E-Biomed, 319

e-mail, 298
*Earth & Life Sciences Editing,* 224
*Earth Interactions,* 301
*Economic Abstracts, Journal of,* 58
economic journals
    blind review policies, 218
    coauthorship patterns, 123
    editorial appointments, 85
    quality of reviews, 160
    rejections, 49, 54, 60–61
    turnaround time, 155
*Economic Review, American,*
        216–217
editor-author networks, 99–100
editorial bias, studies of, 98–100
editorial boards
    appointment of, 81, 83–84
    function of, 79–118
    prestige of, 111
    professional productivity, 88
    professional status, *86–87*
    prominence of, 91–92
    role of, 81–82
editorial peer review
    areas for future research, 315
    conclusions, 307–324
    cost of, 27
    definition, 15–16
    by disciplines, *102–103*
    editors description of process,
        *18–24*
    electronic environments, 295–304
    evolution of the process, 3–8
    improving studies, 315–316
    lack of standardization, 7
    literature on, 8–10
    models of, 316–321
    necessity of, 321–322
    references by decade, *10*
    strengths of studies, 312–315
    studies of process, 101–105
    studies on, 10–13
    today's process, 1–3
    value to authors, 133–136

weaknesses of studies, 310–312
editorials, lack of review, 7
editors
    appointment of, 83
    appointment of editorial boards,
        81
    biases, 96–100, 97
    blind anonymous review policies,
        209–214
    citation patterns, 91
    control of communication, 26
    decision-making processes, 49–54
    guests, 236
    guidelines for statistical analysis,
        274–277
    networks, 99–100
    override of review, 97
    part-time, 79–80
    peer review process, 16–27,
        *18–24*
    prestige and, 111
    problems encountered by, 81
    professional productivity, 88
    professional status, *86–87*
    prominence, 91–92
    publication criteria, 92–96
    rejection reasons, *50*
    and reviewer consensus, 191
    roles of, 79–118, 80–81, 111
    statistical guidelines, 275–276
    statistical reviewers, 249–251
education, statistical, 274–277,
        280–281, 284
education journals, 83–84, 93, 171
ejournals
    peer review, *297*
    postpublication review, 301
    studies of peer review, 301–303
electronic environments
    emerging models, 300–301
    model in medicine, 296–298
    model in psychology, 300
    model in the high-energy physics-
        theory, 298–300

peer review, 295–306
peer review models, 317–318
publication, 3
*Emergency Medicine, Annals of,* 252
errors
    statistical, 257–262
    type I, 259
    type II, 259
    types of, 283
ESPERE, 298
ethical standards, 82, 97–98,
        108–109, 120–121
ethics committees, 275
ethnicity biases, 225–232
European Association of Science
        Editors, 14
*Exercise and Sports Review,*
        *Research Quarterly for,* 197
*Experimental Psychology, Journal of,*
        267
expertise
    and citation rates, 91
    of reviewers, 154
exposure, journal selection, 130

**F**

fabricated documents. *See* manu-
        scripts, fabricated
*Family Relations,* 153
favoritism, 44
Finn's *r,* 185, 190
Flesch-Kincaid index, 53, 170
formats, of manuscripts, 97
fraud, 120–121
funding, and coauthorship, 126–127,
        127–128, 142

**G**

gender
    biases, 225–232, *228,* 239, 312
    editorial appointments, 83
    editorial board appointments, 84
    of reviewers, 228–230
*General Internal Medicine, Journal*
        *of,* 158, 234
generalizability, 95
*Glacial Geology and*
        *Geomorphology,* 301
graduate students, 162, 164
guarantor listings, 141
guest editors, 236
guidelines
    benefits of, 313
    *BMJ,* 278
    editorial, 105–110
    publication of, 25, 81, 276
    *Requirements for Manuscripts*
        *Submitted to Biomedical*
        *Journals,* 13–14
    reviewer agreement, 197–199
    reviewer scoring, 192
    for reviewers, 160–166, *163–164,*
        234–238
    statistical analysis, 273–277
    statistical review, 281–283
    suggested, *106–107*
Gunning's Fog Index, 53, 170

**H**

*Health and Social Behavior, Journal*
        *of,* 190, 196
Higher Education, American
        Association of (AAHE),
        130–131
*Hospital Pharmacy, American*
        *Journal of,* 154, 161

*Human Organization,* 232
humanities journals, 5


# I

ICMJE. *See* International Committee
    of Medical Journal Editors
ideas, and coauthorship, 125–127
ideologies, biases against, 223–224
illustrations, 214
impartiality, 44
inadequate theories, 95
*Index Medicus*
    editorials, 26
    index of coauthors, 122
    information about peer review, 7
    journal selection, 58
    medical journals and review
        reports, 154
    peer review information, 11
    peer-reviewed journals, 105
indications, and Internet, 321
*Infectious Diseases, Journal of,* 260
information systems journals, 123
Ingelfinger rule, 44–45
innovative ideas. *See also* controver-
    sial topics
    author caution about publication,
        119
    electronic media, 321
    at meetings, 45
    publication criteria, 95
    response of reviewers, 62
    suppression by peer review, 14
insignificant results, 95
Institute of Physics, 58
institutional review boards, 48, 275
institutions. *See* academic affiliations
instructions to authors
    and acceptance, 92
    editorial comments, 25

editors response, 96
guidelines, 105–110, 136–141
inattention to, 51
publication of, 17, 142–143
and rejection, 53
self-citations, 217
integrity, editors, 81
intellectual honesty, 120–121
intellectual theft, 210
interclass correlation coefficients ($r_1$)
    (ICC), 185, 188, 190, 192
interests, publication criteria, 95
internal medicine, 281
*Internal Medicine, Annals of*
    benefit of review, 171
    clinical trials, 282
    rating of reviews, 170
    reviewer consensus, 194
    statistical review, 281
    study of clinical relevance, 183
    submission policies, 45, 46
*Internal Medicine, Archives of,* 4,
    281
International Committee of Medical
    Journal Editors (ICMJE)
    authorship principles, 137–*138,*
        140
    blind review, 236
    electronic publications, 297–298
    history, 13–15
    recommendations, 110
    reviewer guidelines, 166
    statistical review guidelines, 281,
        *282*
    support for structured abstracts,
        198
international journals, 90, 92
Internet, 296, 321

# J

*JAMA. See American Medical Association, Journal of the*
John Bates Clark Medal, 62
journals. *See also* specific journals
    author's selection of, 129–132, *131*
    editorial boards, 81
    ejournals, 295–304
    humanities, 5
    paperless, 295
    peer review definition, 15–16
    statistical review, *252*, 277–281

# K

kappa statistic (K), 185, 189, 191
Kendall's coefficient, 185, 192
knowledge, publication criteria, 93

# L

*Laboratory and Clinical Medicine, Journal of,* 233
*Lancet*
    authorship guidelines, 141
    coauthorship patterns, 122
    fast-track model, 318–319, 321
    level of statistical review, 280
    manuscript selection, 6
    part-time editors, 79
    publication bias, 270
    publication decisions, 11
    statistical review, 255, 261
language journals, 60–61
length, of manuscripts, 99–100

letters to the editor, 7, 133, 303–304
*Library Literature,* 58
library science journals, 157, 214
life tables, 265
linear regression, 265
literature journals, 60–61
literature review, *10,* 53
logical flow, 95
Los Alamos National Laboratory (LANL), 299

# M

management journals, 60–61
manuscripts
    approved studies, 270–272
    author's selection of journals, 129–132
    benefits of review, 134–136, 170–171
    coauthorship, 128
    editorial board review, 81
    electronic submission, 298–299
    fabricated, 223–224, 237, 272–273
    final disposition, 311
    formatting, 97
    length of, 99
    prediction of outcome, 194
    preparation of, 47–48, 125–127
    publication criteria, 92–96
    reasons for rejection, 49–54
    rejected, 43–78
    review process, *2,* 100–101
    review time, 155
    reviewer consensus, *182*
    solicitation of, 79–80, 81
    solicited, 7, 105
    statistical review, 251–254, *252*
*Mathematical Society, Bulletin of,* 303

*Medical and Pediatric Oncology,* 250
*Medical Care,* 321
*Medical Journal of Australia (MJA),*
    300
medical journals
    anonymous review, 314
    articles without statistics, *266*
    blind review, 214
    coauthorship patterns, *122, 124*
    concern with process, 26
    editorial appointments, 90–92
    fate of rejected manuscripts, 68
    and the news media, 44–46
    publication bias, 268–269, 269
    reviewer consensus, *182*
    statistical review, *250*
    statistical tests, *264*
    studies of, 59
meetings. *See* conferences
methodological problems
    publication criteria, 96
    and rejection, 53, 54
    studies of bias, 224
methodology, biases, 208
multicenter collaborations, 126, 137
multiple submissions, 53


**N**


National Clearinghouse for Mental
    Health, 11
National Institutes of Health (NIH),
    319
National Psychosis Research
    Framework, 137
National Science Foundation (NSF),
    14
*Nature,* 3, 107–108, 209–210
necessary model, 318
negative results, 49, 259, 267–268,
    279

*Neuropathology and Experimental
    Neurology, Journal of,* 216
*Neurosurgery, Journal of,* 4
*New England Journal of Medicine,* 4
    acknowledgments section, 126
    authorship guidelines, 139
    burden of reviews, 151
    coauthorship patterns, 123
    cost of peer review, 27
    double-blind review, 214
    ejournal models, 297
    publication bias, 270
    publication of negative results,
        268
    rejection letters, 47
    rejection rates, 61
    signed reviews, 233
    statistical analysis, 265
    statistical review, 255, 260, 261,
        280–281
    studies of clinical relevance, 183
    submission policies, 45, 46
*New Zealand Journal of Medicine,*
    136–137
news items, 7
news media, 44–46
Nobel Prizes, 62
nonparametric statistics, 265
null hypothesis, 259, 267, 270
*Nurse Midwifery, Journal of,* 6
*Nursing and Allied Health,
    Cumulative Index to the
    (CINAHL),* 57–58
nursing journals
    blind review, 214
    definition of peer-review, 15
    editorial appointments, 89–90
    editorial peer review, 6
    peer review process, 101
    reasons for rejections, 49
*Nursing Outlook,* 15

# O

objectivity, publication criteria, 93
*Online Journal of Current Clinical Trials (OJCCT)*, 298
*Online Journal of Knowledge Synthesis for Nursing*, 298
open reviews, 235, 302. *See also* anonymous reviews; blind reviews
*Ophthalmology*, 265
*Ophthalmology, American Journal of*, 265
ophthalmology journals, 265
Optical Society of America, 298
*Optics Express*, 298
organization, and rejection, 53
Organization for Economic Cooperation Development (OECD), 303
organizational behavior journals, 134
otolaryngology journals, 264–265

# P

page charges, 132
*Parapsychology*, 6
particularism, in reviews, 170
Pearson's correlation coefficient, 265
*Pediatric Neurosurgery*, 161
*Pediatrics*, 263
*Pediatrics, Journal of*, 4, 218
Peer Review in Biomedical Publications, International Conference on, 12
peer-reviewed journals, definitions, 15–16
peers, definition, 15–16
persistence, and publication, 70–71
personal biases, 208

*Personality and Social Psychology, Journal of*, 189, 221, 223–224, 266
*Personality and Social Psychology Bulletin*, 67, 189
pharmaceutical companies, 49
pharmacy journals, 92
*Philosophical Transactions of the Royal Society*, 1
*Physical Medicine and Rehabilitation, American Journal of*, 265
*Physical Medicine and Rehabilitation, Archives of*, 265–266
*Physical Review*, 4, 61, 100–101, 124, 184
*Physical Review Letters*, 4–5
    author recognition, 214–215
    coauthorship patterns, 124
    manuscripts handling, 100–101
    rejection rates over time, 61
    studies of reviewer consensus, 184
*Physical Therapy*, 197
physics, high-energy, 298–300
physics journals, 58, 84, 95
*Physics Today*, 161, 167
*Physiologia Plantarum*, 159
*Physiological Zoology*, 191
*Plastic and Reconstructive Surgery*, 234
policies
    definition of bias, 97
    and editorial boards, 81
*Political Economy, Journal of*, 226, 274
political science journals, 84, 95
*Political Science Review, American*, 62
politics, and reviews, 97
position papers, 93
postdoctoral fellows, 127
practicality, 95

presentation
  correctable, 50–51
  and rejection, 53
prestige
  academic affiliations, 221, 239
  biases, 208
  editorial, 83
  editorial boards, 81–82, 84, 111
  journals, 132, 196, 302
  and quality of reviews, 158
  and rejections, 44
previous publications, 51
proceedings, publication criteria, 95
*Proceedings of the National Academy
    of Sciences,* 122
procrastinator, reviewer, 169
productivity, measures of, 91–92,
    119–120
promotional activities, 7
*Protein Science,* 107
*Psychiatry, American Journal of,* 5, 260
*Psychiatry, Australia and New
    Zealand, Journal of,* 260
*Psychological Abstracts,* 11
*Psychological Medicine,* 217–218
*Psychology,* 33
psychology journals
  author recognition, 215
  editorial appointments, 88–89
  editorial board appointments, 85
  ethical guidelines, 108
  publication bias, 268
  publication criteria, 95
  replication studies, 273
*Psychology of Women Quarterly,* 51,
    184
Psychonomic Society, 134
*Psycoloquy,* 300, 317, 321
public, definition of, 301
*Public Health, American Journal of,*
    67, 155, 227
  author recognition, 217
  blind review, 211
  coauthorship patterns, 123

conference presentations, 7
*Public Health, Canadian Journal of,*
    258
publication biases, 208
  approved studies, 270–272
  published article studies, *269*
  research project outcomes, *270*
  statistical review, 249
  statistical significance, 267–268
publication criteria, 92–96, *94,* 111,
    313
Publications of the Modern
    Language Association
    (PLMA), 225–226
*PubMed Central,* 319–320

**Q**

quality
  blind *vs.* nonblind reviews, *219*
  and coauthorship, 128
  evaluation of, 51
  Los Alamos eprints, 299
  manuscript improvement,
    170–171
  published management, 52–53
  rejection rates, 43–78, 55
  and reviewer consensus, 194
  reviewer input, 154
  reviewers reports, 158–160

**R**

*Radiology,* 68, 162, 170
radiology journals, 95
randomization, 255, 278, 280
randomized controlled trials (RCTs),
    262, 270, 271, 276

rapid publications, 4
readership, 26–27, 130, 132, 153
recruiters, and coauthorship, 126
refereed journals, definition, 16
reference lists, 49
registries, 275
regular columns, 7
rejections. *See also* acceptances
    appeals processes, 63–64
    author's experience of, 48, 64
    author's response to, 62–67
    conclusions about manuscripts,
        70–71
    correctable problems, 50–51
    discipline-specific, 54–60, *56–57*
    editorial comments, 25
    feedback to authors, 46–47, 133
    final disposition of manuscripts,
        64–67
    final publication outcomes, *66*
    gender bias, 228–232
    journal policies, *18–24*
    manager publications, 311
    of manuscripts, 43–78
    negative results, 49
    options, 2–3
    publication criteria, 92–96, 96
    publication of, 25
    rates over time, 60–62
    rates within disciplines, 59–60
    reasons for, 47, 49–54, *50, 52*
    reviewer consensus, 190–191,
        192, 199
    statistical review, 253
    threshold, 51
    time spent on reviews, 157
replication studies, 95, 96, 208,
    267–268, *269*, 273
*Reporting of Clinical Trials*, 282
reprisals, open review, 235
reputations
    journals, 130
    publication criteria, 95
*Requirements for Manuscripts*

*Submitted to Biomedical*
    *Journals,* 13–14
research designs, publication criteria,
    93, 96
*Responsible Conduct of Research in*
    *Health Sciences, The,* 137
resubmissions
    American Psychological
        Association's Council of
        Editors, 63
    journal selection, 130
    new ideas, 15
    rejected articles, 3, 64–67
    review of, 162
    revisions, 67
reviewers
    advantages to, 308
    age of, 313
    anonymity, 25, 209–210
    author recognition by, 209
    author recognition of, 217–218
    biases, 207–246, 218–223,
        236–237, 238–239
    blind *vs.* nonblind, *219*
    characteristics of, 154–158
    comments, 47
    consensus, 181–205, 186–187,
        199–200
    editorial override, 97
    editors and, 81
    editors options, 92
    electronic media, 302
    gender of, 228–230
    graduate students as, 162, 164
    guidelines for, 160–166, *163–164,*
        192, 197–199, 234–238,
        274–277
    interrater reliability, 312
    length of reports, 169
    motives of, 151–152
    qualities of, 154, 169
    quality of reports, 158–160
    recruitment of, 17
    role of, 2, 151–179

reviewers *(continued)*
   scoring guidelines, 192
   selection, 2, 152–154, 195
   signed agreements, 160
   signed reports, 232–234
   statistical, 249–251, 274–277
   status and quality of reviews, *159*
   thanking of, 25
   value of reports, 166–173, *168*
   workload, 155, *156*
reviews
   automated systems, 153–154
   electronic submissions, 298–299
   evaluation of, 197–198
   particularism in, 170
   postpublication, 301
   signed, 232–234
   statistical, 247–293
*Roentgenology, American Journal of,*
      67, 126–127, 160
Royal Society, 107–108


**S**


satisfaction, author's, 134
*Science,* 301
*Science Citation Index,* 11, 91,
      122–123, 124
Science Editors, International
      Conference of, 11
Science Editors, International
      Federation of, 14
science journals, 54, 90–92
scientific achievement, measures of,
      88–89
Scientific Unions Abstracting Board,
      International Council of, 5
search engines, 295–296
secrecy, 235
self-citations, 217
*Serials Directory, The,* 7

*Sharing Research Data,* 321
single-reviewer reliability, 180
*Social Forces,* 128–129
*Social Issues, Journal of,* 223
*Social Problems,* 93
*Social Science & Medicine,* 225
social science journals
   double-blind review, 314
   editorial appointments, 85
   publication criteria, 95
   rejection information, 54
   replication studies, 273
*Social Sciences Citation Index,* 11
*Social Service Research, Journal of,*
      215
*Social Work,* 63–64, 88
*Social Work, British Journal of,* 262
*Social Work Research,* 192, 194–195
societies
   conferences, 7–8
   membership, 44
*Sociological Quarterly,* 189
*Sociological Quarterly, The,* 60
*Sociology, American Journal of,* 60,
      128–129
sociology journals
   coauthorship patterns, 122–123
   editorial appointments, 87–88
   rejection information, 54
   rejection rates over time, 60–61
   turnaround time, 155
*Sociometry,* 128, 224
software, statistical analysis, 260
*Southern Medical Journal,* 5
speed of publication, 132
sponsored conferences, 49, 69
statistical analysis
   articles lacking, *266*
   and coauthorship, 125–127
   complexity of, 263–266
   error categories, 255, *257–262*
   errors, types, *257*
   errors in, *256–257,* 314–315
   guidelines for, 273–277, 313

inaccurate, 51
knowledge of reviewers, 153
power of tests, 276
publication criteria, 95
published guidelines, 281–283
and rejection, 53
review by individual journals,
    277–281
reviewer consensus, 183,
    185–193, 186–187
significant results, 267–268
software, 260
statistical reviews, 247–293
conclusions about, 283–285
editorial comments, 25
limitations of studies on, 282–283
published studies, 254–263
statisticians, 274, 275, 279–280, 283
statistics, tutorial, 276–277
*Statistics in Medicine,* 281
statistics journals, 91
*Stealing into Print: Fraud,
    Plagiarism, and Misconduct
    in Scientific Publishing,* 308
*Structure of Scientific Revolutions,
    The,* 321
study design
    control groups, 220–221
    editorial peer review, 309–310
    Institutional Review Board atten-
        tion, 275
    planning stage, 279
    statistical methodology, 258
study monitors, and coauthorship, 126
subject matter
    journal selection, 132
    previous publications, 51
    prioritization, 53
    reviewer selection, 152
    timeliness, 51
submissions, journal selection,
    129–132, 300
support staff, 81
*Surgery, Archives of*

editorial board appointments, 84
editors, 96
meeting communications, 49
rejection letters, 47
reviewer guidelines, 161
*Surgery, British Journal of,* 260, 261
*Surgery, Gynecology, and Obstetrics,* 3
survival analysis, 265
symposia, 7

**T**

*t*-tests
    misuse of, 259, 260
    students, errors, 255
    use of, 248, 265
tact, of reviewers, 161
technical help, 125–127
tenure decisions, 302
terminology, literature searches, 8, 10
timeliness
    publication criteria, 93
    publication process, 318–319
    review turnaround, 155
    of reviews, 161
    subject matter, 51
topic selection, 93
*Transfusion,* 261
turnaround times, 155

**U**

*Ulrich's International Periodical
    Directory,* survey of editors, 7
*Uniform Requirements for
    Manuscripts Submitted to
    Biomedical Journals,* 49,
    140, 281, *282*
URLs, maintenance of, 296

# V

validity, 162, 248
Vancouver Groups. *See* International
        Committee of Medical
        Journal Editors (ICMJE)
*Vascular Interventional Radiology,*
        *Journal of,* 192
*Veterinary Medicine, American*
        *Journal of,* 261
*Virology, Comprehensive,* 233
volunteer reviewers, 17, 153


# W

*Web of Science,* 152, 212
*William and Mary Quarterly,* 211
World Association of Medical
        Editors, 14
writers. *See* authors
writing, and coauthorship, 125–127
writing style
    and acceptance, 92
    editorial bias, 96
    publication criteria, 95
    and rejection, 53, 54
    in reviews, 162

# More Great Books
# from Information Today, Inc.

## ARIST 34
## Annual Review of Information
## Science and Technology

Edited by Professor Martha E. Williams

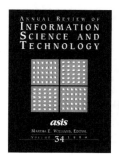

Since 1966, the *Annual Review of Information Science and Technology (ARIST)* has been continuously at the cutting edge in contributing a useful and comprehensive view of the broad field of information science and technology. ARIST reviews numerous topics within the field and ultimately provides this annual source of ideas, trends, and references to the literature. Published by Information Today, Inc. on behalf of the American Society for Information Science (ASIS), ARIST Volume 34 (1999) is the latest volume in this legendary series. The newest edition of ARIST covers the following topics:
• The History of Documentation and Information Science (Colin Burke) • Applications of Machine Learning in Information Retrieval (Sally Jo Cunningham, Jamie Littin, and Ian Witten) • Privacy and Digital Information (Philip Doty) • Cognitive Information Retrieval (Peter Ingwersen) • Text Mining (Walter Trybula) • Methodologies for Human Behavioral Research (Peiling Wang) • Measuring the Internet (Robert Williams and Bob Molyneux) • Infometric Laws (Concepcion Wilson and William Hood) • Using and Reading Scholarly Literature (Donald W. King and Carol Tenopir) • Literature Dynamics: Studies on Growth, Diffusion, and Epidemics (Albert Tabah).

**Hardbound • ISBN 1-57387-093-5**

**ASIST Members $79.95**          **Non-Members $99.95**

## Introductory Concepts in Information Science

Melanie J. Norton

Melanie J. Norton presents a unique introduction to the practical and theoretical concepts of information science while examining the impact of the Information Age on society. Drawing on recent research into the field, as well as from scholarly and trade publications, the monograph provides a brief history of information science and coverage of key topics, including communications and cognition, information retrieval, bibliometrics, modeling, economics, information policies, and the impact of information technology on modern management. This is an essential volume for graduate students, practitioners, and any professional who needs a solid grounding in the field of information science.

**Hardbound • ISBN 1-57387-087-0**

**ASIST Members $31.60**          **Non-Members $39.50**

# The Web of Knowledge:
# A Festschrift in Honor of Eugene Garfield

Edited by Blaise Cronin and Helen Barsky Atkins

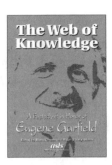

Dr. Eugene Garfield, the founder of the Institute for Scientific Information (ISI), has devoted his life to the creation and development of the multidisciplinary Science Citation Index. The index, a unique resource for scientists, scholars, and researchers in virtually every field of intellectual endeavor, has been the foundation for a multidisciplinary research community. This new ASIST monograph is the first to comprehensively address the history, theory, and practical applications of the Science Citation Index and to examine its impact on scholarly and scientific research 40 years after its inception. In bringing together the analyses, insights, and reflections of more than 35 leading lights, editors Cronin and Atkins have produced both a comprehensive survey of citation indexing and analysis and a beautifully realized tribute to Eugene Garfield and his vision.

**Hardbound • ISBN 1-57387-099-4**

**ASIST Members $39.60**          **Non-Members $49.50**

# Knowledge Management
# for the Information Professional

Edited by T. Kanti Srikantaiah and Michael Koenig

Written from the perspective of the information community, this book examines the business community's recent enthusiasm for Knowledge Management (KM). With contributions from 26 leading KM practitioners, academicians, and information professionals, editors Srikantaiah and Koenig bridge the gap between two distinct perspectives, equipping information professionals with the tools to make a broader and more effective contribution in developing KM systems and creating a Knowledge Management culture within their organizations.

**Hardbound • ISBN 1-57387-079-X**

**ASIST Members $35.60**          **Non-Members $44.50**

# Electronic Styles
## A Handbook for Citing Electronic Information

Xia Li and Nancy Crane

The second edition of the best-selling guide to referencing electronic information and citing the complete range of electronic formats includes text-based information, electronic journals and discussion lists, Web sites, CD-ROM and multimedia products, and commercial online documents.

**Softbound • ISBN 1-57387-027-7 • $19.99**